Contemporary Chinese Politics

Contemporary Chinese Politics considers how new and diverse sources and methods are changing the study of Chinese politics. Contributors spanning three generations in China studies place their distinct qualitative and quantitative methodological approaches in the framework of the discipline and point to challenges or opportunities (or both) of adapting new sources and methods to the study of contemporary China. How can we more effectively use new sources and methods of data collection? How can we better integrate the study of Chinese politics into the discipline of political science, to the betterment of both? How can we more appropriately manage the logistical and ethical problems of doing political research in the challenging Chinese environment? In addressing these questions, this comprehensive methodological survey will be of immense interest to graduate students heading into the field for the first time and experienced scholars looking to keep abreast of the state of the art in the study of Chinese politics.

Allen Carlson is an associate professor in Cornell University's Government Department. He is the author of *Unifying China, Integrating with the World: Securing Chinese Sovereignty during the Reform Era* (2005) and the coeditor (with J. J. Suh and Peter Katzenstein) of *Rethinking Security in East Asia: Power, Identity and Efficiencies* (2004). His articles have appeared in the *Journal of Contemporary China* and *Pacific Affairs*.

Mary E. Gallagher is an associate professor of political science at the University of Michigan and the director of the Center for Chinese Studies. She is also a faculty associate at the Center for Comparative Political Studies at the Institute for Social Research. She is the author of *Contagious Capitalism: Globalization and the Politics of Labor in China* (2005), and her articles have appeared in *World Politics*, *Law and Society Review*, *Studies in Comparative International Development*, and *Asian Survey*.

Kenneth Lieberthal is a senior Fellow in Foreign Policy and in Global Economy and Development and also is director of the John L. Thornton China Center at the Brookings Institution. He has written and edited fifteen books and monographs, most recently *The U.S. Intelligence Community and Foreign Policy: Getting Analysis Right* (2009) and (with David Sandalow) *Overcoming Obstacles to US-China Cooperation on Climate Change* (2009). He is also the author of about seventy periodical articles and chapters in books and has published in the *New York Times*, *Washington Post*, *Los Angeles Times*, *Financial Times*, *South China Morning Post*, and numerous other newspapers.

Melanie Manion is a professor of political science and public affairs at the University of Wisconsin–Madison. Her publications include *Retirement of Revolutionaries in China* (1993) and *Corruption by Design* (2004). Her articles have appeared in the *American Political Science Review*; *Comparative Political Studies*; *Journal of Law, Economics, and Organization*; and *China Quarterly*.

Contemporary Chinese Politics

New Sources, Methods, and Field Strategies

Edited by

ALLEN CARLSON
Cornell University

MARY E. GALLAGHER
University of Michigan, Ann Arbor

KENNETH LIEBERTHAL
Brookings Institution

MELANIE MANION
University of Wisconsin–Madison

CAMBRIDGE UNIVERSITY PRESS

CAMBRIDGE UNIVERSITY PRESS
Cambridge, New York, Melbourne, Madrid, Cape Town, Singapore,
São Paulo, Delhi, Dubai, Tokyo, Mexico City

Cambridge University Press
32 Avenue of the Americas, New York, NY 10013-2473, USA

www.cambridge.org
Information on this title: www.cambridge.org/9780521155762

© Cambridge University Press 2010

This publication is in copyright. Subject to statutory exception
and to the provisions of relevant collective licensing agreements,
no reproduction of any part may take place without the written
permission of Cambridge University Press.

First published 2010

Printed in the United States of America

A catalog record for this publication is available from the British Library.

Library of Congress Cataloging in Publication Data
Contemporary Chinese politics : new sources, methods, and field
  strategies / edited by Allen Carlson ... [et al.].
    p. cm.
  Includes bibliographical references and index.
  ISBN 978-0-521-19783-0 – ISBN 978-0-521-15576-2 (pbk.)
  1. China – Politics and government – 2002– 2. China – Politics and
  government – 2002– Methodology. 3. Political science –
  Methodology. I. Carlson, Allen, 1968– II. Title.
  JQ1510.C68 2010
  320.951–dc22   2010018862

ISBN 978-0-521-19783-0 Hardback
ISBN 978-0-521-15576-2 Paperback

Cambridge University Press has no responsibility for the persistence or
accuracy of URLs for external or third-party Internet Web sites referred to in
this publication and does not guarantee that any content on such Web sites is,
or will remain, accurate or appropriate.

Contents

Tables and Figures — *page* vii
Contributors — ix
Abbreviations — xi

Introduction — 1
Allen Carlson, Mary E. Gallagher, and Melanie Manion

PART I SOURCES

1 State-Generated Data and Contentious Politics in China — 15
   Xi Chen

2 Why Archives? — 33
   Neil J. Diamant

3 The Central Committee, Past and Present: A Method of Quantifying Elite Biographies — 51
   Victor Shih, Wei Shan, and Mingxing Liu

4 Experimental Methods and Psychological Measures in the Study of Chinese Foreign Policy — 69
   Peter Hays Gries

5 Internet Resources and the Study of Chinese Foreign Relations: Can Cyberspace Shed New Light on China's Approach to the World? — 88
   Allen Carlson and Hong Duan

6 Information Overload? Collecting, Managing, and Analyzing Chinese Media Content — 107
   Daniela Stockmann

PART II QUALITATIVE METHODS

7 The Worm's-Eye View: Using Ethnography to Illuminate Labor Politics and Institutional Change in Contemporary China — 129
   Calvin Chen

8 More Than an Interview, Less Than Sedaka: Studying
   Subtle and Hidden Politics with Site-Intensive Methods   145
   Benjamin L. Read

9 Cases, Questions, and Comparison in Research
   on Contemporary Chinese Politics   162
   William Hurst

PART III   SURVEY METHODS

10 A Survey of Survey Research on Chinese Politics:
    What Have We Learned?   181
    Melanie Manion

11 Surveying Prospects for Political Change: Capturing Political
    and Economic Variation in Empirical Research in China   200
    Bruce J. Dickson

12 Using Clustered Spatial Data to Study Diffusion: The Case
    of Legal Institutions in China   219
    Pierre F. Landry

13 Measuring Change and Stability over a Decade in the
    Beijing Area Study   236
    Mingming Shen and Ming Yang, with Melanie Manion

14 Quantitative Research and Issues of Political
    Sensitivity in Rural China   246
    Lily L. Tsai

Reflections on the Evolution of the China Field
in Political Science   266
Kenneth Lieberthal

Glossary   279
References   283
Index   311

Tables and Figures

Tables

3.1	Tracking Chen Yun's positions in the 1950s	*page* 55
4.1	Structures of national identity: Pattern matrix loadings for principal axis factor analysis with Promax rotation for American and Chinese samples, 2009	79
4.2	Descriptive statistics: Correlations, significance levels, means, standard deviations, and scale alphas and Ns for 2009 Beijing sample (minimum N = 156)	81
6.1	Percentage of 100 samples falling within one and two standard errors of the population mean in two newspapers	115
10.1	Probability sample surveys on Chinese politics resulting in publications analyzing original datasets	186
10.2	Mainland partner institutions for probability sample surveys on Chinese politics	191
11.1	The trade-off between goals of development among officials and entrepreneurs	211
11.2	Perceived threats to stability among private entrepreneurs and local officials	213
11.3	Distribution of private entrepreneurs in local people's congresses	214
11.4	Probit regression: Determinants of private entrepreneurs in people's congresses	216
12.1	Conditions for institutional diffusion	230
12.2	Impact of court adopters on the mean propensity to go to court	231
12.3	Probit estimates of going to court in civil, economic, and administrative cases	233

13.1	Questions asked annually in the Beijing Area Study	239
13.2	Overview of sampling and survey implementation in BAS first decade	243
13.3	Incomplete interviews due to unmet requirements in BAS first decade	244

Figures

3.1	Average age and 25th and 75th percentile age of Central Committee members, 1921–2006	61
3.2	Average birth year and 25th and 75th percentile birth year of Central Committee members, 1921–2006	62
3.3	Percentage of Central Committee members with Long March experience and the number of Long Marchers	63
3.4	Average education level of Central Committee members, 1921–2006	64
3.5	The share of Central Committee members with common experience with Hu Yaobang and Hua Guofeng, 1970–1990	66
4.1	International anxiety as a function of nation, domain, and frame, 2006 samples	74
4.2	International pride as a function of nation and frame, 2006 samples	75
4.3	Final Beijing path model, 2009 sample	82
6.1	Percentage of Xinhua news articles among all articles about the United States published in the *People's Daily*, September 2001–July 2002	118
12.1	The ILRC survey of China (2003–2004)	222
12.2	Example of a county map displaying township boundaries and basic infrastructure overlaid to the Google Earth model, with grids coded in KML displaying three TSUs in each sampled township	224
12.3	Example of a spatial sampling unit (half-square minute) drawn in a low-density rural area in western China	225
12.4	Example of spatial sampling units in an urban area	226
12.5	Impact of the combined presence of court adopters in the community and the respondent's level of trust in the courts on the probability of adopting courts as a dispute resolution venue in a civil case	234

Contributors

Allen Carlson is an associate professor in the Government Department at Cornell University.

Calvin Chen is an associate professor of politics at Mount Holyoke College.

Xi Chen is an associate professor of political science at Louisiana State University.

Neil J. Diamant is an associate professor of political science and Asian law and society at Dickinson College.

Bruce J. Dickson is a professor of political science and international affairs at George Washington University.

Hong Duan is a Ph.D. candidate in the Government Department at Cornell University.

Mary E. Gallagher is an associate professor of political science and director of the Center for Chinese Studies at the University of Michigan.

Peter Hays Gries is the Harold J. and Ruth Newman Chair in U.S.-China Issues and director and associate professor at the Institute for U.S.-China Issues at the University of Oklahoma.

William Hurst is an assistant professor of government at the University of Texas at Austin.

Pierre F. Landry is an associate professor of political science at Yale University.

Kenneth Lieberthal is a senior Fellow in Foreign Policy and in Global Economy and Development and also is the director of the John L. Thornton China Center at the Brookings Institution.

Mingxing Liu is an associate professor at the China Institute for Educational Finance Research at Peking University and research Fellow at the China

Economics and Management Academy at the Central University of Finance and Economics.

Melanie Manion is a professor of political science and public affairs at the University of Wisconsin–Madison.

Benjamin L. Read is an assistant professor in the Department of Politics at the University of California, Santa Cruz.

Wei Shan is a postdoctoral Fellow at Duke University.

Mingming Shen is a professor of political science and director of the Research Center on Contemporary China at Peking University.

Victor Shih is an assistant professor of political science at Northwestern University.

Daniela Stockmann is an assistant professor of political science at Leiden University.

Lily L. Tsai is an associate professor of political science at the Massachusetts Institute of Technology.

Ming Yang is an associate professor of political science and associate director of the Research Center on Contemporary China at Peking University.

Abbreviations

APA	American Psychological Association
APSA	American Political Science Association
BAS	Beijing Area Study
BB	bulletin board
CASS	Chinese Academy of Social Sciences
CATA	Computer Aided Text Analysis
CC	Central Committee
CCP	Chinese Communist Party
CFI	Comparative Fit Index
CICIR	China Institute of Contemporary International Relations
CIIS	China Institute of International Studies
CNKI	China National Knowledge Infrastructure (database)
CNNIC	China Internet Network Information Center
CPPCC	Chinese People's Political Consultative Conference
CSE	collective self-esteem
CYL	Communist Youth League
FBIS	Foreign Broadcast Information Service
FSU	Final (spatial) Sampling Unit
GPS	Global Positioning System
HSM	half-square minute
ILRC	Institutionalization of Legal Reforms in China
IQRM	Institute for Qualitative Research Methods
IRB	Internal Review Board
IWEP	Institute of World Economics and Politics
KML	Keyhole Markup Language
KMT	Guomindang
MFA	Ministry of Foreign Affairs
MOE	Ministry of Education
MR	military region
MVD	Ministry of the Interior (Russia)
NBS	National Bureau of Statistics

NFI	Normed Fit Index
NPC	National People's Congress
NSF	National Science Foundation
PAF	principal axis factoring
PC	party congress
PLA	People's Liberation Army
PPS	probability proportionate to size
PSC	Politburo Standing Committee
PSU	Primary Sampling Unit
RA	research assistant
RC	residents' committee
RCCC	Research Center for Contemporary China
RMSEA	Root Mean Square Error of Approximation
RWA	right-wing authoritarianism
SASAC	State-owned Assets Supervision and Administration Commission
SEC	State Education Commission
SIIS	Shanghai Institute of International Studies
SIM	site-intensive method
SMA	Shanghai Municipal Archives
SOE	state-owned enterprise
SSU	Secondary Sampling Units
TLI	Tucker-Lewis Index
USC	Universities Service Centre

Introduction

Allen Carlson, Mary E. Gallagher, and Melanie Manion

At a workshop at the University of Michigan in November 2006, three generations of scholars met to discuss and debate the study of Chinese politics and how new and diverse sources and methods are changing the field. This volume is the culmination of that workshop. Drawing on diverse research experiences, we present a wide range of sources, methods, and field strategies for the study of Chinese politics in the new era. As political scientists, we place our distinct methodological approaches in the framework of the discipline and point to particular challenges or opportunities (or both) of adaptation in the context of contemporary China. With the main focus on methodological concerns and the discovery of new data sources, the chapters in this volume are also richly substantive illustrations that demonstrate how to adapt method to context innovatively and appropriately. Thus, this book illustrates the benefits of the emerging cross-pollination between China studies and the broader discipline.

Three major themes emerged from our workshop discussions: (1) how to effectively use new sources and data collection methods, (2) how to integrate the study of Chinese politics into the discipline of political science to the betterment of both, and (3) how to deal with logistical and ethical problems of doing research in a challenging environment. In this Introduction, we discuss these themes in the sections below in the context of the initial workshop, the substantive chapters in this volume, and the field more generally. As only sporadic attention has been paid to the nuts and bolts of the study of Chinese politics, we hope this volume will spark future debates and other publications, conferences, and graduate training on research design and methodology in challenging fieldwork sites. We recognize that this volume joins an existing ongoing debate (Baum, 2007; Harding, 1994; Heimer and Thøgersen, 2006; Manion, 1994; Perry, 2007 and 1994b; Shambaugh, 1993; Wank, 1998). Collectively the following chapters illustrate that although much has changed

The editors would like to thank the American Council of Learned Societies, the Chiang Ching-Kuo Foundation, the Center for Chinese Studies at the University of Michigan, and the Department of Political Science at the University of Michigan for their generous support.

in the realm of studying Chinese politics, many of the fundamentals that previous scholars learned about this endeavor still apply. Language skills and familiarity with China strike us as remaining core prerequisites for scholars wishing to make sense of any given aspect of Chinese politics. Moreover, local knowledge – that is, knowing China – is increasingly insufficient. Each of the contributors to this volume has also utilized a wide variety of research skills in his or her work. These skills cover a broad set of approaches to politics and include the use of sophisticated quantitative techniques, the production and utilization of survey data, the application of new technologies, searching out and making use of previously closed archival sources, and even conducting quasi-experiments. Although such approaches cover many tools in the political science kit, and are illustrative of the impressive and at times conflicting directions in which the study of Chinese politics is headed, all contributors to this volume have made use of such methods with a common purpose in mind: to amplify their ability to describe and explain key aspects of politics in contemporary China. As such, the volume shows the rewards of bringing together scholars with diverse backgrounds, yet who share a collective commitment to pushing both China studies and the discipline forward in an inclusive and mutually beneficial manner. Thus, although the volume focuses on mainland China almost exclusively, we believe that the methodology and research design strategies presented here are relevant to scholars in many other places around the globe.

AN ABUNDANCE OF RICHES? DEALING WITH DATA

The study of China within the discipline of political science has changed dramatically over the past thirty years, reflecting in many ways the events and transformations that have occurred in Chinese politics. From a period of near total isolation from one's subject of study when China was closed off from Western scholarship, to a new period in which China's engagement with the world has become a source of wonder, political scientists studying China have gone from a dearth of sources and data to an overwhelming abundance.[1] Moreover, this recent surge in the access that scholars have to a staggering array of sources relating to the Chinese state represents a rather fundamental change in the way in which scholars come to know China. In other words, although the use of new methods is laudable and receives a good deal of attention in this volume, it is also clear that the contributors have been able to apply more advanced social science techniques to the study of Chinese politics only as they have gained access to a historically unprecedented wealth of information within China relating to domestic politics, foreign relations, and national security.

---

[1] See Baum (2007) on the generations of political scientists studying China in the post–World War II period.

The increasing diversity, amount, and complexity of data on Chinese politics require that scholars pause to think about and debate how to use the data effectively and responsibly. The availability of new, often more systematic, data presents researchers with new opportunities not only to use these data effectively but also to combine these riches with more established data sources. Such opportunities can increase the external and internal validity of our arguments and also effectively bring the Chinese case to bear on debates in comparative politics and political science. Several of the chapters in this volume deal explicitly with strategies for using multiple methods and sources to achieve these goals. Lily L. Tsai discusses field strategies to improve the quality and reliability of survey data. Pierre Landry applies new methods of statistical sampling using Global Positioning System (GPS) spatial technology, allowing him to show the patterns of legal diffusion and the actual mechanisms of changing popular opinion toward China's legal system. Victor Shih, Wei Shan, and Mingxing Liu present a new database on members of the Central Committee of the Chinese Communist Party, which permits more systematic analysis of China's key political elite. Neil Diamant and Xi Chen demonstrate the value and increasing accessibility of state-generated data in Chinese archives.

Changes in sources and data also impact how we interpret and evaluate older methodologies and sources. Although few China scholars would accept the comparison to the "Kremlinologists" of old, some of what we study still necessarily includes attention to and analysis of important facets of Chinese politics that do not lend themselves to systematic study. Although the elite politics examined by Shih, Shan, and Liu in Chapter 3 comes immediately to mind, other important social phenomena, such as collective violence, corruption, tax evasion, and ethnic conflict, are also critical research topics that must be studied with limited, often flawed data, and in a political atmosphere that at times entails overt government suppression and at other times astoundingly effective self-censorship on the part of informants, local officials, and in-country colleagues. Many of the authors here provide detailed explanations of how they deal with important topics that can yield insufficient or flawed data. Xi Chen's typology of "upstream" and "downstream" state-generated data provides helpful strategies on how to interpret and assess the reliability and accuracy of government reports and statistics regarding contentious actions by Chinese citizens. He also details how clear knowledge and familiarity with the bureaucratic structure and politics of the government units in charge of monitoring citizens' collective action are critical for measuring accurately the value of one's data. Calvin Chen's ethnographic study of Chinese factories provides a critical look at the seamy side of the "workshop of the world" on China's southeastern coast. In addition, Neil Diamant's contribution illustrates how digging deeper into previously unavailable archival sources can shed new light on past events and challenge conventional wisdom about politics during the early years of the PRC. Many of these strategies should be a more visible part of any political scientist's toolbox in challenging fieldwork locales, in China and elsewhere. Daniela Stockmann utilizes the vast wave of new print media sources that have flooded China during this period. Although China's newspapers and wire reports may be dismissed by some as doing no more than reproducing official rhetoric, Stockmann shows that via the use of new technology, specifically Yoshikoder, it is possible to find in these publications a great deal of new information about trends in contemporary Chinese politics. Allen Carlson and Hong Duan turn to Internet resources related to Chinese foreign policy and national security, and although they find that there is less here than initially meets the eye, these sources too are promising.

COMPARATIVE POLITICS AND COMPARING CHINA

The study of Chinese politics in recent decades has also been profoundly influenced by the political science discipline. This is evidenced not only by the ongoing lively debate about appropriate methodology but also by renewed attention to placing area studies in the broader context of comparative politics. Increasingly and appropriately, graduate school training in political science requires acquisition of strong methodological skills, offering new opportunities for students of Chinese politics. At the same time, application of these methods requires sensitivity in the field to take into account the different context – a developing economy, an authoritarian polity, and an Asian culture. There is then a delicate balancing act to be maintained in the training of graduate students working on China. Increased knowledge of methods (quantitative or qualitative) is a must, but so too are language and cultural training. It is now clear that both of these skills are required, that is, walking on two legs, to conduct successful research on Chinese politics. The nuances of such adaptations are not commonly acquired in the classroom.

Moreover, in recent years, the study of specific places (especially single countries but even specific regions) has been deemphasized in the field of political science. Whether or not this constitutes progress, comparative politics, and to a certain extent international relations and security studies as well, now aspire to develop theories and arguments that can be investigated in and applied to any locale. Ideally, theories with the greatest amount of breadth should be developed to explain important political and economic transformations, for example democratization, rapid economic growth, efficient public goods provision, and ethnic peace and conflict. In most places around the globe, comparative work has absorbed traditional "area studies," and specialists on a single country or region are encouraged and rewarded professionally when they show their ability and inclination to go "cross-national." Although cross-national comparison has long been a hallmark of comparative politics, the methods of comparison have changed as better data have become available, as many recently democratized countries have produced electoral data waiting to be analyzed, and as computing programs have become more powerful. Combined with the growing emphasis on quantitative research methods in graduate school training, studies in comparative politics increasingly employ large-N datasets and sophisticated statistical analysis to compare countries. For various reasons, these methods are often regarded as more effective and powerful than comparative case studies or other small-N comparisons (but see Schrank, 2006).[2]

In general, specialists on Chinese politics have not gone down this path, or at least have not gotten very far down this path. There are several reasons that the study of China remains somewhat apart from these broader trends. They include the problem of making relevant comparisons, China's significant internal diversity, and the challenge of finding or producing high-quality data for cross-national comparisons. Given that these problems are not unique to China and are often present in many other regions and countries, the strategies used to enhance comparison in China may also be applied elsewhere.

The countries most commonly compared to China in earlier periods either collapsed or democratized (or both) during the 1990s as socialism failed in countries from Eastern Europe to Central Asia. The end of the Soviet Union in particular complicated the previously active field of comparative communism. Although comparisons between China and Eastern Europe, Central Europe, and the former Soviet Union continued into the 1990s and beyond, apt comparisons have become more difficult as the political systems have diverged markedly. Even in the resurgent authoritarian states of the former Soviet Union, a number of the political systems remain more democratic and more open than the one-party state of the Chinese Communist Party. As many studies across the globe now focus on elections and party politics, China's one-party system and dearth of competitive elections beyond the grassroots level leave China out of many cross-national studies. In some cases, the availability of systematic electoral data has redirected research away from questions that cannot be probed this way. As Lieberthal notes in the conclusion, research questions should be developed that are interesting and relevant rather than simply because they can be answered through available data. This exclusion of important questions, and by extension some countries, because the data are not comparable to those available in developed democracies is regrettable. In the Chinese case, both quantitative and qualitative research on grassroots elections, and semicompetitive elections at other levels, have yielded important, perhaps pathbreaking, insights into the nature of elections in nondemocratic societies (e.g., Manion, 1996; Shi, 1999a; Tsai, 2007b). However, because Chinese data remain difficult to integrate into mainstream comparative politics research on elections (which is overwhelmingly drawn from democratic countries), the Chinese case does not have a large impact on the field.

Because China does not conform to the path hewed by other socialist states that experienced socialist breakdown – first economic, then political – before

---

[2] We cannot do justice here to the ongoing, vibrant debate on the strengths and weaknesses of different methodologies. Despite the increased reliance on quantitative methods in political science over the past two decades, qualitative methods have enjoyed a renaissance of sorts. These include comparative case studies, process tracing, ethnography, and others. All of these methods are highlighted in this volume.

moving on to democratic transitions with varying success, the range of countries to which China can be appropriately compared remains unclear, particularly as cross-national work often aims to classify countries by regime type. China's extraordinary economic successes in the past twenty-five years place it solidly among the tigers of the developing world. Therefore, comparisons to the economies of its East Asian neighbors across time or to Brazil, Russia, and India (the other "BRICs") today are becoming more common. In its politics, however, China's atypical path of sustained authoritarian rule by an unreformed Communist Party presents researchers with problems of both theory and method. To what other nations should China be compared? How should we accurately code China's regime type in large, cross-national studies? How can we avoid the ontological goal of democratic transition when most of our theories treat democracy in some form as the normal state of politics? In other words, how can we examine China for what it is rather than for what we hope it to become?

Second, comparative research on China as a single entity often masks the remarkable and sustained regional diversity within China itself. Although aggregate statistics for China demonstrate its economic success, the rapid decline in poverty, and the impressive numbers in rural-to-urban migration, urbanization, and industrialization, they often mask the huge and growing regional inequalities. Chinese coastal cities are now reaching the levels of development and standards of living of some of their wealthy developed neighbors whereas the interior still struggles with high levels of poverty, illiteracy, and underdevelopment. Economic diversity is matched by cultural, linguistic, and social diversity that in some cases approaches differences between countries in other parts of the globe. As William Hurst argues in this volume, scholars of comparative politics should be encouraged to pursue any kind of comparative research that yields interesting theoretical and empirical findings. Subnational comparisons can be as fruitful as some of the cross-national research that is so highly esteemed in the discipline. Indeed, many of the authors in this volume utilize China's rich internal diversity to test hypotheses or to explore causal mechanisms of general theories in political science about the nature of economic development, changes in state-society relations, or developments in civil society.

Finally, even though the quantity and quality of Chinese data have improved markedly over the years, it remains difficult to find high-quality data that are easily comparable to data compiled in other countries by international agencies, national governments, academic organizations, or commercial companies. The Chinese government regards much information as politically sensitive and continues to obstruct the collection of systematic political data, broadly defined. In some cases, the government manipulates data for political purposes, which makes it difficult to be confident about the accuracy of government figures. As a result, statistical data from China are rightfully regarded with a healthy degree of skepticism by many researchers. Numbers, although of utmost importance in studying Chinese politics, have to be placed in context, used only when it is clear how they were generated and for what purposes. Indeed, tracing the origins of statistical data generated within China is an exercise that can reveal a great deal about how the modern Chinese state works, as Chen and Diamant show in their chapters on state-generated data in Chinese archives. Although China is surely not unique in this regard, the Chinese Communist Party's attention to the importance of both information and organization can translate into tight controls over survey research and access to some government documents and certain archives. Even some regulations and laws are official secrets. This control continues to limit the creation of accurate datasets, which in turn reduces the integration of China into comparative studies.

Although the study of Chinese politics is not wholly integrated into the subfields of comparative politics and international relations as a whole, the contributions to this volume show that engagement with the theory and methods of the discipline are now the norm for political scientists who conduct research in China today. The problems discussed in this Introduction and the sense of distance between the field of Chinese politics and the discipline are diminishing as scholars trained in the historical, cultural, and institutional context of China deploy standard methods of social science research. The chapter by Peter Hays Gries exemplifies this trend. His scholarship is grounded on a particularly close read of Asian culture yet is informed by a highly critical understanding of work in the vein of political culture that has forwarded rather unsustainable generalizations about differences between East and West. Rather than simply perpetuating this mythical divide, Gries explores recent advances in the field of political psychology and then conducts a series of social experiments in Asian and American settings to determine the degree to which his subjects "see" the world differently. His findings are then applied to developing a more rigorous frame for analyzing the role of leadership psychology in the interaction between states (including the United States) in the Asian security sphere.

POLITICAL RESEARCH IN CHALLENGING ENVIRONMENTS

China's sustained authoritarianism also presents political scientists with logistical, ethical, and political problems when undertaking research that touches on sensitive topics, uses new and innovative data collection methods, or reaches results that may be unsettling or dangerous for powerful domestic interests. As in many other places around the world, studying politics in China is still difficult, at times dangerous, for researchers and research subjects alike, and is wrapped up indelibly with the practice of politics. This work highlights the value added of making use of new sources and methodologies. However, it became clear during our discussions at the workshop that alongside such accomplishments, there is a need for a more candid discussion of the trade-offs when doing fieldwork in difficult locations or on sensitive topics. Although as social scientists we strive for robust internal and external validity, we are routinely presented with situations that require compromise. There are risks in the study of Chinese politics. Researchers who strive to gain access to data that are considered to be "internal" (内部), or related to state secrets, may put themselves at odds with the Chinese state. This is particularly so when the research delves into areas of political sensitivity in China (topics that include ethnic minorities, democratization, religious freedom, etc.). At the same time, carrying out interviews, conducting surveys, and working with officials to gain access to archival sources may also put one's subjects and colleagues in harm's way. Thus, although we do not intend to overemphasize these challenges, at the same time the challenges confronting political scientists working in China extend beyond the issues of increasing explanatory power.

The logistical and ethical problems of doing research in China have become more complicated as our research access and opportunities have widened. As with the treatment of foreigners generally in China, foreign scholars are now much more autonomous from their official sponsors and somewhat better integrated into Chinese society at large. In addition to a more receptive environment for scholarly work, there are new avenues for collaboration with mainland scholars and a better infrastructure for large-scale projects – sample surveys, archival research, and construction of large databases. Such integration and more frequent collaboration require additional attention to the ethical problems of social science research, including protection of informants, attention to the needs and concerns of local collaborators, and striking a balance between the requirements for human subject protection in Western universities with the more informal approaches often taken by scholars working in the field. Several of the chapters here provide effective strategies to mitigate the problems that occur when one is doing research on sensitive topics. Lily L. Tsai examines interviewing techniques that may reduce response errors or misunderstandings between survey enumerators and respondents, particularly with sensitive questions about local government performance, clan relations, or the enforcement of unpopular policies such as birth control or tax collection. Bruce J. Dickson shows the importance of the local partner to ensure on-the-ground cooperation with the survey team. Local partners and colleagues better understand how topics can be presented to reduce political sensitivity, limit self-censorship, and encourage support by local officials. Benjamin L. Read's reliance on "site-intensive methods" allows him to gather information and participant-observation experience at the grassroots level in urban China, the critical point where citizens encounter the state most often and most intimately. Without a considerable amount of time and energy spent intensively studying a few places, Read argues, we often miss the hidden and subtle aspects of power in an authoritarian regime.

ROAD MAP

One of the more exciting developments in much of the recent scholarship on Chinese politics is the exploitation of different sources of evidence and multiple research methodologies in a single study. Indeed, although we have organized the following chapters according to their main methodological themes, a number of them draw from research that illustrates multiple research methods at their best. We hope this volume contributes further to this development and to fruitful collaborative relationships among scholars to exploit more fully the new sources, methods, and field strategies in investigating important questions of Chinese politics.

The chapters in Part I focus on new sources for the study of Chinese politics. Chapters 1 and 2 are companion pieces. In Chapter 1, Xi Chen examines the promise and pitfalls of utilizing *xinfang* (信访 i.e., petitioning) archives. This chapter then meticulously outlines a road map of the kinds of documents available, where they are located, and how accessible they are likely to be, and also presents a series of strategies for maximizing the chances of successful use of such materials. More broadly, Chen assesses the reliability of Chinese archival data. Neil J. Diamant's Chapter 2 echoes and expands upon this conclusion. With a focus on the utility of making more direct use of open archival sources, he crafts a compelling case for broadening the temporal scope of Chinese politics, that is, for bridging the divide between historians and political scientists. Building on this observation, he demonstrates how newly available archives that detail aspects of the personal lives of veterans can provide a new understanding of broad issues in Chinese politics, including controversial questions such as citizenship and patriotism.

Whereas Diamant and Chen examine the Chinese state in the past, and do so largely at the level of local politics, in Chapter 3, Victor Shih, Wei Shan, and Mingxing Liu look to the present and turn attention to the study of elite politics. Shih et al. show how bringing more rigor to the study of elite politics has its own rewards. More specifically, they develop a comprehensive database of the Chinese leadership dating back to the founding of the Chinese Communist Party in 1921. They argue that previous studies of Chinese elite politics lacked such a detailed foundation for studying how and why the careers of China's leaders progressed (or declined).

Chapters 4 through 6 redirect attention to how the consideration of new data sources can deepen understanding of Chinese politics. In Chapter 4, Peter Hays Gries looks for sources in an entirely new direction, mainly by turning to experimental methods and psychological measures to study Chinese foreign policy. In so doing, he seeks to push the discussion of political culture's role in China's emerging relationship with the rest of the world beyond the earlier flawed work in this vein. More specifically, he first outlines the approach he developed in two separate psychological studies. He then utilizes this work to inform a broader discussion of the challenges and limitations of experimental work and psychological measures in the study of Chinese foreign policy. In Chapter 5, Allen Carlson and Hong Duan examine the apparent surge in cyber activity related to Chinese foreign policy. They argue that this development has been poorly understood by researchers, and, ultimately, has tended to be overhyped in the field. Rather than finding a revolutionary development unfolding in China's Internet space dedicated to foreign affairs and national security, they uncover a limited set of new sources in this terrain. Although these data are valuable to scholars, they appear to be less extraordinary than initially expected. In Chapter 6, Daniela Stockmann casts a broad net to reach a somewhat different conclusion. She explores the vast number of Chinese news media sources that are now available online and contends that they provide scholars with new opportunities to conduct content analysis across media sources, across regions, and over time. Stockmann explores the problem of choosing the appropriate sample size for content analysis of Chinese daily newspapers. Drawing on insights from communication methodology, she compares the effectiveness and efficiency of various sample sizes for content analysis in the Chinese context. Although focusing on sample size, Stockmann also includes suggestions for sampling frames for content analysis that involve comparisons across media sources, across regions, and over time.

Part II focuses on qualitative methods in the study of Chinese politics. Qualitative methods of varying kinds have been the hallmark of the study of Chinese politics since American researchers were allowed back into the field in the early 1980s. This volume builds on this strong tradition, but the authors also look beyond the study of Chinese politics to the larger discipline, demonstrating how the study of politics in China can contribute to larger debates on the nature of state-society relations in authoritarian regimes (Read), workshop politics in a rapidly developing economy (Calvin Chen), and the comparative political economy of unemployment (Hurst).

In Chapter 7, Calvin Chen demonstrates how ethnography is a useful tool to understand contemporary Chinese politics. Although some scholars consider the approach inadequate to meet such a challenge, Chen suggests that ethnographic research can go beyond the simple provision of "thick description" and afford a stronger grasp of the multiple and sometimes hidden factors that trigger, sustain, or obstruct change. In focusing on and dissecting developments in communities and institutions at the micro level, ethnography provides a means for generating deeper insights into how macro-level forces influence the interactions and lives of ordinary Chinese citizens and vice versa. Indeed, this approach can aid conceptual development and refinement not only by offering an empirical "reality check," but also by identifying and evaluating the factors that contribute to the social and political outcomes in reform-era China that we seek to explain.

In Chapter 8, Read expands on this approach by arguing for research designs that incorporate "site-intensive" research. His methodology, used in a project on the changing nature of residents' committees in urban China, combines an ethnographic approach that is broader than a single case but still not a large-N study. Read argues that this approach is integral to political science as it allows researchers to develop new hypotheses, expose causal mechanisms, and even falsify existing hypotheses in the literature. His argument builds on the wider literature that has employed these methods, under different names and in other subfields, including American politics. Read also

Introduction   11

shows that in authoritarian and some cultural contexts where politics is often hidden, these methods are even more important.

In Chapter 9, Hurst argues for greater attention to subnational variation across China to develop research questions and effective research designs. Building on a long tradition in Chinese studies to divide the Chinese polity into distinct political economies, he develops a cross-regional research project to explain the wide variation in unemployment policies and outcomes. He discusses the superiority of this approach over single-city case studies, which are not broadly representative, and large-N survey projects, which are often hampered by political sensitivity and unavailable data. Hurst also makes his case by engaging the literature in comparative politics on case studies and the comparative method.

The chapters in Part III consider the place of survey research methods in the study of Chinese politics. In a political environment that remains (at best) officially skeptical about the enterprise, the number of representative sample surveys on Chinese politics nonetheless has grown substantially in the past two decades: political scientists trained and based outside mainland China conducted only two such surveys in the 1980s, but the number of surveys increased more than tenfold in the 1990s and continues to rise steadily. In Chapter 10, "A Survey of Survey Research on Chinese Politics," Melanie Manion reviews these surveys and their products, and evaluates their achievements, with attention to their cumulativeness, contributions to knowledge, and fit in Chinese area studies. Chapters 11, 12, and 13 present findings as they discuss methods of exemplary original survey studies of Chinese politics. In Chapter 11, "Surveying Prospects for Political Change," Bruce Dickson discusses how his surveys of private entrepreneurs and local officials make use of variations across the span of time, geographic region, and key individual-level characteristics to illuminate in the unusual Chinese context a major question of comparative politics: the role of capitalists in democratization. In Chapter 12, "Using Clustered Spatial Data to Study Diffusion," Landry demonstrates the advantages of spatial sampling using GPS technology to analyze the diffusion of formal legal institutions through networks of small communities across the country. In Chapter 13, "Measuring Change and Stability over a Decade in the Beijing Area Study," Mingming Shen and Ming Yang, with Melanie Manion, examine the first decade of the Beijing Area Study (BAS), an ongoing annual representative survey of Beijing residents, conducted since 1995. The measures of change and stability in the unique longitudinal perspective of the BAS allow the authors to gauge the underlying temper of Beijing residents, isolating general patterns of confidence and satisfaction with particular trends of discontent. In Chapter 14, "Quantitative Research and Issues of Political Sensitivity in Rural China," Tsai draws from her qualitative fieldwork and survey research in the Chinese countryside to discuss the implications of political sensitivity for the process and products of our research on Chinese politics, and for our colleagues and interview subjects who remain after we leave to begin the work of evaluating evidence and analyzing data.

Finally, in a concluding chapter, Kenneth Lieberthal reflects on the evolution of the China field in political science. Lieberthal describes the obstacles confronting the study of Chinese politics over the decades and celebrates the current methodological richness and institutional maturity of the field. At the same time, Lieberthal cautions scholars about new problems that will require our ongoing attention if we are to continue to contribute to a broader and deeper understanding of Chinese politics.

PART I

SOURCES

1

State-Generated Data and Contentious Politics in China

Xi Chen

China specialists in the reform era are blessed with much better accessibility to data than previous generations (Perry, 1994b: 704–713). In particular, much information that was collected and maintained by governmental agencies has now become available to researchers. However, because of scholars' unfamiliarity with such sources, uncertainty about collecting them, and long-existing skepticism of their reliability, so far very few scholars have taken full advantage of this opportunity.[1]

In China, many topics on state-society relations are regarded as "sensitive" by the government. Consequently, researchers are faced with various restrictions on their empirical inquiries. Those who study popular contention often find themselves in a difficult situation: interviews or surveys are difficult to arrange, and little information can be found in the media. Under such circumstances, governmental materials, if available, often provide the best sources for the study of state-society interactions. After all, for a long time the party-state not only monopolized political power but also tightly controlled the flow and distribution of critical information.

This chapter will address two major concerns about collecting and using state-generated data: accessibility and reliability. The accessibility of such data is often underestimated. In the reform era, the Chinese government has actually relaxed its control over archival materials. Many documents are published or are available to the public in national or local archives. Various governmental agencies are also willing to share certain materials with researchers. However, the entire archival system is still severely underinstitutionalized, and researchers still face considerable uncertainty about what might be found.

There are also some pitfalls and biases in state-generated data. The reliability of governmental data has long been a concern when studying one-party authoritarian regimes. It is generally believed that such political systems seriously constrain the flow of information, not only between the state and

---

[1] Two notable exceptions are Perry (1994a), and Walder and Su (2003).

society but also within the bureaucratic system. This will certainly affect the data we collect. In order to evaluate the reliability of governmental materials, we need to understand the political processes by which such materials are generated. As some sociologists have noted, "the more we know about the structure and sources of bias in our data, the better prepared we will be to avoid erroneous interpretations of its patterns" (Earl et al., 2004: 77). Therefore, this chapter also examines the structures and processes in which state agents produce archival materials. In particular, we will discuss two sorts of constraints: features of the political system and the process of government-citizen interactions. As Charles Tilly suggests, social researchers need not only develop theories explaining the phenomena under study but also develop theories explaining the generation of evidence concerning the phenomena (Tilly, 2002: 248–254).

This chapter mainly draws on my own experience of collecting and using data from the petitioning (信访) system. During my 2002 field research, I visited four petitioning agencies in Hunan province, including one provincial-level bureau, two prefecture-level bureaus, and one county-level bureau. On my 2008 field trip, I visited several local archives in Guangdong, Hunan, and Hubei. Data generated by other state agencies may not be similar to the petitioning data in every respect, but a discussion of petitioning data can certainly help us think about how best to work with state-generated data in general.

TWO ADVANTAGES

Compared with interviews, surveys, and newspapers, state-generated data have several advantages for the study of contentious politics. Here I will highlight two of them. First, state data can bring the state into focus for our understanding of state-society relations. Second, they make it possible to conduct event analysis, which has made significant contributions to social movement theories in recent decades.

Most scholars of contentious politics in China have focused their empirical studies on social groups rather than on the government. This is understandable, as it is considerably easier to conduct interviews or surveys involving societal actors. To be sure, it is possible to interview or survey government officials, but such interviews or surveys are not easy to arrange and the researcher also faces the difficulty of eliciting candid and informative answers. Those who study popular contention often find a stark contrast between the attitudes of protesters and the attitudes of government officials. Most protesters are eager to talk to researchers – one of their greatest grievances is that no one listens to them. By contrast, government officials are generally reluctant to engage in conversations of any substance on sensitive topics with researchers, especially researchers from foreign countries. With more officials being reprimanded for talking to the media and to others, government officials in most places in China have become increasingly cautious.

Governmental data may be a shortcut. If available, they can provide rich information at a relatively low cost. In particular, they can shed light on the government as an actor in contentious interactions. This is especially important considering that the dominant theoretical paradigm of social movements – political process theory – largely attributes dynamics and outcomes of popular mobilization to the features of the state and their changes. Governmental data, including meeting minutes, leaders' instructions, communications among agencies, and investigation reports, can help us open the black box of the bureaucratic system. For instance, the governmental data that I collected in Hunan province enabled me to conduct systematic studies of governmental responses to popular contention (Chen, 2009; Chen, 2008).

Governmental data not only help us treat the state as an actor but also show us how the state views the relationship between the government and its citizens. Rich governmental archival materials often provide us with a feeling of "seeing like a state" (Scott, 1998). Like social scientists, the state is curious about some social facts and often spends abundant resources to investigate them. State perspectives can help to enhance our understanding of social phenomena. Of course, this is not to suggest that such perspectives are necessarily superior to academic views, but they are often inspiring and illuminating. Take the study of the rising trend of popular contention as a case in point. To explain the dramatic rise of popular contention in China since the 1990s, many studies focus on specific social groups, such as workers or peasants. This is not a problem in itself. But some of these studies tend to overemphasize group-specific conditions and grievances and fail to understand that such social change is a cross-sectoral phenomenon. Government data can help researchers avoid such narrow perspectives since they are concerned with change in the society as a whole. The petitioning system has tracked the rise of collective action for every notable social group. For example, in Hunan province, petitioning data show that social protests on a variety of issues, from pension arrears to environmental pollution, grew substantially and simultaneously from 1994 to 2001.

Although governmental data do have distinct advantages over interviews and surveys, they work best when used together with other data. The state shares a sense of curiosity with social scientists, but its main interests are somewhat different. For example, when the state reports the behavior of protesters, it does so mainly for the purpose of surveillance, and it is very likely to ignore some facts that researchers may find interesting. No matter how rich and comprehensive the governmental materials are, researchers often still find them inadequate for systematic studies. It is therefore necessary for them to collect additional data. Yet, researchers can benefit greatly from governmental data when conducting interviews or surveys. For example, with a complete list of petitions and protests from a certain period, researchers can select and locate interviewees and respondents in a rigorous way. In addition, governmental data can also help researchers frame questions more effectively. In fact, interviewees are generally more willing to talk candidly when researchers appear to have a good grasp of the issues. This is especially true for interviews with government officials.

Another major advantage of Chinese governmental data is that they make event analysis possible. Although archival data are often associated with qualitative methods, they are also suitable for quantitative research or mixed methods, such as content analysis and event analysis.[2] For researchers of contentious politics, event analysis is a particularly important research tool. The methods of collecting and processing data have contributed significantly to the shifting of theoretical paradigms in the field of contentious politics. The two most important theories in recent decades – the resource mobilization and political process models – have substantially benefited from the method of event analysis, which Charles Tilly and his associates pioneered in the 1960s. Based on extensive protest event data collected mainly from newspapers, a number of scholars have conducted cross-regional and cross-period quantitative studies. As the Tillys remarked more than thirty years ago, this method can provide a sounder procedure than "piling example on example, citing informed observers, or reporting strong impressions" (Tilly, Tilly, and Tilly, 1975: 16).

A critical procedure in this method is to compile event catalogs. Such catalogs provide information about occurrence, timing, intensity, sequencing, outcomes, and other aspects of claim-making events. With such information, researchers can answer some important questions about the influence of timing, organizational dynamics, and the political environment on the rates of collective action and on the success of social movements (Olzak, 1989: 120). According to Tilly, analysts can use such catalogs in three ways: aggregate, incidence, and internal regularity. First, they can *aggregate* counts or selected aspects of events into overall measures for times, places, or social categories, and then attempt to explain variation over time, place, or social category. Second, they can also study *incidence* by examining "whether distinguishable features of the phenomenon measured by event catalogs co-vary with characteristics of settings, participants, or associated events." Finally, they can use such catalogs to search for *internal regularities*, such as recurrent sequences or causal links among apparently separate events. The last task is particularly demanding for the data. Analysts have to "break down and recombine narratives of episodes and descriptions of their settings into elements that analysts can then reassemble into representations of the associations or causal connections they have theorized" (Tilly, 2002: 252).

Most scholars have used newspaper data rather than governmental data. In their study of Germany, Italy, and France, the Tillys found that "a continuous run of a national newspaper is a somewhat more reliable source (and a more practical one) than any major archival series we have encountered, a much more reliable source than any combination of standard historical works, and

---

[2] For a good example of content analysis, see Shapiro and Markoff (1998).

superior to any other continuous source it would be practical to use" (Tilly, Tilly, and Tilly, 1975: 16). Indeed, newspaper data are often better than governmental data in terms of scope and reliability. We can hardly expect to find governmental archival materials that can match such newspapers as the *New York Times* in these two respects.

However, there are circumstances in which governmental archival materials may be a better source. For example, in his study of strikes in Russia, Graeme Robertson mainly relied on a protest dataset compiled from unpublished daily text reports of the Interior Ministry (MVD). In order to evaluate the data's reliability, he compared them with the published data and found that "they are a considerable improvement on published strike statistics" (Robertson, 2007: 790). This is because the MVD has both motivation and resources for writing reliable reports, which are primarily used for national security purposes, compiled by officials responsible for actively monitoring levels of disruption in the areas under their supervision. Consequently, "comparisons between the MVD data and official sources show the same macro-trends over time while suggesting higher levels of activity than published sources" (Robertson, 2007: 791).

Likewise, in contemporary China where the media are under very strict constraints regarding reporting popular collective action, governmental data are clearly superior to newspaper data. To be sure, we can still find sporadic reports of popular collective action in the international and domestic media as well as on the Internet. Careful researchers may collect possibly hundreds of such reports. However, these reports can hardly be used in a systematic way as most such events took place in settings that are unrelated. A more useful strategy is to conduct an analysis of a smaller scope but with more solid evidence. For instance, because the event catalog in City Y, which includes all reported events in an internal circular for ten years, provides a variety of information about protest events, such as the number and identity of the participants, forms of action, protest tactics, grievances, ways of framing, and government response, it can be used to answer a wide range of questions. With a statistical study of this dataset, I examined which protest tactics enhance the likelihood of a substantial Chinese government response (Chen, 2009).

WHERE AND WHAT TO LOOK FOR?

Scholars can access state-generated data from three main sources: (1) published materials, (2) national or local archives, and (3) other central or local governmental agencies. In addition, there are some less common ways to locate governmental documents. For example, governmental materials can sometimes be garnered from petitioners. Petitioners are often well aware that such materials may enhance their bargaining power. Despite the government's efforts to withhold critical information, on occasion petitioners have managed to obtain governmental documents. Even many classified internal documents may be circulated among petitioners. Petitioners may sell them or share with other petitioners for free. Some documents are highly informative. A notable example is an internal speech by Deng Pufang, chairman of the Federation of Disabled People in China, in March 2000. Handicapped petitioners in many provinces used this document to exert pressure on local governments in order to obtain favorable policies.

Accessibility is a big advantage for governmental publications. For the field of contentious politics, the most useful among such publications are the various county gazetteers and provincial yearbooks. One reason that such publications can be quite informative is that the boundary between publications for internal use and publications for external use is sometimes vague and fluid. Take the county gazetteers, for example. Although they were originally compiled for internal use, since the 1980s they have been available for public use (Thøgersen and Clausen, 1992; Vermeer, 1992). A local governmental document states that the primary reason for compiling gazetteers (地方志) was "to provide the local leaders with scientific information so that they can make correct decisions" (Thøgersen and Clausen, 1992: 165). Shortly after publication, however, the gazetteers were freely circulated in China. The vagueness as to the audience allows for some degree of openness.

Some local governments are more open than others. As Walder and Su note, the interpretation and implementation of general regulations on information openness is primarily a matter for the local authorities (Walder and Su, 2003: 80). If we compare the Henan yearbooks with the Hunan yearbooks in the 1980s and 1990s, we find that those from Henan include much richer information about petitions and appeals. Of course, even the most informative publications omit information that can be found in local archives or other governmental agencies. Hence there is a trade-off: governmental publications are most accessible, but they are the least informative on sensitive issues.

Accessibility to local archives is usually not a problem. The Chinese government has evidently improved its archival system since the 1990s. The Archives Law was amended in 1996, and a new version of the guidelines was promulgated by the State Council in 1999. Most, if not all, local governments at the county level and above have set up local archives. In recent years, most local archives have not only increased their collections but have also opened more materials to the public. Of course, despite the Chinese government's efforts to institutionalize the archival system, local archives vary considerably in their interpretation of what should be included in their archives. Thus, it is still highly unpredictable as to what is maintained in the local archives and what researchers are allowed to read and photocopy. Some local archives maintain only very old and incomplete materials because other governmental agencies are reluctant to transfer their archival materials to them. Even for those archival materials that are supposed to be open, some special restrictions may be imposed. For example, in the archives of Zhijiang City, Hubei province, researchers who want to look up archives from a specific agency need to obtain the approval of that agency. Therefore, if a researcher wants to read archives that were transferred from the petitioning bureau, he or she needs to be approved not only by the archives but also by the petitioning bureau. The situation is even more complex for foreigners. In some local archives, however, researchers may find relatively new and quite complete archives. In my trip to the municipal archives of Yiyang City, Hunan province, in 2008, for instance, I was astonished to find that many "sensitive" internal governmental documents from the petitioning bureau dating as late as 2000 were open to the public. Among the most valuable was an internal circular called "Petitioning Express," which was originally intended to be provided only to top local leaders.

Archival materials in other governmental agencies are more difficult to collect. Generally, the higher the level of the agency, the more reluctant it is to open its filing cabinets to researchers. Therefore, it is more difficult to collect materials from provincial agencies (and even more so from the central government) than from prefectural-level or county-level agencies. Scholars who are lucky enough to access archival materials directly from governmental agencies can expect to find a variety of data. The following is a brief description of what can be found in the cabinets of the petitioning bureaus: (1) registration forms for letters and visits; (2) case files that include petition letters, meeting minutes, and investigation reports; (3) governmental reports on petitioning events; (4) periodic summaries and analyses of petitions, work reports by petitioning officials, and speeches by local or central leaders concerning petitioning work; and (5) statistical data compiled by the petitioning bureaus. Regarding the extent to which these materials have been processed, they can be roughly classified into raw materials (such as petitioning letters), partially processed products (such as reports of events and summaries of petitions), and well-processed products (such as work reports and statistical data). They are also officially classified into short-term, long-term, and permanent archives according to how long the government intends to keep them. Petitioning bureaus can keep the long-term and permanent archives in their own offices for a certain period of time and then send them to the local archives. According to the Archives Law, county-level bureaus can keep their archives for ten years before transferring them to the local archives. In practice, however, some bureaus may keep them for an even longer period. Most raw materials are regarded as short-term archives and will be disposed of within a year or so. Consequently, they cannot be found in the local archives.

Each of these five types of materials has its strengths and weaknesses. From the first type of material, registration forms, researchers can establish a comprehensive database about all petitions addressed to the petitioning bureaus. Yet the information about each case is limited. There is little information about how the petitioners made their claims and about how the government responded. The second type of material, case files that provide rich information on each case, is suitable for more in-depth case studies. With the petition letters, registration forms, leaders' written instructions, meeting minutes, and investigation reports on file, one is able to reconstruct the entire process of contentious interactions.

The third category of material is especially valuable for event analysis. It usually takes two main forms: (1) special reports sent to local leaders that are titled "important petitioning issues for review," and (2) a special internal circular published by almost every petitioning bureau at each level. It is worth noting that most petitioning bureaus simultaneously publish two different types of circulars. One is purely for internal use whereas the other is more public. For example, in Tianjin City, the first type is called *Petitioning Information* (信访信息), and the second *Tianjin Petitioning* (天津信访), which is a monthly journal. The internal circular is usually much more informative than the public circular. In City Y, the internal circular is issued regularly, about two issues each week. Yet during important periods, such as during the local people's congress annual meetings, it is published almost daily.

The fourth and fifth types of materials are well processed by petitioning officials to inform local leaders or the upper authorities about the basic facts regarding petitions and protests. They often include a large amount of information that is convenient to use. But they have two shortcomings. First, as well-processed materials, they are more vulnerable to distortion. Second, they are not processed as academic research and therefore cannot be used directly. For example, many statistical forms use a variety of official jargon and many basic terms are not clearly defined. Therefore, researchers need to interpret these materials carefully before using them for academic research.

THE STATE, INFORMATION, AND PETITIONING DATA

Like their accessibility, the reliability of governmental data is also cause for concern among scholars. Compared with other data, it is well recognized that using governmental data requires special caution. As Paul Starr rightly points out, "Administrative data are also particularly sensitive to vagaries of bureaucratic policy or procedure unrelated to the external social phenomenon they may be taken to measure. For example, changes in budgets, personnel, and internal incentives and controls such as quotas for cases opened or closed are likely to influence administrative measures of crime, illness, and other forms of civil deviance" (Starr, 1983: 30). Similarly, Earl et al. argue that reporting may be particularly susceptible to error and bias when information about an event is collected from authorities (or participants) because "these actors often have a stake in how the event is portrayed" (Earl et al., 2004: 73). Unlike news agencies, the governmental agencies that produce the data are also actors in state-society or intrabureaucratic interactions. In this sense, using governmental data requires more caution than using newspaper data.

A variety of events in the history of the People's Republic of China (PRC), from the Great Leap Forward to the recent severe acute respiratory syndrome (SARS) crisis, suggest that China specialists may have more reason to be cautious. Even Chinese leaders seem to be well aware of the unreliability of governmental data. Yao Yilin, the director of the General Office of the Central

Committee from 1980 to 1982, expressed his unhappiness with the existing channels of information:

> The most difficult thing for a leadership unit to do is to collect accurate information at the basic level. Various departments also conduct their own investigations but their investigations sometimes have a departmental bias or partiality. Now the reports from the localities are written after repeated deliberations and they have been perfected so that you cannot see anything in them (Huang, 1995: 832).

The tendency toward distortion or even falsification of information in the Chinese political system has been well discussed by academics. For example, Richard Baum and Alexi Shevchenko argue that "lower-level officials in Leninist systems have a strong incentive to lie to their superiors, hiding assets and under-estimating capacity, the quality of information available to leaders in such systems is generally poor" (Baum and Shevchenko, 1999: 337).

However, we should not exaggerate the problems of governmental data. After all, except for a few tumultuous periods, the mechanisms for information generation and circulation have worked at least well enough to sustain the political system. In order to accurately evaluate the quality and reliability of government information, we need to examine the institutional structures and political processes for information generation and circulation. In particular, we need to determine why and how the state agencies have produced the data that we are going to use.

Why does the Chinese government produce so much petitioning information? Every state, especially a modern state, is hungry for information about social facts. This is why James Scott claims that the legibility of the society is a central problem in statecraft (Scott, 1998: 2). Similarly, Paul Starr notes, "that the word statistics comes from the same root as 'state' testifies to an important stimulus of development: the demands of the modern state for social and economic intelligence" (Starr, 1983: 15).

Different regimes may have different strengths and weaknesses for collecting information. Authoritarian regimes such as China have three advantages. First, they often have strong power to simplify and standardize the society to make it more legible (Starr, 1983: 15). Second, some regimes, especially totalitarian regimes, have a strong capacity to mobilize ordinary people to provide information. Third, their deep penetration into the society also facilitates surveillance. In China, grassroots institutions such as work units have long worked as state agents to supervise the population (Walder, 1986).

However, these advantages can sometimes turn into disadvantages. For instance, deep penetration of the society and an all-encompassing structure may actually hinder the collection and flow of information. When most social institutions are under its direct control, it is difficult for the party-state to find any independent sources of information. Moreover, the lack of protections of freedom of speech and of freedom of the press further exacerbate this problem. The media, supposedly the most important source of external information, usually remain silent on critical issues.

Small wonder then that many authoritarian regimes rely heavily on citizen complaints as sources of information. In order to redress their grievances, petitioners have a strong incentive to provide information to the state. Also, because most complaints only bear on trivial issues, relatively few political risks are involved in making complaints. Therefore, Liu Shaoqi, former president of the People's Republic, once commented that he felt more comfortable reading petition letters than reading bureaucratic reports (Diao, 1996: 157).

Generally, the state collects two types of social information: one focuses on the subjective state of the population whereas the other focuses on purely objective facts, such as demographic and economic statistics. The information at stake in the SARS crisis was mostly objective. For example, how many SARS cases had been found? The information provided by petitioners is not confined to objective facts and also may include subjective facts. It is especially important for the state to understand the feelings and opinions of its citizens.

The party-state in China collects information from petitions and appeals for three main purposes: responsiveness, accountability, and surveillance. Those authoritarian regimes that care about political responsiveness work hard to collect information about popular preferences, albeit in a different way from that of liberal democracies. When little reliable information is available from elections and public opinion polls, petitions and appeals constitute an important source of information about popular preferences. Another purpose is to hold governmental agents accountable. With few alternative sources, such as a reliable media, the party-state must identify the misdeeds of its agents through negative feedback from petitioners. For example, various statistics indicate that this channel has provided clues for at least 70 percent of the corruption cases taken by legal enforcement agencies in any period of the PRC.[3] Finally, the party-state can also garner information about the most volatile segments of the population by monitoring the petitioning activities. This is because many petitions or protests have the potential to develop into more rebellious action and violence.

Although petitions and appeals are regarded as external information, by the time they reach the party and government leaders, they have already been processed by the bureaucracy. Therefore, like media information in China, such so-called external information sources are also subject to the constraints of bureaucratic politics. At least two features of the political system may affect the tendency for information falsification and distortion: alternative information sources and responsibility systems. When the leadership relies heavily on one particular information source and has no alternatives, the situation can be best described as "information dependence." Wang Shaoguang, writing on China's fiscal system, attributes information manipulation to such a dependence. As he explains, "the center has to rely upon agents spread widely across the nation for information. In a hierarchical system, those at the bottom have little choice but to pursue their objectives by manipulating the supply of information to the

---

[3] For example, see Diao (1996: 39).

center. Therefore there is always the danger of information transmitted to the center being distorted" (Shaoguang Wang., 1995: 87). Furthermore, there is a variety of local responsibility systems in China that impose rewards and sanctions based on the information generated within the bureaucracy. In particular, it is widely accepted among Chinese officials that "numbers affect positions."

Therefore, we can make two assumptions. First, a higher level of information dependence implies a stronger tendency for information distortion. Second, when the information is more closely tied to political responsibility, the tendency for information distortion is higher. Fortunately, judging by these two criteria, information distortion has not been a big problem for most governmental data from the petitioning system since the 1990s. The petitioning system is only one of many information channels. As to claim-making activities by ordinary people, there are at least five agencies that routinely provide such information to leaders: (1) the police department, (2) the Social Stability Maintenance Office (维稳办), (3) the Politics and Law Committee (政法委), (4) the petitioning system, and (5) the 610 Office for activities related to Falungong followers. In addition, one of the most striking features of the petitioning system is that there are many "skip-level" petitions. Petitioners may deliver their petitions not only to local governments but also to their superiors. Because the petitioning system is not the only agency providing information, and petitioners often send information directly to upper-level governments, it is more difficult for the petitioning agencies to hide and distort information.

Second, the connection between petitioning data and political consequences does not create particularly strong incentives for information distortion. Although the Chinese government holds local governments strictly responsible for handling petitions and protests, the mere occurrence of petition and protest events does not warrant reprimand; political consequences result only when such events are handled poorly. To be sure, at times many local governmental policies have viewed high rates of petitions and complaints as a negative reflection of the performance of local leaders. In recent years, however, there has been an attempt to detach responsibility from the local government for petitions and protests. This became a trend particularly after Premier Zhu Rongji's speech in 1996 when he claimed that a higher frequency of petitions and appeals was not necessarily a negative indication.[4] Rather, it might suggest that local leaders have a more democratic work style and that ordinary people trust them. Of course, leaders in different localities still have different interpretations. For instance, some types of petitioning activities – such as repeated petitions over a long period – may indicate that the local governments are unresponsive or otherwise flawed. In general, however, the motivation for manipulating information about petitioning activities in governmental reports for internal use is not overwhelming.

---

[4] Comrade Zhu Rongji's Opening Speech at the Fourth National Conference on *Xinfang* Work, 1996. This is a document kept by the Xinfang Bureau of County H in Hunan province.

This is not to suggest that we can ignore the information distortions caused by bureaucratic politics. As has been widely observed, protesters tend to overreport, whereas governmental agencies tend to underreport. Protesters often exaggerate the number of participants in order to demonstrate their strength or legitimacy. By contrast, governmental agencies, such as the police, are likely to underreport events or participants in order to reduce the impression of social disorder. This rule also applies to the petitioning system. For example, when I visited the petitioning bureau in County H, Hunan province, I noticed that not every large-scale protest had been reported as required. An official tried to justify such behavior: "That event should not count as an event with over fifty petitioners since most of the participants were only onlookers. They came to the county seat to go shopping, and only unintentionally gathered before the county government."[5]

Indeed, a general discussion of the reliability of petitioning data is insufficient since some types of data are more reliable than others. For instance, raw materials in petitioning bureaus suffer relatively minor problems. Registration forms or case files are seldom distorted. By contrast, those well-processed data are more likely to be manipulated.

Bureaucratic constraints are not the only challenges to information generation and circulation. The contentious interactions between government and petitioners may also affect the process. Historically, it is not uncommon for the state's search for social information to result in political contention. For example, many premodern censuses in Western societies met with strong resistance (Kertzer and Arel, 2006: 665–666; Starr, 1983: 15). Also, as mentioned above, one of the foci of struggles between government and petitioners in China is information about relevant policies and about the petitioning activities of other groups. Therefore, consideration of the possible impact on social actors may also constrain the process of data generation.

For instance, the method of categorization can affect the behavioral patterns of the petitioners. Petitioning data use categories such as "collective visits," "skip-level visits," "repeat visits," and "abnormal visits" to identify petitioning activities. Such categories in fact constitute the basis for norms concerning permitted and forbidden activities. Indeed, the methods of data collection often involve trilateral interactions among upper-level authorities, lower-level authorities, and petitioners. When upper-level authorities implement a certain statistical method, they must often consider the impact on the two other actors: their subordinates and the real or potential petitioners. They are thus often caught in a dilemma – data collection for the purpose of exerting pressure on lower authorities may be exploited by the petitioners, and yet the neglect of such statistical work may reduce the sense of responsibility of the lower-level authorities.

The Hunan Provincial Bureau once experimented with abolishing the counting of repeated petitioning activities by so-called long-term petitioners.

---

[5] Interview, July 2002.

Such activities had been regarded as a negative factor since a large number of repeated petitions to the upper authorities was thought to indicate the failure of local governments; the provincial bureau's counting of such activities therefore exerted pressure on the local governments. However, this method was then exploited by savvy "long-term petitioners." They understood very well that each time they petitioned the provincial government their action reflected negatively on the local government. Therefore, to prevent such activities, the local governments were under greater pressure to negotiate with these petitioners. Conversely, if these activities were not counted, they would not have such leverage. To eliminate the incentive for long-term to visit the upper authorities, the Hunan Provincial Government decided not to count such activities. Yet the policy lasted for only a few weeks, and the previous practice was reinstated. Although the intended effect had largely been achieved (weakened incentives for petitioners to appeal to the upper authorities), the policy had a strong and undesired side effect: lower-level authorities began to work less diligently to prevent long-term petitioners from petitioning to the upper authorities. In sum, the process of data generation about contentious politics is itself a part of contentious politics. A good understanding of intrabureaucratic and government-citizen interactions is therefore helpful for us in evaluating the availability and quality of the data.

THE PETITIONING SYSTEM AND ITS ADAPTATIONS

After a discussion of the general political process of data generation, we can now shift our focus to the specific governmental agency that collects, processes, and maintains petitioning archives. A closer examination of the petitioning system, especially its organization and operating procedures, will further help us evaluate the quality and reliability of petitioning data. In general, petitioning bureaus with strong incentives and abundant resources can produce reliable and high-quality data, but the converse may also apply. The evolution of the petitioning system has been a process that integrates institutional continuity and change. On the one hand, the petitioning system's basic functions and its relationship to the local leadership have hardly changed. On the other hand, since the dramatic rise of popular contention in China in the 1990s, the petitioning system has undergone remarkable adaptations. In order to handle petitions and protests more effectively, the organizational structures have been adjusted and some new procedures have been implemented. Such continuities and adaptations have had a significant impact on the data.

Petitioning agencies still play a role in the bureaucratic system as it was designed more than fifty years ago. As part of mass-line politics, the petitioning system was designed to facilitate communications between party leaders and the masses. Therefore, petitioning agencies are highly dependent on party-state leaders. Indeed, they were never meant to fulfill any function other than that of assisting the leaders. The primary goal of their information work is to serve the local leadership. Each year the information materials in the petitioning bureaus are evaluated, and the officials who produce "useful information" are praised or rewarded. The primary criteria for evaluating "useful information" are whether the materials have attracted the attention of the local leaders and whether written instructions have been issued based on them. In the relationship between 条/部门 and 块/政府, 块 is much more important for the petitioning agencies (Lieberthal, 1995; Unger, 1987).

Such dependence of petitioning bureaus on local leaders has caused considerable variation in the quality and style of petitioning work across localities. In those areas where local leaders care more about the petitioning work, petitioning agencies enjoy more resources and tend to produce better data. In contrast, petitioning bureaus in some localities are clearly poorly equipped and staffed. In one county bureau that I visited, no official was specifically assigned to handle petitioning information. Although most of the original case files were maintained, few reports or statistical data were produced. More important, local leaders also tend to have different understandings about whether information on petitions will affect their performance evaluations. Those leaders who still regard a high rate of petitioning events as a negative factor will discourage petitioning bureaus from providing accurate information.

Overall, however, since the dramatic rise of collective petitioning activities in the 1990s, the petitioning system has been strengthened. It has obtained a higher status in the bureaucracy and it enjoys more resources. For example, in the late 1990s, the Hunan Provincial Government elevated the rank of officials in the provincial petitioning bureau by half a level. Consequently, the bureau chief, whose rank had previously been one-half level lower than that of other department chiefs, began to enjoy the same rank. In addition, since the late 1990s, petitioning bureau chiefs have been concurrently appointed the deputy secretary generals of the government at the county, city, or provincial levels.[6]

In addition, there have been several remarkable adaptations of the procedures for information collection and processing. First, since the mid-1990s the petitioning system has set up procedures for reporting urgent information. For example, in Hunan province, "must report" issues include (1) collective petitioning of over fifty participants that has been addressed to the county government or above; (2) potential collective petitioning activities of over one hundred people; (3) information about collective petitioning events to the provincial government or Beijing; and (4) events that evolved from ordinary petitioning into "explosive mass incidents" (突发性群体事件) that have disrupted normal work, production, business, and daily order. The former three should be reported within the same day; the latter should be reported instantly. The

---

[6] It seems that this is a measure that was adopted nationwide. In Zhejiang province, for example, all petitioning bureau chiefs at the city and county levels had been concurrently appointed deputy secretary general or deputy director of the General Office before the end of 2001. See *Zhejiang nianjian* (2002: 72).

report should include the time, location, number of participants, forms of action, claims, governmental responses, and trends (动态). When necessary, the local petitioning bureau should send follow-up reports.

Second, petitioning agencies are also required to screen "elements of instability" periodically. One of the tasks of the petitioning agencies is to provide information about the targets of social control. There are two main targets: long-term petitioners (老户) and collective petition organizers. Before the rise of collective petitions, long-term petitioners were the primary targets. Since the mid-1990s, however, the primary target has shifted to collective petitioners. Screening "instability factors" is not temporary work. The petitioning system tried to institutionalize it as standard procedure. It was thus written into the Regulations on Letters and Visits in 2005.

Lists of "instability factors" are usually made shortly before important occasions: New Year's Day, the Spring Festival, the "Two Conferences," National Day, and so on. These events are targeted because it is generally believed that collective petitions are more likely to take place on such occasions and that they will have a relatively greater impact on society. Therefore, local governments have often designated such periods as "specially protected periods" (特护期). In some years, petitioning agencies have been especially busy during these occasions. In 1999, for example, besides the regular "important periods," there were other special events during which collective petitioning activities were to be strictly prevented: the crackdown on Falungong, the tenth anniversary of the crackdown on the student movement, the handover of Macau to China, and the fiftieth anniversary of the founding of the PRC. In that year, the municipal bureau and seven county-level bureaus in City Y compiled 43 lists in which they identified 739 "instability factors."

Third, the procedures for compiling statistical data have been substantially improved and standardized since the mid-1990s. Provincial bureaus have established some standard forms that all bureaus at the county and city levels must fill out each month. In City Y, for example, the petitioning bureaus of the five counties and two districts must complete the standard forms each month and send them to the municipal bureau. When the municipal bureau receives the information from the counties, it will complete the same standard forms with the information about the entire city. When the various cities send their forms to the provincial bureau, the provincial bureau will fill out the same forms with the information about the entire province and then send them to the national bureau.

The quality of statistical work by petitioning agencies has improved considerably since the mid-1990s. More extensive information has been collected, and the methods have become more refined. For example, events with five to twenty-nine participants are differentiated from events with over thirty participants on the statistical forms of collective petitions. Similarly, among non-collective petitions, petitions with one to two participants are differentiated from those with three to four participants, which are called "group petitions" (群体访). Previously, this subtle differentiation did not exist.

Finally, petitioning agencies have begun to produce better analytical reports. Although the statistics can speak for themselves, petitioning agencies regularly write all kinds of reports to help the leaders understand the general situation. Many of these reports are based on statistics. There are special reports, which may focus on a special period, area, or issue, and comprehensive reports, which survey the situation about all issues for the entire area. The quality of the reports has also improved considerably since the mid-1990s. Most reports before the mid-1990s were superficial and written in a journalistic style. The reports after the mid-1990s are more extensive and solid. They not only present and analyze statistical data but also provide some background and even offer suggestions for tackling problems.

IMPLICATIONS AND SUGGESTIONS

The above analysis of the process of data generation carries some encouraging messages for researchers. The authoritarian system has not created fatal problems for governmental data. Many governmental materials, especially raw or semiprocessed materials in the petitioning agencies, do not suffer from serious distortion. The regime has also proven to be very adaptive. When the leadership was alerted to the rise of popular contention, the organizations and procedures of the petitioning system were substantially improved. Consequently, the petitioning system has begun to produce richer and better data. Furthermore, the archival system has become more open.

This is not to suggest that governmental data are readily available to everyone. Some conventional strategies for conducting fieldwork in China are still very important. For example, it is helpful for foreign researchers to be affiliated with a Chinese university or research institute. Personal connections are especially important for collecting governmental archival data. Furthermore, researchers are advised to pay more attention to lower level agencies, which are generally more open than higher level agencies. To be sure, higher level agencies usually maintain materials of a larger scope. However, for some "sensitive" topics, data from a county government may be very valuable. Finally, because different local governments may have quite different policies, it is important to try different agencies and locations. Often valuable data cannot be found until researchers have explored a number of possibilities.

But the above analysis also reveals some problems. Because information work in the petitioning system (as well as in most other public agencies in China) generally has not been well institutionalized, there are remarkable variations in the available data across time and region. Differences in the scope and content of collection often make it difficult to conduct cross-time and cross-regional comparisons.

In addition, the irregular variations make the biases in the data somewhat unpredictable. Fortunately, there are some measures to partially remedy the problem of uncertainty. First, we can seek some indicators to measure the quality and reliability of the data. As Walder and Su's (2003) study of county gazetteers indicates, the quantity of information is often an indictor of its quality. This is because the quantity reflects the approach of the local leaders regarding information collection and processing. Where the leaders stress the importance of information work, governmental agencies tend not only to collect more information but also to collect it more carefully. Other indicators may also be helpful. For example, if a bureau has received an award for its information work, usually the data it has produced are of higher quality. Of course, this may also raise questions about bias in the data.

Second, we can investigate the reliability. One advantage of using contemporary data is that it is more convenient to examine how these data have been produced. Government officials in charge of compiling materials can sometimes be interviewed. We can also evaluate the reliability by comparing different sources. Since governmental data include multiple sources, they can be used for cross-checking. For example, important petitioning events can be reported in different forms: they will be reported in the "important petitions for review," the internal circulars, the reports on "screening elements of instability," and the periodic reports. In addition, the reliability can be evaluated by examining outside sources. For example, we can compare governmental data with information from interviews. In this sense, triangulation of different sources is especially useful.

Third, problems are less serious if we use upstream sources. The more the data have been processed, the more biased they tend to be. As analyzed earlier, analytic reports and statistical results are likely to be more biased. When upstream information sources, such as petition letters, registration forms, and original reports about the events, are available, researchers are advised to process the data by themselves as this can yield more reliable outcomes. The statistical data in the petitioning system have multiplied in recent years. Although they are rich and very informative, there are some risks and difficulties in using them. The definition and measurement of key categories are often vague and inconsistent. For example, the term "collective visits" for some years referred to petitions delivered by three or more participants, but in other years it referred to petitions delivered by five or more participants. In addition, the official jargon, which is very common in statistical data, may not only confuse researchers but may also lead to inconsistent information. This is because officials from different agencies may interpret it in different ways. For example, petitions related to illegitimate fees imposed by local schools are sometimes classified as issues of "三乱" but at other times as "issues of peasant burdens." It is uncertain whether these vaguely defined and sometimes overlapping concepts are interpreted consistently by local petitioning cadres. In contrast, with upstream materials researchers can control the methods of codification and aggregation.

These risks and difficulties also apply to information sources from higher level governmental agencies. Higher level agencies usually enjoy much better resources and facilities and therefore produce obviously much better archival materials. However, it should be noted that most of the aggregate data come from below. As Leo Orleans suggested long ago, "the greater the number of administrative plateaus which serve as resting places for statistics as they are moved up the line, the less accurate are their figures" (Orleans, 1974: 51).

Of course, even upstream sources have some selection or description biases. For instance, in the petitioning bureaus we can find files only on those cases that have been regarded as important by the government. Similarly, internal reports of the petitioning system are more likely to cover protests that took place near a government compound or that caused considerable disruption. It is important for us to evaluate and state explicitly these biases in our research.

Fieldwork in China is often like an adventure. No good map is available for the hidden treasure of state-generated data. There are also pitfalls along the road. For those undeterred adventurers, however, other explorers' reflections, such as those in this chapter, may sometimes provide valuable clues.

2

Why Archives?

Neil J. Diamant

Like many of the contributors to this volume, I began graduate school roughly a decade after China began its "reform and opening-up" process. At the time, the field of Chinese politics was, temporally speaking, reasonably well demarcated. Those of us in political science departments were expected to say something novel and significant about the post-1949 period. Within this rather narrow range, however, an even more contracted time span – post-1978 politics – drew the largest number of students, as well as generated the most interest among the broader public and departmental colleagues. To be sure, this temporal border was somewhat porous,[1] but because it was also vigorously patrolled by tough-minded historians, who were reluctant to define the 1949–78 period as "history,"[2] the "present-ism" in the study of Chinese politics was difficult to ignore. More recently, thanks to the growing interest in China's "rise," the gravitation of political science toward the present has become even stronger. Students of politics overwhelmingly concentrate on events in the last thirty years, whereas historians, with some exceptions, still focus on the pre-1949 period, leaving the other three decades of the People's Republic of China (PRC) politics (1949–78) in a disciplinary twilight zone. In this chapter I suggest that presentism has not been cost-free in terms of our ability to understand Chinese politics and that these costs can best be recouped by broadening the temporal scope of Chinese politics and making archival research a far more integral part of scholarship than is currently the case.

---

[1] For example, political scientists such as Elizabeth Perry, James Tong, Joseph Fewsmith, Andrew Nathan, and David Strand crossed it, survived, and made their names concentrating on pre-1949 politics.

[2] The Chinese history field still does not have its equivalent of a Strand, Nathan, or Perry – someone who wrote an award-winning study of the 1960s or 1970s. In contrast, American historians can write books about the civil rights movement or "Berkeley in the '60s" without any special justification.

These musings about disciplinary boundaries were stimulated by Roderick MacFarquhar and Michael Schoenhals's study of the Cultural Revolution, *Mao's Last Revolution* (2006). The book is exceptional in several respects. The authors collected fascinating data from a dizzying array of sources, among them Red Guard personal diaries, broadsheets, handbills, big-character posters, and minutes from Politburo meetings. It is difficult to imagine a more dogged pursuit of data on such a sensitive topic. Unsurprisingly, the book is jam-packed with politics (which they view as driven by personal and family agendas, with "institutions" and "organizations" playing bit roles). At the same time, *Mao's Last Revolution* is atheoretical; I doubt it would pass muster as a "job talk" in most American political science departments, let alone provide the ballast to cross the tenure threshold. Last is the topic itself. Although some historians and sociologists and their graduate students have been encroaching upon the Cultural Revolution, it would be the intrepid graduate student in political science who would venture into the mid-1960s to pen a dissertation about civil-military relations in, say, Sichuan province. As if snubbing their noses at the fads and scientific pretensions of political science, MacFarquhar and Schoenhals present a balanced *political history* of those fateful years. The extended commentary on the credibility of sources, the discussion of how to weigh a particular piece of evidence, and their digging for valuable data nuggets would make both authors highly attractive candidates on the history job market!

But aside from these speculative scenarios – both authors have received tenure at well-regarded institutions – *Mao's Last Revolution* is noteworthy for something even more important, and directly related to the discussion of the role of archives in the study of politics: The authors' ability to marshal thousands of *new* sources on a topic that in many libraries occupies only several shelves demonstrates the exciting possibilities to generate new knowledge about critical events in PRC politics (with legacies lasting decades) if researchers take up the challenge of shifting the temporal frame backward toward the prereform era. Equally significant, *Mao's Last Revolution* was researched *without* access to the central party archives, the "mother-load" of Cultural Revolution material. Imagine the scope of data, and new insights about politics, that could be gleaned from a year-long immersion in this and other archives, or if local archives opened their doors to researchers examining other seminal political events in the PRC, such as land reform, the Korean War, the Great Leap Forward, or diplomatic relations with the USSR! These sources would activate tremors in the field; to stay intellectually honest we would have to revise our lectures, textbooks, and "consensus" histories of the period (such as the *Cambridge History of China*, vols. 14 and 15). We would also have to recalibrate our interpretation of the *post*-Mao period, particularly if scholars offer "path-dependent" and historically grounded explanations for political and economic phenomena, or alternatively, argue that the present represents a sharp break from the past.

Fortunately, we do not need to overstretch our imaginations to envision this scenario. In recent years, some scholars of the PRC, like some of their historian counterparts,[3] have taken advantage of archives to press for significant revisions of the received wisdom about a host of topics. Mark Frazier's (2003) thesis on the Republican-era origins of the work unit (单位) system, Julia Strauss's (2002) work on early 1950s political campaigns, Eddy U's (2003) study of Shanghai teachers, Patricia Thornton's (2007) analysis of efforts to control corruption during the Qing dynasty, the Republican period, and the PRC, Elizabeth Perry's (Perry and Li, 1997; Perry, 2006) studies of labor, and my own on the 1950 Marriage Law (Diamant, 2000) all relied extensively on newly accessible archival data. These archive-based studies, I argue, should be the jumping-off point for a much-needed modification of the received wisdom about politics in the PRC. However, as the situation currently stands, historians willing to "push" history up to the 1970s and 1980s, and not political scientists, most of whom are reluctant to "pull" politics back to this period, will be the main beneficiaries from the rapid declassification of materials now under way in PRC archives at all levels, *sans* the Center; to wit: most of the scholars named above are not employed by political science departments at large American research universities. This would be unfortunate. Given the short history of the PRC, and that much of what we have learned about its politics is based in the "pre-archival era," it is far too soon to relegate the foundational years and critical events of the prereform PRC to "history." Think about this: what would the field of American politics look like if anything that happened prior to the Carter administration was considered "historical," or if political scientists eschewed research in the Nixon Presidential Library and Museum because colleagues and others were more fascinated by the Obama administration? Most Americanists would consider these propositions fairly ridiculous.

In this chapter, I want to make the case for the vital utility of archives to the study of Chinese politics, past and present. I will do this by examining some documents that provide an unprecedented look at the politics surrounding a high status, but personally vulnerable, population: the wives/fiancées of People's Liberation Army (PLA) soldiers during the 1950s and 1960s. Even though these old memos and investigation reports (the proverbial pot of gold for historians) represent a smidgen of what is available in archives, they can open a window onto larger, more conceptual, "political science–friendly" issues – in this case, patriotism and nationalism. They also call into question much of the conventional wisdom about the high status of the PLA and its personnel during this period.

Before moving onto the nitty-gritty of this topic, however, I want to expand a bit on archival research. What are some of the pitfalls? What documents are

---

[3] The fields of Ming, Qing, and Republican legal history have been thoroughly revitalized by archival research. See the works by Philip Huang, Kathryn Bernhardt, Melissa Macauley, Matthew Sommer, and Janet Theiss, among others.

available, and how should researchers use them? As we will see, the volume and level of detail in archival documents can stimulate us to look at old issues in new ways, and draw attention to aspects of the state and society that are easily brushed under the carpet in sources that pay more attention to elites.

ARCHIVAL RESEARCH: PITFALLS AND OPPORTUNITIES

Unlike many methodologies in political science (or the social sciences more generally), there is little by way of official guides for conducting archival research in China. Like the National Archives in the United States, some archives in the PRC publish their own guidebooks (指南) – the Shanghai 指南, for instance, fills 850 pages – but most do not. Wa Ye and Joseph Esherick (1996) compiled a useful overview of archives based on information in county gazetteers, but this volume already is somewhat dated, does not include information on materials that might be made available upon request, or the contents of district (区) archives in cities. Thankfully, Esherick and others have created a Web site with updated information on various archives[4] as well as a very helpful compendium of "Archive Users' Experiences." It is also possible to write to an archive prior to one's visit to request information and to ask if foreign scholars can access certain materials. For sensitive topics, however, it is probably best to work through a research institution or university; connections (关系), of course, help a great deal, as can reciprocal exchange opportunities and conferences. For instance, archivists at the Yunnan Provincial Archives were receptive to my requests for material because their director had recently been hosted by the National Archives.

The successful mining of archives, much like other methodologies, depends upon many factors. The background, education level, and cosmopolitanism of archive personnel can make a significant difference in access. The topic matters as well: given the many political events in PRC history that are considered politically sensitive, how one frames a subject and presents it to Chinese hosts and archivists can affect the outcome of research. Generally, it is important to frame one's subject in as noncontroversial language as possible. For example, a study of land reform might be pitched as a study of changes in land-holding patterns. Since land-holding patterns were partially shaped by land reform, there is greater justification to request these materials. I framed my study of veterans and military families under the more general rubric of "providing preferential treatment for the worthy." It is also important to arrive in China with ample financial resources since it often takes time to collect enough material to produce an article or book-length study. As might be expected, it is beneficial to develop and cultivate ties with archive officials. And last but not least, archival research requires patience. Sometimes the best materials suddenly surface after several months of persistent requests. I definitely recommend *taijiquan* or yoga for relaxation.

---

[4] See http://orpheus.ucsd.edu/chinesehistory/chinese_archives.htm, accessed August 2009.

Since any one of these factors could be problematic, researchers should always have a backup plan in case one archive does not allow access or simply not enough access to justify an extended stay. In Shanghai, Beijing, and other areas that have had more exposure to researchers (who occasionally pressure archivists for more openness), it is possible to procure documents without worrying too much about surcharges and added fees. The same can be said for counties that have hosted foreign researchers; one definitely should not assume that "rural" implies greater conservatism. In Shanghai, researchers can search a database of "open archives" (开放档案) based on keywords. Because all of the declassified documents will appear on the screen, researchers do not have to search for material by work unit, which is how most data are organized. For instance, typing in 复员军人 (veterans) will bring up documents from Civil Affairs, the Shanghai Garrison, the Labor Bureau, factories, and the party committee, among others. This is not the case for archives with fewer patrons and resources, however. Even large provincial archives, such as Shandong and Jiangsu, still use folders labeled with the titles of documents, access information, and page range. When the documents are found in the indices, researchers have to write them down on a form and present them to the officials in charge of the reading room, who, in turn, pass them up to the director of "user services" (利用处).

This is when things can get interesting, and messy. In some instances, officials will deny the request, citing "privacy rights" or some other reason. In others, materials will be furnished, but researchers will not be permitted to photocopy them. This can be a minor or major inconvenience, depending on how much time one has to pore over the materials. In this event, time-rich doctoral candidates, or senior faculty on sabbatical, will have an advantage over those who have flown in during semester break or two weeks in the summer. Despite this problem, the struggle is usually worthwhile: some documents can be very revealing about post-1949 politics,[5] small pieces of evidence from one area can confirm findings from other regions and thus enhance generalizability, and the battle might make it easier for subsequent researchers.

These problems, however, are not necessarily universal. Archive officials will be less skittish when presented with topics that are perceived as less "political." But even with more sensitive topics, such as veterans and military families, it is not a foregone conclusion that photocopy requests will be *categorically* denied; sometimes one has to make repeated visits to the same archive to procure more and better materials.

Unfortunately, Chinese officials are not the only ones raising obstacles to successful political science–oriented archival research. Unlike historians for whom archival research is a badge of professional métier, political scientists in the China field (less so in American, Latin American, or European politics, for whom forays into history are common) who rely on these sources

---

[5] For instance, in Shandong I found the minutes of a meeting of county chiefs. Many told their superiors about uprisings in the province led by Korean War prisoners of war and veterans.

might encounter a number of discipline-related hurdles. First, archival data can be very detailed and descriptive, which can militate against "parsimony" in explanation, the gold standard for some political scientists. Second, despite the dismal record in predicting major political events, political science tends to reward "theoretical innovation" more than the discovery of new information per se. Third, archival research is associated with "historical" or "qualitative" methods, which, in some quarters, are more suspect than methods such as survey research. Finally, there is the presentism issue. With all the news about China "rising," many political scientists, like the lay public, want to know what is happening in China *now*. The rosier contemporary scene – not the brutal and poor Maoist period – is "hot." As a result, topics that get defined as "historical" and that rely on methods drawn from "history" need to be legitimated in ways that more contemporary topics using quantitative methodology do not.[6] My point here is not to dissuade scholars from using archives but rather to note that the incentives for engaging in intensive archival research are not well aligned with the professional incentives in political science (with the exception of the most cosmopolitan departments). For the budding historian the opposite situation prevails; history departments praise the researcher who pries open an archive. This incentive structure is highly problematic, since archival documents, when used in conjunction with other sources, can shine a bright light on many of the dark corners of PRC politics.

WHAT'S IN THERE ANYWAY?

Once having gained access to archives and having limited time and money, what sort of documents are worth pursuing with rugged determination, and which can be given up with little loss of sleep or increased blood pressure? The criteria I have used most frequently in requesting materials are (1) the less censored the better; (2) the more local, the better,[7] and; (3) get everything with the words 调查 (survey) or 检查 (inspection) in it. These guidelines encompass a fairly wide range of documents, so it is worthwhile to get into the specifics: what can researchers expect to find in archives, and why are these materials more useful than other sources? Below is a brief survey.

Minutes of Meetings

Minutes can be a very useful source, since, unlike more official sources such as newspapers, they are usually unedited and uncensored. I am not certain at

---

[6] For this reason, archival research is somewhat more risky for doctoral candidates in Chinese politics than for established scholars. This can be problematic, because, as noted above, it is these researchers who tend to have the time required to plumb through the archival materials.

[7] This is important because most indices only provide the title of the document, so searching for keywords referring to a specific place, or "minutes," can save a great deal of time and hassle.

which level of government it is mandatory for a secretary to take notes, but the practice is widespread. In my own research, I have seen transcripts of meetings of work teams discussing the implementation of the Marriage Law, judges' deliberations, Civil Affairs officials learning about the marriage registration process, and mediators' sessions with veterans embroiled in disputes with local officials. My guess is that many factory archives include comparable materials for workers' conflicts. Like reading recordings of Kissinger's phone calls to foreign leaders in *The Kissinger Transcripts*, minutes provide an unvarnished representation of how the state operates, a central concern in political science. At the same time, reading minutes is labor-intensive, particularly for those not accustomed to reading handwritten Chinese with various shortcuts for characters. It is probably best to have these materials photocopied because time is a precious resource.

Investigation Reports

These sources are probably the most valuable. First, many satisfy my "local rule" because investigations occur at all levels of the party-state apparatus. Trade unions, factory party committees, courts, hospitals, and military units have all been ordered, at one point or another, to investigate something. When the State Council ordered an investigation (on veterans in 1956–57, for example), investigation teams were formed nationwide, which means that archives in Shanghai and Yunnan will have materials on the same problem. This can facilitate interesting comparisons between locales. These materials may be printed or handwritten. Second, investigations have been common. To our immense benefit, the PRC has been obsessed with research. Although their findings are never couched in terms other than Marxist or Maoist, the quotes from officials and ordinary people provide a candid look at the interface between state and society. Third, because investigation reports have never been intended for outside eyes, they are not heavily censored, if at all. Even better, one can sometimes read multiple drafts of the same report to see what parts have been excised.

At the same time, investigation reports should be handled gingerly since they are almost always focused on *problems*. To assess just how extensive these problems are, researchers should look for corroborating evidence from other sources (interviews, the press, gazetteers, or other documents in the archives).

Work Reports

Most of us have complained at one time or another about bureaucracy, but researchers should always remain grateful that bureaucrats have meetings and routinely issue reports about what they are up to. PRC archives are full of this type of document; they were issued quarterly, biannually, and annually, often in multiple drafts. Work summaries (总结报告) tend to be broad-stroked but also include muted criticism of an agency's work, broken down by subcategories. (For instance, Civil Affairs will be broken down into sections on disaster relief, refugees, local elections, veterans, and minorities.) Compared to investigation reports, work summaries have more empty verbiage (空话) and provide a shallower sense of context and the specifics of a problem. Because of this, they can be read fairly quickly. Work summaries generally begin by providing basic information, continue with two or three examples of success (typically model individuals praising the party/Mao), and then shift into critique mode. The transition between sections two and three is clearly marked by the word "however" (但是). Weighing which of this information is closest to the truth of the matter can be a bit challenging: the "achievements" sound exaggerated, but the "problem" section can also be overly harsh. I have generally discounted examples of "models" in the achievement section and have waited for further confirmation from other sources to determine whether the "problems" in these summaries were in fact pervasive.

Policy Documents

Since archives are repositories of official activity, policy documents unsurprisingly represent a substantial share of their content. Although they are not as comprehensive as central archives, researchers can still find most or all important policy documents relevant to research in large provincial archives or in urban archives that have provincial status. In some respects, archives at the latter level are better for looking at issues of policy *implementation* because they receive key policies and reports from the center (these sometimes include materials from other provinces), devise their own policy documents, *and* collect materials from their districts, suburban areas, and rural counties. If one does not have the time to work in a rural archive, or would rather avoid the hassle of securing permission and letters of introduction, it is still possible to conduct a rural/urban comparison in a large municipal archive.

But even without this sort of comparison, archives open a wide window into officialdom, allowing political scientists to see the state "in action." In addition to policy documents, there is also the more mundane back-and-forth correspondence between agencies, letters and complaints from individuals about problems that are too small to be included in work summaries, and answers to queries submitted by lower level officials. The downside of all this, of course, is that it is fairly easy to be overwhelmed by the quantity of data. It is advisable to come prepared with a clear idea of what you are looking for prior to a visit to an archive.

But enough said of these "how to" matters! In what remains of this chapter I want to provide a glimpse of how I am trying to bridge the gap between the more theoretical concerns of political scientists and the "informational" strengths of archives (more prized by historians). Although my focus happens to be on patriotism and how it relates to military service, I would venture that many of the "large" issues that concern political scientists – power, justice, status, distribution of resources, and so forth – can be addressed as fully and provocatively with archival documents as with any other source.

PATRIOTISM, IN EVERYDAY PRACTICE

Patriotism, as well as its sister concept in the scholarly literature, nationalism, has been frequently evoked in the study of Chinese politics. It has been used to explain the victory of the Communist Party over the Guomindang, the split between China and the USSR in the late 1950s, and the resilience of the CCP after the collapse of Marxism-Leninism in the late 1980s and early 1990s.[8] Although used in a number of different ways, the literature on patriotism and nationalism has been consistent in (1) focusing on writing by elites, rather than more popular sources; and (2) focusing on musings, ideas, and ideologies, rather than on action or behavior. These two items are not disconnected: because elites are those who record their sentiments, feelings, and thoughts about a topic in any depth, the literature as a whole is far more likely to focus on *elite cognition* than on other facets of patriotism. Unsurprisingly, the search for evidence about patriotism and nationalism has gravitated in this direction. I argue below that this conceptualization is problematic, and that archival materials, by focusing our attention on behavior and *everyday interactions* among people, shine a far brighter spotlight on what patriotism and nationalism actually mean in practice. Archival materials help ground these concepts – and subsequent theories – in people's *experiences* (generally a research topic affiliated more closely with social historians and cultural anthropologists). To the extent that archives zero in on *political* experiences, we can narrow the gap between what Clifford Geertz (1983) and others have called "experience-near" and "experience-distant" concepts in political science.[9] In my view, studies of nationalism and patriotism lean far too heavily toward the latter.

How would one know to what extent citizens in China, or anywhere else for that matter, are "patriotic"? Any assessment of this question must begin with at least a rudimentary effort to define the term. This isn't easy: patriotism is a value-laden and politicized term. Despite the eminent political theorist George Kateb's warning that patriotism is "inherently disposed to disregard morality" and a "grave moral error" whose source is "typically a state of mental confusion" (2000: 901, 909), American surveys repeatedly show that most

---

[8] In China, for example, many have cited the rise of "nationalism," 民族主义 but in Chinese the more appropriate term, and the one used in propaganda and education, is patriotism (爱国主义).

[9] According to Geertz, experience-near concepts are ones that "someone ... might himself naturally and effortlessly use to define what he or his fellows see, feel, think, imagine and so on." In an "experience-distant" concept, "specialists of one sort or another ... forward their scientific, philosophical or practical aims." Love, he suggests, is an example of the former and "object cathexis" the latter.

people consider themselves to be "patriotic,"[10] probably because its antonym connotes dishonorable behavior; few people relish being labeled "unpatriotic" even if they do not agree with government policies. Political baggage, however, should not deter us from trying to get a better sense of what the term involves; it should not be any different from the key concepts in comparative politics that scholars often debate, such as "democracy" or "corruption." A reasonable place to begin, it seems to me, is the most common and seemingly straightforward definition of it, and the one that was translated into Chinese: "love of country-ism." "Love" is sometimes padded with qualities such as loyalty or pride, "an attitude of sentiment and devotion" to a state or nation (Fletcher, 1993: 17, 140), an "acquired sentiment" (Druckman, 1995: 58), "ongoing civic concerns" for fellow citizens (Tamir, 1997: 21–33, 37), or "identification with others in a particular common enterprise" (Taylor, 1989: 166). Maurizio Viroli (1995: 1) suggests that historically patriotism has been used to strengthen or invoke "love of political institutions and the way of life that sustain the common liberty of a people," whereas Walter Berns argues that patriots in the traditional ("Spartan") sense are "citizens who love their country simply because it is their country" (2001: 10, 65).

From the perspective of archival research on how officials and ordinary people treat the wives of military personnel on active duty – those who are actually fulfilling what the government itself deems a "patriotic duty" to serve – these definitions of patriotism are problematic. First, to the extent that "love," "sentiments," and "devotion" can be considered emotions, it is fairly commonsensical that *all* emotions vary in intensity across time and the "object" of desire or affection. What do they actually mean in the context of states or nations? Should we "love" a country like a father loves a son or like a teenager loves his girlfriend? Second, and more problematic, they are all low thresholds for claiming or assigning patriotic status to any individual or group. Is it really enough for someone to simply express sentiments such as "I love my country" to be considered patriotic? How should we view someone who says "I love my country" in the morning, but that same afternoon has an affair with the wife of a special operations officer risking his life abroad? "Loyalty," for that matter, is also too easy. As Morton Grodzins (1956) argued over fifty years ago, the overwhelming majority of citizens are "loyal" simply because they do not actively join ranks with a country's sworn enemies. Loyalty is a *passive* sentiment (which, of course, usually makes charges of "disloyalty" highly suspect). On a day-to-day basis, love, loyalty, and sentimentality do not *demand* any sort of *behavior* from citizens; their excessively low threshold is somewhat comparable to a regime that claims to be a "democracy" just because people have rights in the constitution.

---

[10] In a 2003 survey (1,200 people contacted by phone) conducted by the Institute of Politics at Harvard University, almost 90 percent of Americans considered themselves to be either "somewhat" or "very" patriotic. The results were the same in 2002. These rates may be higher because of September 11. See http://poll.orspub.com. This database is available only via subscription.

Why Archives? 43

This problem also applies to the concept of "nationalism," particularly when scholars adopt, either implicitly or explicitly, Benedict Anderson's wildly popular definition of nationalism as an "imagined community" based on the perception of some sort of shared identity[11] – a "recognition of similarity" in the Chinese word for "identity" (认同). Imagination, like identity, essentially is a *cognitive* process – it "tells" us that we share a commonality with fellow citizens, much like "emotions" and "sentiments" also occur at this "intra-cranial" level. Even among scholars who question whether Anderson's causal argument can be applied to an underdeveloped country like China, or whether his focus on the "nation" as the sole object of loyalty and identity is sufficient given the prominence of regionalism in many areas of the world,[12] few have noted this "threshold" problem: one becomes a "nationalist" either through an "act" of imagination (can the firing of neurons count as an act?) by suggesting, usually in speech or writing, that one has this identity, or what Adam Smith, in *A Theory of Moral Sentiments*, calls "fellow feeling" with other citizens, or that other citizens *should* "awaken," and/or embrace a higher degree of cultural or ethnic homogeneity.[13] But, as Ronald Krebs insightfully comments, "Nationality is assuredly an imagined construct, but that does not imply that the mechanisms by which its boundaries are drawn and redrawn are best grasped through models emphasizing cognition and mental creativity" (Krebs, 2006: 11).

The methodological consequences of this conceptualization are far-reaching. Much of the work on patriotism and nationalism tends to focus on the short-term protests of elites[14] or their sentiments, ideas, ideals, and ideology, since they are the ones who leave the most coherent records of their musings.[15] Jonathan Unger, for example, argues that Chinese peasants "had little *notion* of China as a whole, let alone being *attuned* to the nationalist *sentiments* that were developing among the educated classes in China's urban areas" (Unger, 1996: xv). The rise of "nationalist sentiments" or "popular nationalism" in China has become the conventional wisdom in much of the recent work on China's international relations.[16] Journalists often use the "trope" of rising nationalism as well.[17]

[11] For an application of this notion to American patriotism, see Bodnar (1996).
[12] See many of the contributions to Unger (1996b). Also see Goodman (2004).
[13] Viroli (1995) argues that *nationalism* focuses on defending or reinforcing the "cultural, linguistic and ethnic oneness" of a people.
[14] It is very common in Chinese history to speak of *patriotic movements* or protests, much like Chinese demands for democracy are often expressed in movements rather than in institutions. See Strand (1990).
[15] For a sophisticated approach to nationalism using intellectuals' writings, see Fitzgerald (1996).
[16] For example, Gries (2004) examines the writings of a new cohort of young, fourth generation "nationalist" intellectuals as well as sporadic incidents of outrage against Japan and the United States. He does not consider whether penning a book or participating in a short-lived, almost risk-free, protest should qualify someone as a "nationalist." In my view, such activities might qualify as "fleeting anti-American sentiments," but not as nationalist in a meaningful sense.
[17] Journalists have adopted this "trope" of rising nationalist "sentiment" uncritically. See "Balancing Act: A Survey of China," *The Economist*, March 25, 2006.

In my view, to be even moderately useful, concepts must include and *exclude* certain behaviors, qualities, and attitudes. Self-definitions, claims of "love," "devotion," and "loyalty," are insufficient since they tend to include most everybody. I would suggest the following: to be meaningful, patriotism should incorporate at least two of the following four criteria: *sustained action*, moderate to long-term *commitment of resources*, some courage, and what a reasonable person would consider a *sacrifice* (not just a "willingness" or "readiness" to sacrifice, which many can easily claim (Druckman, 1995: 58). These dimensions of patriotism are not new by any stretch of the imagination, maybe just unfashionable in an age that is highly materialistic, focused on the rights of individuals and groups, and largely devoid of any integrative experience such as conscription or some other form of national service. Usually promoted by military leaders (far more than intellectual elites) in the context of mass protracted wars (Porter, 1994), they harken back to a long tradition of *republican* or *martial patriotism* which stresses the notions of "self-sacrifice for the good of all" (Bodnar, 1996: 7; Krebs, 2006: 28), a "framework of duty" (Ben-Eliezer, 1995: 265) that treats military service "as the preeminent civic obligation and identifies the good citizen as one willing to die on the battlefield for the political community." Much like the emphasis on *ma'asim* (deeds) in scripture, it implies that speech, cognition, right-minded thinking, sentiments, love, and imagination do not a functioning society, nation, or state make. Political theorist Michael Walzer, for example, argues that "men are bound by their significant actions, not by their feelings and thoughts; *action is the crucial language of moral commitment*" (Walzer, 1970: 98). But such commitments cannot be fleeting. "The nation's existence is a *daily plebiscite*," notes Ernest Renan in "What Is a Nation?" which he defines largely in terms of *actions* and the *memories* created around them, especially shed blood: "the culmination of a long past of endeavors, sacrifice, and devotion" (O'Leary, 1999: 4–5). Nor is this perspective necessarily Western. Korean nationalists at the turn of the century penned eloquent essays on "virtues," such as bravery in action and the "sacrificial spirit," that they saw in both Western and Asian civilizations, citing figures as diverse as Jesus Christ and Bismarck and Zhuge Liang (Tikhonov, 2007: 1030). One of the most revered figures in Chinese civilization, Qu Yuan (c.340 B.C. – 278 B.C.), achieved iconic status as a "patriotic poet" because he sacrificed himself for the principle of loyalty and opposing corruption in government; Yue Fei, a Song dynasty general (1103–1142), is currently revered as a patriot because of his loyalty and for devoting years of his life and taking significant risks in combat for the state. Of course, from the early 1960s until the end of the Cultural Revolution, soldiers of the People's Liberation Army were praised for precisely these qualities as well, as were the families that supplied them to the state.

From this reconceptualization of patriotism we can extract several methodological prescriptions, particularly regarding the sources that might be used in research. Definitions of patriotism and nationalism that emphasize abstract ideas (e.g., imagination) over the *institutional* and *behavioral* will necessarily privilege *elite* sources. Less attention will be paid to the smaller scale *actions* of the *lower classes*, such as soldiers, veterans, and military families – the populations that usually pay a significant price for service on behalf of the patriotic causes the elite support in rhetoric. (For instance, the family of a soldier from a peasant family sacrifices the labor of a healthy young man.) The emphasis on love and imagination also shifts our analytical lens away from *interactions among people* – the *actual treatment* of those whose sacrifices and commitments have been elevated to "patriotic" status. In other words, claiming "love of country" should be analytically differentiated from committing sufficient budgetary resources to the military (proper armor), veterans (favorable legislation), or supporting military families.

This is precisely where archival sources should be mined. Archives, far more than articles and speeches by elites (many of whom are in the employ of the state), enable us to part the velvet curtain that hides and protects national and heroic narratives and peer at the "backstage" of patriotism where people interact. They both ground and fill out abstract ideas in messy reality and local interpretations. Archival sources – particularly the obscure memos, minutes, and investigation reports – do *not* draw our attention to various expressions of pride in country ("mouth patriots"), flag waving at sporting events, or words that reveal "mental constructs" about the nation, but instead zero in on how flesh-and-blood people behind patriotic discourse were treated in more mundane or "everyday" circumstances: in villages when military families needed help with the harvest; when veterans needed time off from work to see a doctor. In short, if patriotism can be conceptualized as Renan's "daily plebiscite," we can get a better sense of its depth and content by examining documents that hone in on the everyday and can explain the gap between official discourse and how the people valorized in it were treated in "everyday" interactions with fellow citizens.

The treatment of military families at the height of pro-military, nationalist discourse can serve as a useful test for the significance of patriotism and the utility of archival research in China. Did the valorization of the PLA as the most patriotic and revolutionary of political institutions in the years prior to the Cultural Revolution (when many were convinced that China would be attacked) translate into positive interactions with the wives and fiancées of the soldiers in military service? Treating military families well, unlike attending a short-lived, state-sponsored protest, may not be easy – which is precisely why it serves as a better test of patriotism. Military families need assistance with harvests; wives and fiancées are left without much protection, requiring other men to stave off their sexual temptations; local financial assistance requires sacrifice. If one were to read newspapers, memoirs, or even to observe the behavior of students during the Cultural Revolution, one could deduce that military families were treated well. After all, Red Guards paraded around in military fatigues, spoke in military-inflected vernacular, and organized their units along military lines.[18] Does a more inductive and grounded approach

---

[18] For an interesting analysis of the military influence on the Red Guards, see Perry and Li (1993).

challenge this fairly widespread view about the status of the military as a patriotic institution and its personnel as exemplars of patriotic commitment? Let us take a brief look at how archival data challenge sources that rely more heavily on the views and short-lived and dramatic outbursts of the more educated classes.

Military Dependents (军属)

In and around Shanghai, the city well known for its leftist radicalism prior to the Cultural Revolution, a flurry of confidential investigation reports threatened to tar its revolutionary reputation. Officials reading these reports in the mid-1960s were probably shaking their heads at the more literal, very risqué twist on the so-called flesh and blood relationship that was said to exist between those who patriotically served in the military and the state: cadres and others were having affairs with the fiancées and wives of PLA soldiers. In a report that was furnished by Civil Affairs to the Shanghai Party Committee, this phenomenon – known as "ruining a soldier marriage" – was deemed "quite serious," affecting soldiers in urban and rural areas (SMA1, 1964:13). In 1963 alone, the report found, some 253 cases had been "discovered" in the greater Shanghai area, including 193 in the rural suburbs and 60 in the city proper. Most of the perpetrators held positions of authority; in the suburbs, 57.4 percent of them were cadres at the township, village, or subvillage ("production team") levels; Communist Party and Communist Youth League members – those *most exposed* to education about the importance of patriotism and the heroic role of the PLA – figured prominently (39 percent) in the overall statistics, although blame was also appropriately apportioned to "bad elements, hooligans, and hoodlums" (SMA1, 1964:13).

Ruining soldiers' marriages was not simply the result of a few bad eggs with inappropriate sexual appetites, however; there were larger, "structural" causes at work as well. According to the report, military families' poverty, which should have been alleviated by government programs and community-based assistance, combined with officials' access to resources, created the opportunity for sexual mischief. Local officials "got close" to PLA wives by expressing "concern about them," and this developed into an exchange of food and entertainment for sex. That the women already were married to soldiers "defending the nation" apparently made little difference. In the Jiangnan Shipyards in Shanghai, a CCP member surnamed Ye was having sex with a Mrs. Yang, whose husband was in the army. To encourage Mrs. Yang to divorce her husband, Ye invoked the high probability of defeat if China were to be attacked: "Do you want to become a counterrevolutionary when Chiang Kai-shek attacks the mainland and returns here?" "You'll be a widow if you're married to a soldier." Some of these relationships were long term. In Songjiang county, a son of a "counterrevolutionary" surnamed Zhang "has been having sex with a woman surnamed Wu since her husband went into the army in 1956." Lacking effective birth control measures or perhaps not caring enough about this, Wu had become pregnant three times by Zhang, and with his help managed to secure a divorce. Divorces and pregnancies were not unusual – fifty-four babies were born from these Shanghai relationships, with another thirty expected in 1965 – and thirty-two soldiers were divorced, in addition to thirty-two who had their engagements broken off because of adulterous sex (SMA1, 1964: 14).

Peasants were well aware of this problem. The praise heaped on the PLA by state propagandists for patriotically defending China against external enemies could not counter the more real, tangible domestic threats faced by PLA soldiers. In contrast to hundreds of memoirs penned by urban students who stressed the attractiveness and patriotic glory of military service in the 1960s, archival documents tell of villages in which youth were warned, "If you're married, you'd better *not* join the army." Soldiers who got wind of these problems requested leave to "visit relatives" but were mainly interested in making sure that village officials had not already seduced their fiancées and wives. Unsurprisingly, municipal officials were concerned because recruiting and military morale were adversely affected, but they did not take much action to change the situation. When confronted, local officials claimed that they were not responsible ("If the soldiers don't lodge a complaint, there's nothing we can do about it"), blamed the PLA soldiers' wives, or argued that sex between PLA wives and villagers was "just an ordinary sex problem" which did not merit further attention. The archival evidence is mixed on the issue of whether this lax attitude spread to the upper echelons of the party. In one account, courts and party organizations rendered 146 verdicts on these cases, with close to half (43 percent) of the perpetrators ordered to undergo "criticism and education," and the rest were punished more seriously (28 percent receiving criminal sentences, ranging from one to five years and more). Because leveling an accusation against a party official was (and remains) no small matter and sex-related offenses can be particularly embarrassing, these cases might represent a fraction of what actually occurred in villages; "lumping it" was probably common (SMA1, 1964: 13–14).

But, however many officials' heads were shaking and pens scrawling, there is little evidence that the situation improved much between 1964 and 1966, the peak years of pre–Cultural Revolution hyping of the PLA. A nationally circulated "Situation Report" authored by the Political Bureau of the Guangzhou Military Region in March 1966 (SMA2, 1966: 24–25) and distributed nationwide (and therefore available in the Shanghai archives) notes that sixteen cases of adultery had occurred "only recently"; six were classified as involving "seduction/rape," whereas eight were said to have been consensual: the soldiers' wives had "low political consciousness and were attracted to material possessions" (SMA2, 1966: 24).

According to this report – classified as top secret – this phenomenon was not limited to South China; Shandong, Shanxi, and other northern provinces reported comparable problems. In Shandong, for example, a soldier's wife named Wen was raped by the village accountant, a man surnamed Wang. Wen reported Wang to the county police, but because "they did not handle the case expeditiously," the accountant "snuck into her bed again." Fighting Wang off, Wen grabbed his leg and held on as he dragged himself from the cooking area toward the door, but he escaped by bashing her finger. Word of this incident leaked out. From his military base, Wen's husband dashed off a letter to provincial-level public security officials, who dispatched an investigation team. Upon arriving in the village, however, they found that Wang already had been tipped off by other officials and escaped. His disappearing act did not last long. Soon enough, he was back in the village, where he once again confronted Wen: "I'm back. Let's see what you can do about it!" (SMA2, 1966: 24).

The Guangzhou Military Region's report seems to have had some impact, at least at the level of pushing paper from one bureaucracy to the next. During the Cultural Revolution's first summer of 1966, the Supreme Court and Ministry of the Interior issued a directive to their subordinate units to look more seriously into the problem of "ruining soldiers' marriages," since many soldiers – whose sacrifices and patriotism were being heralded across the land – were "unsatisfied" with the situation. In response to this directive, the Shanghai High Court and Bureau of Civil Affairs convened a joint meeting, which was also attended by officers from the Shanghai Garrison (SMA3, 1966: 28).

Despite the urgent tone in the correspondence leading up to this meeting, garrison officials were already well aware of this problem – they had sponsored a large-scale investigation of twenty-eight work units in Nanhui county only two years earlier and had reported on the situation in 1965. That earlier investigation, also preserved in the archives, found that of those twenty-eight units, twenty-three (82 percent) had soldiers whose wives or fiancées were involved with other men, with sixty-one cases in total. Garrison officers fingered civilian party officials as the primary perpetrators (a bit over 50 percent of the cases) but also blamed the courts (whose educated officials were better at "imagining" the nation) for not taking the issue seriously; the verdicts were "too lenient" they complained, and "many objections" were raised to them. One example they provided involved a township accountant, a man surnamed Su, who was having affairs with two PLA wives (separately or in a ménage-à-trois is not clear). Local officials were aware of Su's indiscretions but decided to look the other way. The case came to light only when one of the soldiers' wives "drowned her baby in the toilet of a bathroom at the commune seat when there was a meeting going on" (SMA3, 1966: 29–30).

The impact on soldiers was unmistakable. Some heard about their wives and immediately went AWOL; some "immediately fainted on their beds and did not get up for several days." Soldiers circulated in the village to encourage the fathers of draft-age boys to quiz recruiting cadres about "whether you've got your eyes on my daughter-in-law again" (SMA3, 1966: 34). In that politically hot summer of 1966 the contrast in images could not have been starker: at the same time that Red Guards were convincing themselves that they were Chairman Mao's "little soldiers" (as we know from photographs, memoirs, and propaganda), *real* soldiers were going AWOL, their families were up in arms about cadre abuses, PLA wives were being raped and aborting babies, and the Shanghai Supreme Court complained of a "very dim conception of national defense and supporting military families" (as revealed by the archives) (SMA3, 1966: 38).

CONCLUSION

How these data are interpreted will, of course, depend on the choice of the analytic lens through which we view them. Perhaps it was a failure of administration, seen in the lack of effective supervision over local cadres, or even a reminder of the power of sex to undermine state goals. Perhaps poverty undermines patriotism, which requires time, patience, and resources to cultivate (unless, of course, one sees these as "natural" political phenomena, which I do not). Certainly there are elements of truth in these arguments.

In my view, however, the larger and weightier issue was the state's failure to cultivate patriotism that was meaningful to the extent that it shaped the behavior of ordinary people and officials, despite numerous efforts in rhetoric, education, and propaganda. In significant ways, this should not be surprising. In many other comparative contexts, nationalism and patriotism have been strongly linked to the military experience, since the military experience, far more than most civilian and economic institutions, encourages selflessness, sacrifice, courage, loyalty, and the pursuit of collective goals. Nationalism and patriotism have also emerged in the context of universal conscription and mass wars, but China has never had a *national* army – only *party armies*. Citizens, therefore, never fought as a "nation-in-arms" (neither the Nationalists nor the Communists were in a position to institute a national draft during World War II; most conflicts were limited wars, or border wars; educated elites rarely served in combat, even during the Anti-Japanese War). Moreover, militaries, especially in the context of mass wars, have been one of the only institutions in society that have brought together people from many social classes, provided opportunities for upward social mobility for the lower classes, and generated sympathy for their plight among elites.[19] In China, the poor treatment of military dependents suggests that the PLA still had low status, and this, in turn, had adverse consequences on the development of patriotism and nationalism.

Virtually none of this chapter's archive-driven "counter-narrative" about the treatment of PLA dependents has appeared in Western scholarship, and certainly not in recently published gazetteers in the PRC, valuable as these are to scholarship on Chinese politics. In part, this can be attributed to the operationalization of key concepts: if patriotism is mainly about love and sentiment, and nationalism focuses on cognition, we will tend to look for sources that document thoughts and feelings, not *action* and the *treatment* of

---

[19] I develop this argument further in Diamant (2009).

others – which are better revealed in archival sources whose texts are closer to the ground. It can also be explained by more prosaic reasons: it is more convenient to study elites simply because they write and publish – note the cottage industry of former Red Guard memoirists and essayists in journals, magazines, and blogs about China's position in the world. Although useful for studying how nationalism and patriotism are understood by elites at a particular moment in time, such sources tell us far less about how these elites actually treat their compatriots, particularly their social "inferiors," which, in my view, is the more important and meaningful gauge of patriotism and nationalism. The contrast between the elite "take" on the military and the view from the archives cannot be starker than in the case I present here. If the PLA and its personnel had high status, and military service was considered patriotic, why were officials so worried about recruitment and morale? Why did judges give lenient sentences to those who violated soldiers' marriages? Why did so few pitch in to help military families avoid poverty? The elite-based narrative cannot easily accommodate the new evidence from the archives.

If even this small cache of archival documents – roughly eleven pages in total – can raise some intriguing questions, think what would happen to the field of Chinese politics if thousands of such documents were brought to light. The impact on pedagogy and research would be difficult to avoid. Would we be able to teach students that the PLA was venerated prior to the Cultural Revolution? Could we portray intellectuals as the primary victims of Maoist rule if archival evidence reveals thousands of "red" and "heroic" veterans committing suicide in the 1950s? And should we continue to divvy up recent Chinese political history by "campaigns" – which mostly affected intellectuals – if sources provide us with far more information about what happened in the temporal interstices *between* them? Much as archival research and oral history about sexuality and divorce have revealed continuity between the Maoist and reform periods, I expect that more archival research will complicate any arbitrary or stark division between pre- and post-reform China (Diamant, 2000; Honig, 2003).

Herein lies the rub. Even though archival sources have the potential to modify previous interpretations of key political events, to suggest new ways of understanding the inner workings of the state and its relationship to society over time, and to provide much-needed insight into the foundational components of state-building and citizenship – traditionally the strong suits of the political science discipline – they might go untapped by political scientists because of the incentive structure in the discipline and the prevailing presentism among many China scholars in the social sciences. I hope that this chapter, by presenting just one effort at definitional innovation with a smattering of new information, will persuade more scholars and students to delve into the archives and not be deterred by the risks. It would be rather ironic if most new insights about key events in Chinese politics were supplied by historians rather than by political scientists, but, sadly, this seems to be the direction in which we are heading.

3

The Central Committee, Past and Present

A Method of Quantifying Elite Biographies

Victor Shih, Wei Shan, and Mingxing Liu

The political elite was an early focus of Western analysis of the People's Republic of China, partly because information about the elite was relatively available in the opaque political system. As China opened up, information about all aspects of Chinese politics became increasingly available, thus decreasing the relative importance of elite studies in China. In this chapter, we first argue that elite studies continue to be important and necessary for understanding authoritarian regimes like China. Further, we introduce a dataset of Central Committee (CC) members that combines traditional elite studies with new coding and statistical methodologies. The data are used to trace several basic characteristics of the CC through the entire history of the Chinese Communist Party (CCP), and to measure the relative influence of Hu Yaobang and Hua Guofeng in the CC. We further discuss the potential of this dataset for providing more systematic evidence of how elite characteristics and elite conflict affect policy and political outcomes in China.

ELITE STUDIES IN AUTHORITARIAN REGIMES

At a time when China was sealed off from the rest of the world, Western scholars of China relied mainly on the official press and in some cases military sources from Taiwan to make scholarly inferences. As the heroic deeds and – at times – the "errors" of senior leaders were often the foci of official press coverage, Western scholars naturally made extensive use of this relatively abundant source of information, thus creating a heavy emphasis on the elite. Today, China scholars have a wide range of sources available to them, ranging from internal government documents to interviews to survey instruments.

We would like to thank Yang Bo and Li Qiang, both graduate students at Peking University, for carefully and accurately coding the data used in this chapter. They have both graduated into government service and will soon become the subjects of our inquiry! We further thank Nancy Hearst at the Fairbank Center Library for valuable help during the final stage of data collection.

The proliferation of new sources has given rise to the study of grassroots-level political phenomena in China and a decline in the relative importance of elite studies. However, the authoritarian nature of the Chinese regime provides compelling reason to continue elite studies.

Perhaps the most important reason to focus on the elite in authoritarian governments is that power in these regimes tends to be concentrated in the hands of one or a few leaders, whose preferences, beliefs, and actions can have a profound influence on political and economic outcomes. In a rigorous study using leaders' natural deaths as an exogenous variable, economists Jones and Olken (2005) find that autocrats have a much more pronounced impact on a country's growth than their counterparts in democracies because they can directly influence fiscal and monetary policies as well as adjust political institutions. Being familiar with the disastrous outcomes of the Great Leap and of the Cultural Revolution, scholars of China hardly need convincing of the importance of individual leaders (Dittmer, 2001; MacFarquhar, 1997; Schram, 1989; Schwartz, 1966). This approach leads scholars to examine the writings and biographical background of key leaders in order to uncover the "thoughts" and experience that guide their action (Schram, 1989; Schwartz, 1966). Alternatively, with the help of in-depth historical analysis, scholars puzzle out how preferences or "thoughts" guide leaders through complex political situations to achieve a set of objectives (Fewsmith, 1994; MacFarquhar and Schoenhals, 2006). Following earlier works on the elite in Western democracies (Aberbach, Putnam, and Rockman, 1981), China scholars are also beginning to uncover the preference of the political elite via survey instruments (Dickson, 2003).

Another reason for elite study in authoritarian regimes is that the selectorate, that is, those with the power to directly affect leadership selection, is a much smaller share of the total population than in a typical democracy (Bueno de Mesquita et al., 2006). Thus, even if authoritarian leaders have some proclivity to provide public goods, they have strong reasons to direct policies toward fulfilling the interests of supporters in the narrow selectorate so as to maintain power (Kang, 2002; Shirk, 1993; Svolik, 2005; Tullock, 1987: 17). A long-standing literature in China studies has built on this understanding of authoritarian politics, and insights developed in this literature have yielded highly robust predictions of policy outcomes (Bachman, 1991; Manion, 1993; Pei, 2006; Shirk, 1993). In this framework of analysis, understanding the backgrounds of the political elite is also important because interests are often determined by institutional affiliation or past experiences (Lieberthal and Oksenberg, 1988).

The general comparative literature also focuses on the dynamic interactions among the elite because these interactions often lead to palpable political or economic outcomes. For example, Ramseyer and Rosenbluth (1998) demonstrate that fierce factional rivalry between the Meiji elite in Japan led to the formation of competitive alliances with forces outside of the oligarchy and to the eventual collapse of the oligarchic arrangement. Although elite rivalries are readily observable in democracies because rivals often belong to different parties and the media provide extensive coverage of competition, this is not the case in most authoritarian regimes. Outside observers are often unaware of competition until someone has been unseated or a coup has occurred.

In studies of Chinese politics, elite rivalry became a focus of inquiry after the outbreak of the Cultural Revolution, which saw Mao systematically purging nearly all of his former colleagues in the Politburo Standing Committee. A seeming "round-table" arrangement among the top leaders instantly slid into a frenzy of mutual accusation and purging (Teiwes, 1993). Clearly, though difficult to observe, elite conflict is an important aspect of authoritarian politics. The Cultural Revolution has spawned an enormous literature that tries to understand its origins (e.g., MacFarquhar, 1997), manifestations at the local and grassroots levels (e.g., Forster, 1990; Perry and Li, 1997), and its long-term impact on society (e.g., Walder and Su, 2003).

In sum, elite analysis remains important in studies of authoritarian regimes because the preferences, values, and background of the elite, and the often competitive interactions among the elite, continue to play a crucial role in shaping political and economic outcomes. With the proliferation of new tools and sources of information in formerly hermit regimes like China, instead of abandoning elite studies, we should use these new sources to expand the scope and depth of them.

THE CENTRAL COMMITTEE DATABASE

In the tradition of elite analysis, this project focuses on the characteristics of an institutionally defined group of the elite – the Central Committee members. Although the Central Committee is by no means the universe of the power elite in China, one can reasonably argue that most officials holding important positions are CC members. There are obvious exceptions – for example, Deng Xiaoping and Chen Yun in the 1990s – but even they had been CC members for a long time. Chen Yun to this day holds the record as the longest serving CC member (1930–1987). CC members further wielded real power by controlling specific bureaucracies (i.e., provinces, ministries, military regions, and so forth) and by exerting influence on the selection of the top leaders of the regime (Shirk, 1993).

Given the importance of Central Committee members, it behooves us to know as much as possible about them. Indeed, various studies already examine the traits of CC members during various periods of time (Bo, 2004a; Cheng Li, 2001; Lee, 1991; Li, 1994; Nathan and Gilley, 2002). Although these studies give us intimate understandings of subsets of the CC elite during various periods, we still lack an overall sense of how members of this elite body have evolved over the more than eighty-five years of CCP history. Furthermore, without data on CC members over time, it remains difficult to make causal inferences on how membership characteristics and the overall makeup of the CC affected political and policy outcomes and vice versa. This has produced a field of study rich in theory but remarkably lacking in quantitative assessments of how the power elite influence policy outcomes. To the extent there has been work (Huang, 1996; Landry, 2008a; Shih, 2004; Su and Yang, 2000), it mainly focuses on a subset of the CC elite, the provincial and municipal leaders.

In the following, we first describe the conceptual underpinnings of a quantitative dataset that tracks the careers of all CC members from the First Party Congress to the Sixteenth Party Congress. We then provide an account of how we implemented the coding, the problems we encountered, and the solutions we devised to deal with these problems. In order to develop a comprehensive database of CC members, one has to overcome several conceptual and practical problems. First, the end-product must allow users to generate various indicators of interest without having to hand-code additional information from printed sources. New information on CC members only needs to be added to the existing database. This is a tall order for two reasons. First, beyond basic characteristics, such as birth year, education level, year of obtaining party membership, and so forth, CC members typically rotated through a series of positions over the course of their careers that are challenging to track. Furthermore, many CC members, especially senior officials, concurrently served in different positions, which need to be expressed in a quantitative database without generating confusion.

Inspired by work done by Adolph (2003) on the career trajectories of central bankers, this database overcomes the above difficulties by coding the positions, start year, and end year of nearly all the positions held by CC members throughout their careers, rather than merely those positions held by CC members at the time that they served in the CC. This produces a database where every row is a CC member. For every position a CC member held, three columns are dedicated to coding it – a numerical code to describe the position, the start year, and the end year. In this manner, if one adds enough columns, one can track their movement over time as well as the positions they held simultaneously. The example in Table 3.1 contains an illustration of how the database codes Chen Yun's State Council career in the 1950s. As one can see in Table 3.1, the multiple positions held by Chen Yun simultaneously do not create any confusion under this coding scheme. We clearly see that Chen Yun served as chair of the Finance and Economic Committee, which overlapped with his duties as vice premier and minister of commerce. The positions held by Chen Yun are arranged in sequential order, although they need not be. With this data configuration, we are able to make logical inquiries such as:

locate all vice premiers who served between 1949 and 1970

or, since we coded the CC members' tenure in a number of different posts:

locate all CC members from the Twelfth Party Congress who had prior military experience and also served as the party secretary of Sichuan

For the ease of coding and data processing, we further broke down the positions into various categories: People's Liberation Army (PLA) posts, State Council

TABLE 3.1. *Tracking Chen Yun's positions in the 1950s*

Name	Chair, Finance and Economic Committee	Start Year	End Year	Vice Premier	Start Year	End Year	Minister of Commerce	Start Year	End Year
Chen Yun	1421	1949	1956	1025	1949	1975	1321	1956	1958

posts, provincial posts, National People's Congress (NPC)/Chinese People's Political Consultative Conference (CPPCC) posts, court positions, university posts, and positions in the CCP itself. For party experience, we coded the membership of the Central Committee and the positions in the central party organs separately. For CC membership, we coded both full and alternate membership, as well as the sessions (from the First CC to the Sixteenth CC). For party positions, we first specified the central leadership positions, such as party chairman/general secretary, Standing Committee of the Politburo membership, membership on the Politburo, and alternate membership on the Politburo. Then we scored the composite units of the central party organization. In addition to the core organs such as the Secretariat, the Department of Organization, the Department of Propaganda, and so forth, we also coded the leadership in party newspapers and journals, such as the *People's Daily*, the *Guangming Daily*, and *Red Flag*, as well as leadership positions in party-directed mass organizations such as the All China Women's Association.

For each position, we assigned a four-digit number to represent it. The first three digits denote the state or party organ in which the position is located. The last digit represents the level of the position. The score 3021, for example, breaks down to 302, which stands for General Political Department of the People's Liberation Army, and the final digit – 1 denotes the highest level in that department – the chief of the General Political Department. In most cases, we used a "1, 3, 5, 7" system in which 1 represents ministerial positions, 3 represents vice ministerial positions, 5 represents departmental positions (司, 局, 厅), and 7 represents those positions below departments. With this coding system, we were able to quantify the promotions of all CC members throughout their careers.

We additionally included some demographic variables, which facilitate analysis of the background of CC members. We coded basic demographic details including birth year, gender, party membership year, level of education, ethnicity, princeling status, and whether and when the person was purged or rehabilitated. For education, we specified the levels of education and, if they attended university, the specific university they attended. To track the changes in the school networks among CC members, we created a list of colleges and universities on the basis of the Inventory of National Universities on the Web site of the Ministry of Education (MOE) and employed the official school code as our scores for the universities.[1] We further traced their majors in university and graduate school, when information was available. We additionally divided the CC members' careers before they entered any government offices into major categories, including employment as workers, teachers, soldiers, and so forth. With this variable, we obtained an image of the person prior to entering politics.

An important aspect of the career trajectories of many CC members was their service in various units before 1949. Because it is too unwieldy to code their participation in specific military units, we coded their participation in the Long March, their main base area before the Long March, and their main base area after the Long March. For base area experience, since the bases shifted substantially over time, we decided to code them according to major regions and revolutionary experience, which were relevant during the various periods of the revolution. These regions' revolutionary experience included the central Soviet area in Jiangxi, the Shaanxi-Gansu-Ningxia area, the northeast area (Manchuria), the North (Northern China and Xinjiang and Qinghai, except Shaanxi-Gansu-Ningxia), the South (Southern China except Jiangxi), the New Fourth Army, the Eighth Route Army, the Hubei-Henan-Anhui-Northern Jiangsu base area, the Southwest (including Tibet), and overseas work. We created additional dummy variables recording crucial experiences during the revolution, including experience in the Anyuan mine in the 1920s, experience in Jinggangshan, teaching or matriculation at the Anti-Japanese University, and military experience on Taiheng Mountain.

For the experience during the 1946–49 Civil War, we coded the field armies (Swaine, 1992). Field army designations contain extremely useful information about the loyalty of some CC members because field armies were formed out of existing units – for example, the Eighth Route Army and the New Fourth Army – and had fairly consistent leadership. We coded five field armies: the Northwest Field Army (or First Field Army), the Central Field Army (or Second Field Army), the East China Field Army (or Third Field Army), the Northeast Field Army (or Fourth Field Army), and the North China Field Army (or Fifth Field Army).

With the inclusion of demographic and career variables, the dataset currently has 1,604 observations (rows) and 261 variables (columns). As new positions of interest arise, it will be relatively easy to append additional codes

---

[1] There are 1,607 universities and colleges on the MOE Web site. We selected the top 102 schools according to the 2003 university ranking by netbig.com (there are ties in the ranking so we selected 102 instead of 100 schools). In addition, we added Peking Union Medical College, the Chinese Academy of Sciences, the Chinese Academy of Social Sciences, and the Central Party School which are not included on the MOE list or on the netbig ranking but are prestigious in their fields. Also, we included the Southwest Union University and the Anti-Japanese Military and Politics University. These two do not exist today but were influential before 1949 and produced a number of CCP leaders. Finally, two general categories are also included: military academies and other schools. In total, there are 110 values in this variable.

or columns to describe them. This configuration of the database makes it easily expandable.

Implementing Coding

The coding itself took place in several stages. We first hired a research assistant (RA), a master's candidate at the School of Government Management at Peking University, to make a survey of the evolution of party, State Council, and PLA organizations over time since we needed to assign a code to nearly every position across these three institutions. After making a complete catalog of the positions we potentially wanted to code, we selected a subset of them and began coding. The main source we used was the *Dictionary of Past and Present Central Committee Members* (*Dictionary*) (Central Organization Department and Party History Research Center, 2004). We supplemented it with various Western and Chinese sources, as well as sources available on the Internet (Bartke, 1997; Bartke and Institut für Asienkunde [Hamburg, Germany], 1991; Lamb, 2003; Mainland China Research Center, 2006; Jianying Wang, 1995). To fill in the missing data, we also conducted some in-depth historical research, collecting biographical details especially on early revolutionaries (e.g., Cai, 1995; Kou, 2008; Xu, 2005).

To ensure integrity in our coding, we hired two RAs – both master's candidates at the Peking University School of Government Management – to code the data. *Each RA coded the entire CC membership independently of the other.* We first composed a coding manual and trained both RAs in our coding concept, and one of them made a trial coding of a 3 percent random sample out of the *Dictionary* to check the feasibility of the coding manual. We then revised the manual according to the problems revealed by the trial coding, and both RAs began to code. We entertained scanning the *Dictionary* into digital format, but it did not prove necessary as the RAs soon became quite proficient in using the paper text. Over the following two years, as the coding progressed, new problems emerged and we continued to revise the coding manual. Despite these changes, the fundamental logic of the database remained the same – position, start year, end year. All three authors of the chapter monitored the coding progress of the two RAs, both in person and through the Internet.

After both RAs completed the coding, we had them cross-check their entries with each other. If their codes matched, we left them as they were. This applied to the vast majority of the cases. If there were any discrepancies between the two, they noted them down, and the three authors "judged" the merits of the two versions. This laborious process was completed in July 2006, when we obtained a preliminary dataset. We then found that there were quite a few missing data points, especially concerning the start and end years for various positions. To fill in the missing data, the authors conducted further research to fill in as many of the blanks as possible. By October 2006, we had fewer than 400 missing data cells in a dataset of over 417,000 cells.

Problems and Solutions

After we began coding, problems emerged, which we dealt with in various ways, some more satisfactory than others. First, as briefly discussed earlier, we discovered that it was extremely difficult to track the pre-1949 military experience of various CC leaders. Units were created and disbanded in days, whereas others were destroyed and reformed under the same name in a totally different place. Furthermore, there was a blur between civilian positions and military positions during the revolutionary period. To a large extent the party was no more than a leadership group of the army. After all, the base areas were not only territorial areas administrated by the party but also military bases for the Communist army. Thus, before 1946, we coded CC members' experience mainly according to their base areas.

This problem became especially serious in the 1945–49 period when the establishment of geographical administration overlapped with military units. With the information we were able to collect we had no clear picture of the relationship between the specific PLA units, the field armies, and the base areas. For example, for a vice director of the Political Department of the Shanxi-Chahaer-Hebei Military Area in 1945–48, Cai Shupan, do we code him as an officer within the North China Field Army or as a local cadre of the Shanxi-Chahaer-Hebei Base Area? Was the military area a subordinate unit of the field army, or an administrative unit of the base area? Because we had insufficient information on these issues, we instructed our coders to adhere to the following principle: although military positions were usually coded as field army experience, when we were unsure of the field army designation of a military position but were more certain about the geographical location of this unit, we coded the position according to the base area and left blank the field army designation. The second major problem we encountered was that there were simply too many positions in the Chinese bureaucracy due to the multiple levels of government. Every ministry has departments (司, 局), which in turn have bureaus (处), which in turn have sections (科). Every province has both functional departments (厅) and geographical jurisdictions, including prefectures, counties, township (brigades), and villages. Of course, within each geographical jurisdiction, the various functional departments are replicated. An attempt to code every single position in the vast bureaucracy would make coding extremely unwieldy. Instead, we anchored our coding to the ministerial/provincial level. That is, for all positions below or at the ministerial/provincial level, we identified them as a position under that ministry or province at one of four levels: below the departmental/prefecture level (司, 局, 厅, 地), at the departmental/prefecture level, vice ministerial/provincial level, or full provincial/ministerial level. We made some modifications to the provincial coding to distinguish between functional departments and the various geographical subunits and to distinguish between the governor and the party secretary. We also devised a similar coding scheme for military regions and the main departments and branches of the PLA.

One drawback of this approach is that we do not track movement of CC members through various prefecture-level cities or departments within ministries. For example, the dataset specifies that a CC member (say, Li Yuanchao) served as a prefecture or county mayor or party secretary in Jiangsu, but does not specify that this person was in fact the party secretary of Nanjing. We feel that this coding strategy does not forgo too much information, especially if one is interested in analyzing elite politics. Usually, promotions above the departmental/prefecture level signal one's entrance into national politics.

The third major problem we encountered was the frequent changes in the State Council bureaucracy and shifts in the military region structure. For example, the First Ministry of Machinery was merged into the Ministry of Machinery before folding into the State Economic and Trade Commission and eventually the State-owned Assets Supervision and Administration Commission. In general, we adopted a principle of successor. That is, in principle, all codes of the party and state organs are based on their latest manifestations after 2002. Since we have tracked the evolution of all organs, we gave agencies in the past the same scores as their successor agency in the current government. For example, we coded both the Ministry of Domestic Trade and the Ministry of Foreign Trade and Cooperation as the Ministry of Commerce because the former two were incorporated into the latter in 2003. This of course leaves out important information, especially in the State Council, where many top leaders emerged out of the now-abolished machinery or petrochemical ministries. Toward that end, we created three general categories to score experience in these agencies: the machinery ministries (including the former 1st, 2nd, 3rd, 6th, 7th, and 8th Ministries of Machinery), the petrochemical ministries (including the former Ministry of Petroleum Industry and Ministry of Chemical Industry), and light industry ministries (such as the former Ministry of Textile Industry). We likewise applied the successor principle to military regions and party organs. A good case in point was the Xinjiang Military Region (MR). This MR became subordinate to the Lanzhou MR, so we coded positions in the Xinjiang MR with the values of the same positions in the Lanzhou MR. We also applied this principle to code provincial revolutionary committees during the Cultural Revolution.

Work experience in enterprises (企业) and institutes (事业) after 1949 also presented a messy problem. During the planned economy era, all enterprises were supervised by governmental organs and behaved like a part of their supervising organs (Naughton, 1996). They had the same bureaucratic ranks as departments or bureaus in the supervising agencies. In our coding, we first tried to link enterprises to their supervising party-state organs because the career paths of many party leaders, especially the technocrats, began in these enterprises. In some cases, finding out the supervising agencies became extremely difficult, if not impossible. We also obtained a list of enterprises currently managed by the State-owned Assets Supervision and Administration Commission (SASAC) and coded these enterprises and their recognizable "ancestors" as under SASAC or various line ministries. This still left many enterprises uncoded. We then created a variable that records the function of an enterprise: service units (事业单位), transportation, electronics/information, electricity/hydrotechnics, petroleum, mechanical/steel, light industry, and others. We followed this coding with the start and end years of the CC members' tenures in these enterprises.

Despite these problems and the less-than-perfect solutions we devised, we still have a firm grasp of the career trajectories of CC members once they took administrative office. We also have nearly perfect information on their party and state posts. For the vast majority of CC members, the solutions we devised gave us a fairly clear picture of their early careers. Most important, with the basic logic of our dataset, if a research project compels it, we have the flexibility to incorporate additional information into the dataset to address new issues.

ANNUAL INDICATORS

Given the dataset, what is one to do with it? As a first step, we generated a number of annual indicators that provide year-to-year descriptions of the Central Committee as a whole. It has become a fairly regular exercise to derive various characteristics of the CCP elite over certain periods of time or for various party congresses (Bo, 2002; Bo, 2004b; Cheng Li, 2004, 1994, 2000, 2001). These exercises have yielded important insights into the social characteristics and preferences of the CCP elite.

Although one can tabulate various characteristics of CC members for certain years, it becomes difficult to hand-count the number of Long March veterans – for example – over half a century. Furthermore, previous works tabulating the characteristics of CC members covered only a small number of years, especially during the years of the party congresses (PCs) (Baum, 1998; Dittmer, 1983; Saich, 1992; Starr, 1976; Wich, 1974). Major changes often occurred during PCs, but shifts in CC membership also took place between congresses. For example, as the analysis below reveals, the 1985 National Party Conference convened by Deng had a major impact on the age and education structure of CC members. Finally, as one examines an increasing number of characteristics, hand-counting becomes unwieldy. Even fully mapping CC members' characteristics for one year becomes a laborious exercise (Bo, 2004a).

Because this dataset records the start and end dates of most positions held by CC members, it becomes a relatively simple matter to derive various characteristics of CC members over time. Granted, devising such indicators still requires a careful crafting of complex logical statements in statistical software (Stata 9). As mentioned above, there are some drawbacks to the dataset, particularly the inability to code many characteristics before 1949. Nonetheless, as the exercises below reveal, a thorough examination of the annual trends of these characteristics provides further empirical support for some of our core intuitions and generates new insights about CC members.

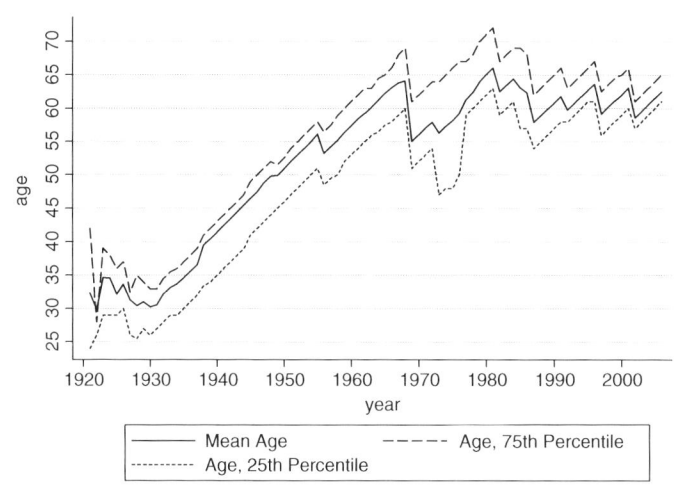

FIGURE 3.1. Average age and 25th and 75th percentile age of Central Committee members, 1921–2006.

Age Structure of CC Members over Time

From a Western perspective, the CCP is often known for its gerontocracy. However, the analysis here reveals that the CCP's tendency to have an elderly elite mainly stemmed from the dominance of the May Fourth generation over the party for several decades. Both Mao and Deng, in their own ways, carried out remarkable campaigns to rejuvenate the elite of the party. By the late 1980s, a system to regularly replace older officials with younger cohorts was firmly in place.

In Figures 3.1 and 3.2, we see that the initial CCP elite did not come from the May Fourth generation, who were born around 1900 or so. In fact, in the early 1920s most CC members from the First to the Third CC were substantially older than that. The Comintern clearly did not trust eager twenty-somethings with the early CCP, preferring more experienced revolutionaries such as Chen Duxiu and Dong Biwu. Once the May Fourth generation took over the party in 1934, however, it remained in charge until the Ninth PC in 1969 (Figure 3.2). Thus, the nearly continuous rise in the average age of CC members from 1934 to 1969 seen in Figure 3.1 was produced by the same age cohort controlling the CC during that period, as seen in Figure 3.2. In that period, the average age of CC members rose linearly from 33.7 to 55, with a minor rejuvenation at the 1956 Eighth Party Congress.

In addition to many other things, the Cultural Revolution represented a substantial rejuvenation of the party. The 1969 Ninth Party Congress saw the formal removal of many of the May Fourth generation from the CC, causing the average age of CC members to plummet from 64 to 55. This spelled the end of the May Fourthers as the dominant generation in the CC. Although the average age of CC members crept upward toward the end of the Cultural

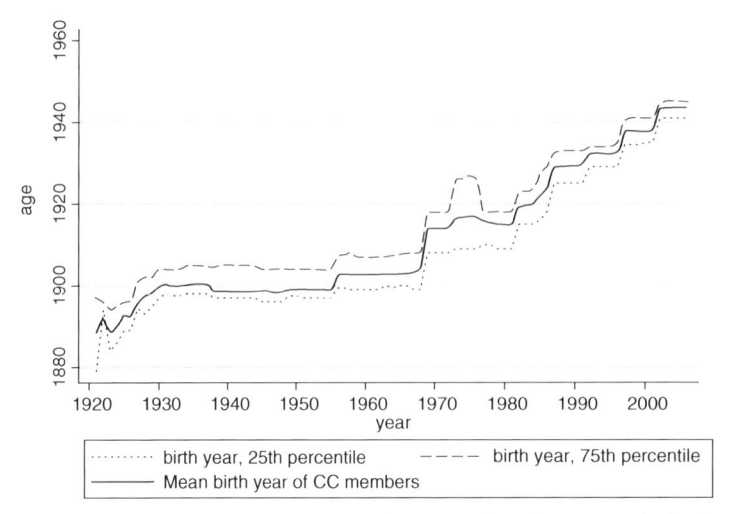

FIGURE 3.2. Average birth year and 25th and 75th percentile birth year of Central Committee members, 1921–2006.

Revolution as many veterans were rehabilitated into important positions, the average CC member nonetheless came from the 1914 cohort instead of an earlier cohort. Clearly, many CC members from the May Fourth generation never returned to active duty.

The rejuvenation effort continued relentlessly into the Deng era (Manion, 1993). The Twelfth PC in 1982 saw the displacement of the 1914 cohort with those born around 1919, which brought the average age of CC members from 66.5 to 62. The most momentous rejuvenation effort engineered by Deng and Chen Yun rivaled even that carried out by Mao. The 1985 National Party Conference and the Thirteenth Party Congress removed wholesale the generation of leaders born before 1919 in favor of much younger officials from the cohort born after 1929. This brought the average age of CC members from 64.5 in 1984 down to 58 in 1987. Thereafter, the age structure of CC members stabilized into the regular pattern of late 50s at the time of a party congress, followed by a gradual rise between congresses toward the low 60s. By these indicators, Deng Xiaoping and Chen Yun were successful in institutionalizing mechanisms to continuously rejuvenate the CCP.

Another way to track the successful rejuvenation of the party is to follow Long March veterans in the CC through time. As Figure 3.3 shows, the number of Long Marchers in the CC rose steadily through the late 1930s and 1940s and enjoyed a dramatic rise at the 1956 Eighth PC. Although the rapid expansion of the CC in 1956 saw a slight decline in the share of CC members who were also Long Marchers, these veterans nonetheless occupied over 60 percent of the seats in the CC. The dominance of the Long Marchers in the CC was maintained until the Cultural Revolution, when the Ninth PC inducted many from a younger generation into the CC. This is despite the fact that the

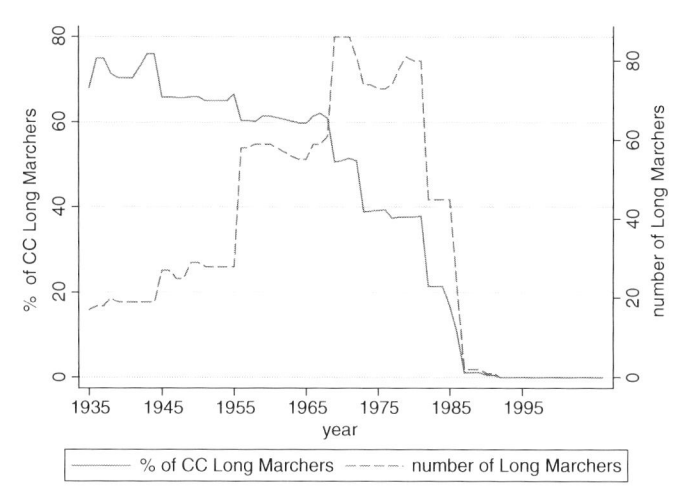

FIGURE 3.3. Percentage of Central Committee members with Long March experience and the number of Long Marchers.

Ninth CC included the highest number of Long Marchers. The high number of Long Marchers in the CC in 1969 is not surprising since many commanders of the military regions took over as heads of the various provincial revolutionary committees, granting them passage into the CC.

Lin Biao's purge in 1971 led to a substantial decline in Long Marchers in 1972 and 1973 as his suspected followers were systematically removed. Long Marchers then enjoyed a brief revival with Deng's rehabilitation in the late 1970s and early 1980s, but policies enacted by Deng and Chen, in addition to illness and death, produced extremely sharp drops in both the number and share of Long Marchers in the CC at the Twelfth and Thirteenth PCs. Although many Long Marchers remained healthy into the early 1990s, the Fourteenth PC did not induct any Long Marchers into the CC, thus spelling an end to the Long Marchers' influence in formal politics. Without an active policy to pressure Long Marchers into retirement, the Long March generation likely would have enjoyed a few more years of formal influence.

Education of CC Members

How did the education level of CC members evolve over time? As seen in Figure 3.4, political events clearly had a substantial impact on the average education level of CC members. In Figure 3.4, the 0 to 3 scale on the Y-axis represents less than a high school education, high school education (or equivalent), college education, and graduate school education. As the figure reveals, the CC began as a highly educated body dominated by cosmopolitan intellectuals. After the CCP split with the Guomindang (KMT), the party inducted into the CC many labor leaders who had participated in anti-imperialist strikes in the mid-1920s, which led to a plummeting of the average education level of CC members to well below

FIGURE 3.4. Average education level of Central Committee members, 1921–2006.
Note: On the Y-axis, 0 denotes less than high school or equivalent; 1 denotes high school or equivalent; 2 is college or equivalent; 3 is graduate level education.

high school level. Many of these new CC members turned out to be highly unreliable and either defected to the KMT or absconded with party funds.

As the party shifted toward a rural focus in the early 1930s, however, the average education level of CC members climbed back toward the mid-point between high school and college. The CCP likely learned not to place too many responsibilities on the shoulders of the uneducated. Although the CCP elite actively recruited peasants during the Jiangxi Soviet period, few of them were immediately inducted into the CC. This accords with Benton's (1992) finding that the southern guerrilla bases in the early 1930s often saw splits between the intellectual "leftist" elite sent down by the party center and the local guerrilla forces of mostly uneducated peasants. Instead of inducting uneducated peasants into the party center, the average education level of CC members remained the same throughout the Long March and the Yan'an period, a mix of high school and college-educated leaders. Some of the peasant fighters recruited in the 1930s, especially those who had participated in the Long March, were finally inducted into the CC at the Eighth PC in 1956, which caused a sharp drop in the education level.

The average education of CC members dropped below high school level during the Cultural Revolution as Mao introduced a mix of veteran peasant fighters and mass representatives into the CC at both the Ninth and Tenth CCs. The lowering of the average education level at both the Eighth and the Ninth PCs likely was a manifestation of Mao's "mixing in sand" tactic of filling the ranks of the elite with loyal, though not necessarily capable, leaders (MacFarquhar and Schoenhals, 2006: 333).

After the fall of the Gang of Four, the average education of CC members slowly recovered, although the pace was much slower than one would expect. Again, due to the active retirement policy pursued by Deng and Chen, the average education level of CC members climbed from nearly high school level just before the Twelfth PC to over half-way toward college level by the Thirteenth PC. As the norm of meritocracy was established, the average education level of CC members climbed with each subsequent party congress. Although the education trend of CC members supports the notion of a transition from revolutionary cadres to technocrats (Lee, 1991), this transition did not have a clear effect on the elite makeup of the CCP until well into the Deng era. The average education level climbed above college level at the Fifteenth PC in 1997 and continued its ascent at the Sixteenth PC. The membership of the CC is now among the most educated elite in the world.

Factional Influence

Finally, this dataset is useful to derive indicators of factional influence. If one believes that factions are formed on the basis of shared native place as well as common education and work experience (Lieberthal and Oksenberg, 1988: 156), then these biographical data would enable us to infer the share of CC members with factional ties with top leaders. The purpose of this exercise would be to track the relative balance of power between various top leaders, which would also provide an indication of how fragmented the party elite is at any particular moment.

In the past, a main challenge of coding factional ties was the enormous amount of work entailed in uncovering how the numerous members of the CC were tied with Politburo Standing Committee (PSC) members. To be sure, it is a relatively simple task to find out all the Tsinghua University graduates or all the Hunan natives among CC members at any given time, and important work on factions has been done on the basis of these simpler biographical coincidences (Li, 1994). Nonetheless, it becomes much more difficult to track job coincidences to capture all CC members who had worked in the same unit as a PSC member, especially one with a rich career. Taking Hu Yaobang as an example – he was a native of Hunan and a graduate and instructor of the Anti-Japanese University. However, he also held the following positions before becoming general secretary of the CCP: a senior cadre in the Communist Youth League between 1936 and 1937 and between 1952 and 1966; a senior cadre in the Central Military Commission between 1939 and 1946; a commander in various units of the North China Field Army between 1946 and 1949; a member of the Southwest Military and Political Committee between 1953 and 1956; one of the party secretaries of the CC Northwest Bureau between 1964 and 1965; the vice president of the Central Party School between 1977 and 1982; the head of the Central Organization Department between 1977 and 1978; and finally the third secretary of the Central Discipline and Inspection Commission between 1979 and 1982.

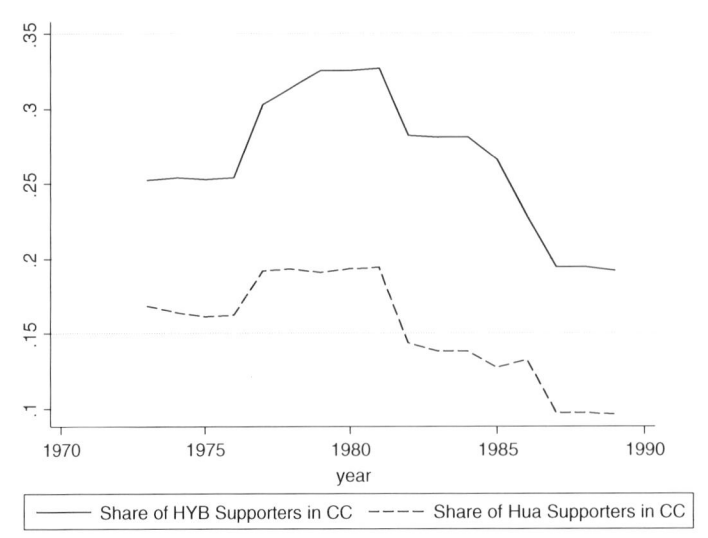

FIGURE 3.5. The share of Central Committee members with common experience with Hu Yaobang and Hua Guofeng, 1970–1990.

To find all CC members who had worked with Hu at the Twelfth PC, for example, one would have to carefully examine the biographies of all CC members elected at the Twelfth PC. If one wanted to track those who had worked with Hu over time, one would have to examine every CC member's biography over a period of time. This exercise would be even more laborious if one wanted to compare Hu's influence with that of Hua Guofeng, whose followers presumably would be quite different from Hu's. Although it took us quite a while to code the CC dataset, because we have the start and end years of most of the positions held by CC members, we can deploy a computer algorithm (in Stata) to search for CC members who had worked at the same time and in the same unit with Hu Yaobang. We can do this for every year during Hu's career, but especially during the years when he served as party general secretary. Although it is by no means a simple exercise, the availability of the data and the use of a computer algorithm make comparing the influence of various PSC members in the CC a manageable task.

In Figure 3.5, we present a comparison of the share of CC members who had common experiences with Hu Yaobang and Hua Guofeng, two contenders for power in the late 1970s. As one can see, Hu Yaobang's wide-ranging experience gave him a large advantage over Hua Guofeng throughout the entire period, even before the Eleventh PC. Hu's wide-ranging experience afforded him shared experiences with a much greater proportion of the CC throughout much of the 1970s and 1980s. In contrast, Hua Guofeng served only in provincial positions in Shanxi, Hunan, and Guangdong, as well as a short stint as the minister of public security before becoming the party helmsman. Thus, although the Eleventh Party Congress in 1977 allowed Hua to induct some cadres with shared experiences into the CC, his influence in the CC still paled in comparison with Hu's, who shared experiences with roughly 30 percent of the CC in 1977.

Why couldn't Hua have blocked Hu followers from entering the CC at the Eleventh Party Congress? Even if we discount Deng Xiaoping's backing of Hu Yaobang, it would have been very difficult to do so given Hu's wide-ranging experience. In order to block all possible Hu followers from the CC, one would have had to exclude cadets at the Anti-Japanese University, officers of the North China Field Army, and senior cadres in the Communist Youth League for much of the 1950s and 1960s. As these cadres made up some of the best human capital in the party at the time, it simply would have been unimaginable to exclude them all. Although one's influence in the CC does not entirely determine one's political fortune, the data in Figure 3.5 are certainly consistent with Hua's eventual fall and the elevation of Hu to the position of party general secretary.

To be sure, Hu later suffered his own fall from power at the hands of a powerful coalition between Deng Xiaoping and Chen Yun (Fewsmith, 1994). Beyond pushing for a liberal line against Deng's wishes and causing instability, Hu's own influence also began to slip by the mid-1980s due mainly to the death and retirement of many in his cohort. This may have made removing him from the party general secretary position easier for Deng and Chen. However, one can see that even after his demotion and the retirement of many of his followers at the Thirteenth PC in 1987, Hu remained an influential figure in the CC.

THE NEXT STEP

In this chapter, we introduce a new database of all Central Committee members that uses an unconventional logic of coding biographies. Instead of focusing on time and sequence, the coding scheme focuses on positions, followed by when the CC members served in a given position. This logic of coding elite biographies provides enormous flexibility both to generate various indicators of elite characteristics and to allow for the expansion of the dataset in various directions. As a preliminary step, we developed a few basic time-series trends in the CC. We hope this chapter will pave the way for other researchers to code other elite bodies in China and elsewhere. For example, it would be fruitful to code all PLA generals, not all of whom were CC members. Likewise, one could code members of the Central Discipline and Inspection Commission to examine their role in Chinese politics.

With the CC data, one can conduct three kinds of analyses. First, with these annual indicators, one can conduct time-series analyses, especially given the numerous data points provided by the database. Elite characteristics can be used as either dependent or independent variables. For example, certain types of political crises might increase the number of PLA representatives in the CC. Likewise, shifting characteristics of the CC, such as the average education level of CC members, might explain the pace of adopting new policies.

At the other extreme, one can conduct individual-level analyses and treat every CC member as an observation. With this dataset, one can infer the characteristics that would earn CC members promotions to the Politburo level. The individual-level data can be augmented by various economic and political indicators to provide a comprehensive look at the factors that drive elite promotions. Instead of focusing only on regional administrators (Landry, 2008a; Li and Zhou, 2005), a general theory of the factors that drive elite promotions *across* the various segments of the CCP regime can be tested rigorously.

Furthermore, this dataset also allows the researcher to segment the CC population into sectors or geographical regions and to correlate characteristics of regional or sectoral elite with various policy outcomes. Regional elite indicators, including regional representation in the CC, provincial factional affiliations, and the average education level of provincial elite, can be used to explain a host of regional economic and policy outcomes. With the development of these various indicators, we hope to make quantitative studies of the Chinese elite a less burdensome task.

4

Experimental Methods and Psychological Measures in the Study of Chinese Foreign Policy

Peter Hays Gries

Do concerns over "face" play a greater role in Chinese than American foreign policy? What is the nature of Chinese national identity? Can it be empirically measured and compared to other national identities, and is it consequential for foreign policy outcomes? For instance, how do Chinese patriotism and nationalism compare with, say, American patriotism and nationalism?

This chapter argues that experimental methods and psychological measures provide valuable tools to the political scientist interested in answering such questions. Experiments have long been the first choice for establishing causality in the hard sciences. The social sciences are catching on, with psychology and behavioral economics leading the way. Political scientists, led by Americanists interested in voting behavior, are beginning to follow suit (Druckman et al., 2006). International relations scholars have taken notice. As Rose McDermott (2006: 356) has recently argued, "experiments offer a unique opportunity to make a clear causal argument ... which is why it has been differentially adopted by the hard sciences, psychology, and behavioral economics as the gold standard method of choice." It is the random assignment of subjects to experimental and control conditions that allows analysts to be confident that variation between groups of subjects on dependent measures was "caused" by variation in the independent variables that were manipulated. By contrast, the majority of quantitative work in political science, which is based on research designs that are correlational in nature, cannot confidently make causal claims.

The postwar histories of comparative politics in general and China studies in particular make the idea of utilizing psychological measures in the study of Chinese foreign policy particularly contentious. In the 1960s and 1970s, modernization theory emerged as a major intellectual paradigm, with the concept of "political culture" at its core. Unfortunately, "political culture" was often used as a residual variable to explain what the theory could not otherwise explain. Its deterministic conclusions – certain nations could not democratize because of their "backward" cultures – also came under sustained criticism.

In the China field, Lucian Pye (e.g., 1968) took "political culture" in a psychoanalytic direction, put the entire Chinese people "on the couch," and declared the Chinese race to be stuck at the anal stage of development. Such arguments rubbed many younger China scholars the wrong way. Many of the Vietnam generation, often organizing around the Committee of Concerned Asian Scholars, revolted against Pye and modernization theory. "Political culture" and psychology in general have largely been taboo topics in the China field ever since.

The China studies taboo on the study of political psychology is extremely unfortunate. Psychology in general and social and cross-cultural psychology in particular have much to offer the political scientist interested in Chinese politics and foreign policy today. In addition to valuable theory, psychologists have developed reliable instruments to measure a variety of phenomena central to the study of Chinese foreign policy. For instance, Luhtanen and Crocker's (1992) collective self-esteem (CSE) scale, developed to study gender, ethnic, and other social identities, can easily be adapted to study constructs like Chinese and American patriotisms, as is done in the second study in this chapter. Instead of "I am proud to be a woman or black," the researcher can use "I am proud to be Chinese or American" and take advantage of the hard work in psychometrics Luhtanen and Crocker undertook to develop a robust 16-item CSE scale. The methodology of psychometrics, furthermore, provides the China scholar with the desire to study new or China-specific phenomena, such as U.S. policy preferences, with the tools to develop their own internally reliable measures to tap such constructs.

To illustrate these methodological and measurement issues, I first introduce selected results from two separate studies. The first shows how an experimental design and survey data can be used to test the popular assumption that Chinese are more driven by "face" in their foreign policy than Americans. The second shows how psychological measures and exploratory factor analysis can be used on survey data to inductively uncover differing Chinese and American structures of "patriotism" and "nationalism." It then uses the statistical technique of path analysis to uncover a possible model of the consequences of variations in Chinese patriotism and nationalism for the perception of U.S. threats and even U.S. policy preferences. In the final section, I draw on these two case studies to discuss the challenges and opportunities of experimental work and psychological measures in the study of Chinese foreign policy.

"FACE" AND FOREIGN POLICY: AN EXPERIMENT

Are Chinese more concerned about "face" in their foreign policy than Americans? This question was addressed in one part of a larger study (Gries, Peng, and Crowson, under review) exploring symbolic and material gains and losses as determinants of (in)security in international relations.

Design

A pair of student surveys was implemented in the United States and China in 2006. The design included both experimental (random assignment) and quasi-experimental (natural group) variables. It also included both between and within subjects designs. In other words, students' responses were compared to each other's as well as to their own responses to other questions. A 2 (domain) by 2 (frame) by 2 (level) by 2 (nation) factorial design with 16 conditions was employed, thus requiring a large sample size ($N = 521$). But this complexity allowed for the analysis of four key issues underlying the security studies debate over the fundamental determinants of (in)security in international affairs.

Independent Variables

The core of the design is an experimental 2 by 2 involving *domain* (material/symbolic) and *frame* (gains/losses). This portion of the design is a pure between-subjects experiment, with student participants randomly assigned to one of four conditions: (1) material gain, (2) material loss, (3) symbolic gain, and (4) symbolic loss. Each condition was operationalized with a set of scenarios that participants read and that differed only on the issues of domain and frame. For instance, "*You have been dating your boy/girlfriend for over three months and realize that you love him/her. You decide to take a risk and tell him/her that you love him/her. He/She responds by saying that he/she doesn't love you anymore and wants to break up*" was a symbolic loss scenario.

Both the materialist and symbolic security studies camps rely on an analogy with individual human needs. Materialists assume that states, like individuals, prioritize survival. Symbolic analysts posit that states are driven by higher human needs for belonging and esteem. Both camps thus appear to share the assumption that the dynamics of security and insecurity are the same at the individual and international levels. To put this assumption to the test, we included a third variable in our design, *level*, by adding to the individual-level scenarios a parallel set of scenarios at the international level. For instance, "*Sports analysts now predict that China will double the American medal count at the 2008 Beijing Olympics. In their view, China will be the only sports superpower in the 21st century*" was an international symbolic loss scenario for American subjects.

The final independent variable, and the one of central interest here, in the 2 by 2 by 2 by 2 design is *nation* (U.S./China). Orientalist notions of a Chinese obsession with "face" persist today and have a direct bearing on the issue of symbolic and material gains and losses. The Chinese, both Western (e.g., Smith, 1890) and Chinese (e.g., Ho, 1976; Hu, 1944) sources have long told us, are culturally predisposed to be sensitive to issues of "face." Americans, meanwhile, supposedly disregard face in favor of a more rational calculation of their material self-interest.

Hypothesis: Chinese are more sensitive to symbolic gains and losses than Americans, and Americans are more sensitive to material gains and losses than Chinese.

To put this hypothesis to the test we first adapted the original English-language survey to the Chinese perspective. For instance, in the Chinese version, the material-gain condition of the energy scenario read, "A Chinese oil company has just purchased monopoly rights to drill in the two largest oil fields in Africa, beating out a U.S. company." This reverses the words "Chinese" and "U.S." from the U.S. material gain condition, thus making the content of the U.S. material-gain version the same as the Chinese material-loss condition, and the U.S. material loss the same as the Chinese material gain. We then translated the adapted survey into Chinese and then back-translated it to ensure comparability. (For instance, "一家中国石油公司刚刚打败美国一家公司，购买了在非洲两个最大油田的独立钻井的权力.")

Dependent Measures

Each of the scenarios used to tap the different conditions was followed by a battery of emotional response items. Each was on a 1 (strongly disagree) to 7 (strongly agree) seven-point Likert-type scale. At its most fundamental level, security means the absence of concern or anxiety. We therefore constructed an *anxiety* score by averaging the self-reported responses to the "I feel worried" (我感到担心) and "I feel afraid" (我感到害怕) items.

Davis Bobrow (2001: 4) has perceptively noted that "threat centered work provides rich ground for security dilemma spirals of action and reaction, measure and countermeasure." He thus urges that the study of threats be balanced with the study of opportunities. To balance our negative anxiety measure with a more positive one, we decided to supplement it with a single item measure of *pride*, "I feel proud" (我感到骄傲).

Participants and Method

Because our 2 by 2 by 2 by 2 design entailed 16 conditions, and we desired at least 30 students per condition (actual $M = 32.56$), a large sample of 521 university students (284 female, 215 male, and 22 who did not indicate their gender) was recruited to participate in the study on a voluntary basis in spring 2006. Among these students, 240 were American at the University of Colorado and 281 were Chinese at Peking University. Participants ranged in age from 17 to 32 (median age = 20), and a *t*-test revealed that the American students ($M = 20.58$, $SD = 4.44$) were only slightly older than the Chinese students ($M = 19.88$, $SD = 2.23$), $t = 2.27$, $p = .024$.

We tested the Chinese and American participants in 15-minute sessions. The experimenter told the participants that the purpose of the study was to assess their reactions to eight scenarios. After assuring the participants that their responses would remain anonymous, the experimenter administered the survey packets. The participants filled out a series of questionnaires individually. After completing the packet, the participants were thanked for their participation, debriefed (i.e., informed that none of the scenarios that they had read were real), and released. The ethical standards of the American Political Science (APSA) and the American Psychological Association (APA) were strictly followed during data collection and analysis.

Selected Results

To see whether nation had any impact on our dependent measures, we ran a series of four three-way (frame X domain X nation) analyses of variance (ANOVAs). The first, with *individual level anxiety* as our dependent variable, revealed the main effects of gain/loss and material/symbolic, but not of nation. Losses ($M = 5.17$) produced much more anxiety than gains ($M = 3.34$), $F(1, 495) = 302.68$, $p < .001$. And material scenarios ($M = 4.84$) produced more anxiety than symbolic scenarios ($M = 3.68$), $F(1, 495) = 121.88$, $p < .001$. The effect size of gain/loss ($\eta_p^2 = .38$) was massive: about twice that of material/symbolic ($\eta_p^2 = .20$).[1] The p value for nation ($p = .49$), however, was not even close to statistical significance. None of the two-way interactions was statistically significant either. The three-way interaction of nation, domain, and frame was statistically significant, $F(1, 495) = 12.66$, $p < .001$, but not in any obviously meaningful way, and the effect size, $\eta_p^2 = .025$, was quite small. The mean overall levels of anxiety were also very close for both the United States ($M = 4.27$) and China ($M = 4.18$), suggesting that there was no method effect impacting the results. At the individual level, in short, the evidence overwhelmingly suggests that the Chinese and American respondents' self-reports of anxiety were not significantly different.

When we ran a second three-way ANOVA on *international-level anxiety*, however, moderate national differences began to emerge. Overall, Chinese participants ($M = 3.54$) reported higher levels of anxiety after reading the international scenarios than did the American students ($M = 3.03$). There were main effects of gain/loss, material/symbolic, and nation (all ps < .001), with effect sizes of $\eta_p^2 = .18$, .15, and .03, respectively. All the interactions were significant as well, although the effect sizes were small. Figure 4.1 reveals that although the overall effect size, $\eta_p^2 = .02$, of the three-way domain by frame by nation interaction, $F(1, 492) = 11.78$, $p = .001$, was on the small side, the Chinese participants ($M = 3.87$) reported much more anxiety in the international symbolic-loss condition than the U.S. participants ($M = 2.43$).

A three-way ANOVA on *individual-level pride* revealed the main effects of gain ($M = 4.74$) over loss ($M = 1.91$), $F(1, 499) = 632.08$, $p < .001$, $\eta_p^2 = .56$, symbolic ($M = 3.64$) over material ($M = 3.01$), $F(1, 499) = 31.49$, $p < .001$, $\eta_p^2 = .06$, and nation, $F(1, 499) = 3.95$, $p = .047$, although the effect

---

[1] Partial eta-square (η_p^2) provides a global index of the size of observed differences in means. Small and medium effects are represented by values around .01 and .06, respectively. Large effects are represented by values around .14 or greater.

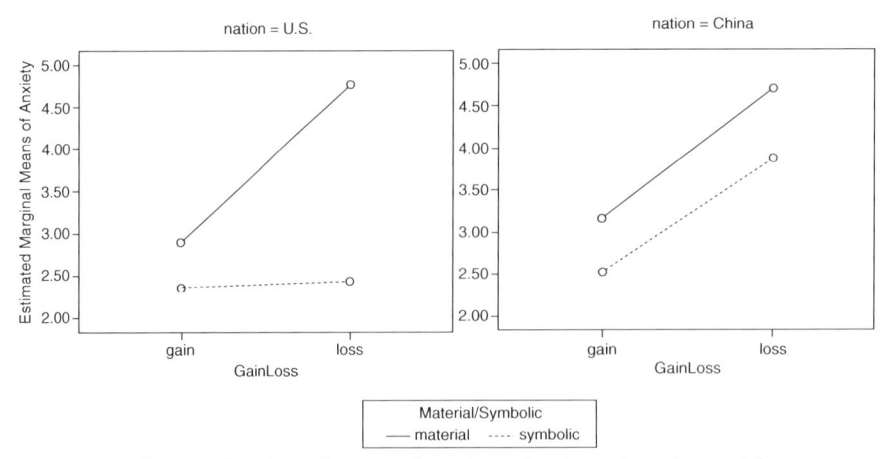

FIGURE 4.1. International anxiety as a function of nation, domain, and frame, 2006 samples.

size for the latter, $\eta_p^2 = .01$, was very small. The only statistically significant interaction was gain/loss and material/symbolic, $F(1, 499) = 25.88$, $p < .001$, $\eta_p^2 = .05$. Both American and Chinese students reported significantly more pride in personal symbolic gains ($M = 5.39$) than in material gains ($M = 4.14$), with symbolic losses ($M = 1.94$) and material losses ($M = 1.88$) virtually indistinguishable.

A three-way analysis of variance (ANOVA) on *international-level pride* revealed the main effects of both gain/loss, $F(1, 497) = 275.61$, $p < .001$, and material/symbolic, $F(1, 497) = 12.73$, $p < .001$, although the effect size of the latter, $\eta_p^2 = .03$, was dwarfed by that of the former, $\eta^2 = .36$. Although there was no main effect of nation, there was a statistically significant interaction, $F(1, 497) = 41.83$, $p < .001$, between nation and gain/loss, with a medium effect size, $\eta_p^2 = .08$. As displayed in Figure 4.2, compared to the Americans, the Chinese reported both higher levels of pride with national gains (China $M = 5.18$; U.S. $M = 4.18$), and lower levels of pride with national losses (China $M = 1.99$; U.S. $M = 2.78$). Indeed, subtracting the losses scores from the gains scores reveals that the Chinese participants (3.19 difference) were over twice as impacted by national gains and losses as the American participants (1.4 difference).

Discussion

Are Chinese more sensitive to symbolic gains and losses than Americans, and Americans more sensitive to material gains and losses than Chinese? The evidence from our experiment is mixed, but revealing. At the individual level, American and Chinese students were virtually indistinguishable when it came to their self-reports of anxiety and pride in response to symbolic and material gain and loss scenarios. For instance, both Chinese and American students

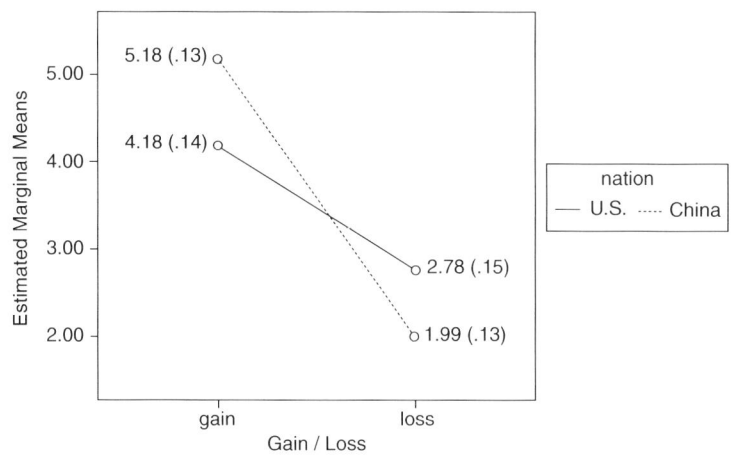

FIGURE 4.2. International pride as a function of nation and frame, 2006 samples. numbers in chart = means number in parenthesis = standard deviations

took more pride in symbolic gains than in material gains. This suggests that scholars should be wary of Orientalist and Occidentalist notions of deep-rooted cultural differences, such as the idea that Chinese have an inordinate cultural sensitivity to issues of "face."

National differences did emerge, however, when we shifted from individual to international scenarios. As Figure 4.1 reveals, Americans reported much lower levels of anxiety in response to national symbolic losses than did the Chinese participants. And as Figure 4.2 shows, Chinese were over twice as sensitive to gain/loss as Americans when it came to national pride.

Two questions arise from these international-level findings. First, were the Chinese levels of national pride and anxiety high or were the American levels low? In other words, is this finding evidence of a Chinese oversensitivity to the plight of their nation, an excessive concern with China's national "face"? Or is it evidence that Americans can more easily disassociate themselves from the fate of their nation, or that they can kid themselves into believing that they don't care? Further experimental work is needed to clarify this issue.

Second, why did our nation variable produce these international-level differences? Are they a product of the distinction between individualist and collectivist cultures, such that Chinese have more of their psychological well-being invested in the good of their groups? Alternatively, could these differences have historical origins, with the Chinese experience of victimization at the hands of Western imperialism during the "Century of Humiliation" making them more sensitive to their international status? Or are they simply the product of the current balance of material power, such that Americans have less to worry about or to take pride in, confident in U.S. global preeminence. Chinese, by contrast, may be more anxious simply because they are confronting the reality of an American military superpower that is ambivalent about China's rise. Although the use of an experimental design allows us to confidently state that nation "caused" these differences in our international anxiety and pride scores, further research is needed to uncover the mechanism of causation.

STRUCTURES AND CONSEQUENCES OF CHINESE NATIONAL IDENTITY: PSYCHOLOGICAL MEASURES AND METHODS

What is the nature of Chinese patriotism and nationalism? How do they differ from American patriotism and nationalism? And what impact do they have on Chinese foreign policy attitudes? To explore the structure and consequences of Chinese national identity, two surveys were conducted in the United States and China in spring 2009 (see Gries, Zhang, Crowson, and Cai, 2010). Using psychological measures, exploratory factor analysis, and path analysis, we found that although American patriotism and nationalism were empirically similar, they were highly distinct in China, with patriotism aligning with a benign internationalism, and nationalism with a more malign blind patriotism. Chinese patriotism, furthermore, had no impact on the perception of U.S. threats or U.S. policy preferences, whereas nationalism did. The role of nationalist historical beliefs in structures of Chinese national identity was also explored, as well as the consequences of historical beliefs for the perception of U.S. threats. Selected methods, results, and discussion are presented below to demonstrate the utility of psychological measures and methods to the study of Chinese foreign policy.

Participants and Procedures

The surveys were completed by 512 Chinese and Americans in spring 2009, among whom 161 Peking University undergraduate students in international relations filled out a three-page hard-copy survey in February, and 351 American adults from around the country took an online survey in March. Both surveys began with an explanation that the survey was about the relationship between personality and international relations, and that the data collected would remain confidential.

The Beijing sample included slightly more women ($N = 89$) than men ($N = 69$), and more students from the "masses" (群众) ($N = 95$) than CCP party members (党员) ($N = 61$). Due to a clerical error, age was not requested, but a survey of the same Peking University class the previous semester revealed a median age of 20. Of these students, 44 claimed to have grown up in the countryside and 114 claimed an urban upbringing.

The national American Internet sample was very well balanced, with slightly more men ($N = 177$) than women ($N = 174$), and slightly more Democrats ($N = 130$) than Republicans ($N = 121$) and Independents ($N = 100$). Ages ranged from 18 to 69, with a mean age of 33.54 ($SD = 14.20$). In terms of ethnicity, the sample was 81.2 percent white, 3.7 percent African American, 2.3 percent

Experimental Methods and Psychological Measures 77

non-Chinese Asian American, 2.3 percent Latino/a, 4.3 percent Native American, and 6.3 percent "other."

Measures

Unless otherwise noted, the questions that composed the following scales were on seven-point Likert-type scales, ranging from 1 ("strongly disagree") to 7 ("strongly agree"). Both samples responded to the national identity items. The Americans were not asked the nationalist history, U.S. threat perception, and U.S. policy preferences items.

National Identities. Twelve items were utilized to tap four distinct types of national identities discussed in the literature on patriotism and nationalism. Higher values on these scales indicate greater patriotism, blind patriotism, nationalism, or internationalism. The Chinese language versions of these national identity items are listed in the note to Table 4.1.

Patriotism. Three items adapted from Luhtanen and Crocker's (1992) collective self-esteem scale were used to tap the positive love of one's own country. They were "I'm glad to be Chinese/American," "I often regret that I am Chinese/American" (reverse coded), and "Being Chinese/American is an important reflection of who I am."

Blind patriotism. Shatz, Staub, and Levine (1999) distinguish "blind" from "constructive" patriotism, arguing that the former represents an unquestioning allegiance and intolerance of criticism. We adapted three items: "China/America is virtually always right," "Chinese/American foreign policies are almost always morally correct," and "I support my country whether its policies are right or wrong."

Nationalism. Kosterman and Feshbach (1989) argue that nationalism goes beyond a positive love of one's own country (patriotism) to a belief in the superiority of one's own country over others. We adapted three items, "China/America is the best country in the world," "It is NOT important for China/America to win international sports competitions" (reverse coded), and "In view of Chinese history and democracy, it is only natural that China lead East Asia/the U.S. lead the world."

Internationalism. Kosterman and Feshbach (1989) further distinguish nationalism from internationalism. We adapted three items: "The alleviation of poverty in very poor countries like Haiti is their problem, not ours" (reverse coded), "Our children should be taught to support the welfare of all of humanity," and "Our foreign policies should pursue the greatest good internationally, and not just pursue the Chinese/American national interest."

Nationalist History. Beliefs about the nature of China's past encounters with the outside world may impact the nature of Chinese national identity (Gries, 2004) as well as beliefs about the intentions of other countries in the present. We therefore included four items tapping beliefs about two distinct Chinese historical encounters with the outside world: (1) the "Century of Humiliation," and (2) the Korean War. The two "Century" items were taken directly from the series preface to the multivolume "Never Forget the National Humiliation" (毋忘国耻) history book series (1992): "China's early modern encounter with Western imperial powers was a history of humiliation in which the motherland was subjected to the insult of being beaten because we were backwards" (中国近代与西方帝国主义列强的历史就是祖国蒙受奇耻大辱落后挨打的惨痛史) and, "China's early modern encounter with Western imperial powers was a heroic struggle by the Chinese people against imperialism" (中国近代与西方帝国主义列强的历史就是中国人民不甘屈服于帝国主义及其附属的英雄斗争史). The two Korean War items were "China won the War to Resist America and Aid Korea" (中国在抗美援朝中得胜了) and "The War to Resist America and Aid Korea was a heroic moment in Chinese history" (抗美援朝是中国历史上的英雄时刻).

Threat Perception. Perception of the threat that the United States poses to China was tapped with four items, composed of two possible subscales. Two addressed military threat: "A growing American military is bad for China" (美国军队的发展对中国无益) and "The recent increase in U.S. defense spending undermines Chinese security" (最近美国国防开支的增长威胁中国安全). Two addressed humiliation threat: "American criticisms of Chinese 'human rights' are really just attempts to humiliate China" (美国政府批评中国 "人权问题" 实际上是在羞辱中国) and "American support of Taiwan and Tibet is really about insulting the Chinese people" (美国支持台湾和西藏是在羞辱中国人民).

U.S. Policy Preferences. Three items were developed to tap respondents' preferred U.S. policies. They were "The Chinese government should adopt tougher foreign policies toward the U.S." (中国政府应该对美国采取更强硬的外交政策), "The best way to deal with the U.S. is to build up our military and seek to contain U.S. influence throughout the world" (应对美国的最好方式是增强我国的军备，削弱美国在世界范围的影响), and "If the U.S. threatens China, we should use military force against them" (如果美国威胁中国，我们应该用军事力量对美国进行反击). Higher values indicate desires for tougher Chinese policies toward the United States.

RESULTS: STRUCTURES OF CHINESE AND
AMERICAN NATIONAL IDENTITY

To compare the structures of Chinese and American national identities, we first conducted exploratory factor analysis on our American and Beijing samples. Principal axis factoring (PAF) was conducted on both samples, followed by Promax rotation with Kaiser normalization to aid in the interpretation of the factors. Table 4.1 displays the results and includes all loadings greater than 0.35.

PAF on the American sample produced two factors with eigenvalues greater than 1 (5.18 and 1.51, respectively).[2] As Table 4.1 reveals, both were clearly

---

[2] Eigenvalues represent the weight of the loadings on a factor. Generally, an eigenvalue of at least one is seen as a necessary but not sufficient condition for viewing a factor as independent.

TABLE 4.1. *Structures of national identity: Pattern matrix loadings for principal axis factor analysis with Promax rotation for American and Chinese samples, 2009*

	American		Chinese	
	Factor 1: Patriotism / Nationalism	Factor 2: Internationalism	Factor 1: Patriotism / Internationalism	Factor 2: Nationalism / Blind Patriotism
Patriotism 1	.908		.466	
Patriotism 2r	.829		.811	
Patriotism 3	.797		.696	
Blind Patriotism 1	.405	.351		.546
Blind Patriotism 2	.433	.388		.669
Blind Patriotism 3	.660			.614
Nationalism 1	.455			.782
Nationalism 2r	.390			
Nationalism 3	.780			.601
Internationalism 1r		−.612	.639	
Internationalism 2		−.725	.500	
Internationalism 3		−.553		
Eigenvalues	5.18	1.51	3.26	2.28
Factor intercorrelation	.558		.269	
Scale α (N)	.88 (9)	.66 (3)	.75 (5)	.78 (5)
Mean (SD)	4.43 (1.16)	5.27 (1.11)	5.63 (1.08)	3.92 (1.17)

Note: Factor coefficients are shown only if > 0.35. Reverse coded items denoted with an "r" and *italicized*. Differences in American/Chinese versions are underlined:

Patriotism
1. "I'm glad to be American/Chinese." 我很高兴自己是中国人。
2r. "*I often regret that I am American/Chinese.*" 我经常遗憾自己是中国人。
3. "Being American/Chinese is an important reflection of who I am." 我觉得作为中国人对我的自我认同很重要。

Blind Patriotism
1. "American/Chinese foreign policies are almost always morally correct." 中国的外交政策基本上都是正义的。
2. "America/China is virtually always right." 中国的决策几乎都是正确的。
3. "I support my country whether its policies are right or wrong." 无论我国的政策对错与否，我都予以支持。

Nationalism
1. "America/China is the best country in the world" 中国是世界上最好的国家。
2r. "*It is NOT important for America/China to win international sporting competitions.*" 中国赢得国际体育竞赛并不重要。
3. "In view of America's/China's history and democracy, it is only natural that the U.S. lead the world/China lead East Asia." 鉴于中国具有悠久的历史，光辉的文明，中国的然应该领导东亚。

Internationalism
1r. "*The alleviation of poverty in very poor countries like Haiti is their problem, not ours.*" 诸如海地这样的贫穷国家所面临的问题应该由他们自己解决，与我们无关。
2. "Our children should be taught to support the welfare of all of humanity." 我们应该教育我们的子孙后代不仅为中国而为全人类的福祉做贡献。
3. "Our foreign policies should pursue the greatest good internationally, and not just pursue the American/Chinese national interest." 我国外交政策应当追求国际主义而不是只追求中国的国家利益。

interpretable. All nine patriotism, blind patriotism, and nationalism items loaded most strongly on the first factor, which has been labeled "patriotism/nationalism." The three internationalism items loaded on the second factor, labeled "internationalism." The two factors intercorrelated quite highly at $r = .56$ and the internationalism items all loaded negatively. Along with our second eigenvalue of just 1.51, this suggests that our two factor solution was close to being a single factor solution. In short, although patriotism, blind patriotism, and nationalism are conceptually distinct, our data suggest that empirically American patriotism and nationalism go together and even approach being part of a single dimension set against internationalism.

PAF on the Beijing sample also produced two factors with eigenvalues greater than 1 (3.26 and 2.28, respectively). Table 4.1 reveals that both were clearly interpretable with no cross loadings. All three patriotism and the first two internationalism items loaded on factor one, labeled "patriotism/internationalism." All three blind patriotism and two of the nationalism items loaded on factor two, labeled "nationalism/blind patriotism." The two factors intercorrelated at just $r = .27$, indicating that these two dimensions of Chinese national identity are largely orthogonal or independent of one another.

The differing structures of American and Chinese national identities revealed in Table 4.1 are truly striking. Where patriotism – love of country – and nationalism – belief in the superiority of one's country over other countries – go together in the American sample, they do not go together in the Chinese sample. Instead, patriotism in China is associated with internationalism and should thus be understood to be more benign than American patriotism. In other words, the more patriotic an American is, the more nationalistic she or he also tends to be. In China, however, patriotism and nationalism do not necessarily go together, such that a highly patriotic Chinese is just as likely to be low on nationalism, and a very nationalistic Chinese to be low on patriotism.

RESULTS: CONSEQUENCES OF CHINESE PATRIOTISM AND NATIONALISM

To explore the consequences of Chinese patriotism and nationalism we first constructed scales for each, as well as for the history, threat, and policy variables. The scale reliabilities and Ns are reported in the last two columns of Table 4.2, which reports the descriptive statistics for the Beijing sample. The Cronbach's alphas ranged from fair ($\alpha = .71$) to good ($\alpha = .82$) internal reliabilities, giving us confidence that the specific survey items composing each scale tapped the same underlying construct.[3]

---

[3] Cronbach's alphas range from zero to one, with higher scores indicating greater internal reliability of the measure; .60 is generally seen as the minimal acceptable alpha. Alphas tend to be higher for longer scales, so our alphas of .71 and .73 for scales of just two and three items might actually be interpreted as quite good.

TABLE 4.2. *Descriptive statistics: Correlations, significance levels, means, standard deviations, and scale alphas and Ns for 2009 Beijing sample (minimum N = 156)*

Variables	1	2	3	4	5	6	M	SD	α	N
1. Patriotism/ Internationalism	–	.19*	.38**	.20*	.29**	.13	5.63	1.08	.75	5
2. Nationalism/ Blind Patriotism		–	.44**	.32**	.38**	.35**	3.92	1.17	.78	5
3. Nationalist History			–	.39**	.45**	.38**	4.71	1.15	.75	4
4. Military Threat				–	.34**	.32**	4.29	1.21	.71	2
5. Humiliation Threat					–	.44**	4.31	1.51	.82	2
6. U.S. Policy						–	3.81	1.26	.73	3

Note:
** Correlation is significant at the .01 level (2-tailed).
* Correlation is significant at the .05 level (2-tailed).

The means and standard deviations for all six of our scales are also listed in Table 4.2. The Beijing sample reported much more patriotism/internationalism ($M = 5.63$) than nationalism/blind patriotism ($M = 3.92$).[4] Given a scale midpoint of 4, we can say that, overall, the Beijing sample was very patriotic but quite balanced in terms of nationalism. The means for nationalist historical beliefs ($M = 4.71$), military threat ($M = 4.29$), and humiliation threat ($M = 4.31$) were just above the scale midpoint of four, whereas U.S. policy preferences were just below the scale midpoint ($M = 3.81$), suggesting a good balance on all of our scales.

Finally, Table 4.2 also reports the zero-order correlations among our six scales. With the exception of the lack of a relationship between patriotism and U.S. policy, all of the correlations were statistically significant and positive. And with the exception of the relationships between patriotism and nationalism, and patriotism and military threat, which correlated at just $p < .05$, the remaining correlations were highly significant ($p < .01$) and substantial in size, ranging from $r = .29$ to $r = .44$.

Given that the zero-order correlations do not account for collinearity, we decided to use path analysis to better understand the precise relationships among our variables. Path analysis has a number of advantages over multiple regression, such as the ability to model mediated relationships among variables, as well as the ability to evaluate the global fit of a model containing those mediated relationships. We used AMOS 17.0 with full information

---

[4] An independent sample *t*-test revealed the difference between the means to be both statistically significant and very large, $t(160) = 15.14, p < .001$.

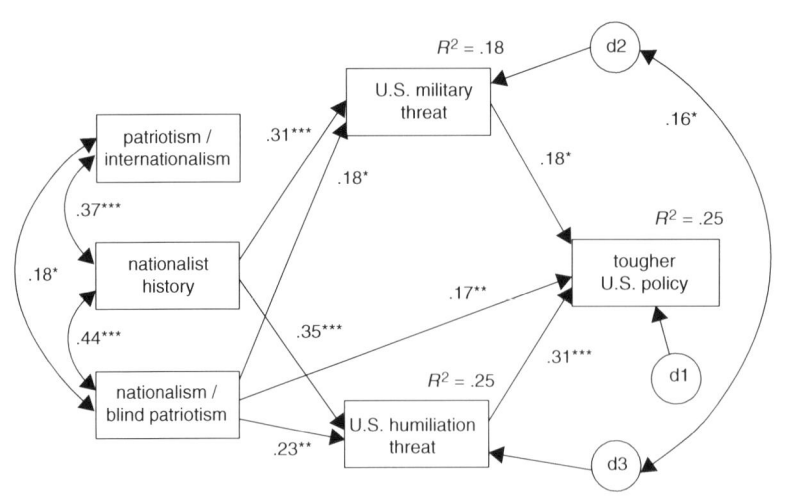

FIGURE 4.3. Final Beijing path model, 2009 sample.
*** Correlation is significant at $p < .001$; ** Correlation is significant at $p < .01$;
* Correlation is significant at $p < .05$

maximum likelihood estimation to first test a fully saturated model in which patriotism, nationalism, and nationalist historical beliefs were treated as covarying exogenous variables predicting U.S. military and humiliation threat, which in turn predicted policy preferences. After removing the statistically insignificant paths, the model displayed in Figure 4.3 emerged as the best fit for the Beijing data.

We examined the fit of our path model based on the χ^2 test, the χ^2/degrees of freedom ratio, the Comparative Fit Index (CFI), the Tucker-Lewis Index (TLI), the Normed Fit Index (NFI), and the Root Mean Square Error of Approximation (RMSEA). Nonsignificant χ^2 values and χ^2/df ratios < 2 or 3 are considered reasonable indicators of a close model fit. Conventional cut-offs for a close model fit are CFI, TLI, and NFI values greater than .95 and RMSEA values less than .06 (see Kline, 2005; Schumacker and Lomax, 2004). Our final model in Figure 4.3 was a very good fit for the Beijing data, with a nonsignificant χ^2 value of $p = .338$, a χ^2/df ratio of 1.135, a CFI of .997, a TLI of .983, a NFI of .976, and an RMSEA of .029.

The most striking aspect of our Beijing path model is that when controlling for nationalism and nationalist history, patriotism had no impact on perceptions of U.S. military or humiliation threat or U.S. policy preferences. Nationalism, by contrast, had a strong impact on U.S. policy preferences, both directly and mediated through perceptions of U.S. military and humiliation threats. Indeed, these three paths combined to account for a full 25 percent of the variance in U.S. policy preferences.[5] From a foreign policy perspective,

---

[5] The "d1" in the path model represents prediction error, or the 75 percent of the variance in preferred U.S. policies not accounted for by the variables included in the model.

therefore, Chinese patriotism appears decidedly benign, whereas Chinese nationalism appears potentially malign in its consequences.

It is also noteworthy that nationalist historical beliefs covaried strongly with both patriotism ($r = .37$) and nationalism ($r = .44$), providing strong support for the argument that beliefs about the national past and national identities in the present are mutually constituted. Nationalist historical beliefs also strongly predicted both perceptions of U.S. military ($r = .31$) and humiliation ($r = .35$) threat.

Finally, Figure 4.3 reveals that perceptions of a humiliation threat had a much greater impact on U.S. policy preferences than did perceptions of a military threat. Indeed, squaring the partial coefficients reveals that whereas perceptions of a U.S. humiliation threat accounted for a full 9.6 percent of the variation in U.S. policy preferences, perceptions of a military threat accounted for just 3.2 percent of that variation. Those interested in the determinants of China's U.S. policy, therefore, would be wise to consider not just the objective balance of military power but also the subjective realm of identity and affect.

Discussion

Allen Carlson (2009) has lamented the lack of rigorous measurement in studies of Chinese national identity and the failure of scholars to place Chinese nationalism in a broader comparative framework. I agree. This case study should demonstrate that the rigorous measurement of constructs like patriotism and nationalism is not only possible but that such constructs can be part of an explanatory social science.

Neil Diamant (2009: 18–23; this volume, Chapter 2) has argued that there is a "threshold problem" in studies of popular nationalism such as my own (Gries, 2004): the patriotism of the self-styled "fourth generation" of urban Chinese does not entail sufficient sacrifice or commitment to rise to the level of true patriotism. Compared to the veterans he studies who have genuine "patriotic standing," Diamant dismisses the urban youth who have been at the forefront of the last decade of popular nationalist protests as inconsequential "café latte" nationalists. Those like myself who have studied the rise of this popular nationalism, furthermore, foster "China threat" discourse.

Diamant's "threshold" approach to patriotism/nationalism is both conceptually and empirically problematic. Conceptually, where should one draw the line? What level of "sacrifice" is sufficient to be included in his "patriot" category? (Or what level of latte drinking is sufficient to be dismissed as an unpatriotic "elite"?) Empirically, reducing concepts like patriotism or nationalism to an either/or binary does violence to the complexity and variability of the concepts. For patriotism or nationalism to be useful in a social science that seeks to be explanatory, we should seek to *maximize* rather than minimize the variation that is empirically measured. Variables should vary – as much as possible. For instance, without the variability of each of our survey items, whose responses were on 1–7 Likert-type scales, and without five items tapping both patriotism and nationalism, increasing each scale's internal reliability, it is unlikely that we would have been able to empirically distinguish between Chinese patriotism and nationalism or to uncover the unique consequences of each.

Diamant is also misguided to dismiss the nationalism expressed by China's young netizens (网民) and street demonstrators as inconsequential. This study has shown that individual differences in "trait" or enduring levels of nationalism impact both perceptions of U.S. threat and preferred U.S. policies. It is likely that temporary or "state" levels of nationalism have similar consequences. Thus when incidents like the 1999 Belgrade bombing or the 2001 Hainan Island plane collision temporarily inflame anti-American nationalist sentiments, Chinese perceptions of U.S. threat likely increase, along with Chinese desires for tougher U.S. policies. During such crises, therefore, inflamed Chinese nationalism could have very serious consequences for Chinese foreign policy, even if temporarily inflamed levels of nationalism dissipate later, as Diamant rightly notes. In short, variations in Chinese nationalism, whether between individuals or across time, appear to be related to variations in both threat perception and even foreign policy preferences, thus warranting further research rather than dismissal.

Diamant's most serious charge is that studies of popular Chinese nationalism, like my own, foster "China threat" discourse. His logic is one of guilt through association: "China threat" proponents frequently refer to the rise of Chinese nationalism to support their arguments; therefore, those who study Chinese nationalism are complicit in the "China threat" project. This logic is problematic: once scholarship has been published, no scholar can completely control its use or misuse. Diamant's charge could also have a chilling effect on scholars, who too often cede the public sphere on sensitive political topics to nonexperts. I would argue that we need to encourage more, not less, academic work and policy outreach on highly consequential topics like Chinese nationalism.

CONCLUSION: OPPORTUNITIES AND CHALLENGES

In the conclusion to their edited volume *New Directions in the Study of China's Foreign Policy*, Thomas J. Christensen, Alastair Iain Johnston, and Robert S. Ross (2006: 387) rightly note that Chinese foreign policy studies have been a "consumer but not a producer of theory and methods." I hope this chapter has made the case that experimental methods and psychological measures offer great promise not just for deepening our substantive knowledge of Chinese foreign policy but also for contributing to the theoretic development of the field of foreign policy analysis. Just as cross-cultural psychology was well positioned at the margins to challenge and reshape the universalism of much of mainstream social and cognitive psychology (see Nisbett [2003] for an overview), China scholars are well positioned to challenge and reshape theories inductively derived from the Western experience that do not travel well to China.

Experimental methods, furthermore, are theoretically neutral. Whether you are a structural realist focusing on the balance of material power like Bob Ross, or a constructivist focusing on sociological theory like Iain Johnston, you can benefit from the rigorous causal explanatory power that experiments bring to empirical work.

The same cannot be said for psychological measures. If you agree with rationalists like Bob Ross (2001: 395) that "common arguments about misperceptions in policymaking ... do not apply to the U.S.-China conflict," you will have no need for psychological measures. If, on the other hand, you agree with Robert Jervis (1976) that perception and misperception are central to the relations among nations, psychological measures may well be indispensable for those who wish to move beyond theory to the empirical examination of Chinese foreign policy.

Psychological measures developed in the West, however, do not always travel well to China. Many core concepts in the psychological literature, such as conservatism, are so bound up in the Western liberal tradition that they simply cannot travel to China. For instance, the widely used right-wing authoritarianism (RWA) scale has idiosyncratic items like *"Atheists and others who have rebelled against the established religions are no doubt every bit as good and virtuous as those who attend church regularly"* that clearly would not resonate with Chinese subjects.

Another problem with using Western psychological measures in China is that the scales tend to be one dimensional, requiring that negative items be reverse-coded. Cross-cultural psychologists have found that due to a greater tendency toward dialectical rather than categorical thinking, Asians are more likely than Westerners to simultaneously hold contradictory attitudes (e.g., Spencer-Rodgers, Peng, and Wang, 2004). Forcing their responses onto unidimensional scales, therefore, is likely to reduce their reliability. For example, a Chinese respondent to a stereotyping or prejudice scale might simultaneously rate Americans as both highly "friendly" (a positive attribute) and highly "disagreeable" (a negative quality), thus reducing the reliability of a unidimensional scale. Greater multidimensional scaling in such a situation would be needed. Similarly, in our second case study, separate items tapping beliefs that China was a victim and beliefs that China was a victor during the "Century of Humiliation" cohered, despite their apparent contradiction. Such empirical findings point to the importance of a fundamentally inductive orientation toward the data gathered from Chinese surveys.

Another challenge is that psychological constructs like threat perception are notoriously difficult to measure, especially when using hard-copy or Internet surveys that rely on self-reporting. People are not always honest, even with themselves, about their actual views and emotions. Through "impression management" or "self-presentation" techniques, we often seek to orchestrate the images we present to ourselves and the world (Goffman, 1959). With sufficient funding, future research could also use physiological techniques, such as measuring blood pressure and galvanic skin conductance as indicators of anxiety and threat perception. A more affordable approach is sentence unscrambling tasks and other methods that can reveal subconscious or implicit levels of various attitudes and affect.

At a broader level, all statistical studies confront two challenges: junk-in-junk-out and gold-in-junk-out. First, regardless of the rigor of the statistical analysis, if the original data are poor, the results will be of limited value. This problem has been well documented in the case of the famous "correlates of war" database once widely used in conflict studies. The coding of even basic issues such as distinguishing between interstate and civil wars or the exact onset or termination dates of hostilities was found to be highly problematic. In the case of the type of political psychology conducted here, good internal reliabilities are vital to the discovery of robust patterns of associations among our variables. For instance, had the internal reliabilities of our measures been lower, the fit statistics for our path model would not have been good enough to give us confidence in the pattern of associations depicted in the model.

Second, even excellent survey data, if not properly interpreted, yield little of value. Statistics do not speak for themselves. One problem is that political scientists overemphasize statistical significance testing (p values) at the expense of effect sizes (η_p^2) and the interpretation of the practical significance and meaning of their statistical results. The focus on statistical significance testing is particularly problematic when political scientists use preexisting datasets, such as the American National Election Survey or the Chicago Council on Global Affairs surveys that generally have very large Ns. With such datasets, it is rare for variables to be completely *uncorrelated*; p values are a direct product of sample size. Another problem with statistical significance testing is the systematic failure to report statistically *insignificant* findings. Empirical falsification, as Karl Popper (2001) has noted, is vital to the accumulation of knowledge. Statistical non-findings can also prove highly instructive, such as the finding reported in the first case study above that American and Chinese students responded similarly to the individual-level scenarios of symbolic and material gains and losses, allowing us to question Orientalist notions of a uniquely Chinese obsession with "face."

Much statistical work also suffers from a lack of attention to the interpretation of the meaning of statistical results. This is likely due to the limits of correlational data and the challenges of interpretation. Correlational designs cannot yield causal explanations. Even our path model presented in Figure 4.3, although an excellent fit to the data, did not prove a causal relationship. It is always possible that there are other configurations of paths that would fit the data equally well or better. Interpretation can also be challenging even with data resulting from experimental designs. For instance, whereas we can feel confident that nation (American vs. Chinese) was the cause of the differing levels of anxiety displayed in Figure 4.2, the precise mechanism of causation remains unclear. Our interpretation of the results, therefore, must remain tentative. In nascent fields like the political psychology of international relations and Chinese foreign policy studies where so little is yet known, translating even rigorous experimental findings into coherent causal arguments remains a daunting task.

The list of challenges, frankly, is humbling. It is not easy to do this type of research. Mastering psychological and international relations theories, experimental and survey designs, psychometrics, and statistical analysis are just the beginning. Another challenge surrounds data collection. Finding partners in China is the critical first step. It is vital to work with groups of people who trust one another and who share common interests and goals. I prefer the coauthoring and sharing of data to purchasing data, although that is not always possible if one seeks a nationally representative sample. Often more challenging are human subjects review boards at U.S. universities – these are difficult to begin with and frequently have misperceptions about China that hinder project approval. Once approval is secured, the procedural details are numerous but manageable. Hard-copy questionnaires must be stored in secure areas, devoid of any identifying information. Electronic data files must be password-protected on computers to ensure participant confidentiality.

A final challenge for political psychologists is that peer review in political science journals will always be challenging because of an arbitrary preference among most reviewers for the external rather than the internal validity of research designs. This is likely due to the dominance of American politics and Americanists' focus on voting behavior, where external validity is obviously of paramount importance. Furthermore, most political scientists have a myopic view of external validity: all they can understand is random sampling. Replication is a fundamental principle of the scientific method. Indeed, the entire discipline of psychology is built on the cross-validation of research using independent samples. And yet I have experienced reviewers who refuse to accept results replicated across four or more independent samples. They were trained in random sampling and are dismissive of other approaches to external validity. Clearly scholars need to be careful about generalizing from nonrandom samples, but there are times when the advantages of measurement and internal reliability outweigh the costs to generalization (e.g., Nicholson-Crotty and Meier, 2002). Research design should follow from research goals, not dogma.

In my view, such challenges to using experimental methods and psychological measures must be overcome if we are to better understand the determinants of security and insecurity in U.S.-China relations – and avoid another bilateral conflict. China and the United States fought twice in the latter half of the twentieth century, and the United States could easily be dragged into another conflict involving either Taiwan or China-Japan relations at the onset of the twenty-first century. As Figure 4.3 makes clear, psychological concepts like humiliation have a powerful impact on the foreign policy preferences of individual Chinese. Rationalist approaches to IR, such as neorealism and neoliberalism, therefore, must be supplemented by approaches that take into account the intersection of politics and psychology. The stakes are simply too high to cover our eyes and simply hope for the best.

5

Internet Resources and the Study of Chinese Foreign Relations

Can Cyberspace Shed New Light on China's Approach to the World?

Allen Carlson and Hong Duan

For decades, students of Chinese foreign policy were confronted with a stark dearth of information relating to China's position in the international arena. In the 1960s, Allen Whiting's seminal work, *China Crosses the Yalu*, while drawing from the author's extensive governmental experience, referenced only a limited pool of official Chinese sources to describe Beijing's stance on the Korean peninsula. In the 1970s, the main source of information for Samuel Kim's book, *China, the United Nations and World Order*, was Chinese votes in the United Nations General Assembly. A few years later, A. Doak Barnett's short, but influential, *The Making of Foreign Policy in China*, was also marked by the use of a limited number of sources. In contrast, in the late 1980s, a new generation of scholars began to gain access to a somewhat broader set of data. The best examples of this trend were Tom Christensen's consideration of newly available documents relating to the Korean War, followed by Iain Johnston, David Shambaugh, and Robert Ross's utilization of extensive interview data. However, this being the case, the general informational frame for researching Chinese foreign policy has remained relatively static since the early 1990s, with researchers repeatedly making use of the same limited set of sources (a handful of Chinese-language journals dedicated to international politics,[1] official statements, a smattering of 内部 documents, and interviews with a small circle of foreign policy elites). In comparison, it is widely perceived that the study of Chinese foreign policy is now poised to enter a new era. Indications of such an incipient development are purported to be found in the expanding availability of new data. The most prominent of these sources is generally seen to be the Chinese Internet, which appears to contain a treasure trove of new information related to China's

---

The research and writing of this paper was generously supported by Cornell University's LaFeber Fellowship, a fund that supports collaborative research between Government Department faculty and graduate students. Ben Brake, a Cornell graduate student, provided additional research assistance for this chapter.

[1] The most important of these are 国际问题研究,世界经济与政治, 现代国际关系.

foreign relations. The question then becomes how significant is the Internet to the study of Chinese foreign policy?

In taking up this issue, this chapter consciously seeks to reorient focus on the Chinese Internet away from its much discussed potential to contribute to societal transformation in China and issues of censorship and freedom of speech. Instead, the chapter concentrates on the more prosaic, yet, for researchers, more elemental issue of whether this space contains new information that can contribute to our understanding of China's foreign relations.[2] On this score it contends that the returns to date are mixed. On the one hand, as Part One of the chapter will show, the main sites in China dedicated to foreign policy issues contain less new data than many may suppose to be the case. Indeed, many of the official statements and elite analysis that have been posted in Chinese cyberspace are not original content but rather reproductions of work that has been previously published in more conventional formats. On the other hand, as discussed in Part Two of the chapter, a number of incremental advances in the collection and analysis of data related to China's foreign affairs can be made within this new space. Thus, the conclusion contends that Internet materials can be used to supplement conventional resources, but they do not appear to be in a position to supplant the interviews, journal articles, archives, and news sources that have come to form the core of the field of Chinese foreign policy studies over the last two decades.

PART ONE: MAPPING CHINA'S FOREIGN RELATIONS–RELATED CYBERSPACE

This section describes the main contours of Chinese foreign policy cyberspace. It defines this terrain as including those sites that consistently contain a significant amount of content related to China's foreign relations. Such an exercise is valuable simply in terms of providing an initial guide to those with an interest in traveling more extensively within this area.[3] Along these lines, the cartographic presentation that follows is divided into four parts: a consideration of the main media and news sources that cover Chinese foreign policy and international affairs, a survey of the Web pages maintained by China's Ministry of

---

[2] For extensive consideration of the societal impact of the Internet on Chinese politics see Taubman (1998), Hartford (2000), Chase and Mulvenon (2002), Yang (2003), Shie (2004), Zhou (2005a), Tsui (2005), Kluver and Yang (2005), Saunders and Ding (2006), Damm and Thomas (2006), Tai (2006), Zheng (2008), and McKinnon (2008). For a skeptical discussion of the broader argument that cyber activity can have real-world impact, see DiMaggio et al. (2001), Thelwall and Smith (2002), and Langman (2005).

[3] This being said, a limited number of previous efforts have been made to create similar maps; among the best of these in the security field are Fravel (2000) and Zhou (2005b). More broadly, Rebecca McKinnon has led a series of groundbreaking workshops that explore various emerging issues in Chinese cyberspace. The most recent such workshop, "China and the Internet: Myths and Realities," was held in 2008 in Hong Kong. Archives of the workshop are available at http://jmsc.hku.hk/blogs/circ.

Foreign Affairs (MFA) and top research institutes and universities, a review of the most important academic sites which exist primarily in cyberspace (rather than as Internet-based affiliates with real world institutions) and are dedicated solely to foreign policy issues, and a survey of Chinese Bulletin Boards (BBs) and blogs that focus on international politics.

Chinese Cybermedia Outlets and Their Coverage of International Affairs

Over the last decade the most prominent and rapidly expanding aspect of Chinese cyberspace related to foreign policy issues has been the emergence of online media sources. This trend was led by Xinhua and *People's Daily*, each of which established major Chinese news portals. However, alongside such sources, new comprehensive Web portals such as Sina Net, Sohu Net, and Netease have also opened news channels and started providing news online.[4] As a result, and following developments elsewhere in the world, the Internet in China has increasingly become an important source of both domestic and international news. The extent of this development is indicated by a recent survey conducted by the China Internet Network Information Center (CNNIC). This report found that by the end of 2007 the total number of Chinese Internet users had reached 210 million, and that reading news online was the fourth most frequent type of activity among Chinese Internet users (CNNIC, 2008). Indeed, 73.6 percent of Internet users who responded to the survey claimed they read online news; moreover, 20 percent said that the first thing they do on the Internet is to read online news (CNNIC, 2008: 16). In other words, the new cyber media has become a crucial conduit for the dissemination of information related to China's foreign affairs. Four main sites are of specific interest.

1. People's Net (人民网) *http://www.people.com.cn*
People's Net is the most visible of the main media sites and is run by the official newspaper of the Chinese Communist Party, the *People's Daily*. The site is organized into a number of issue specific sectors. For example, it contains channels dedicated to news about the party,[5] the government,[6] the National People's Congress,[7] and the Chinese People's Political Consultative Conference.[8] In addition to the regular news channel, more detailed and categorized news is also available on channels with titles such as *politics*, *world*, *military*, and *Taiwan*. Moreover, full-text versions of the print edition of most of the

---

[4] For Sina Net visit http://www.sina.com.cn/; Sohu Net's site is http://www.sohu.com/; Netease is found at: http://www.163.com/ .
[5] See http://cpc.people.com.cn/GB/index.html.
[6] See http://gov.people.com.cn/GB/index.html
[7] See http://npc.people.com.cn/GB/index.html.
[8] See http://cppcc.people.com.cn/.

newspapers and magazines published by the People's Daily Press, including 人民日报 (domestic and overseas editions), are also accessible via this site and archived back to 2000.[9]

Beyond these general channels, People's Net also contains an impressive array of sites dedicated primarily to issues related to international politics. For example, it maintains a channel that catalogs all the speeches and talks of foreign ministry spokespersons dating back to 1997. In addition, the site also repeatedly invites Chinese foreign policy experts to discuss topical issues and to conduct online dialogue with Internet users. The list of scholars who have participated in such forums is constantly expanding and includes some of the most influential students of foreign policy within China. Among those who have been involved are Wang Jisi, Yan Xuetong, Jin Canrong, Shi Yinhong, and Liu Jiangyong.[10]

2. *Xinhua Net* (新华网) *http://www.xinhuanet.com*

Xinhua Net is run by the government-owned Xinhua News Agency, and, in many respects, it is similar to People's Net. It also contains a wide variety of dedicated news channels. For example, in its "Data Channel" there is information about the structure of the Chinese government, the CCP, nonruling parties, civil associations, China's economic development, legal system, human rights, education, national defense, and diplomacy.[11] The site also offers full texts of the print edition of the newspapers and magazines that belong to the Xinhua News Agency, including *Xinhua Daily Telegraph*. Moreover, like People's Net, Xinhua Net's world channel invites government officials and scholars to talk with Internet users about particularly controversial issues relating to China's foreign relations. The transcripts of these online talks are then posted on the site in a channel entitled "International Interview."[12] Beyond such content, Xinhua Net also places a relatively prominent emphasis on links to other sites. For example, its homepage highlights links to each of the other major Chinese news portals and to thirty-five regional news portals.[13]

3. *China Net* (中国网) *http://www.china.com.cn/*

China Net differs from the other sites discussed in this section in that although it is a news portal, it is directly sponsored by the State Council's Information Office. China Net publishes both world news and, perhaps of greater interest, news about Chinese foreign policy. Along these lines, a main source of

---

[9] Until recently, the *Global Times*, a popular weekly newspaper with a focus on international issues and published by the People's Daily Press, was available as well. However, this publication launched its own Web site in September 2007 and has become a separate news portal (http://www.huanqiu.com/). As such, it is no longer accessible via People's Net.
[10] For a list of the topics and transcripts, see http://world.people.com.cn/GB/8212/115071/index.html.
[11] See http://news.xinhuanet.com/ziliao/2004-11/04/content_2177717.htm.
[12] See http://www.xinhuanet.com/world/gjft.htm.
[13] See http://www.xinhuanet.com/dfwl.htm.

content on this site is reports about Chinese diplomacy, exchanges with other countries, foreign trade, and cross-Strait relations. As abundant as such coverage is, it is necessary to note that the site's Chinese-language version contains significantly more information than its English-language mirror site. For example, its 国情, or "National Conditions," channel contains an encyclopedic directory of other Chinese-language sites and archives related to both national defense and diplomacy but lacks an English-language companion of comparable scope.[14] The same holds true for sections of the site that provide "statistical reports" (统计公报),[15] annual reports on global politics, and reports on national security.[16]

4. *China Military Online* (中国军网) *http://www.chinamil.com.cn/*
China Military Online is run by 解放军报 and acts as a conduit for the cyber publication of the People's Liberation Army's (PLA's) own position on both general issues in world politics and specific military concerns. The site has both an English- and Chinese-language homepage (as do most other Chinese news sites). As in the case of China Net, on Chinese Military Online there is a noticeable difference in the content of these two pages. The English site is clearly organized into a number of distinct channels, including the following topics: national defense, army building, political works, logistics, military diplomacy, armaments, information technology, science and technology, military training, disaster relief, frontier and coastal defense, and the history of the PLA. The Chinese site is basically organized in the same fashion but contains significantly more information. For example, it offers full texts of the print edition of 解放军报 and the other newspapers and magazines affiliated with the PLA. This list is expansive and includes publications that range from the authoritative, such as *PLA Daily* and *China's National Defense*, to both popular and technical publications like *China's Militias*, *PLA Pictorial*, *Military Correspondents*, and *Global Military Affairs*. In most cases, back issues of these papers have been archived online dating to 2004. In addition to being a valuable warehouse for the Chinese military press, the site also contains an extensive survey of the structure and organization of the Chinese military. Along these lines, it includes a detailed database introducing China's current military leadership, its military regulations, armaments, and other information.[17]

Web sites of the Ministry of Foreign Affairs, Universities, and Research Institutes

Over the last decade China's Ministry of Foreign Affairs (MFA) and each of the main foreign policy research institutes and universities with major

---

[14] See http://www.china.com.cn/aboutchina/node_6175014.htm.
[15] See http://www.china.com.cn/economic/zhuanti/06gongbao/node_7014958.htm.
[16] See http://www.china.com.cn/zhuanti2005/node_6087279.htm.
[17] See http://www.chinamil.com.cn/site1/database/index.htm.

international studies programs have launched their own Web sites. Although these sites were initially quite skeletal and still vary quite significantly in terms of content, they have expanded in recent years and have become a durable facet of China's foreign policy-related Internet. Five of these sites, along with a cluster of university Web pages, merit specific mention.

1. **Ministry of Foreign Affairs** (中华人民共和国外交部)
http://www.mfa.gov.cn/
The Chinese-language version of this site contains rich information regarding China's diplomacy.[18] The "diplomatic developments" channel consists of a comprehensive and current news archive on high-level diplomatic activities and MFA press briefings.[19] The "resources" channel is composed of foreign policy speeches by Chinese leaders and high-ranking officials, Chinese foreign policy communiqués, and a list of treaties.[20] In addition, the site also posts detailed information about the MFA itself. The "ministry" channel lists each ministerial-level official's name, biography, and the issue areas within his or her portfolio.[21] This channel also offers information about the foreign ministry's organization. Not only are all the general departments under the ministry listed, but each department's contact information and the names of its directors are also provided. It is also of note that the site is well connected. It lists links to Chinese missions overseas, other central government organizations, local governments and local foreign affairs offices, and major Chinese Web news portals.

2. **Foreign Policy and International Affairs Research Institutes of the Chinese Academy of Social Sciences**
As China's "highest academic research organization in the fields of philosophy and social sciences," the Chinese Academy of Social Sciences (CASS) is a vast organization that employs almost 3,000 researchers and encompasses 31 research institutes and over 50 research centers (CASS, 2009). Although the majority of academic activity and policy analysis that takes place at CASS falls outside the scope of this chapter's focus, a number of China's most prominent foreign policy and international relations research institutes are located here. Whereas in the 1990s learning about these centers and gaining access to

---

[18] The MFA site also has versions in English, Russian, French, Arabic, and Spanish. The English version (http://www.fmprc.gov.cn/eng/) is somewhat different from the Chinese version. To begin with, the Chinese version tends to be more current. Moreover, the "countries" channel is organized somewhat differently on the two mirror sites. Whereas the Chinese version of this channel (http://www.mfa.gov.cn/chn/pds/gjhdq/gj/) offers mainly political and economic profiles of individual countries and regions, the English version (http://www.fmprc.gov.cn/eng/gjhdq/) focuses on their bilateral relations and bilateral exchanges with China, which is probably more useful for students of China's foreign policy.

[19] See http://www.mfa.gov.cn/chn/pds/wjdt/.

[20] See http://www.mfa.gov.cn/chn/pds/ziliao/.

[21] See http://www.mfa.gov.cn/chn/pds/wjb/.

researchers working in them required repeated phone calls, letter writing, and personal visits, today all of the main CASS institutes maintain Web sites that contain detailed data on the organizational structure as well as the contact addresses of their hosts. However, beyond such information, these sites are generally quite sparse. For example, one of the most significant of the CASS sites is maintained by the Institute of World Economics and Politics (IWEP) which introduces the institute's history, its organization, and its leading researchers (including resumes, e-mail addresses, and a list of major publications).[22] Yet, beyond these data, the few articles and papers posted on the page have been previously published. The Institute of American Studies page is organized in a similar fashion and contains only a handful of articles published by the institute's researchers.[23] However, the contact information on the site is not as comprehensive as that which appears on the IWEP Web page. The Institute of Asia-Pacific Studies site has a complete list of information regarding its researchers, but beyond such data, this site is also quite skeletal.[24] Of even less substance is the site maintained by the Center for China's Borderland History and Geography Research, which fails to provide detailed information on the researchers employed there or to post research publications.[25]

3. *China Institute of International Studies (http://www.ciis.org.cn/)*
Although the China Institute of International Studies (CIIS) is the main research institute of the MFA, the site which it maintains contains relatively little substantive information. Indeed, the CIIS Web page does little more than provide a scant outline of the organization, brief biographies of its main researchers, and links to the table of contents of each issue of 国际问题研究 (CIIS's flagship journal).

4. *China Institute of Contemporary International Relations (http://www.cicir.ac.cn/)*
Like the CIIS site, the China Institute of Contemporary International Relations (CICIR) Web page is not especially informative. It does little more than offer brief introductions to each of its research divisions and provide the table of contents and abstracts of articles published in 现代国际关系 and 国际资料信息.

5. *Shanghai Institutes of International Studies (http://www.siis.org.cn/)*
This site is more informative than the CICIR site. It offers introductions to the Shanghai Institutes of International Studies (SIIS) itself and to each of its research divisions. It also provides biographical information on each of the institutes' researchers. Moreover, it contains introductions to research

---

[22] http://www.iwep.org.cn/.
[23] http://ias.cass.cn/.
[24] See http://iaps.cass.cn/.
[25] See http://chinaborderland.cass.cn/.

6. University Sites

The handful of Chinese universities with significant international relations programs now all maintain their own Web sites. However, such sites are, generally, of minimal substance. For example, the main pages of Peking University's School of International Studies,[26] Renmin University's School of International Studies,[27] Fudan University's School of International Relations and Public Affairs,[28] Tsinghua University's Institute of International Studies,[29] and China Foreign Affairs University[30] all consist of little more than lists of each program's main organizational attributes and faculty members.

International Relations Professional Web Portals and Scholarly Discourse

The number of reports and traffic on sites produced directly by the Chinese media and on official sites of the main foreign policy institutes is staggering. Yet, it is also the very volume and scope of the sites discussed above that makes navigating them so daunting. In addition, as the main media sites cover such a wide variety of issues, their discussion of foreign policy tends not to be particularly well focused and is largely episodic (driven by the latest news cycles and government directives). Moreover, with only limited exceptions, these outlets rarely expand their coverage of either China or the world beyond the limits set in official government statements. In contrast, in recent years a handful of more specialized academic sites dedicated solely to foreign affairs and international politics have come online in China. Although these sites are less traveled, they possess a singular focus and have shown the potential to stretch (if not directly challenge) the discursive limits for the discussion of foreign policy set by China's leaders. As such, it is these nascent sites that appear to be of even greater value to students of China's foreign relations.

Before delving into specifics, it is important to emphasize that these portals share a number of common characteristics. To begin with, each is designed to cater to those with a pronounced interest in the study of international relations in general and Chinese foreign policy more specifically. They are clearly not intended for a broad readership, and, in light of the fact that all of the sites also have much more content in Chinese than in English, they seem to be created mainly for consumption within China. Beyond such broad issues, these sites share a number of additional similarities. First, they are all organized in a

---

[26] http://www.sis.pku.edu.cn/.
[27] http://sis.ruc.edu.cn/.
[28] http://www.sirpa.fudan.edu.cn/.
[29] http://166.111.106.5/xi-suo/institute/index.htm.
[30] http://www.fac.edu.cn/.

similar fashion. Content is divided into substantive issue areas, including topics such as international relations theory and more policy-oriented discussions involving national security concerns, Chinese diplomacy, and more detailed studies of China's main bilateral relations (particularly with the United States and Japan). Second, all of the sites have tended to highlight Western international relations scholars (including Morgenthau and Waltz, among others). Indeed, it is worth noting that works by established contemporary Western scholars are not only available but are also reviewed, and even downloadable on these sites. Third, these portals tend to contain extensive reviews of the leading scholars and research institutes working within China. Finally, the sites are all quite interlinked to each other (while also providing linkages to sites outside of China as well). Although the list of such portals is likely to expand over the next several years, at present two sites are of particular importance.[31]

1. IR China (中国国关在线) *http://www.irchina.org*
IR China was founded by the Institute of International Studies at Nankai University located in Tianjin. Zhang Ruizhuang, a senior scholar at Nankai, is widely perceived as having been a prime force behind the development of the site, but it is governed by an academic board composed of established scholars from dozens of prominent foreign policy–related think-tanks, academic departments, and institutions within China. Among those in this organization from Beijing are Jia Qingguo, Qin Yaqing, Men Honghua, and Li Shaojun. Shanghai participants include Yang Jiemian, Zhu Mingquan, and Su Changhe. Indeed, this group encompasses virtually all of the best-known scholars working on international relations in China and can generally be seen as a shorthand list of who is inside the inner circle of China's foreign policy elite. In this sense, IR China is clearly the best established and influential of the Chinese IR Web portals.

Such influence is underscored by the scope of content featured on the site. The creators of the site have collected approximately one hundred Chinese scholars' works in various forms – journal articles, commentary pieces published in newspapers, interviews, conference papers, book chapters, and others. Such an array of sources has not been matched on any other Chinese site and as such further sets IR China apart from other portals. Nonetheless, the value of these postings may not be as great as they would first appear. Indeed, upon close inspection the majority of publications that are placed on the site are simply duplications of articles that were previously posted elsewhere. For example, of the first five articles posted on the English version of the site's "International Observation and Hot Issues" page in the spring of 2009, all

---

[31] When this chapter was first written, a third site, Chinese IR Study Network (中国国际关系研究网) http://www.sinoir.com/, appeared to be poised to develop alongside these two sites. However, underscoring the transitory nature of the Chinese Internet, the link to this site is now inactive.

were reproductions of articles that had appeared in print.[32] The first five articles in the lead subject category on the site's Chinese-language page, "学科建设," at this time were also all reprints.[33] In other words, not much of the content on this site is new. Instead, it mirrors quite closely the discussions that have been featured in recent years in the main academic journals published in China dedicated to foreign policy and international relations. In this sense, the site appears to be less innovative and pathbreaking than initial consideration might lead one to believe it to be.

Nonetheless, IR China also features two characteristics that are of interest to students of China's foreign relations. First, it is self-consciously concerned with the development of the field of international relations in China. The channel mentioned above, "学科建设", or "constructing the discipline,"[34] contains more than 100 scholarly articles on the study of international politics. Second, it is widely connected to other sites related to the study of international relations in China. It offers links to dozens of universities and research institutes.[35] Beyond these academic links, the site also provides linkages to major Chinese foreign affairs and international politics journals and magazines.[36]

2. *TECN Academic Net* (天益学术网)
http://www.tecn.cn/academic/index.php.[37]
In contrast to IR China, TECN Academic Net is administered not by a formal academic institution but by a group of individuals. The site covers a variety of fields within the social sciences and humanities, and its international relations channel is especially impressive. The organizers of the site have established a network of top Chinese scholars and worked to then post specific examples of their works online. As with IR China, much of what is published simply copies articles that have previously appeared in various print sources. However, the overlap on this site is not as pervasive as is common on other Web sites. Indeed, quite a few of the works posted on TECN are originals. Of even greater interest to students of Chinese foreign policy, TECN's cyber papers have frequently pushed the envelope established by official sources for the discussion of sensitive issues in international politics. Among the most prominent examples of this trend are the following papers: Zhang Wenmu's article on the American "Tibetan Plan" and its failure,[38] Wu Xinbo's article on the U.S. and East Asian integration,[39] Wang Jisi's article on the historical lessons of the

[32] See http://www.irchina.org/en/news/hot.asp?cataid=25.
[33] See http://www.irchina.org/news/xueshu.asp?cataid=22.
[34] See http://www.irchina.org/news/xueshu.asp?cataid=22.
[35] See http://www.irchina.org/xueke/inchina/jigou.asp.
[36] See http://www.irchina.org/xueke/inchina/kanwu.asp and http://www.irchina.org/guancha/link.asp.
[37] Since late July 2009, this site has been inactive, leading to speculation that the site has been closed. This is unfortunate for it contained relatively more original/unpublished works by scholars than other available sites.
[38] See http://www.tecn.cn/data/detail.php?id=18165. See footnote 37, above.
[39] See http://www.tecn.cn/data/detail.php?id=18243. See footnote 37 above.

Soviet-U.S. hegemonic competition and the road to China's rise,[40] Xu Yan's talk on China's military buildup and national security,[41] Song Wei's article on Diaoyu Island and China's policy toward Japan,[42] and Liu Junning's article on nationalism.[43]

IR-Focused Bulletin Boards and Blogs

Whereas media portals and academic Web sites largely represent an extension of the sources of which students of Chinese foreign policy have been making use since the 1980s, in recent years cyberspace has also emerged as a forum for the expression of broader public opinion about foreign policy and international affairs. Indeed, although views from the general population about foreign policy were almost entirely opaque through the end of the 1990s, nonspecialists in China are now using the Web to discuss China's place in the world. The most pronounced facet of this development has been the emergence of bulletin boards and blogs that focus on international relations.

1. Bulletin Boards

Most Chinese Web portals provide bulletin boards. To post on BBs, Internet users have to register; however, many BBs allow unregistered Internet users to read postings. Moreover, it is now quite apparent that a large number of Chinese netizens frequently post on such sites. For example, according to a survey report released in January 2008, 35.4 percent of respondents reported that they had posted information or replied to postings on online forums and/or bulletin boards (CNNIC, 2008:54). Many of the sites discussed above maintain BB pages. Three BB pages are of particular note.[44]

The most prominent BB is maintained by People's Net and named, 强国, or Strong Nation forum. The 强国 forum had its beginnings in May 1999 when the then online edition of 人民日报 launched its first bulletin board – "the protest forum" – to facilitate Chinese Internet users' publication of their opinions on, and protests against, the bombing of the Chinese embassy in Belgrade during the course of the Kosovo war.[45] This temporary site was then replaced by 强国论坛, a forum that rapidly developed into a lasting virtual community. It now contains dozens of categorized lists and has more than 680,000 registered users.[46] Most recently, 强国论坛's already prominent profile in Chinese

---

[40] See http://www.tecn.cn/data/detail.php?id=5947. See footnote 37 above.
[41] See http://www.tecn.cn/data/detail.php?id=2216. See footnote 37 above.
[42] See http://www.tecn.cn/data/detail.php?id=364. See footnote 37 above.
[43] See http://www.tecn.cn/data/detail.php?id=6810. See footnote 37 above.
[44] Note that Chinese Military Online also maintains an expanding BB. See http://bbs.chinamil.com.cn/site1/gwgfsq.
[45] For a more detailed report, see http://www2.qglt.com.cn/fuwu/dt/hm99/hm9905.html.
[46] See http://bbs1.people.com.cn/. A widely held belief is that a large number of unregistered Internet users read postings in this community, particularly during periods when interest in world affairs is most pronounced within China.

cyberspace was boosted when Chinese president Hu Jintao visited People's Net and conducted an online dialogue with Internet users via this forum.[47]

The second set of BBs of special significance is maintained by China Net, which hosts a number of discussion forums dedicated to foreign policy issues. The most significant of these is the 和平论坛 (Peace Forum) that contains forty subdiscussions, five of which focus on international affairs, Taiwan, and military/security concerns. In 2008, the forum had more than 120,000 registered members.[48]

The final BB of note is maintained by the MFA. The forum, entitled 中国外交论坛, is only maintained in Chinese. Like the other BBs, those wishing to post on this page must register, but guests can monitor the forum without taking this step. The forum, although appearing to be more closely monitored by the authorities than either 强国论坛 or 和平论坛, is particularly interesting because it has often been mentioned among the new technologies that China's leaders have begun to develop to gauge public opinion within China on foreign policy–related issues. In addition, MFA officials regularly log onto the forum to answer questions from forum participants.

Although knowledge of these BBs is useful, it is essential for any student of Chinese foreign relations to also consider the overall popularity of such forums within the broader space of the Chinese Internet. However, gauging interest in these sites is not a particularly straightforward process. To do so it is necessary to first locate the most visited Chinese Web sites, which, according to a 2007 survey conducted by CASS's Research Center of Social Development, include Sina Net and Baidu.com, and the top Web search engines in China were Sohu Net and Netease (CASS, 2007: 39). In addition, according to China Web sites Ranking, a specialized Web Sites–ranking site sponsored by the Internet Society of China, the top five most visited comprehensive Web sites include Baidu.com, Tencent (the official Web site of QQ, the most popular instant messaging software in China), Sina Net, Sohu Net, and Netease.[49] Using this information as a guide, the authors of this chapter examined recent postings on 中国外交论坛 [50] and 和平论坛 [51] and compared them with the number of postings on popular BBs on the portals mentioned above. This survey found that these two forums have not attracted all that much Internet traffic. In other words, in terms of visits and postings, both of these forums lag far behind mainstream BBs. This finding suggests the limited influence and appeal of such BBs in China, and should stand as a cautionary observation for any scholars who attempt to draw broad generalizations about Chinese public opinion via use of the messages that are posted on them.

---

[47] For the transcript, see http://www.people.com.cn/GB/32306/33093/125024/index.html.
[48] See http://forum.china.com.cn/ciicbbs.
[49] For this ranking, see http://www.chinarank.org.cn/top500/Rank.do?r=1213942617523.
[50] See http://forum.china.com.cn/ciicbbs/thread.php?fid=71.
[51] See http://bbs.fmprc.gov.cn/board.jsp?bid=6.

2. Blogs

Since the concept of blogging was introduced into China in 2002, the number of blogs in Chinese cyberspace has expanded at a rapid clip. Indeed, according to a recent CNNIC survey, by the end of November 2007, the number of bloggers in China was about to reach 47 million, among whom almost 17 million were considered to be active bloggers (CNNIC, 2007: 9–10).[52] With the rapid growth of blogs, it may not be a stretch to say that an alternative, individualized, less-censored, and freer outlet of views and opinions has emerged in Chinese cyberspace. However, the existing evidence seems to imply that this form of online expression has not yet extended much in the direction of China's foreign relations and national security. To begin with, compared with other topics, "international affairs" and "foreign relations" are far from a popular focus of discussion for most bloggers or blog readers. In fact, according to the CNNIC survey, the majority of blog postings in Chinese cyberspace are bloggers' records of their own experiences and life stories (CNNIC, 2007: 18). This is not to say that there are no Chinese netizens who blog on international politics, but rather that BB forums have been a more popular format for the discussion of these topics.[53]

PART TWO: MAKING USE OF CHINESE FOREIGN AFFAIRS–RELATED CYBERSPACE

The previous section of this chapter treats the Chinese foreign affairs–related Internet as a relatively static entity. Admittedly, this is a somewhat artificial approach as it portrays a dynamic terrain as if it were unchanging and thus it precludes any consideration of the ebbs and flows that are constantly at play. However, as so little is known within the China-watching community about this facet of the Chinese Internet, mapping out this territory represents a necessary first step in beginning to explore its potential value for the study of Chinese foreign policy. As noted above, such a space, especially when viewed as an inert form, does not contain as much new or groundbreaking data as one might expect. Thus, compared particularly to the access scholars and analysts gained starting in the late 1980s to Chinese foreign policy elites, Internet sources do not appear to offer a significant new pathway for conducting research in the area of Chinese foreign relations. However, scholars are also ill advised to simply ignore these resources, as they do contain useful

---

[52] Also note the growing number of English-language sites that track blogging activity in China; in particular, see http://www.virtual-china.org/, eastwestsouthnorth at http://www.zonaeuropa.com/archive.htm, and the University of Heidelberg's Digital Archive for Chinese Studies, http://www.sino.uni-heidelberg.de/dachs/.

[53] Moreover, compared to experts and scholars in other disciplines, IR scholars and experts have been slow to take advantage of this new channel for publishing their work. Few established IR scholars write blogs. Although a handful of scholars have blogged, including Pang Zhongying (http://blog.sina.com.cn/m/pangzhongying), most of these blogs have not been active in recent years or have stopped altogether.

data. In general, the significance of these virtual sources is located in the ease with which they may be accessed (in comparison to print resources or elite interviews) and in the fact that they constitute a database on China's foreign relations that is in motion (rather than stationary). That being said, the fluidity of this terrain, and the breadth of the materials posted within its limits, can be challenging. In light of such promise and perils, there are then at present three primary approaches that researchers may consider to maximize the research potential of China's foreign affairs–related cyberspace.

Treating Web Pages as Windows into the MFA, Think-Tanks, and Research Institutes

Even though the Internet sites maintained by the major foreign policy institutions in China do not contain an abundance of new data on Chinese foreign policy, they still constitute a useful source for the initial stages of conducting research on China's foreign relations. The main utility of such sites is that they contain readily accessible outlines of the organizational structure of both the formal institutions and informal ties that form the core of China's growing community of foreign policy elites. On the first of these fronts, that of organizational structure, transparency has been incrementally increasing ever since the late 1970s. However, as recently as the mid-1990s, it was possible to track institutional development only through painstaking library-based research, interview data, and reliance on a handful of authoritative secondary sources. In contrast, by monitoring the Web pages these organizations host, it is now a relatively straightforward exercise to locate the individual departments within these institutions, the formal responsibilities with which they are charged, their personnel, and even their publication records. For example, when studying the MFA's Web page in the spring of 2009, it was a simple endeavor to note that the organization had established a new department, the Department of Boundary and Ocean Affairs, and to learn that the director of the department was Ning Fukui.[54] Looking beyond the MFA, the structure of each of the main foreign policy–related institutes may also be traced quite easily online. For example, as noted, the State Council's CICIR Web site lists each of the organization's departments and department chairs.[55] The same holds true for the sites maintained by the MFA's Chinese Institute of International Studies and the various CASS research institutes.

It is also possible to track movement by individual scholars between various universities and research institutes via the Web. Thus, by accessing Peking University's Web site, it can be confirmed that Zhang Qingmin, a prominent foreign policy analyst and Sino-U.S. watcher who had been affiliated with China Foreign Affairs University for much of his career, had become a

---

[54] See http://www.fmprc.gov.cn/eng/wjb/zzjg/bianhaisi_eng/.
[55] See http://www.cicir.ac.cn/tbscms/html/jgsz_En.asp?rid=jigou_en.

member of the faculty at Peking University (Beida).⁵⁶ Of even greater utility, Zhang's Web page at Beida contains contact information that ten years ago would have been available to a researcher only after extensive phone calls and the use of preexisting social networks. Moreover, Zhang is by no means unusual in this regard. Indeed, over half of the professors listed on Beida's site provide contact information on their personal Web pages. Virtually all of the scholars with pages on Tsinghua's Institute of International Studies Web site include their contact information.⁵⁷ Although the Web pages maintained by the plethora of think-tanks in Beijing and Shanghai are not quite as proficient in providing similar information on individual researchers, each of these sites does maintain institutional e-mail addresses and phone numbers. In short, although some of the data posted on these sites appear to be dated, and even when current there is no assurance that meetings or interviews will be forthcoming, at the very least it does greatly ease the process of making initial contact with scholars working in China. This development represents a significant change in the manner in which elite interviews, long a staple in the field of Chinese foreign policy studies, can be arranged.

Using New Technologies to Track Changes in Internet-Based Collections of Print Sources

The use of elite interviews and Chinese-language sources made an obvious contribution to the study of Chinese foreign policy in the 1990s. However, as the vast majority of this work was heavily qualitative in nature and often lacked any direct consideration of issues of data collection or methodological concerns, it was also rather open to challenges regarding the representativeness of the views that were culled from such sources. Iain Johnston helped lead the field past such perceived limitations. More specifically, Johnston (1996) developed a social scientific frame for the qualitative analysis of elite Chinese views on foreign policy and national security issues in his work on China's historic realpolitik strategic culture and its imprint on the more recent past (particularly Mao's approach to military conflict). Although much of this work focuses on the issues of cognitive mapping and symbolic analysis, in other publications Johnston repeatedly returns to the technique of conducting content analysis (searching out specific terms and key phrases) within large open-source datasets. Over the last ten years, a growing number of scholars followed Johnston's move and made use of content analysis in attempts to discover new trends and tendencies within Chinese foreign policy statements and analysis. However, such endeavors were exceedingly time-consuming and difficult to replicate due to a pair of limitations. First, as few of the sources that were of interest to researchers were available in electronic form, print data

---

[56] See http://www.sis.pku.edu.cn/web/Teacher_Browse.aspx?ID=101. For a full list of those working at Beida see http://www.sis.pku.edu.cn/web/Teacher.aspx.
[57] See http://rwxy.tsinghua.edu.cn/xi-suo/institute/english/faculty/faculty.htm.

had to be coded by hand (a process that introduced the likelihood of human error). Second, when data first became available via CDs and other electronic formats, search engines for exploring them were rather rudimentary. As a result, until recently the broader use of content analysis techniques has been limited. However, over the last several years, the rapid expansion of online collections of both Chinese- and English-language sources, and the emergence of new technologies for tracking the data contained within them, have gone a long way toward overcoming such difficulties. Indeed, these dual developments have now made content analysis, a task that was once particularly onerous, a relatively straightforward task.

Daniela Stockmann's chapter in this volume explores the use of many of these new technologies with reference to the process of conducting content analysis of Chinese media sources. In light of the comprehensive nature of Stockmann's survey, this chapter will not dwell at length on these issues. However, two particular programs are of note. First, the Yoshikoder program, which allows users to conduct relatively quick and sophisticated counts of the frequency with which specific terms appear in texts, may be utilized to examine electronic collections of official Chinese foreign policy statements.[58] Second, the China National Knowledge Infrastructure (CNKI) database maintained by EastView in the United States, a foundational resource in Stockmann's own work, is of special use. To begin with, CNKI, via its "Core Chinese Newspapers Database," contains a readily accessible, and searchable, collection of official statements relating to Chinese foreign policy. More important, CNKI's China Academic Journals Full-Text Database, especially its subcollection "Politics/Military Affairs/Law," contains a comprehensive archive of elite analysis of Chinese foreign policy and international affairs. Indeed, whereas gathering articles from the major Chinese foreign policy journals, let alone publications from provincial universities, was once a difficult and time-consuming chore, now all of these materials are available online for any subscriber to CNKI. Moreover, as CNKI's search function is easy to navigate, the site readily lends itself to rudimentary content analysis of such publications. For example, the rapid emergence and subsequent decline of the peaceful rise (和平崛起) debate in China can easily be traced through a search of article titles appearing in CNKI's "Politics/Military Affairs/Law" subsection. In 2002, no articles with 和平崛起 in their titles were in the database; in 2003, there were 8 (included Xia Liping's influential contribution on this subject in 国际问题研究), whereas the following year there were 201 articles, and in 2005 there were 307 – but by 2008 only 72.

Employing New Technologies to Track Changes in Cyber Terrain

The techniques discussed in this section so far may generally be seen as extensions of conventional research strategies. Each promises to ease the collection

---

[58] This technology can be downloaded at http://www.yoshikoder.org/.

of data related to Chinese foreign policy, but neither breaks new ground in terms of recognizing and managing the notoriously turbulent realm of cyberspace. Indeed, until recently the shifting and transitory nature of this space has largely defied categorization and measurement across the social sciences (not only in the China field) as the technology to map this terrain was so underdeveloped. However, during the last several years a growing number of rudimentary research tools have been invented that are designed to more systematically track Internet data. Through exploring the utility of these tools, scholars can begin to develop more accurate understandings of the flows of information and networks that have formed in China around foreign policy issues. Two specific new technologies appear to be particularly promising.

The first of these tools is the program Touch Graph, which uses a Java application to track the way Internet sites are linked.[59] The free downloadable version of the program provides users with a relatively easy to use device for observing how popular sites are by presenting links in an active graph matrix. It is also possible to make use of an online version of the program with reference to Google's online search engine. For example, via utilization of the Google application of Touch Graph the connectivity of the Chinese MFA was examined for this chapter. This was accomplished by pasting the MFA site's URL[60] into Touch Graph's search function, and the program produced a graph that succinctly captured the centrality of this site in Web discussions of Chinese foreign policy. The graph showed the MFA's Web page to be quite closely linked with the Chinese media, state, and the main Web page of the PRC. Beyond governmental sites, a similar test was run on China's premier academic Web site dedicated to foreign policy issues, IR China. Once more Touch Graph's technology underscored the connectivity of IR China, particularly with reference to organizations within China, such as the Ministry of Education's University of International Relations[61] and IWEP, and also with worldwide foreign policy research initiatives.[62]

The second tool is Technorati, which is used to collect online aggregate data by tracking over 100 million blogs and the linkages between them.[63] This program was originally designed to search English-language blogs and its scope and ease of use make it a powerful tool. Thus, it is possible to utilize Technorati technology to search the number of times a topic is discussed or a

---

[59] This program is available at http://www.touchgraph.com. Ben Brake made a significant contribution to the research and writing of this paragraph.
[60] See http://www.fmprc.gov.cn/eng/.
[61] See http://www.uir.cn.
[62] Other programs which perform comparable functions include (but are not limited to) SocSciBot, which is described at length by the leading information scientist Mike Thewall in his handbook on online network analysis, available at http://linkanalysis.wlv.ac.uk/; UCINET's social network analysis/cultural domain analysis software: http://www.analytictech.com/; and VOSON's peer-produced tools for social science research of online networks, available at http://voson.anu.edu.au/.
[63] Available at http://technorati.com/chart/.

word is used during a given time period, and garner a better sense of which issues are attracting the most attention in cyberspace at any given point in time. For example, using the program's online site, a search was conducted of the frequency with which all English-language blogs mentioned the phrase "North Korea" during a 180-day period in the spring of 2009. The resulting graph traced a surge of blog activity related to this term during a time period that neatly maps with the escalation of tensions on the Korean peninsula.

The significance of such capabilities for students of China's foreign relations is even greater now that the program also allows for the searching of Chinese language–based blogs. As an early test case of such utility, during a thirty-day period in the fall of 2007 the Technorati program was used to track the frequency with which the Chinese blogosphere contained postings containing the Chinese characters (布什) in President Bush's name. During this period, over 6,000 blogs made use of this combination of characters. In contrast, in a subsequent search for the same term during a 180-day period in the winter of 2008–2009, Technorati generated data that revealed that Bush's name had, not surprisingly, disappeared from the Chinese blogosphere. Of perhaps greater interest, a parallel search of the Chinese term 朝鲜 (North Korea) was also conducted during a period that mirrored that used for the English-language search discussed above, and produced a similar pattern of activity.

In sum, Touch Graph and Technorati should do much for those wishing to make use of Chinese cyber data in their studies of China's foreign policy. Nonetheless, as useful as such programs appear to be, there remains a particularly steep challenge facing any scholar who seeks to employ Internet postings as an indication of Chinese popular sentiment regarding foreign affairs. Directly stated, broad questions loom about the overall representativeness of views posted online as such a forum is available only to those who have Internet access and who also engage in Web discussions. Although the sheer number of Internet users in China has been increasing rapidly, this segment of the population remains largely urban and educated, and the larger rural population and less-well-educated population might have been left out.

CONCLUSION

The significance of the issues considered in this chapter is particularly acute since over the last several years a new round of debate about China's place on the world stage has begun to unfold. Although such a discussion is far from new, this is the first time it has taken place during a period when Chinese Internet-based sources are readily available. Thus, a more pointed reprise to the query posed in the Introduction involves asking whether reliance upon such sources has afforded researchers with greater insight into the nature of China's current rise.

In this vein, it is first readily apparent that the use of Internet resources in analyzing Chinese foreign affairs at least has made for fuller, richer descriptions of Beijing's policy decisions and the motives underlying them. However, not surprisingly, it has done little in regard to creating a consensus about China's rise. For example, on the one hand, China security expert M. Taylor Fravel recently surveyed Chinese military Web sites to construct an argument about the posturing of PLA forces in China's frontier regions. Fravel uses these sources to support the claim that there is a decidedly defensive rationale informing the deployment of Chinese troops within China (Fravel, 2007: 701–737). On the other hand, Paul Mooney, an established journalist, surveyed other facets of Chinese cyberspace in 2005 and concluded that the Internet was "fanning the flames of nationalism" (Mooney, 2005).

Such contrasting observations point to the remarkable diversity of Internet resources related to Chinese foreign relations. They are also illustrative of the fact that these new data have done little to bring analysts together in regard to the portrait that is now painted of China's rise. This being the case, it is too much to ask of any type of source, particularly one as fluid as Chinese foreign policy cyberspace, that its value be gauged primarily by the degree to which it can create consensus among those who make use of it. However, at the same time, it is not unfair to critically examine the ways in which scholars have utilized such new resources. Unfortunately, on this score the majority of the existing work in the foreign policy field was designed with little reference to methodological concerns or consideration of basic issues regarding the collection and use of empirical data. In other words, although there is much promise in mining cyberspace for the study of Chinese foreign relations, so far scholars have failed to fully realize its potential. This chapter, then, is designed to provide researchers with the main coordinates of this terrain and with suggestions on how to develop more effective research approaches to it.

In closing, as China's foreign relations–related Internet continues to expand in the coming years, the researcher's ability to make use of it will likely continue to be hobbled by numerous difficulties. Chief among these, the appearance of data in cyberspace tends to be fleeting, and the volume of content published there is massive. In addition, questions over the reliability and representativeness of the information that appears on the Chinese Internet (especially with reference to issues of access, firewalls, and censorship) will continue to pose vexing problems for researchers. Moreover, especially in the realm of BBs and blogs that make use of rather stylized, colloquial versions of standard Chinese, language issues will remain a challenge for non-native speakers. Finally, as few students of Chinese foreign policy are trained to make use of advanced computer programs and software, technological challenges will persist. Nonetheless, most of these obstacles may be overcome through close monitoring of this terrain, coupled with a utilization of the strategies discussed in this chapter. As such, the Chinese Internet is poised to emerge as an increasingly useful tool in the study of China's foreign relations.

6

Information Overload?

Collecting, Managing, and Analyzing Chinese Media Content

Daniela Stockmann

Only two decades ago the main information source for China scholars abroad was the Foreign Broadcast Information Service (FBIS), an open intelligence source of the CIA. FBIS collected, translated, and disseminated available news and information from Chinese media sources. During the Cultural Revolution most foreign researchers were not allowed to conduct fieldwork in China; the five-times-weekly FBIS report thus constituted one of the main sources for information about events in the mainland. Since original media sources only became available during the reform era, those interested in Chinese media reporting usually relied on the information selected and translated by FBIS. Aimed at the U.S. intelligence community, FBIS did not draw an unbiased and representative sample of the Chinese news, but, at the time, it constituted one of the best information sources available to the research community abroad.

Today, the situation could not be more different. Since China's opening up to the outside world, we have the opportunity to spend extensive time in the country reading, listening, and watching the same news as Chinese citizens. Even when we are not in China, we can access a large number of Chinese media sources electronically using the Internet, cable, or satellite dishes. In addition to increased access, we also have the opportunity to store this information. We can mail abroad newspapers, magazines, and DVDs from China, scan documents, download files, and record television and radio programs. Most of this information is stored electronically. Once preserved, the data gathered in countless hours sit on our hard drives, waiting for analysis. Instead of reading the FBIS report, we simply access a folder on a computer and immediately have data available for research. What a wonderful world for doing research on China – or so it would seem.

For insightful comments and suggestions I would like to thank Allen Carlson, Iain Johnston, Will Lowe, Zhang Jie, Jonathan Hassid, Jessica Weiss, and Jamie Reilly. For sharing data I am grateful to Ku Lun-wei from National Taiwan University and Deborah Cai from the University of Maryland. Many thanks as well to Wang Mingde for research assistance.

The amount of information available inside as well as outside of China has increased tremendously over a relatively short time. Inside China, the media sector grew by about 100 percent between 1978 and 2008.[1] Outside China, information about the country has increased as well. A growing number of Chinese publications aimed at propagating China's policies abroad have been established since the 1980s.[2] There is also more and more news about China in the foreign press.[3] Today, it is a challenge to keep track of the news on China simply because there is an enormous amount of information out there that cannot all be processed simultaneously.

A second challenge is that the available information turns over rapidly. Some newspapers close while others are newly founded; electronic search engines suddenly appear on the Internet but disappear quickly. Therefore, many China specialists have started to become collectors of data, not only accumulating data directly related to their current research projects but preserving other interesting materials for fear that the information will never be found again. As a result, we are not only dealing with the challenge of trying to handle and process the information out there but also with large chunks of data stored in offices and on hard disks queuing up to be analyzed.

None of these developments is necessarily specific to China. One aspect of globalization has been an increase in information and a more rapid pace of information turnover. The success of search engines – such as, for example, Google – demonstrates that there is a demand for services that assist people in locating information. Similarly, decreasing prices of technology that allows storage of information combined with the higher speed of the Internet and the increased opportunities for file-sharing have resulted in huge chunks of unorganized data on many computers. Software firms are therefore in the process of developing file-storage systems that facilitate data management on computers. Hence, what we observe in China is part of a broader trend. What is specific to China, however, is the rapid pace with which we have moved from information scarcity to overabundance.

China scholars have had difficulties adapting to the changes resulting from the information revolution. Up to the present, there has been little scholarly discussion about the methods and techniques that can be employed to cope with the rapidly increasing and changing information environment. In this chapter, I explain the usage of electronic aids to collect, manage, and analyze data originating in the Chinese news media. Since electronic aids to analyze

---

[1] Newspapers increased from 186 to 1,943, periodicals from 930 to 9,549, television stations from 32 to 287 (excluding *guangbo dianshitai*), radio stations from 100 to 263, and Web sites from 0 to 2,878,000. See http://www.gapp.gov.cn; http://www.drcnet.com.cn; http://www.stats.gov.cn; http://www.cnnic.cn; http://number.cnki.net; http://press.gapp.gov.cn.

[2] The *China Daily*, an English newspaper, was established in 1981. The *People's Daily* Overseas Edition was founded in 1985 (information taken from each newspaper's Web site).

[3] See, for example, Ethan Zuckerman's Global Attention Profiles, at http://h2odev.law.harvard.edu/ezuckerman/, accessed January 24, 2008.

Chinese texts qualitatively have so far not been developed, the focus of this chapter is only on content analysis. The main advantage of relying on the techniques described in this chapter is that they assist us in conducting research in a systematic fashion. Random sampling automatically leads us to ask questions about the nature of the data available for our research and the generalizability of our conclusions to China as a whole. Content analysis software enables us to remain consistent across a large number of texts. Therefore, electronic aids help us to gain a more accurate understanding about China and to strengthen our conclusions about where China is heading.

The explanations laid out in this chapter are relevant to those planning to use content analysis in their work. Content analysis quantitatively analyzes messages, broadly defined (Neuendorf, 2002). It is therefore different from qualitative text analyses, such as, for example, discourse analysis or grounded theory (Charmaz, 2006; Wood and Kroger, 2000). Content analysis best answers questions of *who, where, how many, how much,* and *the relationship between specific variables.* Although these questions are raised across different subfields in Chinese politics, so far content analysis has been primarily used to examine Chinese media content. Such studies are conducted for two reasons: first, researchers use the press as a social indicator – as a window to understand opinions of intellectuals (see, for example, Gu, 1996; Johnston and Stockmann, 2007; Li and White, 1991). Second, scholars aim to understand the causes and consequences of propaganda through the news media (see, for example, Esarey, 2009; Hassid, 2007; Stockmann, forthcoming-a; Stockmann and Gallagher, forthcoming; Wang and Tan, 2008).[4] However, content analysis can also be applied to other sources. Political scientists have used content analysis of speeches, letters, party manifestos, textbooks, government bills, and court rulings to study beliefs of political elites (Burden and Sanberg, 2003), citizen opinions (Lee, 2002), the political ideology of parties (Laver and Garry, 2000), international conflict (Bar-Tal, 1998), political agendas (Martin, 2004), and the relationship between different legislative institutions (Kilwein and Brisbin, 1997), to name just a few examples. Apart from the media, content analysis can therefore be applied to a wide range of texts. In Chinese politics we now have access to diverse sources, many of which are in electronic format, such as, for example, political speeches, government documents, court rulings, governmental Web sites, textbooks, lectures, and Chinese scholarly work. Although this chapter focuses on the Chinese media, the techniques explained here can also be applied to other sources relevant for the study of Chinese politics.

This chapter will proceed as follows. In the first part, I provide an overview of electronic sources of the Chinese news media, focusing on Web sites and archives that provide useful tools for collecting news media sources. Next, I lay out sampling techniques for content analysis and show how to investigate the

---

[4] Before the reform period, content analysis of content was also used to understand elite politics (Walder, 1979).

representativeness and efficiency of the sampling size. Subsequently, I explain techniques of data management and analysis. In particular, I explain the use of a software program for content analysis of texts in simplified Chinese characters. I conclude by discussing the limitations and potential of the use of electronic sources in content analysis for further advancing our understanding of Chinese politics.

ELECTRONIC SOURCES OF THE CHINESE NEWS MEDIA

When collecting news articles, researchers of advanced industrial democracies can usually rely on data archives, such as, for example, Lexis Nexis or the Television News Archive at Vanderbilt University in Tennessee. China scholars are not so fortunate. Most datasets for research on Chinese politics are not archived. However, China scholars are usually willing to share existing datasets when personally contacted. In recent years, a number of datasets of Chinese news content have been created, which are, in principle, available for further research. One of the first datasets was collected by the University of Maryland for the U.S.-China Security Review Commission (Maryland Study, 2002). This dataset sampled newspaper articles on the United States in six newspapers between 2001 and 2002. Stockmann (2007) created a dataset of all articles relevant to labor law in three newspapers in Chongqing during a period of three months in 2005. Esarey (2009) collected information about propaganda in newspapers in Shanghai, Beijing, and Guangzhou. Hassid (2007) analyzed aggressiveness in twenty-six newspapers between 2004 and 2006. More recently, Stockmann (2009) examined reports on the United States in three newspapers in 1999 and 2003. The usefulness of these existing datasets for further studies of Chinese news media content is, however, limited. All of these existing datasets sample news articles published only in newspapers, excluding other media sources; they also encompass relatively short periods of time; and most deal with specific issues, such as legal news reporting about labor or international news reporting about the United States. These features make it difficult for other researchers to use the data for further inquiry. Original research involving the Chinese news media will therefore often require the collection of news reports for content analysis. Below I explain which electronic sources may be used for data collection.

Search Engines of News Web Sites

The obvious place to sample from the Chinese news media is the Internet. Many (but not all) traditional media make their news reports available online. CCTV, for example, has a search engine for transcripts as well as video-clips of previous reports going back to 2000. Similarly, newspaper content can often be searched online starting as early as 2000. Online news Web sites that selectively display news articles by other news organizations, for example, Sina, allow researchers to see which articles were displayed on the Web site on a particular day (going back to 1998). Finally, Xinhua news reports can be searched online from 2000 on. A list of useful electronic search engines of influential national and local media sources, such as those mentioned above, is available on www.daniestockmann.net. When using these search engines, however, researchers should be aware of the following problems.

First, news content displayed on Web sites of traditional media outlets, including newspapers, magazines, television, and radio, is not necessarily the same as that broadcast or printed in traditional media outlets. Some articles are published in online editions only, and media staff have more leeway in writing these articles (He and Zhu, 2002; Stockmann, forthcoming-b). The choice of a search engine depends on whether researchers want to explore online news content or news content in traditional media. As a rule of thumb, search options directly available on the Web site's "home" tend to search online news content, whereas search engines of broadcast or printed news content can be found through links named "advanced search" or "electronic edition."

Yet even when located correctly, search engines of traditional media outlets differ in terms of how they search and return news content. Some search engines allow full-body searches based on keywords, returning txt-files, whereas others allow searches based on publication date, returning pdf-files.[5] These differences may be irrelevant when scholars aim to select articles solely based on publication date since all search engines share this feature. Most of the time, however, we are looking for specific keywords in the body of a text. In these cases, we may introduce a selection bias in our data collection. Media outlets in certain regions are more likely to use search engines that return txt-files. For example, most newspapers in Beijing use search engines that allow keyword-based searches and return txt-files, whereas those in Chongqing are usually limited to searching by date only, and they return pdf-files. Therefore, we should keep in mind that we may introduce systematic biases into our research when relying on one kind of search engine as opposed to another.[6]

The same is true for solely relying on online news Web sites to collect news reports. Clearly, those traditional media outlets that have online news editions with functioning search engines are also the ones that are more profit-oriented and commercialized. For example, local metro and evening papers are more likely than local official papers to have online editions. And newspapers from the more developed areas on the east coast are more likely to be present on

---

[5] These features do not necessarily go together, but in practice they often do.
[6] Inaccurate results may also result from three kinds of measurement error: first, they sometimes return texts that do not match actually printed articles 100 percent. To double-check, researchers can compare a sample of results retrieved electronically with broadcast or printed texts. Second, the same article is sometimes returned multiple times, in which case the researcher needs to correct the number of "hits." Finally, error may be introduced when search engines differ with respect to the techniques used to identify keywords. The same article may be a "hit" in one search engine but not in another. To hold techniques for keyword searches constant, one can select search engines that simultaneously search a number of media outlets. Newspaper conglomerates sometimes offer this option.

the World Wide Web than those located in the western inland regions (He and Zhu, 2002). To get a representative sample of news content of a particular region in China, it is therefore advisable to rely on additional means to collect news reports. Some of these means are also available electronically, as explained in the next section.

Other Electronic Sources

Selection bias due to search engines and the media outlets' presence on the Internet can be partially overcome using other electronic resources. To my knowledge, publicly available databases for television and radio do not exist in China. My focus in this section is therefore on traditional print media.

Most official papers can be accessed through the China National Network (CNKI.net). In total, the "China Core Newspapers Full-Text Database" (*Zhongguo zhongyao baozhi quanwen shujuku*) includes over 700 newspapers, starting from 2000. Most newspapers in this database are so-called official or party papers; evening and metro papers are rarely found. Nevertheless, this dataset complements online news Web sites. More complete but also more costly is a newspaper database by Apabi.[7] In addition, the *People's Daily* can be searched from 1946 to the present using the "Renmin Ribao Full-Text Archive," accessible through many libraries.

Electronic versions of many newspapers that cannot be found on the World Wide Web are available on CD-ROM. This option is particularly interesting for researchers who intend to do time-series analysis. For example, the *Beijing Evening News* can be searched on the Internet beginning from 2005, but can be purchased on a CD-ROM for all years between 1997 and 2004.[8]

Electronic databases as well as CD-ROMs constitute additional electronic sources that can be used to complement data collection based on the search engines of news Web sites. Although these sources help us overcome a selection bias when relying solely on news Web sites, the correction may only be partial. In order to collect representative material, researchers may still need to go back to hard-copy versions of print media or tape-recordings of broadcasting media, followed by subscriptions to these materials into electronic formats when using computer-assisted content analysis. A smaller random sample of hard-copy material can be used to assess the magnitude of the selection bias, thus allowing the researcher to make corrections (Heckman et al., 1998). However, there is no doubt that the electronic sources available greatly facilitate data collection. Since the exact nature of these electronic sources,

---

[7] Available at www.eastview.com/Online/AsianProducts.aspx. A free (but more limited) version of Apabi is available at www.press.idoican.com.cn, accessed May 26, 2009. Another newspaper database called WiseNews appears to be using CNKI.net. See www.wisers.com/corpsite/global/en/products/wisenews.html, accessed January 8, 2010.

[8] Contact information and prices for the *Beijing Evening News* and *Beijing Daily* are available at http://www.bjd.com.cn/com/2001gp.htm, accessed January 24, 2008.

especially news Web sites, changes rapidly, however, my final advice for data collectors is to plan to finish the data collection within a short period of time, especially when relying on the Internet. If data collection extends over several months, some useful Web sites may have already been lost in the data jungle of the World Wide Web.

DRAWING REPRESENTATIVE AND EFFICIENT SAMPLES

Given the vast amount of information available to China scholars today, it is hardly possible to examine all materials on a particular research topic. Unless one's research question is narrow enough to limit the number of documents to one that is manageable, the best solution is to randomly select a sample from the "population," the set of units about which the researcher wishes to generalize. Nonrandom, so-called nonprobability, samples should be used only if no other options exist since we cannot generalize findings from nonrandom samples to a population. For content analysis, the unit of analysis is often a message (broadly defined), but depending on the research question the researchers may also break it down into message components or choose a broader unit, such as, for example, media sources. Once the population is defined, it must serve as the basis for the sampling.[9]

At present, two kinds of sampling techniques are primarily used by China scholars when analyzing media sources. The first one is called systematic random sampling which selects every *xth* unit from a list of all units in the population (also called the sampling frame) or in some flow of occurrence over time. For example, the Maryland Study of Chinese news content about the United States selected the issue of six newspapers every second day over a period of several months (Maryland Study, 2002). A big disadvantage of using systematic random sampling when working with media sources is that the format differs depending on the day of the week. For example, the *Beijing Youth Daily* publishes a special edition on Mondays, which is especially popular among Beijingers (CPCR, 2005). If this periodicity matches the skip interval of systematic random sampling, the representativeness of the sample may be negatively affected. Therefore, studies employing systematic random sampling often lower the skip interval and thus increase the sample size. This, however, may result in oversampling: researchers analyze more data than are needed to retrieve estimates representative of the population.[10] To avoid this problem, Esarey (2009) and Stockmann (2009) have used a second sampling technique, called constructed-week sampling, for the analysis of daily newspapers. According to this technique, all weeks during the period of interest to

---

[9] For a detailed introduction to different definitions of populations and sampling for content analysis, see Neuendorf (2002).

[10] If the size of the population and the desired sample size are known, researchers can divide the population size by the sample size to calculate the skip interval to avoid oversampling (Neuendorf, 2002).

the researcher are numbered, and subsequently one Monday, Tuesday, and so on is randomly selected until one, or several, weeks are constructed (Lacy et al., 2001; Stempel, 1952). The procedure works similarly for weekly publications (Riffe, Lacy, and Drager, 1996) and online news sites (Wang X., 2006).[11] Constructed-week sampling is especially attractive for research that involves multiple years because it relies on a small sample size while, at the same time, retaining representative results.

Yet how do we know how many constructed weeks to sample? Ideally, we would like to draw a sample size which is "just right." That is, an efficient sample size is achieved at a point when increasing the number of cases will not significantly reduce the sample error, whereas decreasing the number will significantly damage the representativeness of the results. In the American context, media scholars have found that two constructed-week samples constitute the most efficient sample size for daily newspapers (Lacy et al., 2001). To test whether the same sample size applies to the Chinese context, I compared the results of the Maryland Study's systematic sample, which oversampled the number of cases, with the results of constructed-week samples over a period of ten months.[12] If the estimates based on the constructed-week samples are close to the estimates drawn from the over sampled systematic sample, we can be confident that these findings are also valid estimates of the population data.

In doing this comparison, I was particularly interested in differences between different types of newspapers. Therefore, I chose the *Beijing Youth Daily* as an example of a nonofficial paper and the *People's Daily* as an example of an official paper. Official papers include papers under direct supervision of state units (such as, for example, the *Worker's Daily*); nonofficial papers are evening and metro papers that are run with a stronger commercial orientation. Chinese urban residents prefer reading nonofficial papers (Stockmann, forthcoming-a). For each newspaper, the Maryland Study allowed me to assess how many articles about the United States were published per day and the average tone in these articles per day.[13] Treating the systematic sample as the population, I examined the likelihood that the sample means of these variables in the constructed-week samples fall within one and two standard errors of the population means. According to the Central Limits Theorem, 68 percent of the sample means should fall within one standard error of the population mean and 95 percent of the sample means should fall within two standard errors of the population mean. Accordingly, a sample size is considered effective only if

---

[11] Riffe, Lacy, and Drager (1996) argue that stratification by month, followed by simple random sampling of two days per month, is the most efficient sampling method for weekday TV network news in the United States.

[12] The Maryland Study includes about 46 percent of all articles published during ten months (September to December 2001; February to July 2002); thus it is highly representative of the population.

[13] These variables were assessed by trained coders. More detailed information about coder training and measurement can be found in the Maryland Study (2002) or in the online appendix available at www.daniestockmann.net.

TABLE 6.1. *Percentage of 100 samples falling within one and two standard errors of the population mean in two newspapers*

	People's Daily				Beijing Youth Daily			
	Number of Articles about the U.S. (per day)		Average Tone of Articles about the U.S. (per day)		Number of Articles about the U.S. (per day)		Average Tone of Articles about the U.S. (per day)	
	1 s.e.[a]	2 s.e.	1 s.e.	2 s.e.	1 s.e.	2 s.e.	1 s.e.	2 s.e.
1 week	20%	32%	22%	39%	22%	35%	15%	34%
2 weeks	32%	51%	29%	55%	25%	55%	25%	49%
3 weeks	28%	56%	39%	66%	35%	60%	32%	62%
4 weeks	47%	72%	44%	69%	51%	78%	37%	68%
5 weeks	65%	90%	49%	75%	46%	75%	48%	83%
6 weeks	53%	90%	57%	81%	53%	78%	47%	83%
7 weeks	48%	86%	47%	87%	56%	86%	47%	88%
8 weeks	60%	91%	50%	89%	65%	92%	60%	88%
9 weeks	60%	87%	62%	93%	62%	96%	68%	94%
10 weeks	69.00	100%	75%	98%	72%	96%	70%	96%
Population Mean[14]	6.43		0.18		9.65		0.15	
(s.e.)	(0.32)		(0.07)		(0.41)		(0.05)	
{s.d.}	{3.81}		{0.81}		{4.83}		{0.60}	

Source: Maryland Data.
[a] By Mean; s.e. = standard error; s.d. = standard deviation.
[b] Tone was assessed based on trained interviewers, ranging between +3 (highly positive) and −3 (highly negative). See the online appendix at www.daniestockmann.net for details. Results do not differ significantly when using sampling weights that account for the sampling design (first drawing a systematic sample from the whole population and then drawing a constructed-week sample). Results can be retrieved from the author at dstockmann@fsw.leidenuniv.nl.

its sample means distribution meets these standards. As displayed in Table 6.1, ten constructed weeks fulfill this requirement when 100 samples are randomly drawn from the Maryland Study data. This sampling size did not differ much between the *People's Daily* and the *Beijing Youth Daily*. When it comes to daily newspapers, constructed-week sampling is preferable to systematic sampling as it significantly reduces the sampling size, in this case by 50 percent, while, at the same time, remaining representative.[14]

Do you always need to draw ten weeks when using constructed-week sampling? The answer depends on the goal of the study. My example here is most relevant for those who intend to generalize from a small number of media reports to media reporting over an extended period of time, in this case about a year. If the purpose of the study is to examine how media reporting changed

---

[14] The Maryland Study collected 140 out of 303 days; 10 constructed-weeks sum up to 70 out of 303 days.

over a short period of time, such as, for example, in response to a specific event, the population of articles may be small enough that sampling is not necessary. Furthermore, my example relates to international news reporting, especially with respect to the United States. When researchers are interested in features with a lower variance in day-to-day news reporting than the standard deviations displayed in Table 6.1, they can reduce the sample size.[15] For any other topics that share the same variance in coverage to ten articles per day, ten constructed weeks should be sufficient.

Now that I have explained how to go about collecting samples, let us consider the next step in conducting content analysis: managing and analyzing the data.

MANAGING AND ANALYZING DATA USING DIGITAL TECHNOLOGIES

At first glance, seventy days do not seem to represent news reporting in one newspaper during almost a whole year. Yet once we consider that each day includes more than one article, our dataset of ten constructed weeks may soon contain about 4,000 articles dealing with one issue area – reports related only to the United States. All of these articles will need to be managed, read, coded, and analyzed.

A common way to deal with the problem of analyzing large datasets is to organize a number of people to help with the coding and content analysis. Although this makes a lot of sense, it also creates potential problems in terms of consistency since different individuals may use different standards to evaluate news content. For example, one person may interpret an article as somewhat negative whereas the other may find it more neutral in tone. Therefore, scholars have placed much emphasis on the training of content analysis personnel and have developed mathematical techniques to test coder interreliability (Perreault and Leigh, 1989; Riffe, Lacy, and Fico, 1998).

Consistency may also be ensured by using digital aids. For many languages there are qualitative and quantitative software programs that can be used for content analysis. So far, there is only one software program that is able to recognize and analyze simplified Chinese characters. Yoshikoder is an open-source software available for free on the Internet.[16] In addition to Chinese, it is available in many other languages and thus allows for comparative content analysis across different languages. More specifically, the program may be used qualitatively to facilitate comparisons of texts that mention specific keywords. Researchers can upload a number of articles simultaneously and

---

[15] This also explains why Lacy et al. (2001) decide that two constructed weeks are sufficient: the variables they examine are characterized by low variance.
[16] The software runs on both Windows and Macintosh operating systems. It can analyze txt-files in UTF-8 format. For general information, see www.yoshikoder.org; for information on how to run Yoshikoder in Chinese, see www.daniestockmann.net.

color keywords of interest. This function comes in handy when comparing the usage and framing of certain words in a single or several texts. However, the program's strength lies in its quantitative content analysis. The software can count specific characters or groups of characters, either in the whole text or within a certain distance to a keyword. This allows the quantification of the use of certain concepts or categories of words. Below, I use two examples to illustrate how these functions may be used in practice.

Assessing the Sensitivity of News Content by Counting Keywords

Researchers of the Chinese media agree that the state generally exerts a considerable amount of control over Chinese media content. However, government control over news reporting in China changes over time. In addition to major political events during which media reporting may be restricted, such as, for example, during the SARS crisis in 2003, each year the Chinese media undergoes a regular cycle of tightening and loosening. At around the time of the Spring Festival and the meeting of the National People's Congress (usually between late January and March), reporting is supposed to be positive. Toward the end of the year there is more room for criticism (Stockmann, 2007). The dynamic nature of space for news reporting potentially creates problems when sampling news content. For example, in my study of news reporting about the United States, I was interested in the tone of the news content. Yet if, by chance, my constructed-week sample overrepresented the period during the Spring Festival, perhaps my results were overly positive.[17] Yet there is a way to account for these changes of space for news reporting over time in the Chinese media.

In my content analysis I am using the percentage of Xinhua articles published on the same topic on a particular day as a means to control for sensitivity over time. Xinhua articles are sometimes reprinted in newspapers as must-carry news. In other words, the Propaganda Department requests that Xinhua articles be published instead of reports written by the newspaper's own journalists. Explicit requests are rare today, but editors still feel that they are on the safe side by publishing Xinhua articles when reporting about sensitive issues. Handbooks distributed by newspapers to journalists for training purposes also recommend that journalists rely on Xinhua material when covering certain issues (Stockmann, 2007). Researchers of the Chinese media can therefore use Xinhua reporting as a proxy for sensitivity over time.

Note that I look at changes in the percentage of Xinhua articles over time, *not* whether an article is equivalent to a Xinhua report. Especially when it comes to international news reporting, newspapers are somewhat dependent

---

[17] This problem is not easily addressed when employing stratified sampling. First, we do not know precisely what news reporting in China would look like if journalists were not to self-censor. It is also difficult to set a precise date marking the beginning and end of periods during which articles are more tightly or loosely controlled.

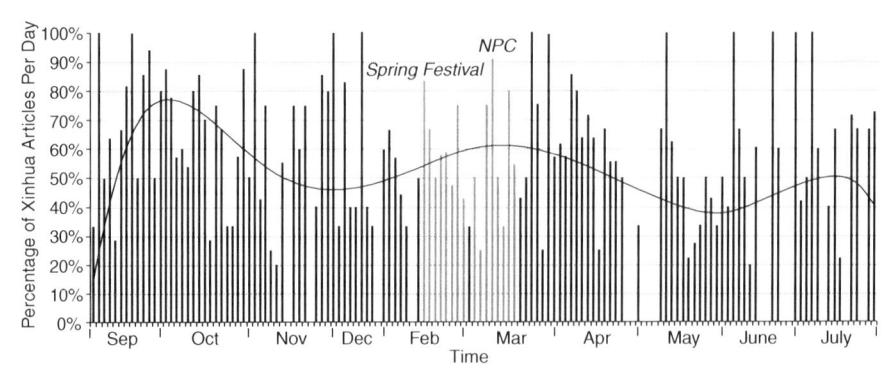

FIGURE 6.1. Percentage of Xinhua news articles among all articles about the United States published in the *People's Daily*, September 2001–July 2002 (no data for January was available).
Source: Maryland Data.

on the Xinhua News Agency as a source of information. Most newspapers do not have permanent correspondents abroad. As a result, editors often publish Xinhua reports, even when the Propaganda Department has not imposed any restrictions. Yet in an effort to attract readers, many newspapers are making an effort to write their own articles. As a result, nonofficial papers, like the *Beijing Youth Daily*, are actually less likely than official papers, such as the *People's Daily*, to simply reprint Xinhua reports.[18] In this case, reporters supplement Xinhua reports with alternative news sources, such as, for example, the Internet and the newsletter of the U.S. embassy. During major events, such as the 2003 invasion of Iraq, media institutions may also temporarily send reporters abroad (Stockmann, 2007). Therefore, newspapers are partially dependent on the Xinhua News Agency. Simply using a dummy variable for being a Xinhua report will be insufficient to assess sensitivity over time. Only when looking at changes in the percentage of Xinhua articles published on the same topic will we be able to identify periods during which editors reprint Xinhua articles to meet the demands of the state.

Figure 6.1 confirms that this measure indeed represents a valid indicator for sensitivity over time. The Maryland data allowed me to investigate how Xinhua news reporting developed over a period of almost one whole year, starting in fall 2001 and ending in summer 2002, excluding only August 2001 and January 2002. In Figure 6.1 the *x*-axis indicates time, the *y*-axis shows the percentage of Xinhua articles related to the United States published each day. As expected, the percentage of Xinhua articles increased during periods of high sensitivity. Immediately after September 11, space for press reporting was relatively open until foreign correspondents in China reported that

---

[18] Compare Figure 6.1 with Figure A1 in the online appendix at www.daniestockmann.net.

Chinese media coverage was not very sympathetic.[19] The state determined that this attitude was not constructive and tried to replace it with a more sympathetic view.[20] After the government stepped in, media reporting related to the United States became highly sensitive (Stockmann, 2007). After September 11, the percentage of Xinhua articles increased visibly when reporting about the United States, covering such topics as politics, economics, culture, society, sports, and entertainment. In mid-November, sensitivity went back to average levels at around 50 percent of the articles per day. In addition to this period of tension in Sino-U.S. relations, sensitivity increased during the period of the Spring Festival and the meeting of the National People's Congress. In February and March 2002, the percentage of Xinhua news articles increased to about 60 percent. By late April, space for news reporting had loosened again, continuing into the summer, although events related to the American war on terrorism in June and July somewhat increased sensitivity again.[21] The same pattern is found when observing the percentage of daily Xinhua reports in the *Beijing Youth Daily*. Overall, the measure responds in sensible ways to changes in the space for news reporting about the United States.

To reproduce this measure using content analysis software, it is necessary to account for whether an article constitutes a Xinhua report. Fortunately, Chinese newspaper articles usually cite Xinhua as the source, especially when an issue is sensitive. Editors have an incentive to print this information since they can hardly be held responsible for content that has been supervised by someone else. To quickly find a reference to Xinhua in an article, I simply asked Yoshikoder to count the term "新华" for me. If Yoshikoder did not find a match, the article was coded as "zero." If there was a match, it was coded as "one." The number of reprinted Xinhua articles was then divided by the total number of articles published on the same day, and each article published on that particular day received the respective proportion in my dataset.[22]

Although assessing the degree of sensitivity on an issue may be interesting in itself, the percentage of daily Xinhua reports may also prove useful as a control variable. When entering this measure into a regression analysis, the relationships between other variables of interest can be investigated while controlling for changes in sensitivity over time (see, for example, Stockmann, 2009).

---

[19] Urban youth and netizens expressed a fair amount of "schadenfreude" immediately after 9/11 (Chen S., 2004; Guo, 2002). For an example of foreign correspondent reporting, see CNN, "China Tries to Keep Tight Lid on Anti-U.S. Feeling," September 14, 2001.

[20] For example, universities were required to show a movie that portrayed the Americans in a more sympathetic light (Chen S., 2004).

[21] In June 2002, the government of the Afghan Transitional Administration was established. In July 2002, the Chinese press started to discuss a potential American military intervention in Iraq.

[22] Using proportions may be preferable to percentages if all independent variables are coded to run from "zero" to "one." This allows for interpretation of the constant in regression analysis.

In this section, I used Xinhua reports as an example to illustrate how Yoshikoder may be a useful tool to count keywords. This function may also be used to examine other features of news reports. For example, researchers interested in how the Chinese media frame certain issues can identify a number of keywords associated with a particular frame. In my own work on the framing of legal news reporting about labor issues, I grouped terms that were associated with workers and their legal representation, such as "employee", "lawyer", "plaintiff", and so forth, and terms that stood for businesses, such as "employer", "factory", "corporation", and so forth. By counting the number of times that these terms were used in news articles, I could assess whether news reports were written primarily from the perspective of workers or of employers (Stockmann, 2007).

In addition to counting individual terms of groups or keywords, Yoshikoder can also be used to count cross-references between groups of keywords. This feature is used, for example, when assessing the tone of news reporting, which I explain in the next section.

Assessing the Tone of News Reporting by Counting Cross-References

How can a computer pick up the tone of a news story? Many words we use can be grouped into having positive or negative connotations. Once words are grouped into "positive," "negative," and "neutral," computers can recognize and count these words around the specific concepts of interest. The trick, of course, is to categorize the language in a meaningful way. Fortunately, China specialists do not need to start from scratch. Numerous psychologists and linguists have developed "dictionaries" to measure tone as well as other categories in text documents (Stone, 1997; Stone et al., 1966). A large number of dictionaries are available for computer-aided content analysis in various languages.[23] Up until recently, we lacked a complementary dictionary in Chinese, but in 2005 linguists at National Taiwan University created the first collection of positive and negative words (Ku et al., 2005).[24] These terms can be entered into the Yoshikoder software program as two separate categories and then compared with the terms immediately surrounding other keywords. Although a mainland Chinese version would be desirable, in practice I have found that the results based on the Taiwanese version match my qualitative reading of mainland Chinese texts fairly accurately.

For example, I was interested in studying the differences in legal news reporting related to labor issues between official and nonofficial papers. In addition

---

[23] See, for example, the homepage of the *General Inquirer* at http://www.wjh.harvard.edu/~inquirer/, accessed January 26, 2008.
[24] This dictionary is composed of a translation of the *General Inquirer* and a collection of colloquial terms used on the Internet. Its validity was pretested using a method to extract positivity/negativity from radicals in Chinese characters. The dictionary can be retrieved in traditional Chinese characters from Ku Lun-Wei at lwku@nlg.csie.ntu.edu.tw.

to the Chinese dictionary of positive and negative valence words, I also created groups of synonyms for all main actors involved in labor disputes, including agents of the state (for example, "government" or "administration"), the law (for example, "contract" or "regulation"), employee (for example, "worker" or "migrant worker"), and employer (for example, "company" or "boss").[25] I then counted the relative frequency of positive and negative words within a distance of eight words to these synonyms.[26] Subsequently, the article's tone was measured by subtracting the number of negative words from the number of positive words in this semantic space surrounding all synonyms for the same concept.[27] Somewhat surprisingly, nonofficial papers actually turn out to be more neutral in tone than official papers. Greater balance in positive and negative expressions create distance from overly positive reports associated with the propaganda of official papers and aids in creating perceptions among readers of nonofficial papers as a credible information source. The data also revealed a stronger pro-business orientation of nonofficial papers. Yet reporting in favor of employers does not necessarily conflict with being in favor of employees: nonofficial papers continuously pointed out the positive treatment of workers when reporting positively about specific corporations; they were pro-business and pro-worker at the same time. My findings demonstrate that the message of the state and commercial orientation can mutually reinforce each other (Stockmann, 2007).

Cross-referencing does not necessarily have to be used to assess the tone of news reporting. Researchers have developed dictionaries for language associated with particular institutions, identities, and values, to name just a few examples.[28] As of 2009, only a limited number of such dictionaries existed in Chinese, including dictionaries for sensitive keywords as well as Chinese foreign politics (Hassid, 2007; Stockmann, 2009). If shared, the creation of new dictionaries would add to the current applications of Yoshikoder and therefore further improve computer-aided text analysis in Chinese studies.

The examples above illustrate that Yoshikoder is a useful tool for assessing Chinese news content. One of the key advantages of the program is that it increases consistency throughout the process of analyzing Chinese-language materials. Compared to human coding Computer Aided Text Analysis (CATA)

---

[25] These groups are called "categories" in Yoshikoder; individual keywords are called "patterns." For useful suggestions on developing categories, see http://www.wjh.harvard.edu/~inquirer/developing_new_categories.htm, accessed January 26, 2008.

[26] In Yoshikoder, first make a "concordance," followed by a concordance report.

[27] Since the number of matching synonyms for a concept of interest affects the number of negative and positive words found in the text, I recommend to either normalize this measure of tone by this variable *or* to control for this variable in the statistical analysis. In some cases, the length of the article (counted by the Yoshikoder) may be preferred.

[28] To develop your own dictionary, first you must define words consistent with the conceptual definition for that construct. Then you need to add variations on those root terms. Finally, check for inappropriate variations and for words too ambiguous to be validly included. For more examples of dictionaries, see http://www.wjh.harvard.edu/~inquirer/homecat.htm, accessed February 20, 2008.

offers reliability and standardization. However, relying on software to analyze texts also has disadvantages. CATA is less nuanced and flexible than human coding as it cannot pick up contextual information: the computer locates co-occurrences while ignoring the semantic relationships between words that co-occur (Roberts, 1989). For example, a 1999 report in the *People's Daily* states "以美国为首的北约袭击中国大使馆，是对中国主权和民族尊严的粗暴侵犯" (The surprise attack on the Chinese embassy in Belgrade by the United States as the main actor is a sincere violation of China's sovereignty and national dignity).[29] In this sentence, the United States is the country taking the initiative and China is the victim. Negative terms such as "surprise attack" and "sincere violation" describe the actions by the United States rather than by China. However, when analyzing the tone surrounding the terms "United States" and "China," Yoshikoder will find one negative term ("surprise attack") close to the United States and one positive and three negative words ("dignity, "surprise attack," "sincere," and "violation") close to China. As a result, the tone surrounding China will be measured as more negative than the tone describing the United States. Therefore, CATA's assumption that co-occurrences correspond to relationships may in individual cases inaccurately measure relationships between different groups of words. In practice, I have found that the average tone of a Chinese text picked up by the software program corresponds to my qualitative reading of the text, even if my qualitative assessment of individual sentences occasionally differs.[30]

In this context, it is important to keep in mind that the use of software does not substitute for reading. When using computer-assisted content analysis it seems as if one could simply insert a document into a machine that subsequently returns numbers in response to a research question. This idea seems tempting, since mindless counting of keywords is a waste of time. Numbers are only of substantive value when they match the concept they intend to measure. Therefore, anyone working with Yoshikoder or any other content analysis software should frequently check to determine whether the software is picking up all keywords and whether important synonyms or categories need to be added.[31] And, of course, counting keywords can never substitute for the in-depth understanding one gets about the interpretation of current events in China from reading the news.

CONTENT ANALYSIS AND CHINESE POLITICS

What, if anything, can researchers of Chinese politics gain from using content analysis? This question was vividly discussed in the 1960s and 1970s. In a study of Chinese press reporting during the Indo-Chinese border crisis

---

[29] See "A Sincere Threat to World Peace," *People's Daily*, May 12, 1999.
[30] A possible solution to this problem is semantic and network text analysis (Roberts, 2000).
[31] To improve the software, please report problems to the developer of Yoshikoder (see www.yoshikoder.org).

of 1962, Liao and Whiting (1973: 81) propose that content analysis offered an "appropriate method of research in which availability of data is a problem or where the investigator is heavily dependent on documentary evidence." They stress three key advantages: first, the method made optimal use of scarce information; second, it provided a "check on impressionistic research" and permitted replication by other researchers; and third, it uncovered patterns that were not intuitively obvious and therefore provided insights on their own (Liao and Whiting, 1973: 97). However, their claim met with strong criticism. Friedman (1975: 538), not convinced that content analysis added to the understanding of Chinese politics, retorted: "the Liao and Whiting model ends up tied to a mechanical model which cannot handle the open, subjective, reflexive realities of politics and politicians." In an earlier publication, Oksenberg (1964: 605) goes further, warning of the dangers inherent in the new methods: "Increased use of computers, quantitative content analysis, and other advanced research techniques cannot eliminate the problems [associated with source bias]; the danger is that they may camouflage them." Revisiting the topic, Walder (1979: 570) agrees that content analysis must begin with an assessment of possible sources of bias but argues that its strength lies in exposing "to the critical reader the set of assumptions and decisions that lead to a particular conclusion – information that is not made explicit in other methods." Walder concludes the discussion on a positive note, emphasizing transparency as a key advantage of content analysis.

Not all the points raised thirty years ago for and against content analysis are still relevant today. In contrast to China experts in the 1970s, we no longer face a shortage of data sources. The information revolution brought about many opportunities for research on Chinese politics. Most important, China scholars no longer need to think about how to make optimal use of scarce resources – a question that Liao and Whiting considered as key in the study of Chinese politics. Instead, a central question in developing a research design today is how to narrow down the information so the research is manageable but still representative of developments in China. It is therefore useful to develop sampling techniques that produce representative results. In this chapter, I have demonstrated that ten constructed-week samples constitute an efficient sample size for collecting international news reports about the United States during a period of about one year. Inferences can be drawn from these findings on daily newspaper content for other topics if researchers have some understanding of the nature of the variation in newspaper reporting. However, they cannot easily be transferred to radio or television reports. To advance research in Chinese politics through the Chinese media, further tests of sampling techniques are needed with respect to other issue areas as well as other media sources. When conducting these tests, researchers can follow the procedure outlined in this chapter, whereby I have relied on a dataset that oversampled news reports and compared the results to a more efficient sampling technique. More broadly, studies that investigate sampling are important for addressing the question of how to reduce the information available on China while simultaneously drawing accurate inferences about China's development.

This central question relates to Oksenberg's worry about source biases when using content analysis in Chinese politics. At present, such a bias is common in studies of Chinese media content. Researchers overwhelmingly rely on official national channels and media outlets located in China's more developed eastern regions when analyzing Chinese media content.[32] These biases in contemporary research are unrelated to research methodology. When investigating Chinese news media content, scholars tend to use qualitative research methods, and the few who rely on quantitative techniques have so far made little use of computer software programs. Therefore, the existing bias in the use of sources has not resulted from using quantitative research techniques or electronic aids as Oksenberg feared. As Walder argues, source bias represents a problem when conducting research no matter which research methodology is employed. At the same time, Oksenberg's observation that electronic aids limit the range of sources that are used in practice by the researcher remains true today. In this chapter, I have shown that electronic sources provide easy access to media outlets from more developed regions and underrepresent less-developed regions. Nevertheless, to date China scholars have not fully explored the opportunities that electronic sources offer to extend knowledge of the Chinese media. They could use electronic sources to extend knowledge about magazines, television, and radio; about local media outlets; and about the media environments beyond Beijing, Shanghai, and Guangzhou.[33] Oksenberg's point is still relevant, but considering the nature of source biases in contemporary research, electronic aids embody more opportunities than limitations.

Given the predominant use of qualitative interpretation of Chinese media content, Friedman's criticism of content analysis still resonates among many contemporary China scholars. There is no doubt that content analysis lacks

---

[32] Among 31 articles that systematically analyzed content of Chinese media sources, 65 percent focused on newspapers, 23 percent on television programs, and only 13 percent on Web sites. I am not aware of any works on radio broadcasting or periodicals. Among studies that analyzed the content of newspapers, 85 percent studied newspapers that circulate nationally; 55 percent local newspapers in China's leading newspaper markets of Beijing, Shanghai, and Guangzhou; and only 20 percent local newspapers in other regions of China. Despite the fact that official papers are not popular among Chinese newspaper audiences, 95 percent of all studies that examined newspapers chose to analyze official papers, though 65 percent also sampled non-official papers. Regarding television, all programs selected for content analysis were broadcast on CCTV. Among four articles that examined online content, only one sampled online Web sites, most of them located on the east coast. For references to these studies, see the online appendix at www.daniestockmann.net.

[33] Although transcripts of radio and television reports are available online, the field would profit from developing electronic aids to transcribe additional audio and video material into text files. Voice recognition software available for Chinese (such as Via Voice) may be a useful start to build new software.

the in-depth and detailed understanding of meaning that qualitative research methods can extract. When interpreting texts, qualitative researchers take into account the context of the text, including detailed information about the source, message, channel, and audience associated with the text (see, for example, Roberts, 1989). Content analysis loses much of this context, but it also yields information that is often not exposed in other methods. Content analysis encourages transparency and consistency, thus producing replicable, reliable, and generalizable results (see, for example, Neuendorf, 2002). Because of these complementary strengths and weaknesses, recent literature recommends a mixed approach to analyzing messages, supplementing quantitative with qualitative research methods (Duriau, Reger, and Pfarrer, 2007). When using computer-assisted content analysis, I have argued that the extraction of qualitative meaning should always be the standard against which to judge the quality of the measurement. Computers are just a tool to help human coders carry out their work more consistently and thus produce more reliable results. Therefore, electronic aids such as Yoshikoder should be regarded more as a helpful supplement rather than as a substitute for qualitative text analysis. By assisting in analyzing texts in a systematic fashion and by allowing us to include a great variety of sources, electronic aids help us gain a more complete and accurate understanding of Chinese politics.

PART II

QUALITATIVE METHODS

7

The Worm's-Eye View

Using Ethnography to Illuminate Labor Politics and Institutional Change in Contemporary China

Calvin Chen

In her 1994 review of the state of the Chinese politics field, Elizabeth Perry notes that the normalization of Sino-American relations in 1979 presented a new generation of American political scientists with an opportunity to "pursue a new brand of scholarship, based upon field work and documentary materials available only in the PRC." Moreover, given the "extraordinary diversity that makes up the Chinese political experience" and the maturation of the field, she argued that Chinese politics might finally "be fertile soil for the formulation of new analytical approaches" (Perry, 1994b: 704, 712).

Since the publication of Perry's article, China has not only accelerated its economic reforms but also has inaugurated a new generation of national leaders, joined the World Trade Organization, and become the world's second largest economy. These profound changes, brought about by a matrix of global, national, and local forces, are opening up more avenues for research, dissolving and reconstituting old boundaries, and forcing us to reconsider how we understand issues that have been central to the field of Chinese politics. For example, how does state action impact economic and social transformation, especially in areas where the "reach of the state" has been historically weak (Shue, 1988)? What forms can increased political participation take and how might they contribute to greater political stability and legitimacy? How are market-oriented activities reshaping institutions, practices, and social structures, especially at the local level? In what sense can reemerging and evolving social identities provide a basis for effective collective action? The Chinese case offers a valuable perspective on these and other questions and may potentially deepen our knowledge of how similar processes affect citizens in other regions of the world.

For many political scientists, using ethnography to explore such issues seems inadequate or inappropriate. Although Clifford Geertz (1973: 3–30) helped make "thick description" a tolerable, even legitimate enterprise within the social sciences, most contemporary political scientists, whether quantitative or qualitative in their orientation, are nomothetic in their aspirations and regard ideographic narratives about local contexts to be of limited value in the search for lawlike regularities or general explanations of significant social and political phenomena. It is true that such approaches as process-tracing (George and Bennett, 2004) and comparative-historical analysis (Mahoney and Rueschemeyer, 2003) do draw attention to the value of local observations in explaining outcomes in particular cases. For the most part, however, political scientists depend on replicable methods to develop causal inferences or parsimonious models that purport to explain uniformities or variations across time and space. In the process, the discipline has left very little space for efforts to develop deep understandings of the *meanings* that individuals and groups attach to their practices, choices, and environments.[1] Certainly, there are inherent trade-offs in applying different methods in the social sciences, but the discipline can only benefit from a greater appreciation of these trade-offs and a better balance between various kinds of nomothetic and ideographic approaches (Sil, 2004).

In contrast, many China scholars, as well as many area specialists, readily appreciate the potential contributions of ethnography. In spite of this, the applicability of ethnography has been limited at best, given that area specialists in political science are aware that this work cannot constitute a "test" of a hypothesis or provide an empirical foundation for general theory. In the case of China, there is an added incentive to eschew ethnographic scholarship because ethnography, even in the post-Mao era, remains largely a hit-or-miss affair. Securing approval from Chinese authorities for such study can be time-consuming and burdensome: the process is rarely consistent or transparent. Even when official approval is granted, a host of challenges awaits, including scheduling conflicts, information gaps, access restrictions, and a reluctance or fear on the part of locals to speak with outsiders. Given such problems, the benefits of hewing to a more conventional research strategy that links general models to measurable variables seems to outweigh the potential risks of conducting ethnographic research. In the process, however, the prospective intellectual gains of ethnographic study in and of itself and as a means of gathering data in larger studies are lost. Consequently, many important questions are left unexamined because they cannot be readily represented in the form of standardized variables or easily subjected to replicable methods of empirical analysis (Sil, 2004).

While recognizing the constraints and pitfalls of ethnographic research in China, this chapter attempts to highlight how such research can improve our understanding of Chinese politics. Although more variable-oriented approaches may offer important insights, I argue that the expanded use of ethnographic research is critical to developing a more comprehensive approach for identifying and exploring different dimensions of Chinese politics and society. I suggest that ethnography can, in fact, shed new light on central issues in politics and aid the development of more empirically grounded, nuanced, and rigorous

---

[1] Michael Burawoy makes a similar point in his review of early anthropological studies. See Burawoy (2000: 9).

arguments. Although ethnography places heavy emphasis on "thick description," it is important to note that in the course of depicting the complexity surrounding particular people in a particular place and time, ethnography also affords a stronger grasp of the multiple and sometimes hidden factors that trigger, sustain, or obstruct change. In focusing on the specific and the concrete, social scientists can avoid exaggerating the significance of a priori deductive reasoning as well as the overcommitment to and misapplication of theoretical constructs and categories.[2] Indeed, I agree with James Scott when he asserts that social scientists in general and political scientists in particular are more likely to make lasting intellectual contributions to debates within the field if they balance their preference for what the ancient Greeks called *techne*, or settled knowledge, with a greater respect for *metis*, or practical knowledge, the facts that defy easy categorization (Scott, 1998: 319–323). Paying closer attention to outliers and anomalies would not only precipitate deeper understandings of local concerns and practices but also provide new opportunities to reexamine, refine, and challenge the assumptions undergirding existing theories and concepts.

Ethnography alone cannot fully resolve these problems, but it does offer a more holistic understanding of interactions and processes that often escape scholarly analysis and establishes a stronger basis for understanding what Charles Ragin terms "multiple conjunctural causation" (Ragin, 1987). In this sense, ethnography is less at odds with current trends in political science and China studies that stress quantitative and variable-oriented research approaches than one might imagine; indeed, more ethnographic research can arguably augment efforts to capture the interactions and effects of macro processes in micro settings and vice versa. In this way, we might not only improve our ability to test one hypothesis against alternative explanations but also establish an epistemological "middle ground" that fosters greater dialogue among scholars across disciplines and even advance the cumulation of knowledge in the social sciences (Sil, 2000a: 166).

THE ETHNOGRAPHIC EYE

The advantages and pitfalls of ethnographic research have been the subject of intense debate in the social sciences. Long associated with anthropologists and sociologists, this research approach has effectively opened up both seemingly familiar neighborhoods and faraway places to scholarly analysis. As Michael Burawoy points out, pioneering works like W. I. Thomas and Florian Znaniecki's *The Polish Peasant in Europe and America* (1918) and Bronislaw Malinowski's work (1922) on the Trobriand community set the stage for the rise of major ethnographic studies that later became the hallmark of the Chicago School (Burawoy, 2000: 7–11). These works examine how ordinary actors perceived and responded to their world as it was beset by unprecedented

---

[2] See Emerson, Fretz, and Shaw (1995: 111).

changes in patterns of economic production, social organization, and political authority. Other studies reveal how more remote communities remained relatively unaffected by such factors. All offered a vital corrective to elite-oriented analyses by focusing considerably more attention on nonelite individuals and groups – their thoughts, strategies, and actions. Through extensive conversations with locals and the scholars' own lived experiences as members of the studied community, these accounts expanded scholarly understandings of the ways in which they coped with, and even resisted, the seemingly invisible macro forces that enveloped them.

Despite such breakthroughs, social scientists often criticize ethnography as a research methodology for its dependence on anecdotes and impressionistic evidence rather than on rigorous empirical analysis or parsimonious theoretical models. The seeming fixation of many an ethnographer on gathering an ever-growing collection of fine details, whose value in generating broader generalizations about political dynamics is puzzling to some, only reinforces the impression that ethnographers are little more than storytellers. This is exacerbated by popular perceptions of ethnographers as dashing figures cut from the same cloth as the celebrated medical anthropologist Paul Farmer, who seems to exude in equal measure daring, idealism, and toughness. Individuals like Farmer achieved rock star status not only because of their personal courage and uncompromising commitment, but more important, because they practiced what Farmer himself calls an "anthropology [that] concerned itself less with measurement than with meaning" (Kidder, 2003: 72) and appealed to a wide readership by revealing how a common humanity still exists in even the most uncommonly wretched and forgotten places.

Other critics point out that the process of ethnographic data collection rarely, if ever, accords with the strictures of the scientific method, which are presumed to apply equally to quantitative and qualitative analysis (King, Keohane, and Verba, 1994). From this perspective, ethnographers are seen as relying too much on serendipitous encounters and personal observations, with little concern for selection bias or sampling errors. Because ethnographers emphasize understanding how multiple factors, material and ideational at both the individual and structural levels, combine to produce specific outcomes in a given context, they do not focus on the causal significance of specific variables in producing a distribution of outcomes. Seeing this as a sign that ethnographic scholarship lacks rigor, critics contend that the conclusions drawn from these works remain at best atheoretical (and possibly subjective) interpretations of particular circumstances. Even proponents of "analytic narratives" (Bates et al., 1998; Levi, 2004), although seemingly intent on combining theoretical models and deep knowledge of particular cases, bypass the complexities posed by the multiplicity of local narratives and ultimately turn to the logic of strategic games for their causal analyses (Sil, 2000b: 375). Efforts to push ethnography in a more theoretical direction have not been helped by the poststructuralist turn in some quarters of anthropology and sociology where the apparent adoption of a more relativistic epistemological stance has called into question the possibility of value-neutral representations by the scholar-observer in the field (Rosenau, 1992). Given these developments, it is not surprising that many political scientists are skeptical that the often delightful anecdotes collected by their colleagues can be anything more than just "stories."

Such criticism is not totally unjustified. Ethnographers concentrate so much on capturing the singular uniqueness of specific people in specific circumstances that they sometimes fail to bring out the full theoretical implications embedded in their work. However, the perceived gulf between ethnographers and political scientists is often overstated. Here, it is important to note that ethnography is not and has never been totally divorced from theory. As Clifford Geertz points out, the ethnographer "confronts the same grand realities that others – historians, economists, political scientists, sociologists – confront in more fateful settings: Power, Change, Faith, Oppression, Work, Passion, Authority, Beauty, Violence, Love, Prestige; but he confronts them in contexts obscure enough … to take the capital letters off them" (Geertz, 1973: 21). To be sure, ethnographers could and should address theoretical issues more directly and deliberately, but the larger point here is that the raw empirical data contained within ethnographic accounts are indispensable to the development of sophisticated explanations. Although ethnographers are justifiably reluctant to generalize on the basis of one study, it is clear that such studies can nevertheless ground and extend the import of theory by testing its relevance in new or previously understudied sociopolitical contexts.

Moreover, ethnographic accounts are valuable because they often force scholars to reevaluate developments and processes with a fresh perspective. The anthropologist George Marcus warns against sticking too closely to established categories and modes of reasoning, for "if there is anything left to discover by ethnography it is relationships, connections, and indeed cultures of connection, association, and circulation that are completely missed through the use and naming of the object of study in terms of categories 'natural' to subjects' preexisting discourses about them" (Marcus, 1998: 16). Similarly, when Kevin O'Brien conducted research on local people's congresses in China, he found that by adopting a "flexible approach to question choice, question order, and follow-up inquiries," it became obvious when "[a question] had been conceptualized incorrectly or [when he] had posed a dilemma that did not exist or missed a dilemma that did" (O'Brien, 2006: 36). This does not imply by any means that ethnographers should or actually disregard key concepts within their respective disciplines; neither should it lead us to conclude that ethnographers are undisciplined in their research methodology. If anything, this search for "cultures of connection, association, and circulation" compels us first to clarify how we define and apply preexisting concepts informing our theoretical frameworks and then to test their analytical utility anew when new data are introduced. For O'Brien, making "mid-course corrections" or changes to the original questions or concepts as a result of conducting field research actually allowed him to refine concepts that extended from a "Western understanding of political reality to a place where it did not apply" (O'Brien, 2006: 30,37). Indeed, by uncovering the systemic regularities that are intertwined with the particularities of highly diverse settings, ethnographic studies demonstrate how the application of an *inductive* approach alongside a *deductive* one can enrich social science inquiry.

ETHNOGRAPHY AND CHINESE LABOR POLITICS

When opportunities to conduct ethnographic research appeared in conjunction with China's post-Mao reforms, scholars were eager to undertake new research but were confronted with a daunting set of challenges. Some involved practical concerns like securing access to field sites, dealing with possible government surveillance, and protecting respondents from potential harassment. Such constraints often made it difficult for many researchers to engage in anything more than what Thomas Gold (1989) has called "guerrilla interviewing." Moreover, given China's sheer size, ethnographers struggled mightily to find field sites that were, on one hand, relatively open to scholarly research and, on the other, representative of a cross-section of the country. Although these issues persist, scholars have nevertheless managed to conduct critical research that has filled in major gaps in how we understand major developments in contemporary Chinese society.

One of the key debates in the field is the nature and trajectory of China's industrial transformation and its impact on the multitude of workers who toil on the shop floor. Some recent works on Chinese labor have been especially illuminating in regard to the sometimes murky world of factory work. Ching Kwan Lee's *Gender and the South China Miracle*, for example, highlights how "diverse patterns of production politics emerge as conjunctural outcomes of the state, the labor market, and differentiated deployment of gender power" (Lee, 1998: 160). Her work shows how global economic forces and state objectives combine with such factors as native-place ties, age, and gender to shape the authoritarian management strategies and grueling work conditions in the two electronics plants she researched in southern China. Similarly, Pun Ngai's *Made in China* (2005) explores how female workers(打工妹) who anchor the factory workforce defy their male superiors despite the trauma they experience while working in an alienating, industrial setting. Both highlight the hidden battles and behind-the-scenes politics that employees engage in on the shop floor. Using the testimony and experiences of female workers, Lee and Pun successfully draw out micro-level data to show conclusively that production politics involves a more complicated, sometimes unseen set of negotiations and processes that simultaneously takes place on individual and collective planes. It is these processes that ultimately mold workers' ability and willingness to challenge work-related injustices and seek redress.

In comparison, my research on institutional origins and practices in rural enterprises was conducted in two townships in Wenzhou and Jinhua prefectures (Zhejiang) that were quite different in many respects from those Lee and Pun studied in southern China. Nevertheless, I also came upon a complex set of organizational dynamics that encompassed a sometimes confusing mix of formal requirements and informal practices. In order to untangle these strands, I first toured all of the major plants of Wenzhou-based Phoenix and Jinhua-based Jupiter,[3] shadowed key managerial staff throughout their work day, labored alongside production workers on the assembly line, and finally conducted multiple open-ended interviews with various personnel. In Wenzhou, I stayed in one of the company dormitories and ate with employees in the canteens. Over time, I became a part of the community and, as such, was never asked for gifts or payments.[4]

My extended stay allowed me to ask key questions about the genesis and implementation of company policies as well as the sources of resistance to them and their eventual evolution. More important, the data I collected prompted me to revise initial hypotheses regarding the linkage between financial incentives and employee compliance with managerial directives as well as the enterprise's overall profitability and efficiency. As a consequence of new discoveries I made through my interactions at these companies, I began to explore the organizational landscape differently, focusing on how official goals often diverged from the informal norms and practices that bind all members of the enterprise community together and how management struggles to bring both into closer alignment.

Scholars employing variable-oriented research approaches to study similar questions often find the incorporation of developments and data that fall outside the purview of their original research design a challenging task. An astonishing example of this emerged during my 1997 research stint in Wenzhou. That summer, a pair of Chinese researchers from the Chinese Academy of Social Sciences (CASS) arrived to conduct surveys of employee attitudes and to investigate management practices at several local firms. During their weeklong visit to Phoenix, they met with a "representative" group of managerial staff for a few hours to discuss their work experiences and the challenges they saw in working at a private firm. Not surprisingly, with their superiors observing the proceedings from the corner of the conference room, every staff member either made positive statements expressing a deep appreciation for the opportunity to better his or herself or said nothing at all. Who in their right minds, some participants remarked afterward, would state their true feelings and risk jeopardizing their jobs for the sake of a survey? Individually and collectively, they decided it was safer to express what they thought the researchers and their superiors wanted to hear.

---

[3] Phoenix and Jupiter are fictitious names I created to protect the identities of the companies and their employees.
[4] I did give many respondents small tokens of appreciation just before I left the field. These consisted of lapel pins, buttons, and school pennants and were symbolic of my appreciation and affection for them.

To their credit, the CASS researchers recognized the predicament of the employees and tried to counteract their reticence by attempting to elicit more candid responses through anonymous surveys. What they did not realize was that the employees saw the survey forms as an onerous burden; the participants had already spoken at earlier meetings and saw the surveys as another chore packed onto their already heavy work schedules. Toward the end of a lunch break one day, I overheard several members of the office in which I was based laughing about the responses some had written. When I asked them what was so funny, they told me that they had engaged in a bit of mischief. On questions regarding age and gender, for example, they deliberately gave the wrong answer. If the person was male, he instead wrote "female." If he was actually 25 years old, he instead wrote "52." On other questions, they simply didn't respond or gave simple "yes" or "no" answers, or even worse gave nonsensical answers. I never found out how extensive such behavior was but there were rumors that staff in other offices responded in a similar fashion. It seems they did so partly because they were upset about wasting their time on a seemingly meaningless task and partly because this became a chance to relieve some of their frustration and boredom without undermining themselves. The CASS researchers were not responsible for such mischief but this undoubtedly distorted the data they collected and, eventually, the findings of their study.

Although this example is undoubtedly extreme and hardly representative of all sample and survey-oriented studies, it nevertheless highlights major differences between more deductive and theory-driven research approaches and ethnography. For example, social scientists aiming to develop arguments that apply to a broad range of cases often cannot avoid making simplifying assumptions about complex social phenomena, whereas ethnographers seek and insist upon greater empirical validation for their assertions. Moreover, although variables and the relationships between them are often rigorously defined in more theory-driven studies, this type of work is less effective in uncovering how and when specific factors contribute to the generation of a particular result (Ragin, 1987: 54–56; Wedeen, 2004: 301). Hence, because the CASS researchers could not fully explore the magnitude or causes of employee mischief, the potential significance of employee frustration on their analysis was lost.

Even though the CASS researchers undoubtedly had little time to conduct a more comprehensive study, they remained relatively indifferent to exploring possible explanations falling outside the realm of their original research design. When, for instance, I asked the researchers whether they planned to hold more candid conversations with employees outside of the company's offices or workshops, neither felt it was necessary. Instead, by retiring to their hotel room in the evenings to analyze the data they had already gathered, they gave up on opportunities to uncover new information through additional discussions in less formal settings like over meals or cups of tea. Their attitude paralleled the behavior of economists, as described by Truman F. Bewley:

In economics there has been a tendency to suppose that you shouldn't ask people what they're doing or what their own motives are because they'll deceive you, or they won't know what their own motives are, they don't understand them, they'll exaggerate their own roles, and glorify themselves, and so on. So what you do is put a distance between yourself and the subject matter. This can be healthy in some circumstances, but it can also be unhealthy. It's like treating the economy as if it were like some distant galaxy and then you are really stuck with using only very indirect theoretical and statistical methods to understand it. I think those are useful but I think you need to have more immediate experience (Bewley, 2004: 382).

Put another way, sticking strictly to their original research design reduced their engagement with "a great variety of people in different circumstances" and made it more difficult for them to see a larger and more logically coherent story (Bewley, 2004: 383). To be sure, this illustration is not meant to highlight how employees at Phoenix were all disingenuous and uncooperative nor is it intended to denigrate the serious efforts of the CASS researchers. What it does underscore are the limitations of a research approach that, however well conceived, is less attuned to uncovering, identifying, and investigating new leads. By contrast, an ethnographer instinctually seeks to take into account the unspoken and the unseen alongside the "official transcript"[5] and to use that data to weigh the significance of what had been presented in a more public and high-risk forum.

The implication here is that devoting greater attention to understanding the relationships in which enterprise employees are enmeshed as well how actors define and understand the challenges before them – the process of "meaning-making" as Lisa Wedeen (2002: 717) calls it – will greatly enrich our studies. In the previous example, employees gave positive responses because they believed that was what the researchers expected and because they feared retribution from their superiors if they said anything that could potentially tarnish the company's image. Their answers masked deep-seated resentment and frustration with the way their superiors treated them. Again, the problem is that given the predilection of survey research methodology for parsimony and rigor, much of the "noise" that could be important in explaining social and political phenomena is filtered out of the analysis before its full significance can be ascertained. Unfortunately, the CASS study did not contain a mechanism by which such factors could be incorporated and considered.

Ethnography is distinctive and valuable not only because it can uncover hidden dynamics, but because it emphasizes "moving pictures" over "snapshots." What Paul Pierson's (2004: 2) observation means is that in studies that are geared more toward theory-testing, political and social developments often appear to be "frozen in time." One-shot surveys certainly reveal a tremendous amount regarding singular moments, but long-term participant

---

[5] The term comes from the work of James Scott. The implication is that accurate reads of power relations in any context require in-depth studies of what goes on behind the scenes, beyond the public record or official transcript. See Scott (1990).

observation captures a fuller sense of process, of how we get from point A to point B. For ethnographers, history not only matters, but, more important, is seen as central to the development of broader and deeper understandings. In the case of Phoenix as well as other enterprises, without past work practices and authority orientations serving as a reference point, it becomes inordinately difficult to understand why some members of the company's managerial staff became emboldened to undermine their superiors' directives, for such patterns are indicative of other underlying disagreements and conflicts at work.

On this score, my research reveals that this behavior is largely connected to changes in organizational structure and management practices, ones that undercut a more personal and trust-based approach in favor of one that is more impersonal, hierarchical, and routinized, that is, bureaucratic. The concentration of authority in the hands of a select group of managers and the concomitant erosion of personal initiative and control among the enterprise's lower ranking members is a major source of friction and strain on all employees: the survey respondents' mischief-making was a means of venting their frustration over being saddled with what they perceived to be time-wasting activities. It was also a way of exacting a small measure of revenge on their superiors without having to suffer any fallout for their actions.

ETHNOGRAPHY, ORGANIZATIONAL CHANGE,
AND INSTITUTION-BUILDING

In addition to providing more accurate understandings of employee attitudes and motivations, ethnographic research provides vital insights into the nature and fault lines of organizational dynamics in China. At both Phoenix and Jupiter, for instance, enterprise executives actually invited local party representatives to establish branches of party-affiliated mass organizations – the trade union, the Women's Federation, and the Communist Youth League (CYL) – during the early to mid-1990s. Why did enterprise leaders unexpectedly bring the party back in when the consensus in scholarly and policy-making circles was that the party should stay out of enterprise affairs whenever possible? Rather than simply assume that the reemergence of party-affiliated institutions in these companies meant that politics was once again in command, my ethnographic approach shows that the party is now in the unusual position of supporting rather than supplanting the directives and policies of management. Moreover, employee commitment to party ideals has also waned considerably, further undermining a possible party resurgence. When I attended an enterprise-wide party meeting at Jupiter in 1998, it was clear that most of the members were uninspired by socialist pronouncements. Despite the exhortations of party officials and company executives to work hard for the development of the country, several young men present snickered and laughed (most of the women were quiet and more respectful) and even ridiculed some of the speakers for their verbal gaffes and doubted their sincerity and commitment. At Phoenix, employees were less boisterous and critical than their Jupiter counterparts, but they too were unmoved by the goals and ideals articulated at party-sponsored events. In 2004, Phoenix held a two-day retrospective commemorating the centennial of Deng Xiaoping's birth. Although all senior staff were present, almost no one paid close attention to the proceedings. In fact, I was amazed when two of my respondents (one was actually a key organizer) answered my telephone calls during the meeting in a low whisper for fear of being too disruptive. They told me afterward that this was regrettable but unavoidable since they were still responsible for critical and pending decisions.

What participant observation and ethnography also uncovered was that the turbulent course of rationalization and the increased number of nonlocal migrants who dramatically altered the workforce compositions of both firms during the late 1980s and early 1990s had precipitated unprecedented social conflict within the enterprises. As management in both firms sought to build upon its earlier success by routinizing and expanding operations, it undercut prevailing work practices that emphasized personal initiative and norms of reciprocity and trust. Employees, especially locals (本地人) who had worked at these companies since their founding, became increasingly frustrated by what they saw as an overly strict work regimen; they also resented heightened job competition from migrants, both skilled and unskilled. To them, their hard-fought gains and status were coming under siege, producing anxiety as well as sporadic but growing resistance. Increasing class and social tensions within the workforce were accelerating the loss of skilled personnel and a decline in productivity. Thus, by bringing the party back into the workshops, enterprise executives hoped to use the party's extensive experience in organization to bridge social fissures they had failed to resolve rather than to resuscitate the party's preeminence within the enterprise.

Similar efforts to quell internal dissension have been documented in such classic accounts as Richard Cyert and James March's *A Behavioral Theory of the Firm* (1992) and more recent studies like Kathleen Thelen's *How Institutions Evolve* (2004). Although neither is an ethnographic study of organizational behavior, each meticulously traces how different actors can build coalitions to articulate and advance their own interests and those of their allies. As new challenges and interests emerge, these coalitions may try to hold their partnerships together through the reallocation of "slack resources"[6] or choose to remake their alliances. At Jupiter and Phoenix, executives adopted a similar strategy with the party serving as its "front man." They used company profits to provide a variety of collective benefits to all employees, ranging from the inexpensive – bars of soap, containers of cooking oil, cases of soda – to the more costly – new clothes, day trips to local attractions, free yearly medical examinations, and subsidized meals. All were designed to convince employees

---

[6] "Slack resources" refers to resources that exceed what is needed to attain organizational goals. These include but are not limited to capital and labor.

that life at the enterprise could be highly rewarding and would remain so as long as all devoted themselves to becoming "good workers" (Edwards, 1977: 147–152).

To win the hearts and minds of employees, union representatives and members of the CYL also worked tirelessly to organize a vast array of events that entertained as well as promoted a strong company identity that superseded workplace rivalries and native-place allegiances. Most of these took the form of "matches of skill" (比武) and employees generally accepted these with enthusiasm. For instance, production line workers were encouraged to take part in contests measuring how quickly and skillfully they could assemble the items they were charged with churning out each day. Similarly, office staff members were challenged on their typing, accounting, and even their communication skills. Later, speech contests in which employees were commonly invited to speak about how much they had grown personally and professionally since their tenure at the company began were added.

For participants and onlookers alike, speech contests can cause both anxiety and excitement. For some entrants, there was enormous pressure to excel; for audience members, office pride and prestige were on the line. One female respondent who worked in Phoenix's public relations office was particularly nervous about the tryouts. If she did not advance to the final round, she felt she was not only embarrassing herself but also letting down her office-mates. In contrast, although the less well-spoken and less-experienced competitors knew they did not have the necessary polish to advance, they were nevertheless determined to share their experiences with the judges and the audience. In fact, they delivered some of the most memorable lines, ones that drew rousing applause because of their earnestness and joy. A middle-aged female custodian, for example, relayed how other employees treated her with great respect and consideration despite her low status in the company. She commented: "All I do is keep the restrooms clean – it's not a very important job. But whenever I run into others, they always ask me how I am doing and tell me not to tire myself out. They are always looking out for me. No one cared about me at any of my previous jobs." Although other employees did not always share such sentiments, they could still appreciate how she felt.

Even as members of the Phoenix community recognized that factory life had many shortcomings, many also understood just how far the company had come. These events provide employees with a venue for releasing pent-up frustration and to come together without worrying about workplace rivalries or competing social allegiances. Others feel that progress on breaking down stereotypes and eliminating at least some discriminatory employment practices has been achieved. A twenty-something female member of Phoenix's Central Accounting Office who is a local, stated flatly:

The company has gotten better about trusting nonlocals with important jobs – it wasn't always this way. In my accounting department, for example, almost one-third of the staff are nonlocals. When I first arrived in 1996, all positions were exclusively reserved for locals.... But now they've changed their views and can accept these staffing changes.[7]

Similarly, an outsider in his early thirties who recently had risen in 1998 from quality control inspector to assistant manager of a division expressed positive sentiments: "Locals don't discriminate against outsiders as much as before; in fact, most of our workers and mid-ranking personnel are outsiders. The leaders have more respect for workers and pay more attention to their needs. There is still some friction on occasion but it's not as bad as in the past."[8]

The party also seeks to boost the morale of newer and younger workers through their affiliates. According to the current CYL secretary,

> the reason we organize events is so that employees don't feel like there is no life beyond work. Of course, their main reason for being here is to earn money – I understand that. But their time here should be more than going to work in the morning and returning home at night – what's the point of that? ... I always tell members that should they leave the company, they can take these experiences and memories with them. It will remind them of good times.[9]

Despite their long work days, many members remain enthusiastic about organizing and participating in CYL events. One male in his mid-twenties commented that organizing events was "a kind of training" (锻炼) and a great way to meet people. It's an opportunity for us to develop our talents."[10] Similarly, the Women's Federation (妇联) representatives have concentrated on improving promotion opportunities for female employees and raising awareness of stress induced by work and personal relationships (or lack thereof). The Women's Federation head, a woman in her early thirties, noted that just listening to women's concerns is an important service because the "employee is sometimes embarrassed or reluctant to talk, especially if the representative is male. So often they call me directly when we talk on the phone. What we do is listen carefully to them. After the worker is done describing her complaint, we analyze the situation and then lay out the consequences of taking a certain action. We try to help them find the best solution to their problem, but it's very difficult. There is only so much we can do."[11]

These findings both complicate accepted understandings of how organizational control is established and provide a significant opportunity for revising such theories. The developments at Phoenix reveal that this process does not simply work in a top-down fashion, but instead it is the result of complicated negotiations involving all segments of the enterprise community. To be sure, employees are reluctant to use anything other than "weapons of the weak"

---

[7] Respondent #94, personal interview, August 11, 2004.
[8] Respondent #42, personal interview, August 18, 2004.
[9] Respondent #128, personal interview, August 12, 2004.
[10] Respondent #132, personal interview, August 17, 2004.
[11] Respondent #87, personal interview, August 7, 2004.

(Scott, 1985) in their struggles against managerial power, a clear acknowledgment of their subordinate status vis-à-vis management. Nevertheless, managerial attempts to restore labor stability and social peace within the organization represent a clear recognition that different thresholds of legitimate behavior not only exist but that they are vital to maintaining social cohesion. In this sense, these findings are consonant with but may also help refine the theoretical import of Chester Barnard's concept of "zones of indifference" as well the insights offered by the moral economy perspective (Barnard, 1968; Scott, 1976). They also suggest that in addition to material incentives, employees view how the company treats them as individuals with an especially critical eye and will constantly recalibrate their demands accordingly. That is to say, the "zone of indifference" may not be as large as we once imagined, nor the floor for trust and reciprocity as low as we once thought.

Indeed, *informal* factors – membership in kinship and native-place networks – have a profound influence on how authority is constructed and perpetuated at the highest levels of the enterprises. Managers are still inclined to select candidates with whom they are most familiar and see as more trustworthy. As one outsider technical specialist at Phoenix suggested, "Management is scared that if we are given more authority and responsibility, we'll learn all of the company's strategies and secrets. They're afraid this information will fall into the hands of competitors if we leave."[12] In 1998, few outsiders served as plant vice managers at Phoenix; in fact, only one outsider made it to the position of factory manager, and this was only by virtue of his long-standing personal friendship with the enterprise founder. Although a 1998 "purge" of factory-level managers removed a significant number of distant relatives and locals from the managerial ranks, closer relations, like the founder's brother and brother-in-law, remain firmly ensconced in high-ranking positions.

This situation reflects the continued influence of what Mark Granovetter calls "strong ties" (1973: 1360–1380), which, in this case, remain nested in the kinship and social networks that anchor the enterprise's personnel core. As long as this group remains on the scene, their prominence in decision making is not likely to wane soon, despite their somewhat diminished numbers. In contrast, the persistence of informal status distinctions was even more pronounced at Jupiter. The managers of each of the enterprise's most profitable subsidiaries are members of the president's inner circle. For example, his son and son-in-law are general managers of critical divisions as is his niece's husband and another close relation who once bailed him out of trouble.[13] Even at lower levels, similar patterns of domination by locals are evident. At the factory manager rank, 142 of 158 managers hailed from the local prefecture; of the remaining sixteen positions, nine were from areas

---

[12] Respondent #29, personal interview, August 21, 1997.
[13] Respondent #110, personal interview, June 30, 1998.

outside the prefecture but within Zhejiang province and seven were from outside the province.[14]

These developments not only suggest that the process of establishing a hegemonic factory regime (Burawoy, 1985) rests on decision-making power, informal status differences, and the distribution of slack resources, but, more important, they underscore how managers link and manipulate such factors that can enhance or inhibit their ability to mobilize collective action and preserve their own interests. Incorporating these insights into the fields of Chinese politics and organization theory and institutions allows us to better understand how the variability of these factors produces and reproduces consequential structures that we often take for granted (Nohria and Gulati, 1994: 550–551).

CONCLUSION

The field of Chinese politics has made enormous strides in recent years. The availability of new research materials, improved access to archives, as well as new information from field studies have allowed scholars to explore and better understand the contours and ramifications of China's current transition from socialism. These data have also provided an opportunity for scholars to apply a number of different research methodologies in the hope of developing more sophisticated theories of political behavior and change.

Although most political scientists consider ethnography to be a rather limited research approach, it offers a powerful and underutilized means of investigating and understanding larger trends and developments in Chinese social and political life that cannot be easily detected or explained through formal models, statistical approaches, or broad cross-national comparisons. The distinct utility of ethnographic research stems not only from its careful attention to how specific actors think and behave in a particular place and time, but, perhaps more important, from an appreciation of how a complex, interconnected set of forces and processes collectively generates the outcomes we seek to understand. As vitally important as untangling these strands is to deepening our knowledge of political phenomena, such efforts sometimes appear to undermine scholarly attempts at developing more rigorous and practical explanations. In focusing on particular causal mechanisms while often neglecting others, competing research traditions a priori overlook the interrelationships between individual-level and structural forces and how they produce consequential shifts in both political and social phenomena. Understanding the complexity of these linkages requires the use of a much wider range of lenses and in that spirit, ethnography offers a fresh perspective and critical insights that are not otherwise possible.

In grappling with the different meanings that individuals and groups accord to their actions, practices, and worlds, the China field is poised to reexamine

---

[14] These data are drawn from Jupiter's 1997 internal reports on its workforce.

and revise not only the assumptions animating existing theories, but more important, to reevaluate the accepted wisdom on how and why specific outcomes are determined. In the process, we are restoring a sense of richness and depth that comes from the close study of specific people in particular circumstances. Integrating the "extraordinary diversity that makes up the Chinese political experience" (Perry, 1994b: 712) into scholarly debates promises to fuel increased exchange and expansion of knowledge in the social sciences.

8

More Than an Interview, Less Than Sedaka
Studying Subtle and Hidden Politics with Site-Intensive Methods

Benjamin L. Read

The field of Sinology has benefited greatly in the past twenty years from a rich array of studies based on ethnography and participant observation.[1] Anthropologists, not surprisingly, have led the way (Bruun, 1993; Chen, 2003; Fong, 2004; Friedman, 2006; Gladney, 1996; Hertz, 1998; Jacka, 2004; Jankowiak, 1993; Jing, 1996; Judd, 1994; Kipnis, 1997; Litzinger, 2000; Liu, 2000; Murphy, 2002; Notar, 2006; Perkins, 2002; Pun, 2005; Rofel, 1999; Schein, 2000; Watson and Watson, 2004; Yan, 1996, 2003; Yang, 1994; Zhang 2001). A number of sociologists also embrace these methods (Calhoun, 1994; Chan, Madsen, and Unger, 1992, 2009; Farrer, 2002; Lee, 1998).[2] Whatever its disciplinary origin, and whether the specific topic is interpersonal relationships or village governance or migrant entrepreneurs, much of this work is strongly *political* in orientation. It hardly seems possible to come away from such books without acquiring immensely valuable knowledge about the workings of power in China, particularly at the local level.

Several political scientists have applied versions of these research techniques in China as well.[3] But these methods have a more problematic relationship with the discipline of political science. Though members of our field have long employed ethnography and participant observation (which I group together below under the term "site-intensive methods"), such approaches have never been seen as mainstream. The discipline is now going through a process of energetic debate over what constitutes important knowledge and what methods usefully contribute to such knowledge. Practitioners of other qualitative methods began some time ago to weigh in with articulate statements explaining

---

Parts of this chapter were published in the Fall 2006 issue of the newsletter of the APSA organized section on Qualitative Methods.

[1] This is to say nothing of earlier work by Fei Xiaotong, Sidney Gamble, and others. Also, this chapter deals only with English-language studies.
[2] I owe thanks to Elizabeth J. Perry, Li Zhang, and Ethan Michelson for bringing to my attention some of the items mentioned here.
[3] In addition to the works discussed later, see Blecher and Shue (1996), Friedman, Pickowicz, and Selden (2005), Hurst (2009), Steinfeld (1998), K. Tsai (2002), (2007).

how what they do fits into the process of building and testing political science theory. A new generation of ethnographers and participant observers has recently emerged as well (Schatz, 2009b). As Schatz notes, members of this group differ among themselves, with those identified as interpretivists challenging multiple aspects of the ontology and epistemology of mainstream political science. Others, he writes, carry out ethnographic work in a qualified neopositivist mode, one that "uses attention to detail to generate middle-range theories, that considers cumulative knowledge a possibility worth pursuing, and that is optimistic about the scholar's potential to offer contributions" (Schatz, 2009a: 14). While I applaud the idea that politics should be studied from many perspectives, not merely those fitting within scientific paradigms, what I have to say here falls within the latter category. I argue that political scientists of many stripes can and should appreciate the value of the fieldwork techniques under discussion.

This chapter draws on examples from research on China as well as other locations. Most of what it has to say is not specific to any one country. It makes an argument that site-intensive methods form a particularly appropriate and often necessary part of the apparatus used to study China, though the argument pertains just as well to other non-Western and other politically repressive settings. I wish to develop the theme that those who use ethnography and related techniques need to build bridges with one another rather than digging moats as is sometimes the case. This means cultivating greater awareness of what specialists of other regions are doing, among other things.

The revitalization of ethnographic work in political science that I am advocating – building on existing studies – has two components to it. The first concerns how we, the practitioners, conceptualize our work, what we do in the field, and how we write up and package our findings. We should strive to come together on accounts of this methodology that can guide what we do and help make the research process as efficient and productive as possible. The second concerns the discipline more generally. To some extent, bringing site-intensive methods to full fruition in political science requires efforts to shape the discipline itself. It is necessary to make more clear to other political scientists how these methods fit into the methodological world with which they are familiar. Only then will this type of work, whether on China or anywhere else, achieve its maximum potential.

This chapter particularly concerns *trade-offs* that are inherent in site-based research, notably the balancing of breadth (studying more units, maximizing variation among them) and depth (getting the most validity, richness, and understanding out of each unit). Although by no means uniquely so in the social sciences, political scientists are obliged to confront issues of generalizability. Our work is expected to speak in abstract terms to conceptual questions of broad interest to our peers, and the explaining of variation is prized. Sometimes the most appropriate research strategy lies at one or the other end of the spectrum: training microscopic scrutiny on a single locale, as in James Scott's (1985) famous study of the Malaysian village he called "Sedaka," or applying thin measures to a large number of sites or respondents, as in much survey research. Often, though, there are reasons for pursuing a compromise approach in which a small or medium number of units is observed in ways that obtain some fraction of the depth that can be achieved in traditional ethnography. Although there can be no formula that resolves this dilemma neatly for all projects, this chapter attempts to conceptualize and clarify some of the factors involved.

Finally, I happen to be a committed proponent of applying multiple or "mixed methods" to attacking empirical questions in political science. In my own work on neighborhood organizations in China and Taiwan, for example, I have adopted an approach that pairs the deeper insights from participant observation and interviews with thinner but more extensive survey data. Some of the other research considered in the pages that follow is also multimethod, and the benefits of exploiting more than one type of information will be evident in the discussion. However, ethnographic and participant-observation methods need to be understood and justified on their own terms as well as in combination with other approaches.

SITE-INTENSIVE METHODS

The methods that generally go under the labels *ethnography* and *participant observation* occupy a somewhat awkward place in political science (Bayard de Volo and Schatz, 2004). Our discipline lays claim to prominent, if rather isolated, examples of scholarly work based on these methods – with perhaps the two most widely read being Fenno's *Home Style* (1978) and Scott's *Weapons of the Weak* (1985). A subset of empirical researchers has always been drawn to them, going back at least as far as the immediate post–World War II generation and presumably earlier (Banfield, 1958). They are discussed on the occasional conference panel. They are actively employed in much exciting research today, by themselves or in conjunction with other methods (non-China examples include Adams, 2003; Allina-Pisano, 2004; Bayard de Volo, 2001; Cammett, 2005, 2007; Galvan, 2004; MacLean, 2004, 2010; Roitman, 2004; Schatz, 2004; Straus, 2006).

And yet, these methods remain marginal. I think it is fair to say that they only occasionally crop up in methodology curricula. Even within the world of the American Political Science Association's organized sections on qualitative and mixed methods and the stimulating ferment that has been fostered in recent years, they have shown up so far as a distant cousin. Very little in this vein appeared on the 2006 Institute for Qualitative Research Methods (IQRM) syllabus, for example. Two of the most important recent books on qualitative methods, although immensely useful to ethnographers and participant observers, also seem to have been written without these approaches particularly in mind (George and Bennett, 2004; Brady and Collier, 2004).

What are the reasons for this marginality? Let me first mention a few obvious ones. Acquiring the skills needed to use these methods and then applying them is time-consuming and costly, particularly when research is conducted in foreign-language settings. They are thus rather difficult to recommend in good conscience to the average graduate student who is under pressure to minimize time to completion. Also, other methods skills are much more in demand within the discipline as a whole.

But clearly there are other reasons as well. Practitioners are split by apparent differences in epistemology, such as the previously mentioned divide between "interpretivists" and "positivists," which looms large in some recent accounts (Burawoy, 1998; Schatz, 2006; Yanow, 2003). There is also a hesitance on the part of many to go beyond describing what they did in their own research to suggesting sets of general procedures for others to follow. Efforts within political science to spell out the benefits of these methods for building and testing theory have so far been limited. Finally, and perhaps most important, there has been no real push to build a coalition behind the critical appreciation, application, and teaching of ethnography and participant observation.

I believe an appropriate step forward would be for researchers who use these methods – either exclusively or in combination with other methods – to work toward building a coalition or users group within the discipline. This enterprise would start by identifying common ground in a related set of *approaches to the gathering of sources, evidence, and data*. This would, one hopes, cross-cut and set aside underlying epistemological divides.

An umbrella term bringing together a set of related methods might be useful. One such term would be *site-intensive methods* (SIMS), referring to the collection of evidence from human subjects within their ordinary settings, where their interaction with the surroundings informs the study just as the researcher's own questioning does. This implies the need for a deeper engagement with a site, context, locality, or set of informants than is obtained from, for instance, telephone surveys or some types of one-time interviews.[4] This term would subsume most of what is referred to as "ethnography" and "participant observation," and perhaps some forms of other practices, such as focus groups. It would also highlight the diverse forms that this research takes, including studies that strive for a high degree of depth in a single locale along with those that aim for breadth as well, and projects in which SIM is the main course, so to speak, as well as others where it is more of a side dish.

I somewhat reluctantly suggest some new term like SIMS in part because I am not convinced that other categories are up to the task of bringing together the most useful and productive coalition of researchers within political science. "Ethnography" on its own has the advantage of a long pedigree within the social sciences and a voluminous methodological literature, especially in anthropology. But it may have drawbacks as well. Some versions of the anthropological model may set the bar too high in implying that months or years of immersion are required to obtain insights. It may connote a holistic orientation according to which the entirety of a community or locale must be

---

[4] In fact, some kinds of surveys and interviews require considerable stage-setting and trust-building; see Posner (2004).

comprehended to make sense of any one part. It should be pointed out that the meaning and practices of ethnography today are undergoing evolution and sharp debate; by no means do all practitioners see ethnography as limited to these forms.[5] Nonetheless, the term seems to me problematic as applied to projects employing shorter stints of fieldwork and less encompassing modes of information gathering.

"Participant observation" would also seem to be a possible umbrella term. Yet here too, the boundaries implied by this concept may not be coterminous with what it is we want to bring together. On the one hand, the researcher "participates" in other kinds of research, such as straight-up interviews. Conversely, to some it may imply that only through a long-term process in which the researcher becomes a part of community life can full or meaningful participation be achieved. Some may feel that this covers only a subset of the practices comprised by ethnography whereas others see the two concepts as interchangeable.

As noted earlier in this chapter, two studies, by Fenno (1978) and Scott (1985), may be the most widely read examples of site-intensive methods in political science. Reflecting on these books in particular provides an opportunity to consider what it might take to promote an initiative within the discipline that incorporates and promotes both types of research. Viewed from one perspective, they can be seen as strongly contrasting, perhaps almost polar opposites in their approach. Scott describes his project as a "close-to-the-ground, fine-grained account of class relations" (Scott, 1985: 41) in a Malaysian village, population 360, which goes under the pseudonym of Sedaka. Situating his methods in the ethnographic tradition of anthropologists (Scott, 1985: xviii, 46), Scott states that he spent at least fourteen months in Sedaka, interviewing, observing, and taking part in village life.

Fenno's (1978) work was motivated by questions concerning the relationship between politicians and those they claim to represent. "What does an elected representative see when he or she sees a constituency? And, as a natural follow-up: What consequences do these perceptions have for his or her behavior?" (Fenno, 1978: xiii). His approach was to spend time in the company of members of the U.S. House of Representatives in their home districts. He famously characterizes his research method as "largely one of soaking and poking – or just hanging around," and situates it explicitly within the tradition of participant observation as practiced by sociologists and other political scientists; ethnography is not mentioned, as far as I can tell (Fenno, 1978: xiv, 249, 295). In the text of the book and its long methodological appendix, Fenno candidly and rather self-deprecatingly explains his modus operandi of accompanying politicians wherever they would let him tag along, building rapport, recording their remarks, and asking questions when possible.[6] Clearly this was

---

[5] Marcus (1998), for example, provides arguments in support of multisited studies, albeit with reservations.
[6] He also discusses his methods in a 1986 *APSR* article and other essays, all reprinted in Fenno (1990).

a far "thinner" form of engagement with a research milieu than was Scott's village study. Relative to a single-site project, Fenno traded depth for breadth, studying eighteen different representatives and thus obtaining substantial variation on characteristics such as party affiliation and seniority (Fenno, 1978: 253–254). The total time he spent with each representative ranged from three working days to eleven, averaging six (Fenno, 1978: xiv, 256), and on some of those days the research subject was available only part of the time.[7]

Despite their differences, these books can readily be seen as belonging to a common category. Both scholars were propelled into the field by strongly theoretical motivations – theories of hegemony and false consciousness in one case, and theories of representation in the other. In both instances, the researchers identified an empirical subject of key importance where (at least as they portrayed it) existing accounts relied on assumptions that needed to be tested or fleshed out through on-the-ground study.

WHEN SHOULD RESEARCHERS USE SITE-INTENSIVE METHODS?

What are the circumstances under which these approaches are particularly valuable – sometimes even necessary – for political research? One way to view it is that such methods are especially valuable when what we are studying is *subtle* (for example, relationships, networks, identities, styles, beliefs, or modes of action),[8] and when what we are studying is *hidden*, sensitive, or otherwise kept behind barriers that require building trust, waiting to observe unguarded moments, or otherwise unlocking access.[9] Scott's and Fenno's projects serve again as examples. In both books, to simplify somewhat, the fundamental subject of study was individuals' perceptions (peasants' views of class relations and politicians' views of their constituents). These perceptions are both subtle and, most of the time, hidden. This fact made forms of research like surveys and short interviews unworkable and necessitated strategies involving trust-building and over-time observation.

Subtlety, as considered here, is in part a relative concept. The ways in which site-intensive methods are best applied to a problem may change significantly depending on the existing state of theory. The success of a project like Scott's, in the way that he framed it, hinged on the scholarly readership accepting false consciousness as a viable explanation or foil. How a specific application of site-intensive methods is pitched depends in part on the sophistication of existing hypotheses and data. If everyone agrees that X_4 has a positive relationship with Y when X_1, X_2, and X_3 are controlled for, and the debate is over the

---

[7] One could go on about the contrasts. Scott is, of course, particularly attuned to the voices and experiences of the subaltern, whereas Fenno does not conceal an often admiring sympathy for the elites whom he studies.

[8] In fact, most concepts I can think of in the realm of politics contain subtleties that probably deserve up-close scrutiny. At the same time, this is not at all to deny that less-intensive methods can also shed light on these topics.

[9] On hidden aspects of politics, see also Scott (1990) and Kuran (1995).

magnitude of the coefficient, whether the relationship is linear or quadratic, and whether an interaction term with X_5 is required, then merely observing that X_4 and Y appear linked does not provide as much added value as it would have earlier in the research cycle. But by no means are site-intensive methods appropriate only for little-studied topics or when existing theories are crude. To continue the above analogy, up-close fieldwork could still usefully point out that X_4 is more complex than we thought it was and requires new measures; that, in real life, the causality seems in fact to run from Y to X_4; or that the relationship is conditioned by other factors that previously had been ignored entirely.

This leads to one answer – in the affirmative – to the question of whether such methods have special applicability in a country like China. It would be a mistake to argue that sociopolitical phenomena in China are somehow "more subtle" than those elsewhere. But one might point out that China has long produced events and things that, at least initially, either confounded or else fit only problematically within the social science categories created in North America and Western Europe. A list would include the CCP's rise to power; the Cultural Revolution; local associations; patterns of interest representation; modes of contention and grievance articulation; rapid economic development under Communist Party rule; the transition from socialism; and even the PRC's current regime type. The question, "What is this phenomenon I am looking at in China a case of?" is not always easily answered.[10] This has created stumbling blocks but also opportunities for innovative contributions. Thus, as in the study of other non-Western systems, empirical phenomena in China need to be analyzed carefully before determining their relationship with existing concepts, and site-intensive methods are well suited for this.

The other part of this answer concerns "hidden" subjects. It should be emphasized again that even in open, liberal political systems, certain important topics remain hidden, such as a politician's true perceptions of his or her constituents. In China, barriers created by state controls lead, in some circumstances, to obstacles to access and concerns about the validity of the data that are obtained. China today is not as open as, say, Taiwan, nor as closed as, say, North Korea or Myanmar. Particular institutions or individuals vary greatly in how available they are. Occasionally, one can obtain what is needed from a government agency just by walking through the front door. For some topics, a short phone or questionnaire survey conducted by a stranger may be adequate. But a common configuration is one of *formal barriers and informal porousness*. In these circumstances, valid or usefully detailed information cannot be acquired in a single visit or conversation but can be obtained through a more patient approach. The proportion of settings in which relatively intensive strategies are required to obtain any valid information is large in China compared to countries with more open political institutions and stronger norms

---

[10] I thank Laura Stoker of the University of California, Berkeley, for insisting that students ask themselves the "What is this a case of" question.

of transparency and disclosure. Conversely, the rewards to approaches that involve trust-building and over-time information gathering are correspondingly large there and in other closed or semiclosed political systems.

For these reasons, certain kinds of projects require extensive cultivation of research sites whether or not they involve traditional aspects of ethnography, such as direct observation of human behavior. For example, Melani Cammett, in her project on Hezbollah in Lebanon, went through an elaborate process of establishing links with the organization in order to lay the groundwork for a series of interviews with its members.[11] Relatedly, studies like Whiting (2001) and Remick (2004), although not ostensibly ethnographic in nature, clearly relied on building rapport and networks within the two or three localities upon which they were based.

In my own work, I have used site-based methods as one way to study the state-fostered neighborhood organizations of China and Taiwan. These are known as Residents' Committees (RC) or Community Residents' Committees (社区居民委员会) in the former and neighborhood heads (里长) and block captains (邻长) in the latter. My research in China took place in seven different cities but focused on the city of Beijing. My goal there was to study several neighborhoods in different parts of the city and in a variety of socioeconomic settings. I wanted to choose my sites more or less at random. I also wished to avoid the "model" neighborhoods that each district establishes; in major cities, local and international visitors alike are routinely shepherded to such showcases. Equipped with a letter of introduction from my "host unit," the Chinese Academy of Social Sciences, but otherwise without special permission, I knocked on the doors of RC offices, identified myself, described my research, and asked to come in and chat.[12] In cases where the committees were receptive, I made repeated follow-up visits and eventually established a set of ten neighborhood sites in this fashion.[13] I spent about thirty half-days (morning or afternoon) with two of the committees, and made twelve to fifteen trips to most of the others over fourteen months of dissertation fieldwork (1999–2000) and during three shorter follow-up stays (2003–2007).[14] On each visit, I sat in the offices, chatted with the staff, and watched and listened as they went about their work.

The most fundamental purpose of my research was to understand the power dynamics of neighborhood communities and the kinds of relationships that

---

[11] As of June 2009, papers from this project were under review but not yet published.
[12] In two cases, initial contact was made informally through acquaintances, and in two other cases I took a more official route involving a personal contact at a Street Office but also obtaining formal permission via the city government and my host unit's foreign affairs office.
[13] In five neighborhoods I was turned away, either by the RC itself or by government officials. In two of these cases I was accompanied by a police officer to the local police station (派出所) and told not to return to the neighborhood. In two of the ten sites, after six successful visits the committees were told by the authorities to discontinue contact with me.
[14] In three of the ongoing sites I offered to teach English to staff members or their children, and for several months I ran a weekly language class in my apartment.

state-sponsored organizations at this ultra-local level have with the residents they notionally represent. These topics are subtle in that they feature complexity and nuance, and in that they vary across places, people, and situations. They are hidden, or at least potentially hidden, in that RCs or constituents might not speak frankly to strangers about these relationships, and in that interaction between them generally leaves no publicly available record. Direct observation does not automatically overcome these challenges. But by building familiarity and trust, by probing gently, and by happening to be present as the committees dealt with all manner of situations and problems, I could learn much about this point of contact between state power and urban society. The RCs thus exemplify the pattern described above: there are formal impediments to studying them, but it is often (though not always) possible to obtain entrée, especially via informal channels.

HOW DO SITE-INTENSIVE METHODS CONTRIBUTE TO THEORY?

In some circumstances, as the previous discussion indicates, gathering any valid data at all requires building ties of trust and familiarity with one's research subjects and the institutions in which they are embedded. This alone is a powerful rationale for site-intensive methods. But apart from this, it may be constructive to spell out at least four ways in which ethnographic work contributes to the building of social science concepts and theory.

First, ethnographic work can *inductively generate new hypotheses*. For Fenno (1978), the choice to conduct his field research by "soaking and poking" was in part driven by his conceptualizing the project as breaking trail through wholly uncharted territory. He argues that political scientists had previously all but ignored representatives' understandings of their districts and how they behaved there (Fenno, 1978: xiii). Given this theoretical tabula rasa, a "totally open-ended and exploratory" approach was needed:

> I tried to observe and inquire into anything and everything these members did. I worried about whatever they worried about. Rather than assume that I already knew what was interesting, I remained prepared to find interesting questions emerging in the course of the experience. (Fenno, 1978: xiv)

Whether it was absolutely necessary for Fenno to cast the project in this way seems open to question. In the course of acknowledging previous research, he states that "political science studies conducted in congressional constituencies have been few and far between," but goes on to cite no fewer than eight books and articles on this topic as just the ones that have been "the most helpful to me" (Fenno, 1978: xvi, n. 9). Moreover, I fear that Fenno's heavy emphasis on the unstructured nature of his project may have helped lead many members of the discipline to believe that participant observation is necessarily speculative and free-form, useful, at best, *only* for the earliest and most preliminary phases of a research cycle.

Nonetheless, this open-ended approach convincingly results in insights that can be taken as new hypotheses concerning politicians and voters' behavior. Though Fenno soft-pedals them somewhat, the hypotheses that he puts forward include these: House members in the early phases of their careers are most attentive to their districts; members focus most on constituents who are most organized and thus accessible in groups; and constituents care about personal attention, respect, and the assurance of access at least as much as they care about the representative's congruence with their own issue positions (Fenno, 1978: 215, 235, 240–242). His book thus provides a good example of the value of participant observation for inductively generating new theoretical claims.

Some of Calvin Chen's findings from his extensive ethnographic studies of Zhejiang enterprises can also be understood as falling into this category. As his chapter in this volume reports, among other things he discovered that Communist Party institutions were being established in these firms. As Chen indicates, without the benefit of the "worm's-eye view," it would be easy to misinterpret this as the authorities imposing their organizational hegemony, or else as the companies going through the motions of compliance in order to get a political pass. Instead, a surprising third possibility emerges: that the firms actively encourage this development in order to enlist the party's assistance in resolving social tensions among the workforce (C. Chen, 2006, 2008).

Second, site-intensive methods can also be used to *test hypotheses by gathering qualitative measures of their observable implications*. This formulation derives from King, Keohane, and Verba's *Designing Social Inquiry* (1994: 28–31). The notion that qualitative researchers can maximize the leverage they apply to the testing of hypotheses by identifying and evaluating as many as possible of their "observable implications," of which even a single case may have many stands, as one of the more constructive and less controversial messages of this book. Naturally, this echoes long-standing practices of case-based researchers.

The fine-grained accounts of villagers' narratives, rituals, insults, and struggles in Scott's *Weapons of the Weak* (1985) can be read as a series of tests of the "false consciousness" hypothesis. The village ne'er-do-well, Razak, provides one: "As a beneficiary of local patronage and charity, however reluctantly given, one might expect Razak to entertain a favorable opinion of his 'social betters' in the village. He did not.... 'They call us to catch their (runaway) water buffalo or to help move their houses, but they don't call us for their feasts ... the rich are arrogant'" (Scott, 1985: 12). Others appear in perceptions of local misers (Scott, 1985: 13–22), the celebration that results when a job-displacing combine bogs down in the mud (Scott, 1985: 163), and the conflict over the village gate that had protected villagers' paddy-hauling jobs (Scott, 1985: 212–220).

In my Beijing research, I used evidence gathered from the neighborhood sites to test several hypotheses about relations between constituents and their Residents' Committees. One such hypothesis concerned clientelism. In China and around the world, relationships between ordinary citizens and power-holders can take the form of patron-client ties, typically involving exchanges in which subordinates provide political support while superiors provide material goods and opportunities such as jobs. But my RC office visits showed that the committees' activists and supporters obtained few or no tangible rewards for helping to keep watch over the neighborhood and conveying information to and from the committees. They often received only token gifts such as towels and bars of soap at annual parties. The committees, closely managed by the Street Offices, had little latitude to channel state benefits toward them, and certainly not career opportunities. Instead, the activists' motivations proved to be similar to those of volunteers everywhere: a sense of pride and importance, and the pleasures of sociability. Private interviews with urban residents and quantitative surveys helped to reinforce this conclusion, but participant observation was crucial. Only by observing the activists day after day, by listening to them converse with the RC staff, by talking about these relationships with committee members who were willing to speak frankly about their work, and by acquiring a firsthand sense of just what material resources the committees control (and how limited these resources are) did I become convinced that the clientelism hypothesis is not the key to understanding this aspect of the state-society relationship.

Although the words, attitudes, and behavior of local interlocutors constitute one form of evidence – essentially, data points – that can be gathered to test hypotheses, this evidence can also take a different form, that of *causal process observations*. Seawright and Collier define such an observation as "an insight or piece of data that provides information about context, process, or mechanism, and that contributes distinctive leverage in causal inference" (Brady and Collier, 2004: 277). The search for such observations is essentially the same as what is meant by "process tracing." In political science, some of the most prominent methodological discussions of process-related evidence have taken place in the context of case-based research using historical sources.[15] The logic is the same for ethnography and participant observation. Indeed, site-intensive methods may be *even better* suited for gathering causal process observations, as they allow for active probing by the researcher rather than relying on the passive analysis of extant sources.

Lily L. Tsai's (2002, 2007a) multimethod research on conditions influencing public goods provision in Chinese villages provides outstanding examples of causal process observations derived through participant observation. In this project, much of the analytic power comes through quantitative evidence, in the form of a survey of 316 villages in four provinces, as well as a survey of villagers. Regression models estimated on these data offer evidence that, ceteris paribus, villages that possessed certain kinds of social institutions – notably,

---

[15] Chapter 10 of George and Bennett (2004) gives an overview of process-tracing with an eye toward research based on case studies drawing on historical documents. See also Sidney Tarrow's chapter in Brady and Collier (2004).

temple associations and villagewide lineage groups – also tended to provide good roads and schools. Tsai further employs a series of focused qualitative comparisons among at least nine villages to elucidate the causal link between these social institutions, termed "solidary groups," and the outcomes of interest. Each village case study is derived from visits of between two and twenty days and is presented in the space of several pages. Together they offer vivid illustrations of the causal processes that are in play. In Li Settlement, for example, leaders rallied their constituents on the basis of a common lineage and community spirit in collecting donations to pave a road; in Pan Settlement, by contrast, long-standing conflict among the sublineages impeded similar efforts.

A fourth way in which site-intensive methods make contributions is by *creating, correcting, and refining theoretical concepts* and the categories within which they are understood, measured, and analyzed. As Henry E. Brady points out in a defense of qualitative methods in political science more generally:

Concept formation, measurement, and measurement validity are important in almost all research and possibly of paramount importance in qualitative research. Certainly notions such as "civil society," "deterrence," "democracy," "nationalism," "material capacity," "corporatism," "group-think," and "credibility" pose extraordinary conceptual problems just as "heat," "motion," and "matter" did for the ancients. (Brady, 2004: 62)

Within the China field, the work of Kevin J. O'Brien and Lianjiang Li on "rightful resistance" springs to mind as embodying the importance of protracted, up-close study for concept formation (O'Brien, 1996; O'Brien and Li, 2006). The authors note that their work to date leaves a number of avenues open for later exploration, such as explaining when governments react negatively rather than positively to these particular calls for justice and exploring regional variations (O'Brien and Li, 2006: 114). The project's major éclat stems from its pioneering elaboration of an important category of contentious collective action, with wide application both in China and elsewhere, along with detailing the causes behind it and the dynamics through which it plays out in interaction with successive levels of government. Although a variety of sources are exploited, not all of which are ethnographic, the authors make clear that a relatively small number of village sites in which extensive access and deep background were available played a crucial role in launching and guiding the study (O'Brien and Li, 2006: xi–xvii, 131–133, 139–141, and personal communication with O'Brien).

TRADE-OFFS: DEPTH VERSUS BREADTH

Would *Weapons of the Weak* (Scott, 1985) have been more compelling (or less) if it had involved multiple village sites? What if Fenno (1978) had tracked just four politicians, but spent months with each instead of days?

All research involves trade-offs. In ethnographic and participant-observation studies, by their very nature, the researcher is choosing to invest time in observing and developing relationships with particular sites and informants. Given a finite amount of time and other resources for the project, there is thus an inherent trade-off between depth and breadth: between working more intensively at a smaller number of sites (or a single one) and developing a larger number of sites but spending less time at each. How many sites, then, should be developed in a given project?[16]

Site-Level Variation

The answer to this question depends in part on the number of site-level independent variables and the nature of variation within them. Scott discusses reasons he chose Sedaka: its apparent typicality as well as the fact that previous studies had established a baseline from which to assess change (Scott, 1985: 90). He does not seem to justify in an explicit way his decision to focus on just one village.[17] Implicitly, the reasons seem to be that long-term immersion in a single place was required to obtain access to "hidden transcripts," and that variation within the village itself (between elites and poor, and among different informants) was a more important focus than, say, interregional variation between Kedah and Johore. The overall framing of the research also seems to discourage the exploring of different sites: the denizens of Sedaka are intended to speak for peasants everywhere.

In the case of *Home Style*, Fenno (1978) adopts a casual tone toward the choice of his eighteen congressional representatives ("I make no pretense at having a group that can be called representative, much less a sample" [Fenno, 1978: xiv]). But it *is* a sample, of course, and he makes clear that he selected it in such a way as to observe members and districts of different parties, regions, races, ages, levels of seniority, and electoral competitiveness. Thus, he pursued the familiar small-n strategy of obtaining variation on a number of potentially important independent variables. The problem of small sample size remained, but Fenno's logic is clear.

Up-Front Costs of Site Development

Each site involves what might be called start-up or up-front costs, referring to expenditures of time and effort as well as other costs. What is the minimum, or optimal, degree of access required to obtain valid information for a

---

[16] An essay by Maria Heimer (2006) contains a useful discussion of the choices she made in her work on local cadres, traveling to twelve counties and pursuing a tightly focused set of questions in each. More generally, the volume in which this appears, *Doing Fieldwork in China*, will be of interest to many readers of this book.

[17] To be more precise: the study is hardly limited just to Sedaka; it brings to bear evidence concerning the region as a whole, and Scott mentions excursions to nearby villages. Still, it is framed as a single-village study.

particular research effort? In my encounters with the Residents' Committees of Beijing and other mainland cities, in most cases it appeared that at least three or four visits were required to begin to cross a relaxation threshold. During the initial visits, the atmosphere was at least a little tense and conversation stilted. Obtaining answers to straightforward factual questions – what's the population of the neighborhood? how many low-income residents are there? and so forth – posed little problem, but open-ended questions typically resulted in guarded, bland responses. In most although not all of the sites, this wariness gradually gave way to a much more accepting and, in some cases, even welcoming atmosphere. Thus the early time investment paid dividends by allowing me to observe something closer to the committees' ordinary day-to-day work and interaction with constituents. For present purposes, the point is that the greater the costs and risks of establishing each site, the fewer sites a researcher can afford to develop given his or her limited resources.

The Nature of the Data Sought

This is, of course, typical for ethnographic research, but what is particularly important to point out is that the amount of time required for building trust and rapport (in this and other settings) depends on the type of information needed. If the point were merely to ascertain basic facts of the sort that the RCs themselves regularly collect and often post on their office walls, such as the number of women of child-bearing age within the jurisdiction, this could probably have been accomplished in a single visit, depending on the credentials one could present. To understand something partially hidden but limited in scope – for instance, the actual and highly state-managed process through which RC elections are run – would have required just a few visits.

On the other end of the scale, to aspire to write a comprehensive "neighborhood study" on the model of the best urban anthropological work (e.g., Bestor, 1989) would have required drastically reducing the number of cases. It would have meant applying much more comprehensive and sustained efforts than I brought to bear at even my most intensive sites. It also would have required a strategy of regularly going out within the same neighborhood and talking to a wide sample of residents, in private and independent of their interactions with the RC itself. This would have been possible in my project, but might have threatened the premises of my tacit understandings with the committees. Instead, I chose to do my citizen interviews and questionnaire surveys (designed to get at residents' opinions in a private way, removed from the RC members' presence) in neighborhoods other than those where I was conducting participant observation.

Optimizing Validity

One question to consider in choosing a research strategy is whether the time and effort involved in ethnographic work are justified relative to what can be obtained through one-time interviews. For many purposes and in many settings, the essential things that the researcher needs to understand can be ascertained in a single session. By minimizing the time spent with each subject, the number of interviewees can be maximized, thus potentially obtaining high degrees of variation and some or all of the benefits of large-n research. Even to many qualitative researchers, the idea of returning to an informant for a second or a tenth encounter may seem like a puzzling waste of time.

Some of the reasons one might want to return to a site multiple times have already been made clear: because trust and familiarity are required to obtain information. But there are other reasons as well. First, even the most cooperative and forthcoming of informants may "change their stories" over the course of a single interview and between interviews. It is well established in the world of survey research that different question wordings, question orderings, and contexts can lead to quite dissimilar responses. Similarly, interviewees can reveal different and possibly conflicting sides to their beliefs and experiences on different occasions. Moreover, if the research site is such that multiple informants are present at any given time, their relationships with one another may strongly condition what is revealed. If the point of the in-depth research is to obtain the truest possible measure of an individual's perspective, the extra validity that can be gained through multiple sessions must be considered.

This is all the more evident when the project relies on critical informants, particularly when their memories must be plumbed for recollections of events that took place years or decades earlier. Peter Seybolt's *Throwing the Emperor from His Horse* (1996) serves as an example. Seybolt constructed a political history of an impoverished Henan village through a series of long interviews with Wang Fucheng, who served as its party secretary from 1954 to 1984. The interviews were clustered in four visits, with the first in 1987 and the last in 1994. Several other villagers also provided information, but Wang was central. As the author describes it, on each visit the relationship between Seybolt and Wang (and between their families) deepened, and further layers of memory and nuance were added to the account. This book simply could not have been written on the basis of the author's first visit alone.

A final circumstance requiring multiple or protracted encounters occurs when the project relies significantly on watching the subjects interact with their surroundings – for instance, by observing events that crop up in the course of the visit. Fenno's (1978) research drew heavily on this practice. He points out that his project would not have been successful had it taken the more conventional form of forty-five-minute audiences in the congressional representatives' Capitol Hill offices. He depended on being at his subjects' side as they careened from one home-district event to the next, on noting their actual behavior and demeanor at these events, and on catching them in reflective moments as they unwound after meetings with one or another part of their constituencies.

Residents' Committee offices present broadly similar opportunities in that they are sites of frequent and highly varied interactions among state intermediaries (the committee staff), residents, and higher state officials. Some days and locales are busier than others, but often a great deal of activity goes on in these offices, and much of it is unpredictable from the RC members' perspective and thus impossible for them to plan or script in advance. Residents and transients drop in for an astonishingly vast assortment of reasons: complaining about noisy neighbors; requesting help in applying for state benefits or documents; paying small fees; negotiating the use of sheds, spare rooms, or open space for commercial purposes; demanding that the committee resolve whatever pressing problem they face, whether concerning housing maintenance, part-time employment, match-making, or any number of other things. At the same time, officials from the Street Office regularly stop by to explain the latest tasks assigned to the RC and check on its performance. Police officers, particularly the "beat cop" (片儿警) assigned to the neighborhood, regularly pull up a chair, sip tea, and have a cigarette while conveying or receiving information about burglaries, parolees, recidivists, or dissidents.

Firsthand observation provides an opportunity to watch how residents and committee members handle all these situations. Naturally, it is always possible that the observer's presence affects the behavior under observation, and thus careful judgment and honest evaluation in one's field notes are required. This also underscores the importance of establishing trust and familiarity, as mentioned earlier. By taking note of body language (imperious or supplicating, for instance) and listening not just to what is said but also to the tone of voice in these interactions, one can infer a great deal about power relations between citizens of many kinds and local agents of the state. Also, such observation allows for follow-up questioning after the fact on the basis of details gleaned from the conversation, which makes it possible to probe deeply into specific, concrete cases rather than settling for general or impressionistic answers. For instance, after a resident came in to demand the committee's help in resolving a dispute with a neighbor, I would inquire about the history of that dispute, the parties involved, which government offices or courts had played a part in dealing with it, and the like. If one were interviewing an RC member outside the context of the office without such cues, she might well never happen to mention that particular dispute and thus the information gained about mediation behavior could be much blurrier.

CONCLUSION

A great deal of political information that matters to researchers, from people's unvarnished opinions to the workings of closed institutions, is *hidden*. Also, much in the political world is *subtle*, in that understanding or coding it is no trivial matter, or in that its relationship to established social science concepts is uncertain. When researchers are confronted by any of the above three situations, or all at once, methods derived from ethnography and participant observation, or "site-intensive methods," may be called for. For the reasons explained in this chapter, these conditions can obtain in any country, but they are especially prevalent in politically restrictive and non-Western contexts like China. The strategy discussed here is not the only way to approach hidden and subtle politics, of course: careful analysis of public texts, unearthing and interpreting written documents, and drawing inferences from published statistics can also bear fruit.

The purpose of site-intensive methods is to gain access to information that would otherwise remain inaccessible and to obtain data of high validity. Space constraints here have not permitted much discussion of the nuts and bolts of how one goes about using these methods. But in essence, the researcher spends time to form relationships with human subjects that are deeper than those possible in a single interview. Rapport and trust are built up to the extent possible. Through prolonged interactions, the researcher aims to get below the surface of things, the "party line," and the vague or evasive or unconsidered answer. Watching people in the context of their natural habitat makes available data that could never be captured through a questionnaire or an off-site conversation, useful though those may be in other ways.

By definition, these methods involve an investment of time and effort that can be greater than other methods on a per-informant basis. But these costs may not be as steep as some think them to be. Full-blown immersion for many months at a single site is not the only form that these methods can take. Political scientists may have good reason to split their time among multiple sites, or to use SIMS in limited ways to augment other methods.

This chapter has shown (or has provided a reminder) that contrary to the beliefs of those who associate these methods with theory-free, barefoot empiricism, they are well suited for critical tasks in the building of theory: generating hypotheses, testing them in at least two ways, and refining concepts. Classic and current examples of this work, both in the China field and in the broader discipline, illustrate its value. To more fully capitalize on the potential of this approach, it will be necessary to promote dialogue among practitioners within political science about how to employ these methods well, efficiently, and with maximum theoretical payoffs. It also means creating coherent, persuasive explanations of the utility of ethnography and participant observation to our colleagues in the discipline so that it will be better understood and appreciated.

9

Cases, Questions, and Comparison in Research on Contemporary Chinese Politics

William Hurst

Not that long ago the opportunity to conduct fieldwork in the People's Republic was greeted with an uneasy combination of euphoric enthusiasm and considered skepticism by political scientists. Well into the 1980s, scholars seriously debated the merits of fieldwork on the mainland versus research conducted exclusively in Hong Kong, Taiwan, or abroad (Thurston, 1983). From the beginning, fieldwork on the ground in China was a touchy political subject and researchers' concerns continue to center on gaining access, ensuring the safety of interviewees and collaborators, and the political impact of their findings inside and outside China.

Frequently left aside, however, are questions of how to choose fieldwork sites and what impacts one's choice of locale or locales have on research designs and outcomes. One recent exception is Maria Heimer's thoughtful essay in support of what she terms a "one-case multi-field-site approach" to fieldwork research design, in which she argues that "authors can gain a deeper knowledge of one phenomenon by probing for similarities, while downplaying variations across place" and emphasizes that "this research design is different from, say, going to four field sites and treating them as four different cases of one phenomenon ... and looking for variations between the four cases" (Heimer, 2006: 62, 69).

In contrast to Heimer, I advocate for the advantages of selecting cases with an eye toward explaining particular kinds of variation. What I term a form of within-case comparison, one specifically based on selecting research sites representative of larger subnational units, is offered as a way to at least partially overcome the challenges of defining the scope of one's findings and guarding against an excessive focus on outliers or small subsets of the true range of variation within China. Though the examples I use are from my own study of Chinese laid-off workers, the arguments are meant to be generally applicable to other research on China and in other branches of comparative politics.

WHAT IS A CASE? WHY STUDY IT?

The term "case" or "case study" is not always deployed or defined the same way. John Gerring has proposed a clear definition of a case study as "an intensive study of a single unit for the purpose of understanding a larger class of (similar) units," where a unit (case) is taken to be "a spatially bounded phenomenon ... observed at a single point in time or over some delimited period of time" (Gerring, 2004: 342). The case study researcher must discern the relevant "unit" as well as the larger class of units (universe of cases) from which it is to be drawn.

We could designate significant phenomena in Chinese politics as our cases, conducting field research in several localities and looking for commonalities. This facilitates crafting descriptive or exploratory tales of how and why we think these outcomes came to be. We could go even further and take "China as a whole" as our case, conducting research on national-level phenomena only. Alternatively, we can choose to view smaller units within China's politics, society, or its administrative hierarchy as our cases for study. In practice, this last approach is probably the most common (and most useful) in the study of Chinese politics.

Adopting it raises several additional questions, however. How does one decide which cases to study? Which research questions can be fruitfully addressed with research on which cases? Is it best to research a single case or might comparison of several cases provide for more reliable generalization? These are just a few of the questions faced by researchers opting for the study of one or several smaller cases in Chinese politics. I propose a solution to some of these questions, which I refer to as systematic subnational comparison. This framework is applicable to research questions about which some variation – rather than Heimer's sought-after commonality – across cases within China can be expected.

Perhaps the most ambitious estimation of the general usefulness of case studies is Stephen van Evera's. He has claimed that case studies can be used for "testing theories, creating theories, identifying antecedent conditions, testing the importance of these antecedent conditions, and explaining cases of intrinsic interest" (van Evera, 1997: 55). Theory testing can only be done with case studies under special circumstances (e.g., the "crucial case study") and a few cases that are really of "intrinsic interest" beyond small subfields. These two uses are thus less relevant for most researchers[1]. My method of systematic subnational comparison can be used to create bounded theories, to specify the "antecedent conditions" (i.e., background variables) required for these theories to operate, and to test the necessity of these background conditions and to estimate the scope of the generalizabilty of the theories inferred.

---

[1] For a strong indictment of these uses of case studies, particularly the "crucial case study," see King, Keohane, and Verba (1994:208–212). The earliest, and one of the best, pieces highlighting the usefulness of "crucial case studies," on the other hand, is Eckstein (1975).

SUBNATIONAL COMPARISON AND CASE SELECTION IN COMPARATIVE POLITICS

Subnational comparative analysis has become fashionable in the broader field of comparative politics (Linz and de Miguel, 1966; Mahoney and Rueschmeyer, 2003: 14). Richard Snyder argues strongly that a focus on units below the national level can help guard against two problems, which he labels "mean-spirited analysis" and invalid part-to-whole mappings (Snyder, 2001b: 98–100). Mean-spirited analysis is the practice, common in cross-national research (particularly, though not exclusively, that which is quantitative) of using aggregate national-level indicators as proxies for more detailed knowledge of different parts of a particular country – that is, assuming that all parts of a country resemble its national mean when in fact no localities may closely match the country's aggregate-level score.

Invalid part-to-whole mappings are often, though not exclusively, linked to qualitative case study analysis. As Snyder puts it, "invalid part-to-whole mappings result when traits or processes specific to a well-studied region or other subnational unit are improperly elevated to the status of national paradigm ... national cases are inappropriately coded as if the whole nation possessed the set of attributes characterizing a specific region or set of localities" (Snyder, 2001b: 99). This problem has been especially common in research on Chinese politics.

Much subnational analysis in the wider field of comparative politics has sought to steer clear of the two pitfalls just described while concentrating on various aspects of institution building, intergovernmental relations, or public administration and policy implementation. From this angle, insightful research on Latin America, Europe, North America, and parts of Asia has examined the shape and functioning of various kinds of subnational governments (e.g., Anderson, 1992; Brace, 1993; Cornelius, Eisenstadt, and Hinley, 1999; Eaton, 2004; Gray, 1994; Heller, 1999; Herrigal, 1996; Kohli, 1987; Kooghe, 1996; Michelmann and Soldatos, 1990; Putnam, 1993; Sinha, 2003; Snyder, 2001a; Stoner-Weis, 1997; Tendler, 1997; Varshney, 2002). The China field has also had its share of research on individual provinces or other subnational governmental units in comparative perspective.[2] When studying the shape and workings of formal political institutions, one finds that the boundaries of subnational cases are often easily defined as congruent with the boundaries of subnational political units – such as states, provinces, cities, counties, towns, or villages.

But what about studying outcomes and processes that do not necessarily fall within the bounds of subnational political units – like social movements,

---

[2] On post-1949 military/administrative regions, see Solinger (1977). On Chinese provinces, see, e.g., Fitzgerald (2002); Cheng, Chung, and Lin (1998); Hendrischke and Feng (1999); and the journal *Provincial China* published by the Institute for International Studies of the University of Technology, Sydney. For a more thorough discussion of recent work on provinces in China, see Dittmer and Hurst (2002/2003: 18–20).

poverty, economic growth, industrialization patterns, crime and terrorism, and many other important forms of political activity? It can be artificial and sometimes counterproductive to maintain rigid adherence to using subnational political units as cases. Rather, socially, politically, or economically meaningful divisions that are relevant to the questions at hand should be adopted as ways of delineating subnational units for comparison.

Notable in the wider field are works that aim to explain macro-processes in terms of subnational units that are purpose-specified especially for their relevance to the research question. For example, Richard Bensel, in his analysis of American industrialization in the late nineteenth century, argues that economic development in the United States was profoundly uneven, with distinct regional political economies discernible in the Northeast and Great Lakes, South, and West (Bensel, 2000: ch. 2).[3] In each region, popular claims against wealth and capital accumulation were structured by this political economy (Bensel, 2000: 12–15, ch. 4). Similar use of purpose-defined subnational units of analysis can illuminate the study of any country's politics.

USING SUBNATIONAL COMPARISON TO STUDY CHINESE POLITICS

The best qualitative case study research in the China field draws only measured generalizations and places its findings in proper context. Still, much work in this tradition suffers from a tendency to draw invalid part-to-whole mappings. Innumerable studies of Shanghai or Beijing – China's most atypical cities – or of Guangdong or Jiangsu – China's most atypical provinces – claim to explain the dynamics of politics across the whole of China.

Since the mid-1990s, new research has explicitly sought to compare several subnational units within China to draw more careful and accurate generalizations. Thomas Bernstein and Xiaobo Lü's work on rural taxation and Kellee Tsai's work on informal finance are notable examples (Bernstein and Lü, 2003; K. Tsai, 2002). These books represent a great leap forward in the quality and systematic nature of subnational comparative analysis in the China field, but their particular techniques may not travel well for the study of all other types of research questions.

Work such as that by Bernstein and Lü begins with a deductive premise that all of China can usefully be divided into "three great belts": Coastal, Central, and Western. Such research must start with the assumption that large, arbitrarily defined (usually divided by lines of longitude or in terms of "how many provinces away from the sea") swaths of China are both internally coherent and distinct from one another in ways that are analytically useful. In the case of the three great belts in China – any one of which may be more populous and in many ways more diverse than the entire European Union, and may contain a land area larger than the U.S. West Coast – this obviously does not hold

---

[3] For more detail on how conflict among regions structured much of American politics for more than 100 years after the Civil War, see Bensel (1984).

true for all research questions. A general disadvantage of this approach is that the subnational units studied are too large and heterogeneous to permit the intensive detailed analysis often needed to tease out causal mechanisms, trace complex processes, or refine concepts.

Kellee Tsai's work is more inductive. Rather than starting with a conception of Chinese regions, she begins with intensive studies of several localities and then inductively suggests types or regions based on her micro-level findings. The problem with this is that little justification is given a priori for the selection of given research sites. Thus, the reader is left wondering whether Tsai perhaps selected localities that are all outliers (and not truly representative of any broader types) or, alternatively, sites that all fall within a narrow segment of the true range of variation across all of China (and are therefore representative only of small subtypes). This issue also arises in other works, such as Susan Whiting's book on local institutions and economic development. It is clear from the outset that her cases display only a small portion of the full range of variation across all of China. This limits the generalizability of the findings, even though Whiting emphasizes that she is mainly interested in inductively suggesting types from a limited set of case studies (Whiting, 2001: 29–37).

This kind of work is useful for building what Alexander George once called "typological theory" (George, 1979: 43–68) and helps advance van Evera's broader goal of theory development. It does not, however, allow researchers to specify the scope of generalizations that can be drawn from their arguments. It also does not promote inferences or arguments about antecedent conditions or background variables necessary for theories to operate.

Scholars could ideally combine Bernstein and Lü's deductive reasoning and a priori justification of case selection with Kellee Tsai's and Whiting's fine-grained, nuanced, and careful definitions of regions and categories. Selecting cases in China is a complex task. Most often it is not feasible to conduct intensive research (especially fieldwork) on the large subnational units (e.g., macro-regions, major branches of the administrative apparatus, etc.) whose behavior we might want ultimately to explain. This means we are left to select cases from among one or more of these units – treated as subpopulations – and ask these to stand in for all cases in their respective populations. If we are interested in regions, we may need to select provinces, counties, villages, or cities for more intensive analysis and ask these to stand in for all provinces, counties, villages, or cities within their regions.

This is a form of what has been called a "typical case study" approach as applied to the comparative analysis of several subgroups within a larger population (Gerring, 2001: 218–219). Such an approach is a "most similar systems" design of subnational comparative analysis within a single country, in which "X-variation" is largely confined to a clearly specified set of attributes, but considerable "Y-variation" is observed (Przeworski and Teune, 1970: 32–34). The key is to select cases that are at least reasonably representative of the larger subgroups they are meant to stand in for. Some readers may object to the idea of setting out for fieldwork in China with a preestablished list of cases. Such a research program would likely be impractical. Some may even accuse those who attempt systematic subnational comparative work of applying the rubric ex post facto to findings obtained by simply following their connections (关系) and "going where their contacts are." Such critics assume that systematic subnational comparison requires all cases to be chosen in advance of landing in China. This is not necessarily true, as I will discuss below.

What is important upon setting out for the field is to know what sets of cases might be suitable. This means being able to recognize a good case or an inappropriate case when it presents itself. My framework does not ignore the improvisational element – the "research as jazz" paradigm – necessitated by the opacities, restrictions, and uncertainties of China research. Rather, it introduces the idea of a standard on which an ensemble of cases can play variations and solos.

LOOKING AT LAID-OFF WORKERS IN CHINESE CITIES

Regions and City Case Studies

State sector layoffs in China and their political and social impact can most usefully be examined through subnational comparative analysis. Specifically, the intensive study of micro-level politics and social change in individual cities, systematically chosen as representative of broader regions, can facilitate the explanation of important outcomes. In addition, this sort of comparative analysis allows the formulation of hypotheses about when and where these explanations are valid. In this section I will outline my explanations for the causes of layoffs and patterns of job losses experienced across several different regions. Elsewhere in my research, I also apply this approach to an analysis of policy responses to layoffs, workers' coping strategies and informal paths to reemployment, and patterns of workers' contention (Hurst, 2009).

A clear understanding of the overall spatial scope of the phenomena is needed to define meaningful regions for comparison (Hurst, 2009: ch. 1). Layoffs were not a significant issue in all parts of China. Reliable information on exactly where and when jobs were lost is surprisingly scant. Even internal government reports and secret statistics were given little credence by responsible officials.[4] Without complete data on how many workers left their jobs voluntarily, how many were reemployed, or how many had difficulties finding ways to make ends meet, we must rely on previous observations, available internal documents, and the opinions of the Chinese bureaucracy. One internal report in 2001 listed twenty-one cities as having experienced significant political and economic problems related to state-owned enterprise (SOE) layoffs. The cities were grouped into what the authors considered to

[4] Interviews with six State Council ministry officials, Beijing, 2000–2002.

be regional categories: the "Northeast," the "lower and middle Changjiang region," "Northern China," and "Western China" (DRC, 2001). In an interview, a State Council ministry official with detailed knowledge of the issue claimed that the central government has "come to the conclusion that we need to focus policy solutions on thirteen provinces and special municipalities."[5]

I maintain that there are four regional political economies in which significant SOE layoffs have occurred: the Northeast (Liaoning, outside of Dalian, Jilin, and Heilongjiang provinces), the Central Coast (Tianjin, Coastal Shandong,[6] Jiangsu, Dalian City, and Shanghai), North-Central China (Shanxi, Shaanxi, Inland Shandong, and Henan provinces, plus the cities of Lanzhou and Baotou), and the Upper Changjiang (Hubei, Hunan, Chongqing, and Sichuan).

These regions exhibit variation on five key dimensions, including (1) local state capacity, (2) the general business environment for SOEs, (3) working-class society, (4) market opportunity, and (5) central-local relations. Local state capacity in this context revolves around fiscal capacity – particularly the ability of local governments to finance spending priorities rather than their ability to collect particular proportions of the taxes they are owed. The SOEs' business environment is determined by how much competition they face from nonstate firms and by their general prospects for profitability. Working-class society is a three-dimensional concept encompassing class identity (i.e., the workers' view of themselves as members of a working class), the structure of workers' social ties, and popular perceptions of the Maoist past. All three are strongly rooted in distinct processes of working class formation. Physical legacies of industrialization, especially housing patterns, also help structure workers' social ties such that they either cut across enterprise boundaries or are concentrated within them. Market opportunity refers to both entrepreneurial and other nonstate-sector employment opportunities. Central-local relations refer to the degree of oversight, assistance, communication, and control from the center over city governments.

This variation has its roots in the historical processes of industrialization and development that were also differentiated by region. Though regional legacies from even earlier periods still exert some influence, the industrialization of these regions occurred primarily during the 100 years between 1880 and 1980. Each region had a distinctive pattern of sectoral distribution of SOEs, timing and manner of industrialization, location of SOEs in particular types of cities, relative presence of market activity and commercial centers, transportation infrastructure, and historical relationship with the central government. As reforms have intensified underlying divergent regional development patterns, each region today thus has its own particular political economy and faces its own particular employment situation.

---

[5] Interview with State Council ministry official, Beijing, 2002.
[6] I define Coastal Shandong as Weihai, Yantai, and Qingdao cities. The rest of the province I define as Inland Shandong. The full argument is presented in much more detail in Hurst (2009: chapter 2), upon which the discussion here is based.

It is worth pointing out, as an aside, that regions of this sort are not the most suitable level of disaggregation for every research question. For issues surrounding many aspects of policy implementation, for example, key dimensions of differentiation would be the urban-rural divide and levels in the administrative hierarchy. Region in some form would have to be considered, but it could certainly turn out to be that rural areas under the jurisdiction of nonprovincial-capital prefectural-level cities implement this or that policy in ways that are broadly similar throughout all of China. Conversely, if one wanted to uncover the micro dynamics and complexities of specific types of cross-national production networks, differentiating between townships or counties *within* one city or across a couple of cities – like Kunshan, Dongguan, or Wenzhou – could be more important than drawing distinctions between regional models of political economy or development. For my study of laid-off workers' politics, however, region was the most salient axis of disaggregation, and the areas with significant layoffs could be divided into four major regions.

In each region, I selected one or two representative cities for case study analysis. But just how does one determine the "representativeness" of a city within a regional political economy? We must start with the legacies of earlier industrialization and development – sectoral distribution of SOEs, timing and manner of industrialization, location of SOEs, relative presence of market activity and commercial centers, transportation infrastructure, and historical relationship with the central government – which produced differentiated contemporary regional political economies. Cities must then be selected whose scores on these key criteria match those for the region at large. The cities' scores on key dimensions of contemporary regional political economy, from central-local relations to the business environment for SOEs, must also not be regional outliers.

When selecting cities, I sought to include cases within the regions I had identified that were broadly representative of their larger regional political economies. Thus, for example, I turned down several chances to conduct extensive fieldwork in Guangzhou since it was outside my regions of interest, even though access there might have been better than it turned out to be in some of the cities I did select. I also turned down chances for research in Dalian, as this city was clearly not representative of the Northeast (I opted for more time in Benxi and a second stint in Shenyang instead and, after much deliberation, ended up categorizing Dalian as a Central Coast city). Finally, I tried without success to arrange fieldwork in cities that would have been good fits for my research design, including Ziyang, Zhuzhou, Jilin, Nanjing, and Wuhan. However, these had to be left for future projects or other researchers.

As stated earlier, no one can reasonably go to the field with a list of perfect fieldwork sites etched in stone and proceed to simply run through an established schedule. Contacts, institutional ties, and chance often influence research access more than the best-laid plans. Those employing my brand of subnational comparison therefore must be prepared to roll with the punches of the field in a way that allows them to cobble together a set of research locales that can serve the broader research design – the way a jazz musician might improvise a path back to a standard theme when faced with surprise harmonizing by her colleagues. This was the process through which I selected and revised my selection of case study cities during my research.

As principal research sites, I selected cities that were as representative of their regions as I could find among those places where I could get research access. In the Northeast, the city of Benxi in Liaoning province was selected. In the Central Coast and Upper Changjiang regions, Shanghai and Chongqing, respectively, were studied. In North-Central China, I selected the two cities of Datong and Luoyang, both representative of the region, so as to provide a rough test of the internal coherence of the regions as I define them (Hurst, 2009: 32–36).

Causes of Layoffs

Deteriorating SOE business environments and divergent patterns of central-local relations produced different patterns of layoffs across regions. Declining profitability and spiraling costs led firms in the Northeast to begin laying off workers in the 1980s. Sector-specific problems in the business environments of some North-Central and Upper Changjiang SOEs led them to lay off workers in the early and mid-1990s, even as many enterprises in other sectors in those same regions added new personnel. The Central Coast and provincial capitals were largely spared significant layoffs until after the Fifteenth Party Congress in 1997, when the central state imposed a new cost-cutting policy on SOEs in an effort to force them to adapt to what it perceived as new competition at home and abroad.

Although other regions of China enjoyed intensive growth in agriculture resulting from decollectivization, the Northeast's efficiency advantage in staple grains eroded. Though rural production has always played second fiddle to urban industry in the People's Republic, the fate of SOEs was not entirely divorced from that of the countryside, as rural surpluses provided investment capital for industry. The Northeast's relative (and occasionally absolute) losses from decollectivization hampered local financing of new industrial development or reform of ailing SOEs well into the 1980s (Luo, 1994: 118). Many Northeastern SOEs faced a version of hardening budget constraints, as they had difficulties balancing their books, fell into wage and pension arrears, and were forced to lay off workers.

Layoffs across the Northeast reached a critical scale during the 1990s. Though nearly all the layoffs remained informal, arrangements like "long vacations" (长假) came to be accepted as a permanent state of affairs (DRC, 1999a). "I was officially laid off in 2000, but I had been on long vacation since 1991. In truth, it is the same thing," said one former mine foreman in Benxi. A retired Benxi miner angrily said, "The leaders told me to take a long vacation in 1988. After that, I was just waiting to retire. I got nothing from the work unit. Then they finally allowed me to retire in 1995 – two years late – and I only got one-fourth of my proper pension."[7] The trend remained broadly the same as that in the 1980s, but it quickened and intensified.

In the cities of the Upper Changjiang, layoffs appeared for the first time. Defense-linked companies and textile firms in particular faced mounting competition from nonstate and foreign firms. Mismanagement under increasingly lax supervision was also a factor. Furthermore, local governments and higher level units were progressively less able to subsidize struggling firms. The Upper Changjiang experienced proportionally more layoffs than North-Central China during this period because the textile and military sectors there employed particularly large numbers of workers. The Upper Changjiang had an especially large concentration of small-size SOEs and urban collective firms. Between 1987 and 1997, these firms experienced a particularly severe worsening of their business environments, largely due to competition from nonstate firms (often rural township and village enterprises). Official statistics show a 15 percent drop in the number of collective-sector workers employed in the Upper Changjiang between 1993 and 1997.[8]

North-Central firms experienced a *net addition* of workers during the first part of the 1990s. Even so, some firms there were laying workers off. Many of these SOEs faced competition from township and village enterprises in the production of coal and textiles as well as declining demand for the region's agricultural machinery. Even though conditions were worsening for certain firms and in certain sectors, profits for others outweighed negative trends across the region as a whole.

Few workers seem to have lost their jobs involuntarily in Central Coastal SOEs during the first half of the 1990s. Without clear fiscal imperatives, and with significant political disincentives from a closely watchful central state, most firms held their workforces at a constant size. Those that shed workers generally lost them to better opportunities in the nonstate sector. As one Shanghai city official explained, "before 1997, some workers left their work units to take up higher paying private-sector jobs or to go into business for themselves. In Shanghai at least, no one was forced out."[9]

Written sources on Shanghai during this period tell a similar story. Case studies of key Shanghai SOEs detail how most workers were retained prior to 1997, and many of those who did leave did so voluntarily (DRC, 1999b, 1999c). Though Shanghai was at the forefront of national policy in admitting to unemployment and instituting official mechanisms of assistance before 1997,[10] the scale of the problem was held well in check through a combination of relatively healthy SOE business environments and particularly generous central government subsidies.

---

[7] Interviews with a 47-year-old male laid-off foreman and a 58-year-old female retired miner, Benxi, November 2001.
[8] *Zhongguo laodong tongji nianjian*, various years.
[9] Interview with Shanghai municipal official, July 2000.
[10] On this, see D. Tang (2003).

In September 1997, the CCP convened its Fifteenth Party Congress in Beijing. Key decisions were taken on many issues relating to SOE reform. It was decided that SOEs were to evolve into profitable firms and that a chief means to achieve this goal would be to lay off workers to cut costs. Ideally, enterprises were to become not just market firms but global competitors (Nolan, 2001), and excessive labor costs were an important obstacle that had to be cleared from their path. With his speech opening the proceedings, General Secretary Jiang Zemin threw down a gauntlet for SOEs, telling them they must become profitable market actors and giving them a green light to do so by any means necessary (with specific endorsement of cutting workers to trim costs) (Renmin chubanshe, 1997: 23).

Within weeks of the party congress, SOEs felt pressure to trim what were suddenly deemed bloated workforces. SOE managers and labor officials on the Central Coast closely heeded the signals from Beijing. Over twelve months in 1997 and 1998, Shanghai saw more than 26 percent of state- and urban collective-sector workers lose their jobs. Roughly another 10 percent went out of work the following year (Yin, 2001: 101). Even though their business environments had not obviously deteriorated, Central Coast SOEs came under pressure from a closely observant central state to trim their labor forces. One Shanghai labor cadre said he felt as though he had been told by the party congress that "crying and complaining gets you nowhere in the market; [i.e., don't ask for subsidies] forced exit [layoffs or firm closure] is the only way." Another Shanghai cadre derided the directives of the congress, chafed at bureaucratic micro-management, and mocked the lack of genuine marketization by quoting a joke that played on his city's thick regional accent, saying, "before, everything depended on the bureau chief, afterward, everyone had to look to the market" (以前什么都靠司长, 后来谁都要看市场)– the terms 司长, bureau chief, and 市场, market, sound nearly identical when pronounced by many Shanghainese).[11]

The CCP's post-1997 policies did not so much harden SOE budget constraints as realign them. Instead of subsidies being tied to vertical connections, political behavior (表现),[12] the attainment of production targets, or full employment, they became linked to workforce reductions and the achievement of other "reform targets." And the effects of this ideological shift in incentives extended beyond the Central Coast to regions that had experienced earlier problems. Before the end of summer 1998, firms in the Northeast were instructed to "open up" previously hidden unemployment and to further deepen workforce reductions. In August 1999, General Secretary Jiang Zemin addressed a conference on SOE reform in Northeast and North China, articulating this explanation for the regions' problems and endorsing layoffs as a favored means of reducing "excessive costs" (Jiang, 1999). This gave managers

---

[11] Interviews with Shanghai Municipal Party Committee cadre and trade union cadre, October 2000 and July 2000.
[12] On the importance of 表现 within the firm, as well as in interfirm relations, see Walder (1986: 132–147, 160–162).

an explicit opportunity to earn plaudits by cutting workers to reduce labor costs, even when this failed to resuscitate their firms' profitability.

North-Central and Upper Changjiang SOEs felt new central pressure to openly reduce their workforces rather than to expand them or conceal cuts. Many North-Central and Upper Changjiang SOEs in the late 1990s also confronted a similar constellation of declining profitability and reduced subsidies to what their Northeast counterparts endured in the 1980s. The difference was that they were encouraged to respond with layoffs whereas firms in the Northeast in the 1980s had been politically constrained from responding with layoffs.

Overall, three distinct patterns of job losses can be observed across the four different regions. Each of these, in turn, was the product of a specific set of causal processes, rooted in the political economy of each region. The Northeast faced deteriorating business environments and strained central-local relations, causing its SOEs to struggle in the 1980s, when firms in most other regions were doing well. North-Central and Upper Changjiang enterprises in certain sectors grappled with increasingly competitive business environments and declining government subsidies in the early 1990s, whereas firms in the Northeast continued to struggle and Central Coast companies boomed.

Finally, after the Fifteenth Party Congress in 1997, the political environment for all SOEs shifted. Layoffs were no longer to be avoided at all costs. In fact, they became highly politically desirable for many SOEs. Some firms in the Central Coast even "stormed" to meet new targets for shedding workers whom managers felt were still needed in the production process. Overall, Chinese SOEs did not trim their workforces in the face of any relentless advance of the market or true hardening of socialist budget constraints. Rather, a multiplicity of factors, combining in different ways across space and time, shaped regional patterns of unemployment and retrenchment.

THE UTILITY OF SUBNATIONAL COMPARISON VERSUS SINGLE-CITY CASE STUDIES IN EXPLAINING THE CAUSES OF LAYOFFS

Single-city case studies, although exceedingly good at illuminating complex causal mechanisms, would do little to explain the regional dynamics just discussed. If I had looked at only Chongqing, for example, I would have come away with a story specific to the regional patterns of the Upper Changjiang region, or even worse, to one or two automotive, defense, or textile factories. Conversely, if I had examined only Shanghai, I would have found evidence for an exaggerated role for top-down administrative guidance and command in the genesis of SOE layoffs.

In fact, reliance on single-city or single-unit case studies can give rise to spurious debates among scholars actually looking at apples and oranges. The researcher who worked in Ziyang or Kaifeng would be just as correct in his view of layoffs as sector-specific phenomena as his colleague working in Jiamusi or Fushun would be in her claim that whole cities had been limping along and sloughing off workers since the early days of reform. This is not to say that either of these would not be able to offer superior nuance in their descriptions of specific causal mechanisms. But if whole research questions are dominated only by such single-unit case studies, we would have no way of knowing who is right or, as in this example, whether both sides of an argument might be valid for regionally or otherwise bounded sets of outcomes.

GENERAL ISSUES OF SYSTEMATIC SUBNATIONAL COMPARISON VERSUS INTENSIVE STUDIES OF SINGLE CASES AND LARGE-N STUDIES OF MANY CASES IN CHINA

Perhaps my brand of subnational comparison spreads precious field research resources and time too thinly. Perhaps if I had spent all of my time in Shanghai, for example, my study could have included many more interviews there, along with extensive archival research and perhaps even analysis of detailed local quantitative data. For comparativists, however, after a certain point it just has to be "turtles all the way down" (Geertz, 1973: 29). Knowing everything there is to know about Shanghai just for the sake of understanding Shanghai may be valuable from some perspectives, but it does not, in itself, advance the study of comparative politics.

No matter how much detail we can assemble about any one given case, it does not help us to generalize from that case. If generalization is the aim, we similarly cannot get very far using Heimer's preferred one-case multi-site method. Even if we study multiple places, if we treat them as forming one unified whole, we cannot venture a decent guess as to how generalizable our findings might be, even within China (unless we could somehow realistically study some very large proportion of *all* possible field sites in the country). The best we can hope for from the analysis of single units or cases is the generation of testable and plausible hypotheses that can later be evaluated in more rigorously comparative work.

In fairness, the type of comparative analysis I advocate takes us only a small part of the way along the journey from hypothesis generation to hypothesis testing. With such small samples, so little real knowledge of the populations from which they are drawn, and no way even to begin to estimate the probabilities with which one's conclusions might hold true, my brand of subnational comparison falls far short of large-N quantitative work for testing hypotheses. It can, however, give us a good idea of where and when certain explanations might be valid. In other words, it lets us generate and evaluate hypotheses about background variables and antecedent conditions. It can also help sort out and reconcile competing claims across different subnational populations of cases and generate much more nuanced, causally complex, and internally consistent hypotheses. Finally, looking at several cases within China can help us rule out invalid part-to-whole mappings drawn from explanations of phenomena analyzed in single cases.

This is not to argue against the utility of doing single case studies under any circumstances. The intensive study of a single case, at a greater level of detail than can be accomplished under most subnational comparative designs, helps elucidate the fine-grained specifics of causal mechanisms and promotes refinement and clarification of concepts perhaps better than any other method. But what is gained in concept formation and the description of mechanisms is lost in explanatory power and generalizability.

At the other end of the continuum are large-N quantitative studies of Chinese localities. These can be undertaken using statistical information (either from published sources or obtained by the researcher), data obtained from various types of surveys, or a mixture of the two. Such an approach promises more rigorous testing of hypotheses, a broader sweep than subnational comparative analysis can offer, and the ability to quantify estimates of both the likelihood any given explanation holds true and the level of generalizability of research findings.

Despite all these apparent advantages, several factors detract from the appeal of such methods in the study of Chinese politics. First, there is the issue of practicability. It is not easy to obtain good quantitative data in China, just as obtaining good qualitative or interview data is difficult as well. But getting quantitative data is more costly in financial terms (something especially important for graduate students in the field) and the process of gathering quantitative data is even more tightly controlled for foreign researchers than the gathering of qualitative data. In order to get good quantitative data, the foreign researcher needs to be relatively well funded and must work with exceptionally talented and determined Chinese collaborators (who, fortunately, have become much more numerous in recent years).

Second, there are some variables in China about which it is exceptionally difficult to obtain or collect accurate quantitative data. An example from my own research is the number of laid-off workers. Different sectors and localities record the number of laid-off workers differently from one another and in ways that often diverge from national guidelines. These guidelines, in turn, changed every couple of years during the 1990s and early 2000s, further complicating the picture. Finally, the reporting of job losses is notoriously fraught with deception, corruption, and political interference – some managers and local officials deliberately overstate the totals, whereas many others deliberately understate them; then higher level officials often "revise" the numbers reported from below to suit their own purposes before passing them to the next level, and so on. Given the political sensitivity of the issue, it would also not be easy to conduct an original survey on unemployment. Even if possible, sampling of respondents would present immense difficulties; it also would be difficult to sort out the respondents' answers because so many people have different understandings of the concept.

Third, large-N work is good for some things but not for others. Just as there are limitations to what subnational comparisons can tell us, so too are large-N studies limited in their ability to examine causal mechanisms, generate concepts, and probe the intricacies of political and social interactions at the most micro level. Though I certainly support the use of quantitative work in the study of many questions in Chinese politics, it is not always the best method for the study of all questions. Perhaps more interesting, there is likely a sequence in which the field as a whole can best benefit from each style of research in a cycle over time.

I suggest that relatively new questions are likely best tackled with subnational comparative analysis. This method is best at balancing fine-grained work on mechanisms and concepts with hypothesis generation and assessing the generalizability of explanations. Once we have hypotheses testable at specified levels of generality along with new concepts and clear ideas about causal mechanisms, we can move on to test the validity and generalizability of competing claims with quantitative studies and to refine our understanding of concepts and mechanisms with single-case intensive studies or ethnographic research.

CONCLUSION: A PROGRAM FOR TAKING SYSTEMATIC SUBNATIONAL COMPARISON BEYOND THE STUDY OF CHINESE WORKERS

A method or analytical approach that is not applicable beyond the specific substantive questions it was developed to study is no method at all. How, then, might one apply the basic framework of systematic subnational comparison outlined earlier to contexts beyond the study of Chinese workers, or even beyond China? The most basic answer is that researchers can usefully divide national cases into subnational subpopulations of smaller cases, select representative cases from each subpopulation, make their case selection rubrics clear up front, and be careful about drawing generalizations that are too broad or not attempting to generalize enough from their findings. Such broad programmatic statements are not entirely satisfactory, however.

Starting from the decision of a researcher to engage in subnational comparative analysis, I suggest four concrete steps that I believe can make such analysis more systematic and enhance the clarity of the results. First, researchers ought usefully to consider various ways of slicing up their national cases into smaller subpopulations. Subnational political units do not always make the best subnational cases or subpopulations. Likewise, political, economic, topographical, or linguistic/ethnic regions are not necessarily natural or appropriate. The specific definition of subpopulations, along with the degree of disaggregation, must be driven by the research question and justified a priori by the scholar in light of both the dynamics of the research question and the relevant work of other researchers. To do a good job of systematic subnational comparison, a researcher need not study *every* potentially relevant subpopulation, but the inclusion of some and exclusion of others must be explicitly justified.

Second, before setting out for the field, researchers ideally ought to have a clear sense of not only the relevant subpopulations of cases but also of what representative cases in each subpopulation might look like. Although it would be impractical, and from this writer's experience usually unwise, to set out for the field with a predetermined list of cases set in stone, one must be able to recognize a good case when it reveals itself and to ration precious fieldwork time and resources judiciously and accurately away from outliers and toward cases that can illuminate the subpopulations of interest. Making a list of necessary attributes of representative cases – or even of example representative cases themselves – for each subpopulation to be studied before beginning one's research would be a very useful step.

Third, researchers could usefully pay more attention to just where the boundaries of their theories lie – that is, to avoid invalid part-to-whole mappings but also to take care not to *underestimate* the generalizability of their findings. They can accomplish both objectives by highlighting and specifying the necessary antecedent conditions and the criteria by which they define the relevant subpopulations. The goal should always be to make *testable* rather than irrefutable or watered-down equivocal statements. By telling future researchers what can properly be tested with which data under what conditions, scholars help the general project of advancing knowledge and useful debate in the field. Failure to do so both inhibits progress in the field and sells short one's own research findings.

Fourth and finally, it is important not to lose sight of the broader unit of analysis: China as a whole. It is always useful for researchers pursuing subnational comparisons to at least speculate on how and why particular sets of antecedent conditions came to be in particular countries as well as on whether and why similar sets of conditions might or might not be important in sorting out subpopulations of cases in other national contexts. By doing this, researchers can postulate "meta-hypotheses" that can travel at least as well as their more grounded, but bounded, "real" hypotheses drawn from their fieldwork. If a template used to define subpopulations and to select good cases in China works or fails to work in research on Russia or Brazil, this finding often can be at least as interesting to both China scholars and Russia or Brazil specialists as the specific findings of the research.

By following these four steps and continuing open and clear discussions of case selection and other issues, researchers not only can usefully develop a more mature tradition of systematic subnational comparison in the study of Chinese politics but also can help promote the integration of the China subfield into wider debates and conversations in comparative politics. By making our research more intelligible to non-China specialists, highlighting our more general findings and hypotheses, and giving some hints as to just how generalizable we think our results are and what kinds of data might be used to test our claims in China and elsewhere, we could make great progress toward becoming a "normal subfield" under the comparative tent, and perhaps even get more nonspecialists to pay attention to important findings and arguments from the study of China.

PART III

SURVEY METHODS

10

A Survey of Survey Research on Chinese Politics

What Have We Learned?

Melanie Manion

In a political environment that remains (at best) officially skeptical about the enterprise, representative sample surveys on Chinese politics have nonetheless grown substantially in number in the past two decades: political scientists trained and based outside mainland China conducted a mere two such surveys in the 1980s, but the number increased more than tenfold in the 1990s and continues to rise steadily. By mid-2008, some sixty articles, books, and book chapters drawing from original representative sample surveys on Chinese politics had appeared – including many articles in top-tier journals of political science and area studies alike. This chapter surveys the surveys and their products. It briefly explains the focus here on probability sample surveys and describes the changing regulatory context within which researchers conduct their surveys. Most of all, it evaluates their achievements, with attention to their cumulativeness, contributions to knowledge, and fit in Chinese area studies. The chapter is not a primer on the conduct of survey research on Chinese politics in mainland China.[1] It is instead a status report and reflection on this research, aimed as much (or more) at its consumers (and nonconsumers) as at survey researchers themselves.

From the corpus of English-language monographs and peer-reviewed journal articles authored by political scientists and published in nonmainland sources through mid-2008, I identify studies that exploit original probability sample survey data.[2] In coauthored works, I include studies that meet these criteria so long as at least one of the authors is a political scientist. I have surely missed some relevant surveys in my search – but not, I think, any represented in studies published in major journals of political science or Chinese

---

I thank Kent Jennings and Kenneth Lieberthal for helpful comments on an earlier draft.

[1] For good overviews, see Shi (1996) and Wenfang Tang (2003, 2005). On survey cooperation by ethnic minorities, see Hoddie (2008). On nonresponse, see Zhu (1996). On political sensitivity, see Tsai, Chapter 14 of this volume. Among new monographs drawing from survey data, a good discussion of methods can be found in Dickson (2008).
[2] See Appendix 10.1 for a precise description of what is (and is not) reviewed for this chapter.

area studies or organized by any of the roughly half-dozen major players in the enterprise of survey research on Chinese politics. I focus in this chapter on original surveys, not the small literature by political scientists who analyze datasets produced wholly or mainly by others. At the same time, the paucity of studies analyzing existing datasets is a sign of the relative immaturity of survey research on Chinese politics, a topic that merits discussion and is taken up below.

PROBABILITY SAMPLE SURVEYS

As mainland China is large and diverse, what we observe in our fieldwork is necessarily a small subset of a range of players, beliefs, and actions. Further, as China is changing rapidly, what we observe is a snapshot that may or may not be relevant beyond a single point in time. More observations, across more space and at more points in time, can improve confidence that our fieldwork observations are not highly unusual, but the problem is inherent and remains fundamentally unresolved. If the goal is to generalize from what we observe, then the argument for probability sample survey research as a method is quite strong: without a probability sample of a sufficiently large number of observations, analyzed with inferential statistics, we can say nothing about the generalizability of our fieldwork observations.

The notion of a probability sample survey implies that survey researchers select localities and individual respondents into their samples probabilistically. This permits researchers to answer basic questions about the population sampled. More to the point, although particular estimates about the population will differ from statistics provided by a complete and perfectly accurate census of the population (which is unattainable), probability sampling allows researchers to associate the estimate with a specific degree of certainty (conventionally, 95 percent or 99 percent) that the true population value lies within a specific range of values. By contrast, estimates of population values based on samples drawn in ways that violate probability sampling differ in unknown ways from the population sampled.

It is not very difficult to select a probability sample of localities in mainland China (although it is more difficult actually to conduct survey research in the selected localities, as this requires the cooperation of the political authorities). By contrast, increased mobility and outdated residence lists have made it more difficult to select a representative probability sample of individual respondents in any selected locality in mainland China.[3] The survey of surveys below reveals that relatively few surveys on Chinese politics select samples that are nationally representative. Most of the surveys are local probability surveys: a probability sample of individual respondents is selected within a locality or localities selected for convenience. Descriptive statistics along any single dimension from a local probability sample are generalizable to the local

---

[3] See the discussions in Chapters 12 and 13 of this volume.

A Survey of Survey Research on Chinese Politics 183

population sampled, of course. These descriptive statistics (unlike those based on a nonprobability sample of local respondents) are unbiased estimates about the local population – but not beyond it. Yet, even local probability samples can permit survey researchers to generalize beyond the locality on the sorts of questions that interest social scientists most: questions about the relationship between variables.[4] Indeed, considering mainland China's diversity and rapid pace of change, these are exactly the sorts of questions that can potentially contribute most to our knowledge. For good reason, then, this chapter focuses exclusively on probability sample surveys.

REGULATORY REGIME FOR SURVEY RESEARCH

One of the earliest high-level official responses to collaborative survey research on Chinese politics ominously signaled its vulnerability: in 1990 the Central Committee instructed political scientists at Peking University to cease work on a collaborative survey project with the University of Michigan; the State Education Commission (SEC) confiscated the already collected data, officially declared as "state secrets."[5] Not long after this incident, the SEC and the Chinese Academy of Social Sciences (CASS) were asked to work out appropriate procedures to guide surveys conducted in collaboration with nonmainland researchers, but little was done. A 1996 Central Committee document apparently indicates that proper approval is required for surveys by CASS and universities if the projects involve nonmainland scholars, but the document does not set out procedures for obtaining approvals.[6]

Since 1999, the National Bureau of Statistics (NBS) has been charged with the creation, refinement, and interpretation of a regulatory regime governing all survey research in mainland China conducted with researchers based outside the mainland – in Chinese 涉外调查, translated here as foreign-affiliated surveys. The term refers to research conducted by Chinese agencies jointly with (委托) or funded by (资助) organizations or individuals based outside the mainland. NBS regulations distinguish between business surveys (市场调查) and social surveys (社会调查). Survey research on Chinese politics falls under the latter category, which is more strictly regulated. It is governed by the Measures for the Administration of Foreign-Affiliated Surveys (NBS, 2004a),

---

[4] This depends on the analysis not being contaminated by local peculiarities in the theorized relationships. See Manion (1994).
[5] The survey drew official attention with a request to transport completed questionnaires to the Institute for Social Research at the University of Michigan for coding and data input. The National Science Foundation (NSF), a sponsor of the project, responded to confiscation of the data with a ban on NSF funding for any collaborative research with mainland China. The ban was lifted in mid-1993, when the data were returned to Peking University for coding and input there. An exportable electronic dataset was apparently viewed quite differently from "documents" such as completed questionnaires. See Marshall (1993).
[6] I have not seen this document. My account is based on discussions with mainland Chinese survey researchers.

which replace significantly more restrictive interim measures issued in 1999. The key principles of the regime governing social survey research are the survey permit and project approval systems.

Survey research involving foreign affiliates may be conducted only by the several hundred mainland agencies that have obtained a permit (涉外调查许可证) for such research.[7] Only the NBS and the statistical bureaus of provincial-level governments have the authority to issue such permits.[8] No organization or individual based outside the mainland is authorized to conduct survey research on the mainland without the participation of an authorized mainland agency.

Approval for foreign-affiliated social survey projects must be obtained prior to implementation of the survey. In addition to a copy of the contractual agreement between the Chinese agency and the foreign affiliate, the application for project approval must include a description of the purpose, content, scope, sample, methods, and time frame of the survey as well as a copy of the questionnaire. If changes are made to the survey plan, including the questionnaire, prior to the survey, further approval must be obtained. The NBS and provincial statistical bureaus are obliged to approve (or not approve) the project within fourteen days of receipt of the application. In particular circumstances, the time for approval may be extended another ten days. A written explanation must be provided if projects are not approved.

The existing project approval system is very significantly relaxed, compared to that reflected in the earlier interim measures.[9] Before 2004, Chinese political scientists could not reliably assure their nonmainland colleagues that they would be able to share survey data with them. The earlier measures required not only prior approval of projects, but also a postsurvey second approval to share data with nonmainland affiliates. Chinese authorities could reconsider the confidentiality of the survey data in what might be a new political context. The earlier measures effectively ruled out an early commitment (in grant applications, for example) to public accessibility of survey data.

Foreign institutional review boards may appreciate that the new regulatory regime requires informed consent. Questionnaire cover sheets must conspicuously note: "The respondent has voluntarily agreed to participate in this survey." NSB measures also prohibit use of foreign-affiliated surveys to harm

---

[7] The *China Daily* noted in 2000 that 29 agencies had received permits to engage in foreign-affiliated survey research. The NBS Web site documents the particular agencies to which it has issued permits over the years. I counted 204 in 2004, 83 in 2005, 58 in 2006, and 186 in 2007. Permits are valid for a period of three years. http:///www.STATS.gov.cn/

[8] Survey research that spans provincial boundaries requires NBS authorization.

[9] Business surveys enjoy an even more relaxed regulatory environment: they no longer require survey project approval as long as the survey is conducted by an authorized Chinese agency. The relaxation for both business and social surveys reflected in the new measures is the result of a State Council decision some six months earlier. That decision was prompted by passage of the Law on Administrative Permits in 2003. See NBS (2004b).

the interests of any individual and require that surveys be designed so as to maintain the confidentiality of responses.

The regulatory regime presents some new difficulties for foreign-affiliated survey research, however. An NBS clarification (2004c) specifies exactly what information must be indicated conspicuously on the questionnaire cover sheet: the term 涉外 (foreign-affiliated) appears five times in a mere four lines. That is, the measures make all but certain that survey respondents and local authorities facilitating the project know that the activity has some sort of non-mainland connection. Such a disclosure may jeopardize official cooperation, affect interview response (rate and quality), or both. This is particularly likely if respondents are elites.

In sum, survey research by political scientists based outside mainland China is less vulnerable today than in previous years. Progress on a regulatory regime has been made since the early 1990s and significant progress has been made in the past few years. At the same time, survey research on Chinese politics remains subject to the vagaries of Chinese politics – in particular, to official sensibilities about what constitutes politically sensitive questions.[10] Survey researchers who operate within (and outside) the regulatory regime governing their research presumably take the political context into account. Undoubtedly, what results is something of a compromise, usually reflected in the questionnaire design. So far as I can tell, however, what has not been compromised in the surveys reviewed below is the integrity of the survey enterprise as social science.

A SURVEY OF SURVEYS

Table 10.1 presents the original probability sample surveys on Chinese politics identified from English-language monographs and peer-reviewed journal articles authored by political scientists and published in nonmainland sources by July 2008.[11] The growth of survey research is evident: the pace in the 1990s is being matched in the first decade of this century and also reflects work by a somewhat broader representation of scholars.

Only three of the surveys are nationally representative – although, as discussed below, two recent additions to nationally representative surveys are not reflected in the table. A large number of the surveys focus exclusively on Beijing, a convenient but highly atypical sample of the urban Chinese population. At the same time, there is fairly good representation of a regionally diverse rural China, which mainly reflects scholarly interest in village elections. Most of the surveys were conducted with face-to-face interviews, but

---

[10] Wenfang Tang (2003) argues that economic interests also partly explain NSB reluctance to relax standards further. If all survey organizations could conduct foreign-affiliated surveys, then the market for high-priced NSB survey data would shrink.
[11] The numbering suggests thirty-two surveys, but survey 15 combines six annual surveys, discussed at greater length below and in Chapter 13 of this volume.

TABLE 10.1. *Probability sample surveys on Chinese politics resulting in publications analyzing original datasets. Based on a review of English-language monographs and peer-reviewed journal articles by political scientists published in nonmainland sources by mid-2008*

	Year	Localities Surveyed	Size	Publications Associated With Survey
1	1986–87	1 city: in Jilin	250	Manion (1991, 1993)
2	1988–89	Beijing	757	Shi (1997, 1999b)
3	1990	4 counties: in Anhui, Hebei, Hunan, Tianjin	1,270	Manion (1996, 2006); Jennings (1997, 1998, 2003); Eldersveld and Shen (2001)
4	1990–91	National probability sample	2,896	Nathan and Shi (1993, 1996); Shi (1999c)
5	1992	44 cities	2,370	Tang and Parish (2000); Tang (2001a, 2001b, 2005)
6	1993–94	National probability sample; also Taiwan and Hong Kong	3,287	Shi (1999a, 2000, 2001); Chen and Shi (2001); Chu and Chang (2001); Kuan and Lau (2002)
7	1995	Beijing	916	Dowd, Carlson, and Shen (1999)
8	1995	Beijing	658	Chen, Zhong, and Hillard (1997); Chen et al. (1997); Zhong, Chen, and Scheb (1998); Chen and Zhong (1999, 2000, 2002); Chen (2004)
9	1996	Hubei, Shaanxi, Shandong, Sichuan, Zhejiang	160†	Oi and Rozelle (2000)
10	1996	4 counties: in Anhui, Hebei, Hunan, Tianjin	1,414	Eldersveld and Shen (2001); Jennings and Zhang (2005); Manion (2006); Jennings and Chen (2008)
11	1996	Beijing	895	Shi (1999b)
12	1997	Beijing	694	Zhong, Chen, and Scheb (1998); Chen (1999, 2000, 2004); Chen and Zhong (2000)
13	1997, 1999	8 counties: in Hebei, Hunan, Shandong, Zhejiang	754	Dickson (2002, 2003)
14	1998–99	Beijing, Chengdu, Guangzhou, Lanzhou, Shanghai, Shenyang	1,543	Tong (2007)

(*continued*)

TABLE 10.1. (continued)

	Year	Localities Surveyed	Size	Publications Associated With Survey
15	1998–2004	Beijing	551–757	Johnston (2004, 2006); Johnston and Stockmann (2007)
16	1999	87 village small groups: in 25 provinces	1,356	Li (2002)
17	1999	1 county: in Jiangxi	400	Li (2003)
18	1999	Beijing	670	Chen (2001, 2004)
19	1999	Chongqing, Guangzhou, Shanghai, Shenyang, Wuhan, Xi'an	1,820	Tang (2001a, 2005)
20	1999	4 counties: in Anhui, Heilongjiang	2,400	Zweig and Chung (2007)
21	1999–2001	4 counties: in Fujian, Jiangsu, Jiangxi	1,600	Li (2004)
22	2000–2001	Rural Shaanxi	306	Kennedy (2002); Kennedy, Rozelle, and Shi (2004)
23	2000	Rural Jiangsu	1,162	Zhong and Chen (2002); Chen (2005a, 2005b)
24	2000	Jiangsu, Shanghai, Zhejiang	1,625	Wang, Rees, and Andreosso-O'Callaghan (2004)
25	2001	8 counties: in Fujian, Hebei, Jiangxi, Shanxi	316[†]	Lily Tsai (2007a, 2007b)
26	2001	2 counties: in Fujian	913	Rong (2005)
27	2002–2003	National probability sample	1,525	Kellee Tsai (2007)
28	2002–2003	12 villages: in Anhui	1,503	Tan and Xin (2007)
29	2003–2005	2 counties: in Fujian, Zhejiang	800	Li (2008)
30	2004	1 county: in Yunnan	700	Davis et al. (2007)
31	2004	Beijing	592	Chen, Lu, and Yang (2007)
32	2005	8 counties: in Hebei, Hunan, Shandong, Zhejiang	1,337	Dickson (2007)

[†] Number of probabilistically selected villages in each of which surveyors interviewed a few purposively selected informants.

Notes: National probability sample surveys exclude Tibet. Except for national probability samples, "localities surveyed" refers to nonprobabilistically selected localities within which surveyors used probability sampling selection methods. Except for informant surveys, "size" refers to number of completed questionnaires.

ten were conducted with self-administered questionnaires, typically with a survey team member present to answer queries.[12]

Six of the surveys have a longitudinal component, of considerable value to our understanding of Chinese politics. One is a quasi-experimental design: survey 17 is actually a preelection and postelection survey of the same villagers. For the most part, however, the longitudinal design reflects an effort to gauge the impact of a rapidly changing social, political, and economic environment. Surveys 3 and 10, discussed later in the chapter, are pairs in a panel study, an effort to reinterview respondents in order to track change over time at the individual level of analysis. The remaining four are longitudinal cross-sections: they return to the same localities, with essentially the same questionnaire, but survey a new representative sample of the population. The Beijing Area Study (BAS), which is discussed below and in Chapter 13, is the most important of these if only because it tracks change annually. Survey 11 returns to the Beijing mass public in 1996 to ask roughly the same questions about political participation as asked in survey 2. Survey 32 returns to the same eight counties six years later to survey local officials and private entrepreneurs on the same issues. Surveys 8, 12, and 18 of the Beijing mass public contain a common core of questions on popular political support for the regime, incumbents, and policies.

Also, several studies systematically survey and compare two different populations: local government administrators and the mass public in Beijing (Chen, 1999), villagers and local officials at various levels in the countryside (Eldersveld and Shen, 2001; Jennings, 2003; Manion, 1996), private entrepreneurs and local officials (Dickson, 2003, 2007, 2008), villagers and village committee members (Chen, 2005b), villagers and village leaders (Tan and Xin, 2007; Zweig and Chung, 2007), and urban industrial enterprise managers and local environmental sector bureaucrats (Tong, 2007).

Of the surveys presented in Table 10.1, five stand out as achievements of particular note, milestones in survey research on Chinese politics. They include surveys 2, 4, and 6, supervised by Tianjian Shi, each pathbreaking in its own way.

Survey 2, conducted in Beijing and initially conceived as the pretest for a nationally representative survey, is the first large-scale probability sample survey of the Chinese mass public.[13] The vision underpinning its design is

[12] Self-administered surveys were used in three samples of elites: retired officials in survey 1, local officials and private entrepreneurs in surveys 13 and 32, and local bureaucrats and enterprise managers in survey 14. Self-administered questionnaires were also used to survey the mass public in Beijing in surveys 8, 12, 18, and 31; in rural Jiangsu in survey 23; and in rural Anhui in survey 28. Considering the relatively low effective literacy and general unfamiliarity with survey instruments in mainland China, self-administered questionnaires are probably better suited to more literate samples.

[13] The national survey was precluded by the events of June 1989. The mainland partner was an independent survey research center, newly established under the Beijing Social Economic Research Institute headed by Chen Ziming and Wang Juntao, both later charged and imprisoned as the "black hands" behind the 1989 protests. Shi flew out of Beijing on June 10, 1989, with the pilot study questionnaires.

also distinctive and controversial for its time. It is a bold vision of "normal science" that poses as an empirical and testable question the view of the passive citizen in authoritarian China. Its questionnaire borrows heavily from a classic study of political participation in comparative politics (Verba, Nie, and Kim, 1971) and investigates activities easily dismissed at the time as irrelevant (voting), apolitical (workplace cronyism), or too sensitive to discuss with strangers (strikes, demonstrations, boycotts).

Survey 4, supported by the National Science Foundation, is the first nationally representative survey on Chinese politics. Indeed, as Nathan and Shi (1993) point out, it is not only "the first scientifically valid national sample survey" explicitly focusing on political behavior and attitudes conducted on the mainland but the first such survey ever conducted in a Communist country. Again, the design is prompted by a classic survey study in comparative politics (Almond and Verba, 1963), this time with a focus on political culture. An underlying question is the relationship between Chinese culture and democracy. In what sense does Chinese culture pose an obstacle to democratization? In the event of multi-partism, what does the distribution of values across Chinese society suggest about how preference aggregation might create opportunities for political parties?

Survey 6 borrows the vision of cross-national comparative survey work and adapts it to study political culture in three Chinese polities, asking essentially the same questions of Chinese on the mainland, in Taiwan, and in Hong Kong. This is a complex collaborative project, involving nine principal investigators based in the United States, Taiwan, and Hong Kong. It also distinguishes itself from surveys 2 and 4 by the greater attention, in the questionnaire itself, to the possibility of Chinese exceptionalism. The concept of political culture investigated in the survey prominently includes features of Confucianism, in particular a hierarchical orientation to the moral state. The mainland survey includes a large enough urban subsample to permit statistically valid comparisons with the Taiwan and Hong Kong samples.

A fourth pioneering effort is survey 3, the first probability sample survey on politics in the Chinese countryside.[14] Other new features of this study are its survey of both local elites and the mass public, using some of the same survey items to permit comparisons; a panel component that returned to the same localities to reinterview the same respondents in 1996; and a survey team that included several American political scientists for whom the study was their first foray into the study of Chinese politics.[15] This is very much an omnibus survey, the product of negotiation among ten Chinese and American scholars with a variety of research agendas.

---

[14] Full disclosure: I participated in this survey project. Politics in the post-1989 conservative interregnum intruded to create unusual setbacks for it. See note 5 above.

[15] For example, Jennings authored (1997, 1998a, 2003) and coauthored with his graduate students (Jennings and Zhang, 2005; Jennings and Chen, 2008) several articles drawing on the survey data and published in top-tier journals in both political science and Chinese area studies. Eldersveld coauthored a study with Mingming Shen (Eldersveld and Shen, 2001), the key force in the survey among mainland participants.

Finally, surveys 7 and 15 represent the BAS surveys, described in Chapter 13 of this volume. Begun in 1995, the BAS is an annual survey of the Beijing mass public. It is modeled on the Detroit Area Study and the Chicago General Social Survey and has similar aims: to gauge change and stability over time across a broad range of social, economic, and political dimensions and to understand their correlates. In addition to the basic questionnaire, a novel feature of the BAS is the inclusion of modules of question batteries provided by nonmainland scholars. The foreign policy questions explored by Johnston (2004, 2006) and Johnston and Stockmann (2007) draw from such a module, for example.

In addition to these five milestones, two recent surveys not listed in Table 10.1 are pathbreaking for their nationwide sampling of geographic space using Global Positioning System (GPS) technology. The spatial sampling used in these surveys produces representative samples, including representative samples of the more than 100 million migrants living in Chinese cities, who are typically missed with conventional methods based on household registration lists.[16] First to use this spatial sampling technique for all China (including Tibet) is a 2004 survey on the institutionalization of legal reforms, described at greater length in Chapter 12 of this volume. Second is a 2008 omnibus multidisciplinary survey organized by Texas A&M University and designed to be a regular multiyear effort. In addition to its use of spatial sampling, this survey is noteworthy because preparation included a broad invitation to the scholarly community to contribute questions to the core questionnaire. This feature is modeled on the American National Election Study and may be an important step in building a larger survey research community.[17] As neither of the two surveys had yielded publications by mid-2008, I do not include them in Table 10.1. Clearly, however, spatial sampling inaugurates a new generation of survey research in mainland China, well adapted to ongoing demographic changes.[18]

All of the surveys listed in Table 10.1 are the product of collaboration with mainland partners, a relationship that ranges widely from full partnership to subcontracting. As shown in Table 10.2, a few institutions dominate among mainland partners. First is Peking University, especially its Research Center on Contemporary China (RCCC), which has partnered with nonmainland political scientists for the greatest number of surveys.[19] This reflects (and builds) its reputation as probably the most competent academic survey research agency

---

[16] For a description of spatial sampling using GPS technology and its advantages over conventional sampling in mainland China, see Chapter 12 in this volume and Landry and Shen (2005).

[17] Questions from eleven scholars outside the core team of survey researchers were added to the survey instrument. Full disclosure: I am a member of the board for the Texas A&M China Survey.

[18] Articles analyzing data from the legal reform survey can be found in a special issue of *China Review*, vol. 9, no. 1 (Spring 2009).

[19] The RCCC also conducted the mainland component of the World Values Survey in 2000.

TABLE 10.2. *Mainland partner institutions for probability sample surveys on Chinese politics*

Mainland Partner	Survey
Peking University, Department of Political Science	1, 11
Peking University, Research Center on Contemporary China	3, 7, 10, 13, 14, 15, 19, 32
People's University, Social Survey Research Center, Beijing	4, 6
People's University, Public Opinion Research Institute, Beijing	8, 12, 18
Beijing Social Economic Research Institute, Opinion Research Center of China	2
Economic System Reform Institute of China	5
Northwest University, Xi'an	22
East China University of Politics and Law, Shanghai	24
Chinese Academy of Social Sciences, Private Economy Research Center	27
Chinese Academy of Social Sciences, Research Group, Mass Participation in Community Residents Committees	31
Unspecified	9, 16, 17, 20, 21, 23, 25, 26, 28, 29, 30

Note: Survey numbers refer to surveys listed in Table 10.1. "Unspecified" means either no mainland partner institution is specified in publications associated with the survey or reference to the mainland partner institution is nonspecific.

on the mainland. It also reflects substantial ties between former classmates at Peking University and the University of Michigan that link survey researchers based on the mainland and in the United States.[20] People's University also stands out as a frequent mainland partner.

For the most part, survey researchers have not worked with nonacademic marketing firms, although such firms are plentiful and some have worked on prestigious American surveys (e.g., Pew surveys by Horizon). Although commercial firms may be subject to fewer regulatory requirements,[21] they may be wary of risking their livelihood with surveys on explicitly political topics. The reliance on academic partners probably also reflects existing substantial ties and common scholarly interests. Further, commercial firms can be less collegial (i.e., transparent) about sharing with clients details of sampling design and survey implementation; this makes it difficult for survey researchers to evaluate the quality of the data provided.

[20] Mingming Shen, RCCC founder and director and Peking University graduate, earned his doctorate in political science at the University of Michigan. Classmates at Peking University include Tianjian Shi, Wenfang Tang, and Yanqi Tong. Classmates at the University of Michigan include Dickson, Johnston, and Manion.

[21] See note 9 above.

It is also worth noting that the mainland partners remain unspecified for more than a third of the surveys listed in Table 10.1. This may reflect a partnership that does not meet all of the official standards of the Chinese regulatory regime for survey research. Where mainland partners remain unspecified, notes in methodological appendices sometimes refer vaguely to a "mutual agreement" or "political sensitivities." Whatever the cause, the lack of transparency is unfortunate. It can be difficult to gauge the quality of survey research based on the scant information provided in many of the journal articles listed in Table 10.1.[22] As anonymity provides protection, identification provides accountability. Accountability for the quality of the work is particularly important to the maturation of the relatively new field of survey research on Chinese politics. Further, mainland partners protected from the vagaries of politics are at the same time deprived of the opportunity to build their reputations.

Arrangements with mainland partners may also partly account for the dearth of publicly available datasets from the surveys listed in Table 10.1. Only three have been publicly archived – from surveys 2, 3, and 6.[23] The dataset from survey 25 is available on the author's Web site. Datasets from surveys 16, 17, and 21 are available from the author upon request.[24] Not surprisingly in this context, analysis of existing datasets remains rare. In my survey of the literature, I discovered only a few studies analyzing data from either these datasets or the mainland data from the publicly archived World Values Surveys and Asia Barometer.[25] In short, the norm for survey research on Chinese politics is for researchers to be involved in every part of the project, from survey design to analysis and write-up. To the extent that there is a division of labor, it is reflected in actual survey implementation by mainland partners. As political scientists increasingly receive their survey research funding from agencies that expect a commitment to public availability of data after a specified time, this state of affairs may change. The routine public archiving

---

[22] Descriptions of methods in monographs are generally much better. Normal length guidelines for journal articles undoubtedly encourage sacrificing methodological for substantive elaboration.
[23] Data from survey 3 are archived at the Interuniversity Consortium for Political and Social Research at the University of Michigan. Data from surveys 2 and 6 are archived at the China Archive at Texas A&M University. Data from the Taiwan and Hong Kong surveys that complement mainland survey 6 are archived at National Taiwan University.
[24] Of course, even where researchers do not publicize the availability of their data, they may make it available upon request. For example, Kent Jennings and I have made available data from the 1990 survey of local officials that complement the rural mass public survey in survey 3. Wenfang Tang has made available data from surveys 5 and 19, as well as data from surveys conducted by the Economic System Reform Institute of China in 33–44 cities in 1987–89 and 1991, analyzed in Tang and Parish (1996, 2000) and Tang (2001a, 2005), and from a survey conducted by the All-China Federation of Trade Unions in 1997, analyzed in Tang (2005) (personal communication, June 12, 2008).
[25] Guo (2007) and Hoddie (2008) analyze data from survey 6. Tang (2005) and Wang (2007) analyze data from the World Values Surveys. Chang, Chu, and Tsai (2005) and Zhengxu Wang (2006, 2007) analyze data from Asia Barometer.

of survey data will be one marker of the maturation of survey research on Chinese politics.

CONTENT AND CUMULATIVENESS

What are the main topics that consume the various products of survey research on Chinese politics? What valuable knowledge about Chinese politics has survey research contributed? When survey researchers examine the same or similar topics, do they explicitly engage one another? To what extent are they building a cumulative knowledge?

Of all the studies identified in Table 10.1, a conservative estimate would place more than half in the category of democratization. The single most popular topic in survey research on Chinese politics is village elections, also popular in qualitative research. It figures in some of the earliest survey studies and continues to thrive. It has garnered the attention of the widest range of survey researchers. For these reasons, a brief review of survey research questions and findings on village elections is a good point of departure.

A few studies (Oi and Rozelle, 2000; Shi, 1999a) seek to explain the substantial variation throughout the country in implementation of the 1987 Organic Law on Village Committees. With grassroots democratization as the dependent variable, these studies measure village electoral democracy as electoral contestation. A greater number of studies inquire into the impact of village electoral democratization. These studies also develop more nuanced measures of electoral quality, conceived as a bundle of variables, including but not restricted to contestation. Although they focus attention on different components of the relationship, their findings are all broadly consistent with the proposition that electoral mechanisms strengthen elite-mass connections. Specifically, village elections of higher democratic quality are associated with greater congruence of views between villagers and village leaders (Jennings, 2003; Manion, 1996); a stronger likelihood of villager appeals through village leaders (Li, 2002); villager satisfaction with the electoral process (Kennedy, 2002); higher levels of external efficacy (Li, 2003); perceptions that village leaders are fair (Kennedy, Rozelle, and Shi, 2004) and trustworthy (Manion, 2006); and greater villager political interest, awareness, and optimism (Tan and Xin, 2007). This is a fairly robust accumulation of evidence across surveys conducted at different times in a variety of localities by a range of scholars employing different measures. The overall conclusion is not particularly surprising, however.

Other studies illustrate not only that survey researchers actively engage one another in building a cumulative knowledge of Chinese politics but also that not all survey research on Chinese politics is simply confirmatory. It can yield surprises that contribute importantly to our basic repository of knowledge. Three examples illustrate this fairly well.

Robust evidence attesting to regime support provides a first example. Findings based on surveys of the Beijing mass public at three points in the

1990s produce the same surprising conclusion: despite only moderate support for government policy performance, the regime enjoys broad and strong legitimacy, based on the elitism and authority orientation of ordinary Chinese (J. Chen, 2004; Chen, Zhong, and Hillard, 1997; Zhong, Chen, and Scheb, 1998). Similarly, examining data from the first nationally representative survey on Chinese politics, Nathan and Shi (1996) find that only a small number support an end to party leadership, even among Chinese who support democracy – a concept that resonates more with traditional notions of leadership than with pluralism. Shi (2001) finds a similar result in his comparative study of political trust, analyzing data from somewhat later representative surveys of Chinese on the mainland and Taiwan: political trust on the authoritarian mainland is strong and based on traditional values, compared to trust in democratizing Taiwan, where it is more contingent on government performance.[26]

A second example draws from survey research on the Chinese business-state relationship. Dickson (2002, 2003) reveals that Chinese capitalists neither possess beliefs nor engage in activities that constitute a challenge to the regime. Theories that identify them as likely activists confronting the ruling Communist Party are not well founded. Moreover, "red capitalists" have not become less embedded in the current political system over time (Dickson, 2007, 2008). Drawing from nationally representative survey data, Kellee Tsai (2007) reaches the same conclusion: Chinese private entrepreneurs do not constitute a politically assertive class (or share a common class identity at all) that poses a challenge to the state – nor are they a likely source of contestation in the near future.

A final example originates in the survey research on political participation. As Shi (1997) demonstrates in his early study, political involvement by ordinary Chinese is wide ranging and intensive, not simply formalistic. Further, its intensity and range are increasing (Shi, 1999b). Jennings (1997) confirms that this picture of frequent, varied, and autonomous acts of political participation also extends to the Chinese countryside.

AN EXAMPLE OF COMPETING PERSPECTIVES

The examples above show that survey researchers engage one another in building a cumulative knowledge. One of the more lively examples of survey researcher engagement unfolded in two *Journal of Politics* articles presenting competing theoretical frameworks, hypotheses, empirical tests, and findings on the same question: why do Chinese vote in local congress elections? The presentations by Chen and Zhong (2002) and Shi (1999c) are particularly interesting because the debate is fundamental, clear, and explicit. As such, the engagement merits particular discussion here.

---

[26] Related but not exactly similar is the finding of Lianjiang Li (2004) in a comparison of political trust in different levels of state power: there is substantially and significantly higher trust in the center than in lower levels.

The articles roughly agree in their observations and characterization of *partial* electoral reform: local congress elections are semicompetitive, but in an authoritarian political context. In both articles, Chinese voters are rational, pursuing their interests as best they can under the circumstances. Both articles present multivariate analyses of voter turnout in local congress elections and include most of the same socioeconomic variables. Shi tests his hypotheses with data from a 1990–91 nationally representative sample survey, Chen and Zhong with data from a December 1995 survey of Beijing residents.

Most interestingly, the articles begin with fundamentally different perspectives on contemporary Chinese politics, reflected in completely different hypotheses on voting behavior, given partial reform. The crux of the different perspectives has to do with how much institutional change is required to produce behavioral change. For Shi, a little institutional change is expected to go a long way: the relevant contrast for Chinese voters is with the noncompetitive elections of the past. Electoral *choice among candidates*, although limited, is the relevant institutional change. For Chen and Zhong, the key contrast is with a nonexistent liberal democracy. Despite electoral choice among candidates, current authoritarian institutions have not dislodged Communist Party electoral management and ideological dominance; in this context, the only important new choice for Chinese voters is the choice to *abstain* from voting. In sum, Shi hypothesizes that the choice to vote will reflect the vote's new relevance in elections with choice, despite the authoritarian context; by contrast, Chen and Zhong hypothesize that the choice to vote will reflect the vote's continued irrelevance in the authoritarian context.

Probably the hypotheses and findings of greatest interest have to do with the impact on voting of democratic orientation and political efficacy – which point in different directions in the two articles. Chen and Zhong hypothesize and find that Chinese with stronger democratic values and sense of internal political efficacy are less likely to vote in the (still authoritarian) local congress elections, compared to those with weak democratic values and weak internal efficacy. Shi hypothesizes and finds the opposite. The analyses also yield different findings (each consistent with the different hypotheses) about the impact on voting of anticorruption sentiment and socioeconomic variables such as age and education.

These differences point to three issues for survey research on Chinese politics. First and most obviously, different scholars can begin at the same point but formulate radically different hypotheses about the implications of what they observe; these different hypotheses may both be plausible, even equally plausible. Indeed, what is most interesting about the Chen and Zhong article is their reframing of partial political reform: they present a different way of seeing semicompetitive congress elections, which is completely at odds with Shi's framework, hypotheses, and findings. The second issue is less obvious without a careful reading of the two articles: different frameworks are interesting in the context of survey research because the rival hypotheses they yield can be tested – but not unless they are set up in a true competition. In their socioeconomic measures, the models are nearly the same (although Chen and Zhong fail to include party membership), but the other variables are completely different in measurement and even conceptualization.[27] Moreover, Shi does not include a measure of democratic orientation (or regime support) in his multivariate model: he includes it only in a bivariate analysis; as such, it is not a strong enough empirical finding for a contrast. Of course, Chen and Zhong do not pretend to replicate Shi's model. At the same time, they miss an opportunity for a persuasive contrast and greater cumulativeness by, for example, presenting one model that mirrors Shi's as closely as possible, given the difference in measures.[28]

The third issue may be the most important. A true replication of Shi's model with the 1995 Beijing survey data might well produce very different results from those presented in Shi's article. These are very different populations: Shi's nationwide sample is 70 percent rural, a far different population from the more highly educated and politically savvy Beijing residents. Timing is also important: for Shi's respondents, the most recent congress elections (in 1986–87 or 1988–89) occurred in a more liberal environment than those recalled by Beijing residents in 1995. The more general point is the relevance of context in thinking about relationships between variables and in interpreting statistical results. The pace and unevenness of change in China requires us to pay attention to geographic and temporal diversity. Some of the implications of this have already been emphasized earlier: the value of longitudinal studies, for example. For large-scale surveys that span localities of different types, it implies taking geographic diversity into account in our statistical models. Finally, it serves as a caution against accepting findings as established facts that require no further examination, even in different circumstances.

SURVEY RESEARCH AND AREA STUDIES

If the small community of survey researchers is indeed engaged in building a valuable cumulative knowledge of Chinese politics, how broad is the community of consumers? Certainly, survey-based studies appear to have made serious inroads in the discipline: roughly a dozen of the articles listed in Table 10.1 appear in top-tier journals of political science. Yet, how big is the divide between survey-based studies and studies based on archival and qualitative research methods, both with a longer tradition in Chinese area studies? Twenty-six of the forty-six journal articles listed in Table 10.1 are published in

---

[27] This is certainly true of internal efficacy and anticorruption support. For example, Chen and Zhong use one question to measure internal efficacy: it focuses on workplace (not national) politics; Shi uses both measures in an index of internal efficacy. Chen and Zhong ask for an evaluation of anticorruption measures; Shi measures abuse of power by local leaders.

[28] This would be simple: it would involve including party membership and leaving democratic orientation and regime support out of the model; internal efficacy and anticorruption support would still be slightly different measures, of course.

journals that focus exclusively on China, East Asia, or Asia.[29] This is hardly a definitive answer to the questions posed above, but it does not suggest a chasmic divide. Nor does a close reading of the research products listed in Table 10.1 suggest a divide.

The overwhelming preponderance of survey-based studies explicitly situate their research questions (and findings) within both the discipline of political science and the field of Chinese area studies, regardless of publication outlet. A few refer only to work in the qualitative tradition in Chinese studies, ignoring other survey-based research on Chinese politics and also eschewing a broader empirical and theoretical context. None ignore qualitative studies in contextualizing their research, however. To the contrary, they typically draw at some length from qualitative studies in setting out the research question, justifying its importance, and interpreting statistical findings.

Engaging the qualitative research does not guarantee a readership among qualitative researchers in Chinese politics. Ideally, in an area studies journal, the account of the research and findings should be accessible beyond the community of scholars with sufficient training to assess the quality of the methods. Most articles do not go the extraordinary lengths of Nathan and Shi (1993) in attempting to educate readers about the relative merits of survey research, but most do make an effort (perhaps with editorial prodding) to explain their substantive findings clearly enough.

A more serious problem, to my view, is an overuse of descriptive statistics, which have an inordinate impact because of their relative digestibility. Nearly one-fourth of the research products listed in Table 10.1 are exclusively, essentially, or mainly descriptive – without any multivariate model estimation or inferential statistical analysis.[30] Summary descriptive statistics are a useful preliminary to analysis and also have inherent value when the survey data are nationally representative or permit a valid comparison across time or populations. Many of the descriptive statistical presentations lack these features, however. Even so, this does not reflect a restraint imposed (or self-imposed) with an area studies readership in mind. Although a high proportion of these presentations can be found in journals with an area studies focus, it is not the case that these outlets shun more sophisticated work. Nineteen of the twenty-six survey-based articles on Chinese politics appearing in area studies journals present multivariate models and employ inferential statistics.

Finally, although survey-based studies engage the qualitative research, relatively few integrate qualitative and survey research in a single project. That is,

---

[29] *Journal of Contemporary China* dominates, with ten articles; *China Quarterly* is next, with six articles.
[30] Some of these present bivariate relationships, but most present only descriptive statistics along a single dimension. More than half of these are fairly recent publications (i.e., 2005–2007), so it is not that scholarship has simply been catching up in methodological sophistication. It is worth noting that the standard (multivariate models or inferential statistics) I use here is by no means a very high one.

if there is not a divide, there does seem to be a division of labor. Two welcome recent exceptions are studies by Kellee Tsai (2007) and Lily Tsai (2007a, 2007b). Kellee Tsai integrates an original large-scale nationally representative survey with some 300 in-depth qualitative interviews with local officials, private entrepreneurs, and mainland researchers to describe and explain "informal adaptive institutions" in the relationship between Chinese capitalists and the state. Lily Tsai works on a smaller scale in the Chinese countryside: from a case study of a few villages in a single province, she develops a thesis on the role of "solidary groups" in public goods provision, then collects administrative data through an informant survey of some 300 villages across four provinces and subjects her proposition to statistical testing. Both works are impressive examples of richly contextual research that successfully employs multiple methods. Combining qualitative and quantitative research findings is more difficult to realize in a journal article, given length restrictions, but examples include studies by Manion (1991), Kennedy (2002), and especially Lianjiang Li (2002, 2004).

CONCLUSION

What is the status of survey research on Chinese politics? This chapter points to many reasons for optimism about the enterprise. Most important of all, the products of survey research reflect a community that is actively engaged in building a valuable cumulative knowledge of Chinese politics. Nor does this community ignore the progress in our knowledge of Chinese politics gained from qualitative fieldwork or nonsurvey quantitative work.

Survey research on Chinese politics is still a fairly young enterprise, however. Some important areas for improvement remain outside the range of influence of American researchers. So long as the enterprise is subject to the intrusiveness of a regulatory regime that reflects a wary authoritarian politics, it will be difficult to develop strong open working relationships in survey research with Chinese colleagues at more institutions. This has several implications, none favorable. It obstructs the growth of accountability in survey research and the emergence of reputations for excellence among more Chinese institutions. Concerns to protect mainland partners are also a disincentive (if not always an absolute barrier) to widespread and systematic sharing of data. In turn, the dearth of publicly accessible datasets constrains the integration of survey data more broadly into research on Chinese politics, limiting it to a fairly small community of survey researchers.

APPENDIX 10.1: WHAT IS REVIEWED HERE

For this chapter, I reviewed English-language monographs and peer-reviewed journal articles authored by political scientists and published in nonmainland sources through mid-2008 to identify studies that exploit original probability sample survey data. This focus eliminates from consideration a substantial literature by sociologists and economists drawing from probability sample survey data, including work that to varying degrees bears on Chinese politics broadly defined. Nor do I review survey-based studies produced and published on the mainland. Mainland Chinese political scientists have conducted a large number of surveys, beginning in the 1980s. Nathan and Shi (1993) observe that most such surveys on which they have information are methodologically flawed. Surveys published in mainland sources appear to have improved in quality, but descriptions of their methods are often too sparse to permit evaluation. This is, of course, true of several survey-based studies published outside the mainland too.

I focus in the chapter on original surveys. Researchers based outside mainland China always work with mainland colleagues, but by "original survey" I imply their participation in the decision-making process that shapes the product in crucial ways. This includes choices about pretests, interviewers, training, sampling, and data input. This decision rule was not always straightforward to implement. In particular, Wenfang Tang typically compares evidence from original surveys and existing datasets in his work. For example, Table 10.1 includes a 1992 forty-four-city survey and a 1999 six-city survey, both of which he designed or played the main role in designing. The table does not include three other surveys in which he did not participate in the decision-making process as described earlier. At the same time, his access to these datasets is a noteworthy event in the history of survey research on Chinese politics. This is especially the case for the surveys conducted by the Economic System Reform Institute of China, disbanded after 1989. A National Science Foundation grant allowed Tang and Parish to recover the data and check them against the original questionnaires. For work based on existing datasets acquired by Tang, see Tang (1993, 2001a, 2005) and Tang and Parish (1996, 2000).

I invite readers to alert me to studies that do not appear in Table 10.1 but do meet the criteria for inclusion noted above. Table 10.1 and its associated references are updated regularly on my personal Web site at http://www.lafollette.wisc.edu/facultystaff/manion/.

As discussed in footnote 24, few of the datasets are publicly archived, but in my experience it is worthwhile to make a direct individual request to survey researchers for access to their data. This can be an especially useful strategy for graduate students to supplement qualitative fieldwork and archival sources, for example.

11

Surveying Prospects for Political Change
Capturing Political and Economic Variation in Empirical Research in China

Bruce J. Dickson

The potential political role of private entrepreneurs in China has been a salient issue in recent scholarship on China. Some see private entrepreneurs as potential agents of political change; others see them as apolitical and even supporters of the current political system. Although the political implications of China's rapid economic development have not yet been fully realized, many scholars, politicians, and journalists anticipate not only that economic development is leading toward democratization in China but also that private entrepreneurs are likely to be key players in that process. They point to China's growing numbers of entrepreneurs and "middle class" as potential supporters or even advocates of democratization (Parris, 1993; White, Howell, and Shang, 1996; Zheng, 2004). Others see private entrepreneurs as the leading edge of an emerging civil society that will eventually transform China's political system (Gold, 1998; He, 1997; Pei, 1998). These views were most prominent in the 1990s, when economic privatization began in earnest. In contrast, empirically based studies of the political interests and behavior of China's capitalists reveal most of them to be politically tied to the state or apolitical: very few exhibit strong democratic beliefs, and few of them engage in political activities designed to promote political reform (Chen, 2004; Chen and Dickson, 2010; Dickson, 2008; K. Tsai, 2007). These studies see China's capitalists not as agents of democratization but as key beneficiaries and supporters of the status quo.

Although much of the speculation about the potential role of privatization in general and private entrepreneurs in particular in fostering democratization in China is based on modernization theory, the comparative literature on the role of capitalists shows that they are very ambivalent about political change. They are rarely the leading edge of opposition to the authoritarian state, but their support can tip the balance between whether the state can withstand the challenge from democratic challengers or whether it will succumb to pressure for regime change (Rueschemeyer, Stephens, and Stephens, 1992). In Eva Bellin's apt phrase, they are "contingent democrats": to the extent that their economic interests are dependent on the survival of the regime, they remain supportive of the status quo (Bellin, 2000: 175–205).

These comparative insights are borne out by the most recent empirical research in the Chinese context. On the one hand, the democratic movement in China is weak and divided with seemingly little public support for the brave efforts of individuals and fledgling groups that face unrelenting persecution by the state. Capitalists are rarely first-movers in the democratization process; but in China, they have virtually no one to support even if they were inclined to do so. On the other hand, China's capitalists have been the main beneficiaries of the Chinese Communist Party's (CCP's) economic reform agenda and have little material reason to press for political change. As Kellee Tsai (2007) has shown, the interests of China's capitalists have been advanced by the CCP without the need for sustained collective action on their part. In addition, they are increasingly integrated into the political system, giving them easy access to policy makers. Under these combined circumstances, we should not expect that China's capitalists would be acting as agents of change, and indeed they are not.

This chapter will describe how the findings of comparative political research can be applied and tested in the Chinese context. It will begin with a description of the design of my survey research project, which was meant to capture some of the most salient aspects of contemporary China: the relationship between political and economic elites, but also divisions within each set of elites; regional diversity; and the rapidly changing nature of the economy, society, and political system. It will then provide some brief illustrations to show how these types of variation are relevant for the research question involved. A survey designed in this manner produces more reliable results than other studies that concentrate on a single locale or a single point in time.

DESIGNING SURVEY RESEARCH

China watchers in the scholarly, journalistic, and policy-making communities often expect that China's private entrepreneurs may be agents of political change. These predictions make two assumptions: first, that the Chinese Communist Party is passive in the face of social and economic changes; second, that China's private entrepreneurs have different policy preferences from party and government officials and would press for greater reform, either from within the state or from the outside. If private entrepreneurs are to serve as agents of political change in China, then they should exhibit views on political, economic, and social issues that are distinctly different from those of party and government officials. Otherwise, their growing numbers and greater integration into the political system will be more likely to support the status quo than to challenge it. Their increased integration into China's political institutions gives them the access they would need to press for change, but do they desire change? If so, what kinds of change would they prefer?

These are substantive questions that require reliable empirical data to confirm or challenge. According to most research done on these questions in China, these assumptions do not stand up very well against empirical evidence.

Rather than being the passive victim of economic and social change, the CCP is actively integrating itself with the private sector to promote rapid growth, thereby boosting its popular support and claim to legitimacy and preempting a potential threat. Rather than being inherent supporters of democratization, China's capitalists exhibit views that are not always substantively different from those of local officials, especially the ones with whom they interact the most. They are generally not supportive of democratic activists to bring about political change and they do not hold demonstrably democratic values (Hong, 2004; K. Tsai, 2007; Zweig, 1999). But these studies are not definitive. Most are either based on a single city or industrial sector.[1] Although insightful in their findings and rich in their details, the findings from single site or single sector studies cannot be generalized to the rest of the country with any degree of confidence. The concern that their findings are idiosyncratic due to peculiar features of their cases cannot be entirely dispelled, even if the findings seem quite plausible. Moreover, all previous studies are based on a single point in time and are therefore not able to assess how ongoing economic, political, and social changes are affecting the relationship between the CCP and the private sector, and the prospects for political change more generally.

An appropriately designed survey project can help address these potential shortcomings. Over the last several years, I have been engaged in an ongoing study of China's capitalists, their basic political and social beliefs, their views on economic policy, and their interactions with the state (Dickson, 2003, 2008). To arrive at more definitive answers, my survey was designed to capture the conceptual issues regarding the presumed link between economic and political change and, equally important, to capture key aspects of the Chinese context.

REGIONAL VARIATION

Because China is a large and diverse country, the design of the survey had to capture key aspects of regional diversity. The most important source of diversity for my study was the local level of economic development. The effects of economic development have been most strongly felt in the coastal provinces; here the growth rates have been highest and the private sector developed early and in some areas became the main source of jobs, tax revenue, and economic output. Conversely, inland provinces did not feel the effects of economic reforms as early or as extensively as those on the coast. The growth rates were lower, the standards of living lagged, and the private sector was less developed. Accordingly, I selected three provinces (Hebei, Shandong, and Zhejiang) and also selected one inland province (Hunan) as a control group. Next, within each province I selected two counties or county-level

---

[1] See Pearson (1994); Wank (1995); Unger (1996a); Nevitt (1996). The exception is Kellee Tsai's (2007) study, which is also based on a broad-scale survey that incorporates both regional and sectoral variation.

cities according to their level of economic development in the late 1990s when the first wave of the survey was conducted: one relatively prosperous and one relatively poor county was chosen in each province. (In all, three counties and five county-level cities were selected; one of the county-level cities had become a district of a prefecture-level city by the time of the second wave of the survey in 2005.) Within each of these counties, three townships were selected where the private sector was relatively well developed for that particular county.

This purposive selection strategy has advantages over the more conventional randomly selected sample. First, with only four provinces and eight counties in the sample, a strictly random selection process might not capture the economic diversity relevant to the research question at hand. Of course, increasing the number of sampling units would alleviate this problem, but primarily for budgetary reasons, this was not feasible. The selection of townships where the private sector was relatively well developed was also done intentionally: because the research question dealt with the role of private entrepreneurs in political change, I had to ensure that there was an adequate number of private entrepreneurs in a given township. If a random sample would have selected a township with a small or virtually nonexistent private sector, there would have been little for me to study.

INDIVIDUAL VARIATION

The final stage of selecting the sample concerned what individuals would be interviewed. The survey targeted two groups of people: the owners of relatively large-scale private enterprises and the local party and government officials with responsibilities over the economy; in other words, the economic and political elites of their local communities.

If capitalists are to be agents of change, a logical assumption is that it would be the relatively large-scale enterprises and not the smaller-scale mom-and-pop shops (individually owned enterprises, or 个体户) that would be most relevant. In other countries, it was large firms that were most politically influential, both as individuals and as members of business associations. Smaller firms in China, as in other countries, have less political clout and larger collective action problems, and therefore are less likely to be drivers of democratization. With that assumption in mind, the criterion for including firms in the sample was that their sales revenue during the previous year had been at least 1 million yuan. In some counties, this threshold had to be relaxed because there were not enough large firms to qualify. This was true not only for relatively poor counties but also for one county in Hebei that had a large private sector, though it was comprised primarily of small and medium-sized firms. In the 2005 survey, the 1 million yuan threshold was relaxed and the size of the sample was increased by about twofold to get a slightly wider range of entrepreneurs.

The final selection of which entrepreneurs to include in the sample was based on lists of registered private firms provided by the industrial and commercial bureaus of the county governments. I restricted the sample to only private firms because the theoretical literature links privatization and democratization, and because comparative studies of capitalists and democratization concentrate on the role of non-state-owned enterprises. Given the changing economic landscape in China, it may no longer be valid to exclude other types of firms from research on the political impact of privatization. State-owned enterprises (SOEs) increasingly have to operate in a market environment, and the ongoing restructuring of SOEs has created firms of hybrid ownership, such as joint-stock companies, limited liability corporations, and joint ventures. Many of these firms are a mix of public and private ownership and domestic and foreign investment. Most studies, like mine, do not investigate the political impact of these types of firms, which may lead us to overlook an important ongoing dynamic. I also restricted the sample to officially registered firms. Although Kellee Tsai estimates that as many as 15.3 percent of private firms are unregistered, they tend to be very small-scale operations, such as street vendors (K. Tsai, 2007: 109). In assessing capitalists' willingness and likelihood of being agents of change, excluding unregistered firms was not likely to skew the results.

To select the sample of private entrepreneurs to be surveyed, these officially registered private firms were ranked according to their reported sales revenue and selected using a random start, fixed interval process. For example, if there were fifty firms in a township that met the sample requirements – registered as a non-state enterprise and over 1 million yuan in sales – and we wanted ten firms to be selected for the sample, the survey team would pick the first firm at random and then select every fifth firm on the list. This guaranteed variation in the level of firm size. Because most private firms are small and medium-scale, selecting firms totally at random rather than from a ranked list ran the risk of not including any large-scale firms in the sample. (On a more practical level, it also prevented local officials from handpicking firms they wanted included [K. Tsai, 2007: 63–64].)

The second group of people included in the surveys was local party and government officials. A purposive instead of random selection was again used. The officials most relevant to the question of whether economic change and privatization were creating pressure for political change were the top executives and those with direct responsibility over the private sector. On the CCP side, this included party secretaries and heads of organization and united front departments; on the government side, it included county magistrates, heads of the industrial and commercial management bureaus, and the local chapters of the official business associations (All-China Federation of Industry and Commerce, Private Enterprise Association, and Self-Employed Laborers' Association). In each county, the people holding these posts at the county level were interviewed, and officials in townships and villages where the enterprises in the sample were located were also interviewed. In each county, approximately thirty officials were selected.

These specific officials were selected because they had primary responsibility over the local economy and were most likely to have regular interactions with local capitalists. They shared the common interest of promoting economic development, so surveying these particular officials and capitalists would indicate a degree of similarity in their views on economic, social, and political issues. If China's capitalists are to be agents of political change, then those views should be quite different; conversely, if the views were quite similar, and if the degree of similarity was becoming stronger over time, then the potential for China's capitalists to promote political change would be small.

These two groups – capitalists and party and government officials – are rather broad, and it would be wrong to assume that either group is uniform in its beliefs. For analytical purposes, I was interested in two types of variation within the two groups. For capitalists, the key source of variation was their relationship to the CCP. The main distinction was between "red capitalists" – capitalists who were also CCP members – and capitalists who did not belong to the CCP. I further divided these two groups to get a more nuanced sense of the relationship to the CCP: among the red capitalists, I distinguished between those who had been party members before going into business (whom I dubbed *xiahai* red capitalists, because 下海 is the Chinese term for going "into the sea" of the private sector) and those who were co-opted into the CCP after being in business; among non-CCP capitalists, I distinguished those who wanted to join the CCP from those who were not interested in joining. The result was a four-level variable that measured the degree of embeddedness in the party-state: *xiahai* red capitalists had the longest and presumably closest relationship with the CCP, followed by those who had been co-opted into the CCP, those who were not yet CCP members but wanted to be, and finally those who expressed no interest in joining the party. The reason for these distinctions was straightforward: some scholars have argued that capitalists will exert pressure for political change from outside the state, others that capitalists will work from within to try to bring about change. Asking whether the capitalists as a whole would support political change seemed too broad; it was more important to identify variations within this group and their implications.

The category of "local officials" was also too broad for analytical purposes.[2] It was necessary to disaggregate county from township and village officials for two reasons. First, bureaucratic level is a key determinant of the organization of political power in China, as it is in most countries. There is little reason to assume that officials at different levels will hold the same views just because they are agents of the state. In a variation of the "where you stand depends on where you sit" view of bureaucratic politics, the level of appointment is likely to influence officials' views on various economic and political issues. The second reason to distinguish county from township and

---

[2] In my book, *Red Capitalists in China*, I did not inquire into differences among officials, and therefore missed an important distinction, as examples later in this chapter will demonstrate. This oversight was duly noted by Jennings (2003). It became a prominent theme in *Wealth into Power* (2008), which compares the results of the 1999 and 2005 surveys.

village officials concerns their proximity to the capitalists in their communities. Township and village officials are likely to have more regular interactions with the capitalists in their communities, and perhaps even ties of friendship and kinship. The degree of similarity of views between officials and capitalists may also be influenced by the degree of proximity: capitalists may have more in common with township and village officials than they do with county officials. As will be shown later in this chapter, these distinctions among capitalists and officials not only allow for greater conceptual precision but they are also empirically important.

TEMPORAL VARIATION

In assessing the prospects for political change, China's rapidly changing economic, social, and political environments must also be considered. This requires observations at more than one point in time. Although this project was not originally conceived as a time-series study, the opportunity to do a second wave of the survey is one of the factors that distinguishes it from others on the same topic. Indeed, most survey research captures a point in time, leaving open the question of whether the findings are still relevant by the time the results are published. The first survey was completed in 1999, but the book based on the survey data was not published until 2003. In the intervening years, the private sector had experienced tremendous growth, the level of political protests – in part driven by the strategy of relying on the private sector to create economic growth – also grew, and the top leadership of the party and government had been replaced. How would these major changes affect the relationship between the CCP and the private sector?

To answer these questions, a second wave of the survey was completed in 2005. The same eight counties made up the 2005 survey, regardless of their current level of development, allowing me to observe trends in the same communities over time. Although the local rates of economic development varied, the rank ordering of the counties by level of development was nearly identical, with the exception of the sixth and seventh (poorest) counties, which reversed places. This was not a panel study. No attempt was made to identify the same respondents who participated in the first wave of the survey. In part, there was no theoretical need: I was concerned with changes in the relationship between the CCP and the private sector over time, not whether individual capitalists and officials had changed their minds on specific issues. In addition, the rapid turnover of party and government officials and the opening and closing of firms made a panel study infeasible.

As will be shown below, the second wave of the survey identified beliefs and values that had changed in light of ongoing events and the changing policy environment. At the same time, it also identified other areas of interest that remained stable over time, giving greater confidence that the survey was tapping into relatively stable beliefs and that the responses given were not ephemeral in nature.

Surveying Prospects for Political Change 207

COLLECTING DATA

Once it was decided who would be interviewed and where, the next task was to determine what would be asked. The questionnaire was written, revised, and finalized over the summer of 1997. The timing was an important consideration for several reasons. First, the CCP's relationship with the private sector was sensitive and controversial. At the time, a formal ban on recruiting private entrepreneurs into the party remained in effect, even though it was routinely violated at the local level. More generally, the propriety of the partnership between Communists and capitalists was repeatedly challenged by party veterans, who believed this partnership was contrary to party traditions and threatened to undermine the CCP's hold on power. Getting the cooperation of local officials and capitalists to research the nature of this relationship therefore seemed risky. That risk was compounded by a second factor: the political atmosphere concerning survey research in China at that time was tense. The State Education Commission had recently issued a policy advisory (or 精神) warning that all surveys by academic units should be approved in advance and that foreign scholars (including Chinese scholars living and working abroad) should not be directly involved in survey work.

The key to successful survey research in China is the local partner. In my case, I was fortunate to work with the Research Center on Contemporary China (RCCC) of Peking University. This is one of the premier survey research teams in China; it is headed by Shen Mingming, who received his Ph.D. in political science at the University of Michigan, widely recognized as one of the top schools for survey research and methodology.[3] It was Shen's suggestion that led me to do a survey of the CCP's relationship with the private sector, and his management of the actual implementation of the survey was crucial to its success. He and the RCCC staff contacted local officials to get their cooperation, visited each site in advance to do the groundwork, and then implemented the actual survey in the eight counties. Given the recent warnings against foreign scholars doing survey work in China, it would have been impossible to conduct this project without the RCCC as my partner. In later years, the political atmosphere has become more hospitable to survey work, but the importance of a local partner remains absolutely essential. Properly conducting a survey involves interacting with multiple government offices, designing the sampling frame, selecting individuals for inclusion in the sample, training numerous people to implement the survey, and finally entering the data. Sloppy work at any stage of the process will doom the project. Unlike interviews or archival research, survey work cannot be done by individual scholars working on their own, and mistakes and oversights can rarely be fixed with a return visit.

The questionnaire was finalized at the RCCC during the summer of 1997.[4] Assembling the questionnaire involved multiple challenges, some common to

---

[3] In the interest of full disclosure, I should note that Shen and I were classmates at Michigan.
[4] The 1997 policy advisory against foreign scholars participating in survey research complicated this process. In order to avoid implicating the center's academic and administrative

survey research, some specific to the Chinese context. First, the questions had to reflect the theoretical questions involved but also had to be intelligible to survey respondents in China. Second, the questions had to be worded carefully to avoid preprogrammed "politically correct" answers or, even worse, no responses at all. There was no point in directly asking respondents if they would prefer democracy to the current political system, even though that was the ultimate research question. Posing the question so starkly would not have elicited honest answers and likely would have led local governments to refuse cooperation on the project at all. (In order to elicit their cooperation, the project was titled "The Private Economy and Party Building.") Third, the questions had to make sense in China's political climate of the time. Even the phrase "political reform" presented a challenge. At the time the questionnaire was written, the Chinese phrase for political reform, 政治改革, was politically sensitive. It was identified with former CCP General Secretary Zhao Ziyang, who had been purged after the 1989 student demonstrations. Asking respondents about their views on political reform ran the risk of cueing them to think of Zhao Ziyang's failed efforts to separate the party from government in the late 1980s, which we did not intend. Instead, the more neutral phrase "improve the political structure" (改善政治体制) was substituted. Similarly, asking about official corruption was deemed too sensitive in the late 1990s, although it became a common survey question in later years.

Separate questionnaires were created for the two groups of respondents – capitalists and officials. Most of the questions were similar, or nearly so. For example, capitalists were asked if foreign competition was a problem for themselves; officials were asked if foreign competition was a problem for entrepreneurs in their communities. Capitalists were asked whether they had made charitable contributions; officials were asked if entrepreneurs in their communities had made such contributions. A few questions were asked only of each subgroup. For example, capitalists were asked about their sales revenue, fixed assets, number of workers, and similar questions concerning their firms; officials were asked about the relative importance of the state, collective, and private sectors of the economy, priorities in party recruitment, and whether they or their families operated a private firm.

When the second wave of the survey was done in 2005, the first question to be decided was whether to use the original questionnaire or to revise it with new questions. The advantage of keeping the original was that it would more readily allow comparison over time, which was the purpose of the second wave. The downside was that it would prevent gathering information about new questions, either because I had not thought of them before or because

staff, I participated in the planning meetings not as the principal investigator but as a colleague of the center's director. It is not clear if anyone was fooled by this subterfuge, but the uncertainty created by the new policy advisory made it seem necessary at the start of the project. By the time the survey went into the field, it seemed safe to reveal my true role to the survey staff, but not to the local officials who approved the project in their communities.

they had become more salient in subsequent years. In the end, the original questionnaire was once again used, with only a minor revision: a set of questions was added regarding the entrepreneurs' involvement in self-organized business associations and their effectiveness relative to the officially sponsored business associations.[5]

When the survey was actually administered, the questionnaires were self-administered by the respondents under the supervision of the survey team from the RCCC. The team also checked the identity of the respondents to be sure they were the actual owners of the enterprise and not a family member or manager. The respondents were promised anonymity, and their identities were not recorded when the survey was conducted. Even the names of the counties in the sample were not identified in the published works to protect the identities of the local officials who agreed to participate in the project. Because their identities were anonymous, there was no need to encrypt or code the resulting dataset. This guarantee of anonymity had a second and related benefit: it made the study exempt from review by my university's Internal Review Board (IRB) for human subjects research. This is an often onerous and arbitrary process that has bedeviled legitimate research, so the promise of anonymity not only directly benefited my respondents but also indirectly benefited the research project as a whole by saving the time and trouble of navigating the IRB.

At the time of the survey, the RCCC team also collected two other types of data. The first came from meetings with the local party and government officials. These were not structured interviews per se but group discussions (座谈会) on questions regarding problems of party building in the private sector, the role of the official business associations, and related questions about the party's efforts to guide and manage the private sector at the local level.

The second type of additional data collected at the time of the survey was aggregate county-level data about economic development and party membership that were mostly not available in statistical yearbooks. These data were necessary to get an objective measure of the importance of the private sector to the local economy and the extent of the CCP's relationship with the private sector. This proved to be more troublesome than expected. Measuring the importance of the private sector could be done by its share of GDP or tax revenue, or the number of people employed in the private sector relative to total employment, but not all counties had this information. Moreover, many statistical yearbooks only report on firms "above a certain scale" and therefore overrepresent SOEs and underrepresent private firms, which tend to be small relative to SOEs. In the end, the only measure that all counties could provide was the number of registered firms in the private, collective, and state sectors. This is imperfect because it does not directly measure the size of the private sector or its impact on the local economies, but it was the closest measure available.[6] Similarly, the CCP's relationship with the private sector

---

[5] This set of new questions was largely inspired by Kennedy (2005). See also Foster (2002).
[6] One reason for the lack of systematic and consistent data on the private sector is terminology. Chinese media and other sources often distinguish the state and non-state sectors, but the

could be measured by the number of red capitalists (party members who were also private entrepreneurs) or the number of firms with party organizations in them. These questions were asked in the survey, but an objective measure for the county as a whole would be useful as a reference point. However, although some counties provided very detailed information, others did not. Even when local officials provided what seemed to be very detailed information in the group discussions, their information did not always match the aggregate data provided by other local party or government offices. The consistency and reliability of data is a problem for most empirical research in China, and it certainly was for this project. On some variables, the information provided by the local statistical office was different from the information in published yearbooks or information provided by other offices. For a question as basic as the size of the private sector, it is remarkable that systematic measures are not readily available.[7]

EMPIRICAL EXAMPLES OF REGIONAL, INDIVIDUAL, AND TEMPORAL VARIATIONS

In this section, I give the findings from the surveys to illustrate the importance of capturing individual, regional, and temporal variations in survey design. These examples focus on priorities among the goals of development, specifically the trade-off between promoting economic growth and maintaining political stability, potential threats to social stability, and election to political posts.

Competing Policy Priorities: Growth versus Equity

One of the most salient differences in development strategy is the trade-off between economic growth and political stability. The need to preserve stability amidst rapid economic development is a primary justification for maintaining authoritarian rule, in China as well as in many other countries (Huntington, 1987). This trade-off has become particularly salient in China as the number of local protests has grown sharply in recent years. The number of public protests more than doubled during the period between the two surveys, from 32,000 in 1999 to 87,000 in 2005 (McGregor, 2006). Many of these protests have been a consequence of the strategy of rapid growth, such as the conversion of agricultural land for industrial development, environmental degradation, and official corruption. This growing threat to stability, and the

---

"non-state sector" not only includes private enterprises and *getihu* but also reformed SOEs such as joint stock companies, limited liability corporations, and the like, where the state continues to be a major investor. Precise and accurate definitions are essential for empirical research, but the rapidly changing Chinese context often makes such precision and accuracy hard to come by.

[7] See Huang (2008: 13–24) for further discussion of the difficulty of accurately measuring the size of the private sector.

TABLE 11.1. *The trade-off between goals of development among officials and entrepreneurs* (percentages of those who prefer growth over stability as the top goal)

	1999	2005
All Entrepreneurs	41.7	44.6
Xiahai red capitalists	39.1	42.9
Co-opted red capitalists	29.9	47.3
Non-CCP, want to join	42.1	42.1
Non-CCP, don't want to join	47.9	47.5
All Officials	60.6	49.1
County officials	76.2	59.3
Township and village officials	39.6	41.6

attention given to it by Beijing, should have helped change the views of local officials, leading them to attenuate their support for growth at the expense of stability.

The survey was designed to determine whether there were differences between capitalists and local officials, as well as within both of these groups, on this trade-off between growth and stability and whether these views changed over time. Both officials and entrepreneurs were asked whether their top priority was promoting growth or maintaining stability. One of the most remarkable findings in the first survey was the apparent cleavage between officials and entrepreneurs on this trade-off, one of the few issues where the two groups were "diametrically opposed" (Dickson, 2003: 132–134). However, as shown in Table 11.1, disaggregating the officials by their bureaucratic level reveals a more interesting story: the difference is not between officials and entrepreneurs but between county officials and the rest of the respondents. In the 1999 survey, county officials were most in favor of promoting growth as their top priority: 76.2 percent favored growth over stability, almost double the percentage of township and village officials and entrepreneurs. In the data from the 2005 survey, a clear majority of county officials remained in favor of growth over stability, even though the percentage dropped relative to that in 1999. The numbers for township and village officials and entrepreneurs showed a slight increase in terms of those who favored growth, but the majority in these groups still had stability as their top priority. In both surveys, differences across subgroups of entrepreneurs and between all entrepreneurs and township and village officials are not statistically significant, but the difference between both groups and county officials is significant (at the 0.001 level). These findings are consistent with those of Kent Jennings and others who have argued that the notion of the state needs to be disaggregated to be most useful, in this case by dividing local officials according to their bureaucratic level (Jennings, 2003). In my previous study, I made much of the difference between entrepreneurs and officials on the trade-off between promoting growth and maintaining stability. By adding the question of bureaucratic level, a more interesting and nuanced picture emerges. Although the differences between the groups narrowed during the time between the two surveys, they remained substantively and statistically significant. The design of the survey project made it possible to reveal these significant differences between levels of the state, political and economic elites, and levels of development on the goals of development.

Perceived Threats to Stability

The survey was also designed to elicit more specific information on what respondents saw as potential threats to stability. All respondents were asked whether increased competition and social pluralism were threats to stability. Specifically, respondents were asked about their level of agreement with the following statements:

- Competition between firms and individuals is harmful to social stability.
- If a country has multiple parties, it can lead to political chaos.
- If everybody does not share the same thinking, society can be chaotic.
- Locally, if there are many groups with different opinions, that can influence local stability.

Responses are shown in Table 11.2, and several trends are worth highlighting. First, on every question in both the 1999 and 2005 surveys, county-level officials have the lowest scores, indicating that on average they are less concerned with threats to stability arising from economic competition and social pluralism than are township and village officials and all groups of entrepreneurs. Second, on the three questions concerning increasing pluralism or diversification, all groups of entrepreneurs saw less of a threat to stability in 2005 than in 1999. In a few cases, the decline is slight, but it is mostly greater than five percentage points. Third, the greatest difference is on the first question, focusing on economic competition. Although the capitalists' concern over social diversity diminished between the first survey and the second, all groups of entrepreneurs were more concerned about the threat of economic competition to social stability than were officials, and that concern grew between 1999 and 2005, both in absolute terms and relative to officials. Finally, both entrepreneurs and officials saw economic competition as less of a threat to stability than political and social diversity. In both surveys, entrepreneurs and officials agreed on the rank ordering of threats to stability: economic competition was lowest, competition between parties was highest, and competition among individuals and groups fell in between. Although the absolute levels varied over time and among subgroups, the rank ordering was the same. This similarity in rank ordering reveals stability over time in the views of all groups. The survey design allows us to see more systematically the differences between layers of the state and changes over time, providing an advantage over studies of one group, one locale, or one point in time.

TABLE 11.2. *Perceived threats to stability among private entrepreneurs and local officials* (percentages who agree)

	1999	2005		1999	2005
1. Competition between firms and individuals is harmful to social stability.					
All Entrepreneurs	24.5	26.4	All Officials	11.9	12.2
Xiahai red capitalists	18.7	22.5	County officials	9.9	10.1
Coopted red capitalists	22.7	27.7	Township and village officials	14.7	13.8
Non-CCP, want to join	25.2	27.8			
Non-CCP, don't want to join	29.2	29.4			
2. If a country has multiple parties, it can lead to political chaos.					
All Entrepreneurs	48.0	45.7	All Officials	40.5	40.4
Xiahai red capitalists	50.8	49.9	County officials	36.9	33.9
Coopted red capitalists	47.7	47.3	Township and village officials	45.3	45.3
Non-CCP, want to join	49.3	44.8			
Non-CCP, don't want to join	42.9	39.8			
3. If everybody does not share the same thinking, society can be chaotic.					
All Entrepreneurs	37.6	30.7	All Officials	22.0	21.6
Xiahai red capitalists	33.9	33.1	County offiials	16.7	18.7
Coopted red capitalists	43.1	26.1	Township and village officials	29.5	23.8
Non-CCP, want to join	43.6	31.5			
Non-CCP, don't want to join	33.8	29.7			
4. Locally, if there are many groups with different opinions that can influence local stability.					
All Entrepreneurs	43.3	34.8	All Officials	33.8	28.8
Xiahai red capitalists	40.0	30.5	County officials	32.3	16.9
Coopted red capitalists	46.5	31.3	Township and village officials	35.8	37.5
Non-CCP, want to join	41.3	38.9			
Non-CCP, don't want to join	44.7	38.6			

TABLE 11.3. *Distribution of private entrepreneurs in local people's congresses*

	1999	2005
All Entrepreneurs of which:	11.3	10.5
Xiahai red capitalists	40.7	58.6
Co-opted red capitalists	29.6	23.4
Non-CCP, want to join	13.0	7.2
Non-CCP, don't want to join	16.7	10.8

Electing Capitalists to Political Posts

The final example concerns the participation of capitalists in China's formal political institutions, specifically local people's congresses. If China's capitalists are to serve as agents of change, one venue for their political activity would be these formal institutions. Indeed, Li, Meng, and Zhang (2006: 318) argue that private entrepreneurs sought representation in local people's congresses in order to assert and defend their property rights. The growing presence of China's capitalists in local legislatures has drawn considerable attention, not only from scholars but from the Chinese media as well (*People's Daily*, 2006). More than 200 private entrepreneurs are delegates to the National People's Congress. At the local level, over 9,000 entrepreneurs have served as people's congress delegates (Zhang, 2004: 318).

Survey data allow us to go beyond these aggregate numbers to see which capitalists are most likely to be politically active. Although delegates to local people's congresses are formally elected positions, the CCP has a determining role in who can be nominated and elected. Accordingly, the relationship of the capitalists to the CCP is the most important factor in determining this type of political behavior. The survey was therefore designed to delineate the capitalists' relationship to the party: for party members, whether they had joined the party before going into business or were co-opted afterward; for nonmembers, whether they were interested in joining the party. As shown in Table 11.3, the vast majority of capitalists in local people's congresses are red capitalists. In particular, the largest single group in 1999 and the absolute majority in 2005 are the *xiahai* entrepreneurs, the ones who were already in the party before going into business. In other words, the capitalists most likely to be people's congress delegates are the ones who were most embedded in the CCP before going into business. Rather than being agents of change, these capitalists are more likely to represent the status quo. In contrast, the group that might have the greatest interest in political change – those who are not interested in joining the CCP – has seen its numbers shrink over time. Expectations that capitalists may promote democracy by introducing new actors into the political system are not borne out by these data: rather than introducing new actors, the political system strongly favors those who are already part of it.

The real value of survey research is not simply in specifying the preferences and behaviors of different groups as a whole, but more important, in analyzing the relationship between variables. This allows us to see what types of individual and contextual factors determine which capitalists are more likely to be local people's congress delegates, not just which communities have relatively large numbers of capitalist delegates or the percentages of different types of capitalists among delegates. The interplay of individual and contextual factors in determining which capitalists are more likely to be local people's congress delegates can be seen from the multivariate analysis presented in Table 11.4.

Among those elected to local people's congresses, red capitalists are more likely to be delegates than are non-party members, even when controlling for a variety of other factors. In addition, they are more likely to be older and to operate larger firms than those who are not deputies. The impact of education is curvilinear: high school graduates are more likely to be people's congress delegates than those with less education and those with college degrees. Since the CCP is influential in deciding who is nominated, these results indicate that the CCP favors its own members, older and better educated capitalists, and those who operate the largest firms – in other words, the local political, social, and economic elites. The coefficient for the size of the private sector is negative, indicating that a given capitalist is less likely to be elected to the people's congress where the private sector is large. This may indicate a quota for capitalists in the people's congresses: if there is a ceiling on the number of capitalists who can be in a people's congress, the more capitalists there are in the community, the less likely any one of them is to be chosen. Alternatively, it could mean that in areas where the private sector is small, the capitalists are more inclined to be politically active in order to defend and extend their interests. More research is needed to determine a more definitive answer, but given the CCP's control over the nomination and election processes, a explanation based on the CCP's interests seems more plausible than one based on the capitalists' interests.

A final factor in the determination of which capitalists are people's congress delegates is the perceived threats to stability discussed in the section above. Those elected to local people's congresses are also more likely to see competition and social diversity as threats to stability. Toleration for pluralist viewpoints, interest groups, and competition among individuals, firms, and parties is generally seen as representing liberal or "modern" values, but these values are in short supply among this select but influential group of capitalists in China. If they were able to turn their political beliefs into policy, they would be more likely to favor limits on competition and diversity, and such steps would be antithetical to democratization.

In sum, on most of the questions examined here, the views of entrepreneurs cohere fairly well. Whereas Kellee Tsai (2007) finds the lack of a uniform viewpoint as indicating that China's entrepreneurs do not constitute a class, the data from my two surveys show they are nevertheless distinctive

TABLE 11.4. *Probit regression: Determinants of private entrepreneurs in people's congresses*

<u>Political Factors</u>	
Xiahai red capitalists	.677***
	(.157)
Co-opted red capitalists	.788***
	(.179)
<u>Individual and Firm Characteristics</u>	
Age	.036**
	(.009)
Gender	−.058
	(.227)
Level of education	1.324**
	(.538)
Level of education²	−.219*
	(.091)
Sales revenue (log)	.187***
	(.039)
Years in business	.027*
	(.013)
<u>Cultural Factors</u>	
Threats to stability	.090***
	(.026)
<u>Contextual Factors</u>	
Per capita GDP, 1000 yuan	−.004
	(.009)
Size of private sector	−.551*
	(.267)
Constant	−6.445***
	(1.040)
N	978
Chi²	146.64***
Pseudo R²	.217

* p< 0.05, ** p < 0.01, *** p < 0.001
Robust standard errors in parentheses

when compared to local officials, and especially to county-level officials.[8] Entrepreneurs may not have a singular voice, as indeed most groups do not, but their views are similar on a range of issues. Entrepreneurs are more likely to favor stability over growth, more likely to see the potential social consequences of economic competition, and more likely to see the risks of emerging

---

[8] This is the main theme of K. Tsai (2005); see also K. Tsai (2007). Besides our difference on this point, our findings are otherwise remarkably similar. Replicated results like these provide greater confidence in the reliability of our findings.

pluralism. More important, the views of *xiahai*, co-opted, and non-CCP entrepreneurs have become more similar over time. If their concerns were reflected in policy, it would most likely be to limit the degree of competition and pluralism. Ironically, officials have more "progressive" views on these matters. If entrepreneurs emerge as agents of change, it is hard to see them advocating either economic or political liberalization. Where the difference among subgroups of entrepreneurs matters most is their integration into the political system: red capitalists are more likely to be nominated and elected as people's congress delegates. Since they are already part of the existing political system, they have less incentive to promote regime change. Furthermore, because they are more concerned about economic competition and political diversity threatening social stability, they seem less likely to favor further liberalization. In contrast to assumptions that capitalists are inevitable supporters of democracy, these findings suggest that they are more likely to support the status quo. The survey design – which captured individual, group, and regional variation – was essential for uncovering these relationships.

CONCLUSION

These findings on the question of the political impact of privatization in China, and the potential for private entrepreneurs to be proponents of democratization, are the result of a survey research design that was sensitive to individual, regional, and temporal variation in the current Chinese context. This design provides greater confidence that the findings are reliable and not specific to one place or one point in time. In particular, the survey design explicitly sought to capture differences across political and economic elites, levels of the state, and levels of development necessary to address the theoretical questions that motivated the project in the first place: are China's capitalists becoming supporters of democratization, and if so, which ones are most likely to support that type of political change? A different design might not have revealed the divisions between officials and capitalists regarding the goals of development and threats to stability, or the preponderance of red capitalists among those who have been elected to formal posts.

Nevertheless, the survey design leaves room for improvement in later research. The number of counties, and therefore the extent of variation in the local context, was small. A single outlier could skew the results dramatically. Moreover, the counties were not a random sample, but were purposively selected. This limits the generalizability of the results. More important, the survey design lacks the kind of contextual details that would bring the survey data to life. In looking at the relationships between variables, it is easy to overlook the importance of local politics, personal relationships, and individual agency, which are better uncovered with other research methods. Most important, given this project's main theme of whether China's private entrepreneurs are likely to be agents of change, the surveys cannot easily identify which individuals are most likely to be motivated to engage in political action, individually or collectively, to bring about change. These two surveys did not directly ask respondents about types of political participation in which they have engaged, types of political reforms they preferred, or ultimately what they thought about democracy in China. At the time the questionnaire was put together, these questions were too sensitive to be asked. They may be more feasible in the current political environment, but that is not much consolation.

In addition, there are questions I did not know to ask at the beginning of this project. For example, whether a firm was a reformed SOE or a private enterprise from the start may be an important factor influencing its relationship to the state and its owner's degree of support for the status quo, but SOE reform was just beginning in earnest at the start of this project. Similarly, whether an entrepreneur formerly had been an SOE manager may be as important as whether he or she joined the CCP before or after going into business, but this also was not asked of the respondents. Unlike interviews and archival work, survey research makes it nearly impossible to go back and ask a few more questions to fill in the gaps. Instead, a new survey would be needed, with the large investment of time and resources that it would require.[9]

These shortcomings were offset by the advantages of the survey methodology. Individual case studies can provide a more in-depth look at an individual or locality, but they run the risk of highlighting exceptions rather than the norm. Research that simply extrapolates comparative findings to the Chinese context runs the even greater risk of drawing invalid inferences. Social science is based on probabilistic statements, not deterministic laws, and there is no guarantee that findings from other countries and other points in time will automatically apply to new cases. Empirical research is needed to test the generalizability of comparative claims and to adapt general concepts to China's rapidly changing political and economic environments. The design also took into consideration how to properly adapt a general research question – the role of capitalists in democratization – to the specific context of contemporary China. The degree of political embeddedness is not unique to China, but the specific way of measuring it – the relationship to the CCP – shows how general concepts can be easily adapted for empirical research in a new setting.

Using the same questions in the same communities at two points in time made it possible to show how multiple factors influenced the respondents' views on the questions examined here: the importance of bureaucratic rank, the distinctions between officials and entrepreneurs, the level of development, and the size of the private sector. The consistency across time in the relationships between the variables provides greater confidence that these results are not ephemeral but tap into substantive matters. The survey research methodology and the specific design of this research project were essential to uncover these relationships and to test comparative insights into the dynamic case of China.

---

[9] A new collaborative project with Jie Chen was designed to address these shortcomings, and the survey was carried out in 2006–2007. The initial results can be seen in Chen and Dickson (2010).

12

Using Clustered Spatial Data to Study Diffusion

The Case of Legal Institutions in China

Pierre F. Landry

As Manion details in Chapter 10 of this volume, social scientists with an interest in China already have contributed a healthy stream of survey research based on national probability samples, but the methodology behind these surveys has historically been dependent on the household registration system, or *hukou* (户口). Since the 1950s, Chinese households have (in principle) been listed exhaustively by village or urban neighborhood; for decades, local officials took great care to maintain and update these lists. This system was an efficient collection of population data, and household registration lists have thus been widely used as the basis of the vast majority (if not all) of probability samples drawn in China since 1978.

China's rapid economic transformation has dramatically undermined the key assumption that *hukou* lists are accurate and complete representations of the population of their respective localities. Until the early 1990s, reasonably reliable lists of residents could still be obtained from villages and neighborhoods, but China's rapid industrialization and urbanization have severely undermined the ability of local officials to track their populations effectively. As a result, survey researchers who sample the countryside face the problem of drawing respondents who, according to official lists, live in a village but in reality have become urban residents; yet, if researchers sample from urban *hukou* lists, they will often discover that migrants are not properly listed unless they happen to hold a formal temporary registration. Given the magnitude of recent internal migration in China, the problem is severe. We can no longer claim that samples drawn from *hukou* lists are representative of the population in a given locality. Nor can we claim that such samples are probability samples.

In this chapter, I demonstrate how the features of spatial probability sampling can overcome the hurdle of population mobility and coverage errors induced by "traditional" sampling methodologies. I also show how a specific feature of spatial sampling (geographical clustering prior to household selection) can be leveraged to test whether diffusion effects take place at the community level, using the specific example of the citizen's willingness to go to court. The chapter proceeds as follows. I first present the rationale and key features of the spatial sample that was drawn by a team of researchers in 2003–2004 for a project on Institutionalization of Legal Reforms in China (ILRC).[1] I then discuss the process of institutional diffusion and how it can be traced by linking individual data to the specific behavior of other respondents interviewed in the same sampling clusters. In the last section of the chapter, I test the argument that even small subpopulations (here, individuals going to courts) can have a large impact on the propensity of other community members to emulate their behavior, and presumably help consolidate these legal innovations.

UNTYING SURVEYS FROM *HUKOU* LISTS

The investigators of the survey on the "Institutionalization of Legal Reforms in China" (ILCR) were concerned that increasing mobility in the population seriously undermines the reliability of lists based on *hukou* and leads to the systematic exclusion of subpopulations that are theoretically important to the study of a rapidly changing society. Since the 1990s, the powerful combination of economic reforms and lax enforcement of household registration rules have gravely weakened the institution of the *hukou*. Rural-to-urban migration is taking place on a massive scale: in 1995, there were about 80 million migrants in Chinese cities, only half of whom had been formally registered by the authorities (Congressional-Executive Commission on China, 2006). Only seven years later, the population census of 2000 counted as many as 125 million migrants, 79 million of whom had crossed provincial boundaries (Liang and Ma, 2004).

As staggering as these numbers are, statistical authorities openly acknowledge that the 2000 census exercise most likely resulted in the most severe undercount of all recent Chinese censuses (by about 22 million people), primarily due to the dependency of enumerators on inaccurate registration lists (Zhang, Li, and Cui, 2005). The National Bureau of Statistics (NBS) estimates that the number of "peasant workers" exploded to 225 million by the end of 2008, 140.4 million of whom no longer work in their township of origin. These 140 million do not include other socioeconomic groups and urban registration holders who also experienced some kind of migration or are within-city movers, resulting in serious mismatches between official registration and actual residence (NBS, 2009).

The emergence of a large migrant population has been widely noted (Goldstein, 1987; Solinger, 1995, 1999; Yang, 1993; Zhang, 2001) but has

---

[1] The ILRC project was undertaken by Professors Shen Mingming and Yang Ming of the Research Center for Contemporary China at Peking University in collaboration with Wenfang Tang (University of Pittsburgh), Yanqi Tong (University of Utah), and the author (Yale University). Financial support by the Ford Foundation in China as well as our respective universities is gratefully acknowledged.

only slowly led to a serious reevaluation of sampling techniques derived from *hukou* lists. A number of studies have attempted to reach different types of migrants. Goldstein et al. (1991) were able to analyze migrants who reside in formally registered households, but they concede that this approach restricts the analysis to a very specific subset of migrants. As Goodkind and West (2002) discuss, migrants include a vast array of types, ranging from long-term residents who are ultimately successful in obtaining a formal registration to the "floating population" of informal, short(er)-term migrants who return to their hometowns regularly.

It is clear that *hukou*-based survey methods result in biased samples and that the problem will only worsen unless both residents and local officials are given incentives to update their *hukou* in a timely manner. These biases are not merely a statistical inconvenience but can profoundly impact theorizing about the extent and the nature of social change in contemporary China. Migrants are after all one of the most dynamic and entrepreneurial segments of the population. Using the ILRC sample, Tang and Yang (2008) have shown that standard assumptions about the behavior of migrants regarding dispute resolution do not hold once they are properly accounted for and included in a sample with some probability of selection as nonmigrants. Clearly, excluding migrants from surveys because they are admittedly hard to reach is bound to skew and polarize findings based on groups that have historically benefited from the "urban bias" of the regime (long-term urban residents) and on the rural nonmigrants who tend to be economically and socially disadvantaged. The ability to capture dynamic subpopulations (whether migrants or within-city movers) is also closely related to any conceptualization of institutional diffusion. People on the move bring norms, habits, and life experiences to their new places of residence, where they are in turn likely to acquire new ideas or norms or to adopt some of the behavioral characteristics of other community members. Seemingly representative surveys based on *hukou* lists make it more difficult to capture these changes when they reach only "permanent" residents.

In addition to the phenomenon of rural-to-urban migration, dramatic changes to housing policy in the mid-1990s ushered in an era of unprecedented urban construction during which millions of citizens became homeowners or rented housing in the private sector (Davis, 2000). The impact of these changes on the reliability of registration lists is almost as powerful as the phenomenon of rural-to-urban migration. Within-city mobility where movers do not feel compelled to change their *hukou* status (because they are already proper residents of the city in which they live) is a serious source of nonresponse: based on the formal registration lists, these "movers" may be drawn, but if interviewers are sent to their official addresses, they are unlikely to make contact as these respondents actually live in a different part of the city. During a proof-of-concept study of spatial probability sampling in Beijing in 2002, we found that 20 percent of the sample consisted of such movers. Adding the migrant population (25 percent of the sample), we concluded that

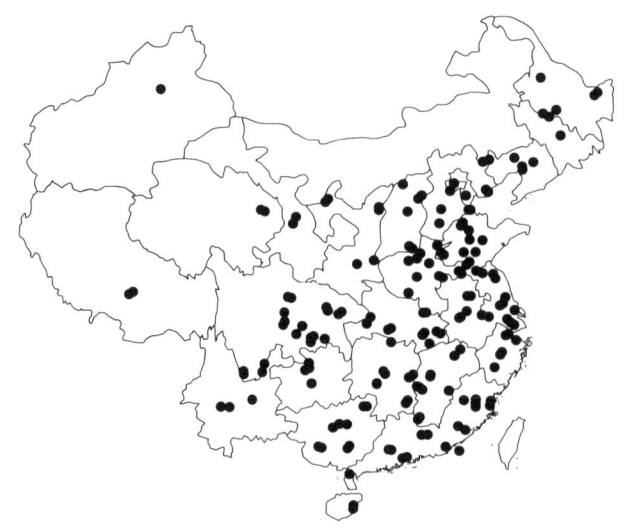

FIGURE 12.1. The Institutionalization of Legal Reforms survey of China (2003–2004). (Dots represent sampled counties and lines denote provincial boundaries.)

only 45 percent of our respondents would have been reached via the traditional *hukou*-based method of selection (Landry and Shen, 2005).

DATA: SURVEY ON THE INSTITUTIONALIZATION OF LEGAL REFORMS IN CHINA

The Institutionalization of Legal Reforms in China is the first national sample of its kind. We collected data on the types and extent of civil, economic, and administrative disputes on a national scale in order to examine in detail the multiple mechanisms by which grievances evolve. The survey is based on a multistage stratified sample in which each province, municipality, or autonomous region on the Chinese mainland is taken as a stratum. Within each stratum, counties (or urban districts) were selected at random by probability proportionate to size (PPS). Within each county, two townships or their *jiedao* (街道) counterparts in urban areas were also selected at random. We used 2000 census data to develop measures of size at the township level. Overall, respondents are thus clustered in 100 county units (Primary Sampling Units, PSUs) and 200 township units (Secondary Sampling Units, SSUs). The PSUs are mapped in Figure 12.1.

SPATIAL SAMPLING

The key methodological innovation in this multistage sampling design took place below the township level. To bypass the household registration system entirely, the spatial approach calls for the random selection of clearly defined sampling units that can be enumerated by the research team. Because this process is time-consuming and costly, it is essential to keep these units as small as possible so that trained enumerators equipped with global positioning system (GPS) receivers can easily locate and survey all final spatial sampling units. Prior experimentation in urban and rural areas suggested that grids of half square minutes (HSM) of latitude and longitude should be developed for all townships.

Whereas primary (counties) and secondary (townships and *jiedao*) sampling units were selected using the traditional two-step sampling procedure based on Probabilities Proportional to measures of Size (PPS) – with county and township population data obtained from the 2000 census – the IRLC project adopted a spatial sampling approach below the township level. In each township, town, or *jiedao*, two spatial units – specifically, HSM of latitude and longitude – were selected by PPS from a geographical grid. The size of each unit was defined in terms of the share of its surface that fell within a township. For example, if only a quarter of a cell fell within the township map, its probability of selection would only be .25/N (where N is the number of HSMs that are inside or straddle the township boundary). If a cell fell entirely within the township, its probability of selection would be 1/N.

Figure 12.2 illustrates the results of this procedure in two townships in western China. The three easternmost rectangles are the chosen HSMs for one township in Huangyuan (H.Y.) county: one unit straddles the railroad near the county boundary whereas the other two are located in more remote areas. In this case, the northernmost block was randomly assigned as the backup unit but in the end was not used.[2] Figure 12.3 shows how the same procedure worked in an urban setting, a district in the capital of a northeastern province. In dense urban areas, units (here, *jiedao*) have rather small surfaces, which leads to heavy clustering among the sampled HSMs.

The respondents were selected from micro-communities, that is, Final (spatial) Sampling Units (FSUS) in which all households were visited for interviews so as to ensure equal probability of selection throughout the entire sample (Landry and Shen, 2005). Each FSU is 1/80th HSM, which is 11.25 square seconds of latitude and longitude. Within each HSM, a varying number of FSUs was drawn completely at random and enumerated systematically by trained surveyors. To yield a consistent set of respondents in each township, the number of FSUs was inversely proportional to the expected population density of the HSM. In the case of Figure 12.4, the population density is high. We thus needed *in expectation* to draw only two FSUs, and enumerate them. By contrast, Figure 12.3 shows how a township of H.Y. county (the easternmost

---

[2] In each township, we drew a third HSM as a backup unit in the event that the first two draws would not yield enough respondents. In the event that the number of respondents per township was still unacceptably low, the initial draw was discarded and two villages were selected at random (by PPS) from the list of administrative villages in the township. These fresh HSMs were centered on the village committee. Final Sampling Units were then drawn using the standard protocol.

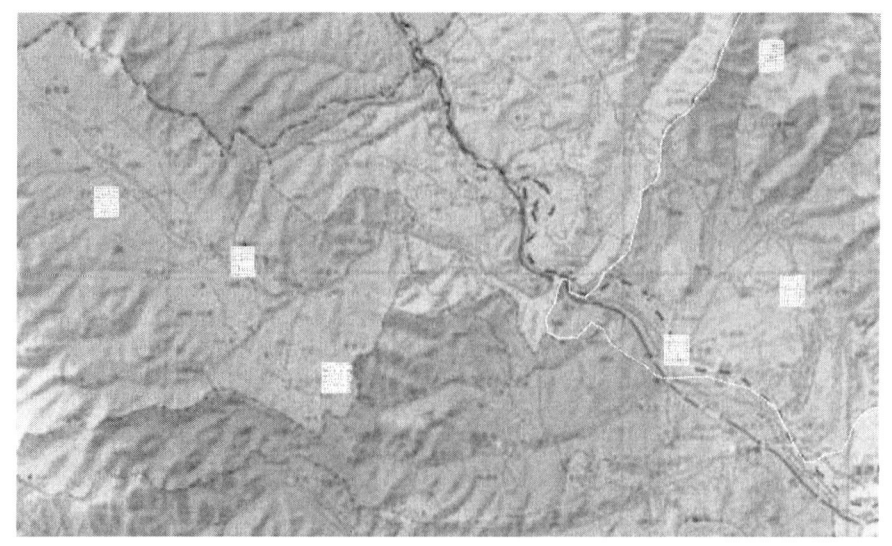

FIGURE 12.2. Example of a county map displaying township boundaries and basic infrastructure overlaid to the Google Earth model, with grids coded in Keyhole Markup Language displaying three Tertiary Sampling Units (TSUs) in each sampled township (one TSU per township was randomly assigned as a backup).

HSM in Figure 12.2) has such a low population density that a census of the entire HSM was required to yield, on average, the same number of respondents. The dots within each cell represent dwellings that were actually inhabited and where interviews were successfully conducted.

In the end, over 16,000 FSUs were surveyed nationwide, and the HSMs that were populated yielded a list of about 12,000 dwellings. Within a few weeks of this enumeration, teams of interviewers selected and interviewed one respondent per dwelling, using the Kish grid method. This procedure yielded a sample of 7,714 valid respondents, drawn with equal probability from a nationally representative sample of Chinese adults. Due to uneven response rates by age and gender as well as the purposeful underrepresentation of respondents drawn in very dense neighborhoods,[3] we used the 2000 census data to devise sampling weights. Finally, we specifically accounted for the design effect of this complex multistage survey at the levels of PSUs (counties) and SSUs (townships).[4]

[3] To control operational costs, if the enumerated lists within a given HSM exceeded 60 dwellings, only 60 dwellings were selected at random. In the final dataset, sampling weights incorporate this component to correct for this purposive but computable unequal probability of selection among these respondents.
[4] We do not account for design effects below the township level. The number of tertiary sampling units per SSU is not only too small to do so (mostly two, sometimes three when the backup unit was used), but numerous studies have also shown that in practice, most of the design effect occurs at the PSU and to a lesser extent at the SSU level; variance estimates are effectively unaffected. See Barron and Finch (1978); Dever et al. (2001).

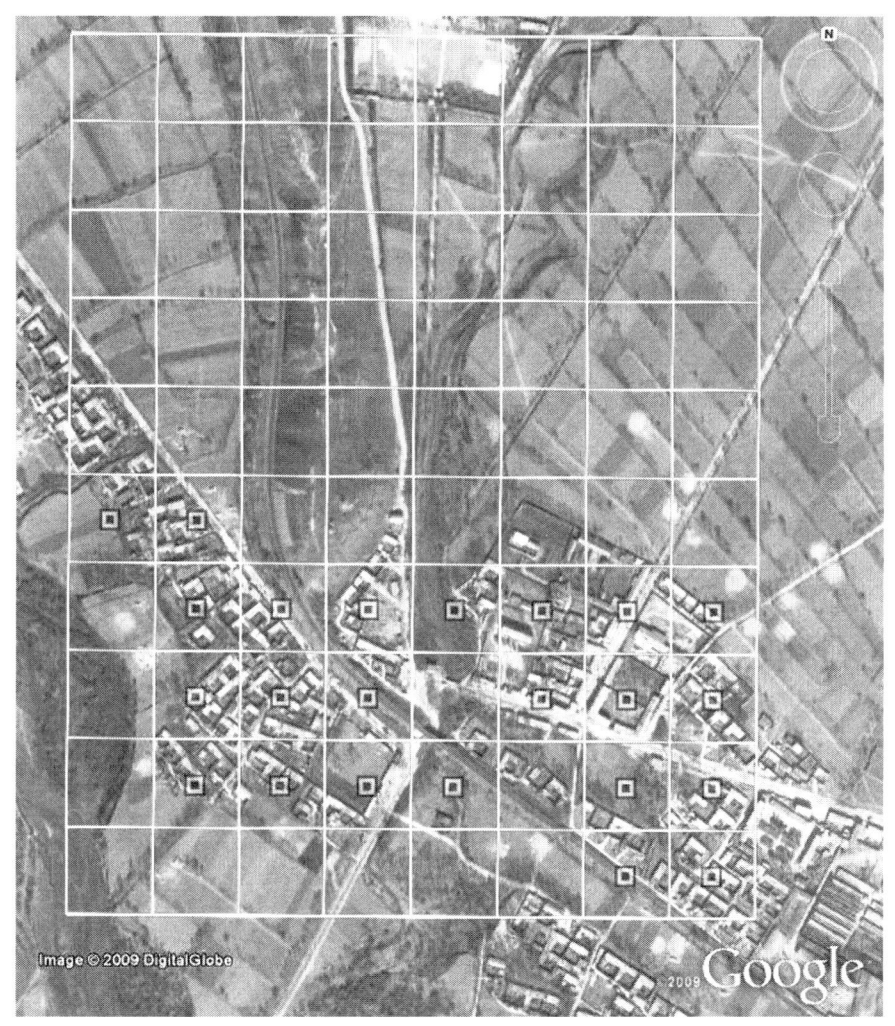

FIGURE 12.3. Example of a spatial sampling unit (half square minute) drawn in a low-density rural area in western China.
(Squares represent FSUs and dots indicate that one (or more) interviews were successfully completed.)

TECHNICAL ADVANCES SINCE 2004

When the IRLC project was implemented, affordable satellite or remote sensing information was neither available nor affordable to most social scientists. Since then, powerful earth visualization software such as Google Earth allows access to remarkable imagery that can be incorporated easily during the preparation phase of a spatial sample.

The images allow samplers to specify more reliable priors on the data. Without satellite imagery, it was not possible to model the distribution of the

FIGURE 12.4. Example of spatial sampling units in an urban area.
Half Square Minutes (HSMs [including backup units]) drawn in one *jiedao* of a large city in northeast China. As the population density is large, drawing two Final Sampling Units (FSUs) per HSM was sufficient to yield – in expectation – the requisite number of respondents. Large squares are HSMs, and small squares are FSUs. Dots within FSUs indicate that one (or more) interviews were successfully completed. The HSM without interviews is the backup unit that was surveyed but not used.

population density precisely below the township level. Some areas were (very conservatively) excluded from the sample a priori in remote regions where the best cartographic evidence and common sense suggested that population density was in effect nil, such as deserts, dense forests, or lakes. Without further details about the specific distribution of dwellings, the number of FSUs – drawn in inverse proportionality to the expected population density of the nonexcluded zones – was large (16,000). This figure was based on the research team's prior experimentation to yield the requisite number of respondents per SSU (townships), a costly and time-consuming process as enumerators had to travel to verify personally whether each FSU was populated.

With satellite imagery, a great deal of work can be accomplished in the office, and in many areas, at a level of detail that allows excluding empty squares a priori with a high degree of precision.[5] If sparsely populated areas happen to be sampled, researchers can literally zoom to an area to confirm ex ante whether surveyors and enumerators must be dispatched to this location.[6] In 2009 high-resolution imagery for China was still not available for the entire Chinese territory, but the data are improving constantly. Even without access to high-resolution information, the default definition is sufficient for coarser exclusion work, with the caveat that higher rates of Type I and Type II sampling errors are likely. It is also advisable to overlay cartographic data or information external to the earth model, which greatly improves the precision of the work (as we did ex-post with Figures 12.2, 12.3, and 12.4). If squares indicate populated points that are not clearly visible from the satellite image, these squares ought to be retained and verified by the enumerators.

To sum up, the ILRC survey provides a solid foundation for testing the validity of prior case-study findings and also allows making point predictions and generalizable propositions about the behavior of ordinary citizens. Furthermore, the sample is large enough that it captures rare events (such as disputes), conforms to the principle of equal probability selection, and is representative of China's varied geographic, demographic, and social and economic environments.

INSTITUTIONAL DIFFUSION

A great deal of the literature on institutional innovation stresses the role of trustworthiness as a key determinant of successful institutional innovation. If, under conditions that need to be specified, people trust an institution, they are likely to rely on it should the need arise; otherwise, they are likely to turn to reasonable alternatives. Trust is also a condition of institutional endurance in the long run (Hetherington, 1998; Levi, 1999; Levi and Stoker, 2000; Ulbig, 2002).

Many scholars have demonstrated empirically that both interpersonal trust and system-based trust are comparatively high in China (Inglehart, 1997; Shi, 2001; Tang and Parish, 2000). However, generalized trust may not be as reliable a predictor of success or failure of a specific institution. Just as trust between individuals can be generalized or particularistic (Uslaner, 2002), Jennings (1998b) has shown that individual trust in government institutions can be highly differentiated. A more recent study by Lianjiang Li (2004)

---

[5] Keyhole Markup Language (KML) is used to overlay data to the Google Earth model and is relatively easy to program. The specifications of the language are available at http://code.google.com/apis/kml/documentation/.

[6] If the satellite image is slightly outdated, it is advisable to retain the seemingly empty squares that are adjacent to populated ones in the sample frame to account for construction or urban growth.

confirms that rural Chinese exhibit highly differentiated levels of trust regarding central and local institutions.

The ILRC survey results demonstrate that these broad findings also hold with respect to legal institutions. We find that trust is institution-specific: whereas organizations that are frequently involved in dispute mediation (such as village committees) fare especially poorly, the courts and the procuracy are held in relatively high regard. Furthermore, most respondents trust institutions that are closely associated with the state to a far greater extent than they trust nonbureaucratic actors: legal professionals are less trusted than public security organs, whereas village committees fare worst of all institutions listed on the survey instrument.

Popular trust is overwhelmingly tilted in favor of central political and judicial institutions. As a follow-up to a general measure of trust (for instance, in courts), we asked respondents to contrast local institutions with central ones. In the case of courts, we asked whether they trust the Supreme People's Court, the local court, or neither. We asked similar central/local comparisons for people's congresses, the Communist Party, and government agencies generally. Although party members tend to be more trusting than nonparty members, central institutions enjoy a considerable degree of support in both groups.

Theorists of trust attach great importance to its relational aspect, but survey research has not been well equipped to test these arguments because respondents chosen at random may or may not be connected to other respondents in the sample. The spatial approach is a better alternative because of the inherent properties of the final sampling units: all households that are located in a small physical space (e.g., a spatial square second of latitude and longitude) are by construction each other's neighbors. Whereas in a typical survey, researchers would ask a respondent whether she trusts other people in the neighborhood, we would be better off knowing whether this trust is reciprocal. In a spatial design, we fortunately interview her neighbors as well.

The spatial sampling design is also a powerful tool for measuring the impact of unusual events within a community, such as going to court. This is a rare event, but the important issue is whether other community members who observe an event affecting a peer are learning anything from his experience.

The role of community networks is especially intriguing given the nature of Chinese society and the structure of the post-Mao state. Considerable research in anthropology (Kipnis, 1997; Ku, 2003; Yang, 1994), sociology (Bian, 1999; Gold, Guthrie, and Wank, 2002; Guthrie, 1999), economics (Krug, 2004; So and Walker, 2006), as well as political science and law (Lee, 1997; Oi, 1986) has been devoted to the extent and impact of social relations (*guanxi* or 关系) and its extent and its impact on individual behavior. If the importance of *guanxi* has indeed endured in the contemporary period, Chinese society should be more prone to the quick adoption (or rejection) of an innovation once it becomes known to members of a tightly knit social network. Dense ties facilitate information flows and rapid diffusion of the benefits and shortcomings of innovations among connected individuals.

TESTING DIFFUSION HYPOTHESES WITH SPATIALLY SAMPLED SURVEY DATA

The ILRC sample is uniquely suited for testing the impact of the small community networks due to its special design. This spatial clustering of the data at the FSU level gives us greater leverage on the analysis of social processes in which neighbors interact with one another. In such small communities, the probability that respondents know each other is very high. If diffusion effects are taking place within micro-communities, the ILCR survey is ideally suited to detect their magnitude.

We can identify respondents in their specific communities who were directly involved in legal disputes, went to court, and were therefore in the position to influence their network based on their experiences with the courts. For each dispute category covered by the instrument – civil, economic, and administrative – we inquired whether the choice of going to court was decisive in the resolution of the dispute. If so, we further asked whether they would be willing to use the same method should a similar dispute occur in the future. We can thus identify the specific communities with which adopters (defined here as past disputants who would use the courts in the future) are present. For each community, we can compute the mean share of respondents ($\bar{x}$) who are "decisive adopters" in each kind of dispute. For additional precision, the computation of s_i excludes the respondent herself, a necessary correction when clusters are small:

$$s_i = \frac{(\bar{x} \cdot N) - x_i}{N - 1} \text{ if } N > 1 \text{ and } s_i = 0 \text{ if } N = 1$$

where x is the variable of interest and N is the total of respondents sampled in the community. These shares are theoretically specific to each community member, although any pair of individuals who share the same behavior has the same share. As the variable of interest occurs rarely, $s = 0$ in most cases and has a theoretical maximum value of 1.

Consider the hypothesis that two parameters are jointly conducive to rapid institutional diffusion: trustworthiness of the court and presence of individuals within small communities who have engaged courts successfully (see Table 12.1). We cannot directly observe social networks, but it is reasonable to assume that members of small communities interact with each other frequently and learn quickly about unusual events. Given its rarity, victory in court certainly qualifies as the kind of news that is likely to spread fast. Rapid diffusion is likely to occur when a high proportion of satisfied and trusting end-users propagate their behavior through dense social networks. If only one of these factors is present, the process will be more gradual. If neither are present, we should observe little or no diffusion.[7]

---

[7] Note that the absence of diffusion does not imply that the number of court users will not rise; it simply means that individuals who use the courts will not be emulated in their communities.

TABLE 12.1. *Conditions for institutional diffusion*

		Trustworthiness of the institution	
		Low	High
Density of adopters	High	Gradual diffusion	Rapid diffusion
	Low	No/very slow diffusion	Gradual diffusion

Community Experiences and Institutional Diffusion

Although diffusion theory assumes that "adopters" are local opinion makers, we must emphasize that these experienced individuals constitute only a small fraction of a community. Using the township as the level of analysis, we encountered very few localities where more than one respondent had actually experienced a dispute that was decisively resolved in court. Indeed, we could not identify any experienced users in most communities: we found 69 townships (out of 200 surveyed) where civil disputes were resolved in court – 47 economic disputes and only 16 administrative disputes. However, the lack of clustering among adopters does not mean that adopters have no measurable impact in their respective communities. As rare as they may be, diffusion research suggests that they may impact the behavior of others if they happen to have strong links with "ordinary" community members.

The survey data suggest that adopters outnumber nonadopters among respondents who have successfully used formal legal institutions. Ninety percent of citizens who have settled an economic dispute in court claimed that they would do so again, against 78 percent in the case of civil disputes. The odds are lower among administrative disputants, probably because the scope of administrative litigation is still quite narrow and success rates remain very low. Overall, these proportions are consistent with the diffusion hypothesis: very few people ever go to court, but since those who do are willing to use the institution in the future, they are likely to diffuse their behavior within their social networks. This would explain the rising proportion of court users among citizens who are engaged in a legal dispute for the first time.

We can gauge the potential impact of these adopters by comparing the propensity of inexperienced respondents to go to court across communities with varying densities of actual adopters. Specifically, we asked respondents who had not experienced a dispute whether they would be inclined to go to court based on a hypothetical situation presented in a vignette of each dispute category. If the diffusion hypothesis is correct, we should observe a greater propensity to go to court among respondents who happen to live in communities where one (or more) of their neighbors has "adopted" the institution.

However, if individual-level variables that predict this behavior change over time, a greater proportion of the population will still adopt the institution.

TABLE 12.2. *Impact of court adopters on the mean propensity to go to court*

	Civil	Economic	Administrative
N	200	200	200
$F(1, 198)$	5.86	0.08	3.85
Model Prob > F	0.02	0.78	0.05
	Coefficient	Coefficient	Coefficient
Share of Court Adopters in Township	1.662**	0.345	4.43**
Constant	0.419***	0.492***	0.30***

***, **, and * denote levels of significance at .01, .05, and 0.1 levels, respectively.

The preliminary evidence is again encouraging for the diffusion hypothesis: using townships as the unit of analysis, two of the three simple bivariate regressions show that in townships where residents have been to court in civil and administrative disputes and are willing to use the institution again, their neighbors who were never engaged in a dispute are more prone to go to court than are residents of communities where no one has any experience with courts (see Table 12.2). However, this does not seem to be the case for economic disputants. To be certain of the net impact of these "adopters" on institutional diffusion, we require a fully specified model that captures both the impact of the individual characteristics of the respondents and the impact of the institution adopters in their community. Such models allow proper measures of the magnitude of these diffusion effects.

Multivariate Analysis: Modeling the Propensity to Go to Court

The propensity to go to court is modeled as a probit equation that takes into account the multistage stratified nature of the sample design and uses probability weights. Separate estimates were computed for each class of disputes that was covered in the ILRC project. We asked all respondents whether they had been involved in civil, economic, or governmental disputes in the past twenty years and whether they chose to go to court to resolve the disputes. The dependent variable is coded 1 if the respondent went to court, and zero otherwise. Those who did not experience disputes were asked to react to a simple vignette and describe the actions they would likely take under such circumstances. This technique is more reliable than asking unstructured questions, particularly since we do not have the problem of cross-cultural comparisons in a single-country study (King et al., 2003). If the respondents never encountered a civil (respectively, economic or administrative) dispute, the dependent variable is also coded 1 if they asserted that they would use the courts in their evaluations of hypothetical civil, economic, and administrative cases presented as vignettes.

On the left-hand side, the model accounts for the disparity between respondents who actually experienced disputes and those who responded to these hypothetical situations.

$$prob(Court)_{|d=0} = \Phi(X\beta) + \varepsilon \quad \text{for individuals who did not experience a dispute of type } d \text{ and,}$$
$$prob(Court)_{|d=1} = \Phi(X\beta + d) + \varepsilon \quad \text{for individuals who did.}$$

The respondents who answered the hypothetical questions after a vignette were more likely to state that they would go to court: their expressed preferences were costless, in contrast to the disputants who actually chose to go to court and faced tangible transaction costs. I interpret the magnitude of the coefficients associated with these actual dispute-specific dummy variables as markers of the transaction costs of going to court.

Since the diffusion hypothesis rests on the impact of two variables (the trustworthiness of courts and the density of adopters in the community), we need to test whether adding these variables to a baseline model actually improves the predictive power and the statistical significance of the model. Since the likelihood-ratio test cannot be performed on probit regressions for a complex survey design, we must instead rely on unweighted probits estimated with the same set of independent variables. Because of a small number of missing observations when these two variables are added to the baseline model, the likelihood-ratio test is restricted to a subset of observations that are common to the saturated and the nested model (Table 12.3).

As shown in Table 12.3, regardless of what kind of dispute – civil, economic, or administrative – these likelihood-ratio tests are all consistent with the diffusion hypothesis. The saturated models are always superior to the nested ones.[8] However, the specific significance of the variable that captures the presence of community adopters varies by dispute category: it is considerable for civil disputes, less so for economic disputes, and insignificant for administrative disputes. The expected dynamics of diffusion hold very well for civil disputes: the coefficients are positive (in the expected direction) for both variables. The propensity to go to court varies across individuals and communities as a function of these parameters. Varying these parameters and holding all other variables at their sample mean yields a more intuitive picture of the joint impact of these variables (as shown in Figure 12.5). The findings of diffusion research through simulations that small networks can have large behavioral consequences seem to apply here as well: even a small share of adopters at the community level greatly increases the likelihood that community members will also adopt the same behavior.

---

[8] Due to space limitations, I do not discuss here a number of control variables measured at the respondent level included under the headings "human capital and information," "political and social capital," and "sampling units" in Table 12.3. Interested readers may consult Landry (2008b) for a substantive elaboration of these variables.

TABLE 12.3. *Probit estimates of going to court in civil, economic, and administrative cases*

	Model 1	Model 2	Model 3
	Civil	Economic	Administrative
Number of strata	24	24	24
Number of PSUs (counties)	100	100	100
Number of observations	7160	7160	7160
Estimated population size (millions)	850	850	850
Prob > χ^2	0.000	0.000	0.000
Control for Actual Disputes			
Civil dispute	-0.841***	–	–
Economic dispute	–	-0.862***	–
Administrative dispute	–	–	-1.062***
Diffusion Variables			
Trustworthiness of courts	0.177***	0.252***	0.208***
Share of court adopters in township			
Civil cases	5.903**	–	–
Economic cases	–	5.845	–
Administrative cases	–	–	3.717
Human Capital & Information			
Formal education (years)	0.023**	0.030***	0.020***
Legal knowledge score	0.061***	0.044***	0.056***
Television	0.119***	0.052**	0.076**
Political and Social Capital			
CYL member	0.172***	0.130	0.005
CCP member	0.229***	0.189**	0.102
Contact w/ Party or Gov. Cadre	0.055	0.091*	0.063
Contact w/ Legal or Public Security official	0.225***	0.174***	0.162***
Contact w/ People's Congress	0.084	0.050	-0.001
Contact w/ lawyer	0.131	0.191**	0.017
Contact w/ Legal Aid Bureau	0.038	-0.181*	-0.176
Contact w/ Labor Union	0.030	0.129*	0.047
Demographic Variables			
Age	0.006	0.008	-0.024**
Age-squared	0.000	0.000	0.000*
Female	-0.019	-0.026	0.105**
Han nationality	-0.016	0.008	-0.102
Urban registration	0.334***	0.123	0.148*
Full-time farmer	-0.040	-0.098	-0.041

(*continued*)

TABLE 12.3. (*continued*)

	Model 1	Model 2	Model 3
	Civil	Economic	Administrative
Constant	−1.548***	−1.356***	−1.133***
LR-test of full vs. nested model without diffusion variables (unweighted probit with 7,160 observations)			
LR $\chi^2_{(2)}$	102.61	131.33	112.15
Prob > χ^2	.000	.000	.000

Because only one PSU was drawn in the smallest provinces, the original strata are grouped in 24 post-estimation strata. Linearized variance estimates account for complex multistage survey design effects, with stratification, first-stage selection of PSUs (counties) and second-stage selection of SSUs (townships). These calculations ignore design effects at and below the third stage.
***, **, and * denote levels of significance at .01, .05, and 0.1 levels, respectively.

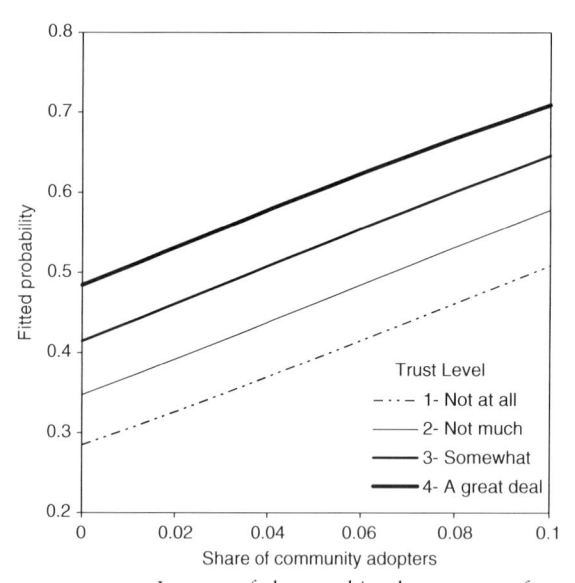

FIGURE 12.5. Impact of the combined presence of court adopters in the community and the respondent's level of trust in the courts on the probability of adopting courts as a dispute resolution venue in a civil case. (All other right-hand side variables are set at their sample mean.)

CONCLUSION

The technology of survey research in China and elsewhere must adapt to rapid social change: in China, migration to urban areas and general occupational and residential mobility greatly complicate reaching respondents drawn at random from official registration lists. This process is not unique to China, but it is especially acute because the history of restricting population mobility from the 1950s to the 1990s through the *hukou* system gave survey researchers extraordinarily reliable sample frames. Given the magnitude of the migration, early approaches have become inappropriate.

Spatial sampling is an effort to solve this problem, by incorporating migrants into sample frames in a cost-effective manner, and to reduce bias induced by coverage errors. This chapter also demonstrates an important secondary benefit of spatial sampling: the ability to investigate diffusion patterns among small clusters selected at random into equal probability samples and to explicitly test hypotheses about the process of institutional diffusion.

The efficiency and affordability of the technique was refined and improved in other projects, including recent waves of the Beijing Area Study, a project on Inequality and Distributive Justice, as well as the latest wave of the World Values Survey (mainland China sample). Better technology combined with the practical experience accumulated by the research teams has greatly improved control over sampling and enumeration costs. There are nonetheless significant challenges ahead. All surveys (spatial or otherwise) face the increasing problem of access to gated communities. As the number of housing estates grows in Chinese cities, even the best spatial sample cannot solve the problem of convincing gatekeepers to allow enumerators into their estates. This risks the loss of entire clusters from the survey, many of which are populated by affluent citizens. Geographical Information Systems and satellite imagery can help researchers understand and perhaps model this process of "community nonresponse," but they cannot solve the problem entirely. It seems advisable to lower these risks by keeping clusters as small as is practical and to increase sampling ratios at the lower stages of selection.

13

Measuring Change and Stability over a Decade in the Beijing Area Study

Mingming Shen and Ming Yang, with Melanie Manion

Descriptive statistics from representative sample surveys conducted in mainland China provide a static picture that is often soon overtaken by the impact of rapid socioeconomic change. The importance of longitudinal data generally, but especially in such a context, cannot be overstated. Survey researchers seem to recognize this: as discussed in Chapter 10, a remarkable number of surveys conducted in mainland China have a longitudinal component. By far the most ambitious of these is the Beijing Area Study (BAS), an ongoing annual representative sample survey of Beijing residents, designed and conducted since 1995 by the Research Center for Contemporary China (RCCC) at Peking University. This chapter begins with an introduction to the underlying vision and goals of the BAS, as conceived in the early 1990s. It then turns to specific issues of questionnaire content, sampling design, and survey implementation. We pay particular attention to the challenges and changes faced over the first decade of the BAS; major changes in sampling were made in 2007, however, and we review these here. For the most part, we do not present survey findings, except to illustrate particular points in the discussion of methods.[1]

VISION AND GOALS

The BAS focuses mostly on socioeconomic rather than explicitly political issues. Indeed, "politics" does not even appear in the full project title: Beijing Annual Survey of Social and Economic Development (北京社会经济发展年度调查). This is not simply because political topics are more sensitive than social or economic topics, with implications for survey implementation, although this is certainly a serious consideration for a project with a long projected life span as opposed to a one-shot effort. It also has much to do with the context of the early 1990s, when the vision of the BAS initially emerged. After 1992, with a renewed policy emphasis promoted by Deng Xiaoping on the role of the

---

[1] For a presentation of findings across issue areas for the first decade of the BAS, see Yang et al. (2007).

private sector in the economy, the pace of economic and accompanying social change in China increased rapidly. In the new historic period of "reform and opening," the broad goal of the BAS designers was to capture, with a continually updated dataset, the impact of the major ongoing reforms on the everyday lives of ordinary Chinese.

An important influence on the BAS as it emerged was a particular American survey experience. While earning his doctorate in political science at the University of Michigan, Mingming Shen gained firsthand experience with survey work as an interviewer for the Detroit Area Study. This study and Chicago's General Social Survey provided well-established models of longitudinal single-city surveys. When designing the survey and questionnaire, BAS organizers also sought the guidance of experienced experts, for example, convening a forum in April 1995 to solicit the views of survey researchers from the University of Michigan's Institute for Social Research.

The influence of the Detroit Area Study and Chicago General Social Survey is reflected in an early decision on questionnaire design. Specifically, in addition to demographic measures, which are repeated annually, the questionnaire is divided into two parts: (1) core items, repeated annually or at regular but less frequent intervals, providing continuity of measures over time, and (2) items designed to change from year to year to reflect changing research agendas or new events. Three other early decisions also set the framework for BAS planning. First, costs dictated the choice of a cross-sectional design rather than a more ambitious panel study (i.e., where an attempt is made to reinterview the same subjects year after year). Second, BAS organizers chose face-to-face interviewing over other implementation methods because of the greater control it offers over accuracy and quality of survey responses. Finally, with few exceptions (described below), BAS questions are forced-choice items. Again, this mainly reflects considerations of cost: before data input, open-ended questions must be systematically coded, a difficult and time-consuming process.

The BAS vision encompasses five goals, targeting different communities. A primary goal is to gauge the impact of the reforms on the lives of ordinary citizens, creating a valuable database by gradually, regularly, and frequently accumulating substantial data on a standard set of indicators. This rich set of empirical materials serves as a basis for systematic investigation into Chinese social change by the scholarly community. Second, the BAS is designed to provide a reliable empirical foundation for policy recommendations to government (and even to enterprises), as relevant. The Beijing Municipal Government Policy Research Office offered highly valued sponsorship in the project's early years. Third, the BAS aims to promote by example the development of quantitative empirical investigation and analysis in Chinese social science. A fourth aim has to do with graduate education. As a major ongoing project of a university research center, the BAS is an educational tool. Many cohorts of graduate students at six universities in Beijing have participated in the project – implementing the sampling design, interviewing respondents, reviewing fieldwork, coding responses to open-ended questions, and entering data. Several cohorts of graduate students associated with the RCCC have honed their statistical skills by analyzing BAS data to produce research papers and graduate theses. Finally, the BAS is a bridge between Chinese and nonmainland academic communities, sharing data on Beijing's social and economic development. The RCCC works with nonmainland scholars to craft appropriate items that reflect particular research interests. These items are "piggybacked" onto the standard BAS questionnaire. Nonmainland scholars can obtain a unique high-quality set of individual-level data that includes their own items as well as a large assembly of standard social and demographic indicators. For example, studies by Johnston (2004, 2006) and Johnston and Stockmann (2007) draw largely from a time series of mainland Chinese views on foreign affairs based on responses to questions designed by Johnston in collaboration with the RCCC and included in the BAS from 1998 through 2004.

Certainly, the most interesting and important feature of the BAS is its extended series of survey data representing the same population, the population most easily accessible to the RCCC at Peking University. Beijing, at the center of national politics, is obviously a distinct environment. Its residents are by no means representative of all mainland Chinese or even of all urban Chinese. At the same time, from everything we know, ordinary Chinese who live in Beijing are probably also more highly attuned to policy changes than are many other urban mainland Chinese. In this sense, then, the views of this distinct population may be of intrinsic interest.

QUESTIONNAIRE CONTENT

As noted above, a key point of departure for the BAS was the policy context: a time of major economic and social change in China. A simple working hypothesis emerged in the early stages of the questionnaire design: if a majority in society have a supportive orientation toward the changes and can accept disruptions brought about by them, then change can be carried out smoothly. Further, to the extent that people see that change has actually brought them benefits, their confidence in prospects for the future, their level of understanding of change, and their ability to accept disruptions brought about by change all increase – and the possibility of successful change is thereby increased.

Core Questions

Core items on the BAS questionnaire include a wide variety of commonly used individual-level social and demographic indicators: sex, age, education, occupation, type of workplace, income, housing, marital status, and length of residency in Beijing, for example. These items, included annually, are not completely unproblematic to design well, but they pose relatively fewer challenges than other questionnaire items.

Measuring Change and Stability over a Decade 239

TABLE 13.1. *Questions asked annually in the Beijing Area Study*

Subjective ranking of household social class
Evaluation of household living conditions compared to last year
Evaluation of relative housing conditions (added in 1996)
Satisfaction with living in Beijing
Evaluation of achievements of "reform and opening"
Level of benefits to household from "reform and opening"
Evaluation of current national economic situation
Estimate of national economic situation one to two years in the future
Estimate of national economic situation five to ten years in the future
Evaluation of Beijing's current economic situation
Estimate of Beijing's economic situation one to two years in the future
Estimate of Beijing's economic situation five to ten years in the future
Evaluation of seriousness of problems in Beijing: market management, health services, income distribution, education, prices, unemployment, social stability, environmental protection, traffic management, communications, energy supply, city government construction, housing, social welfare, city appearance and sanitation, "floating population"
Among the above problems, the three most serious problems in Beijing
Whether Beijing government has taken action on most serious problems
If action taken, effectiveness of action
Whether Beijing government has enough power to address most serious problems
Whether Beijing government has enough resources to address most serious problems
---

As respondent fatigue affects response, interviews cannot be too long; this means that every questionnaire item carries an opportunity cost. Initial decisions on core items to be included annually affect the future of all BAS questionnaires as they take up space that might otherwise be used to pursue changing research agendas or to explore the impact of new events. Some core items that seem highly important in the mid-1990s may lose their importance after a number of years. Should these items then be dropped, losing continuity in measurement and gambling that they will never regain importance? Question wording is also relevant here: whether expressions such as "reform and opening" (改革开放) are easily understood by ordinary Chinese decades after their introduction depends in part on policy changes. BAS core questions mainly reflect caution (i.e., little or no change) on both these issues.

Core BAS items include questions asked annually since 1995 and questions asked every few years. The former sorts of questions number about two dozen, depending on how one counts items. These are listed in Table 13.1 and can be grouped into five categories. A first set of questions has to do with household living conditions, subjective social class, and satisfaction with living in Beijing. The question on housing conditions, added in 1996, is an example of learning from previous findings: housing emerged as one of the three "most serious problems in Beijing" in another question. More generally, the BAS designers reasoned that growing sales of commodity housing would produce significant variation across urban Chinese residents on a basic livelihood issue. A second short set of questions asks respondents to evaluate the achievements of the "reform and opening." A third set of questions asks for evaluations of the current and future economic situation, both in Beijing and nationally.

The last two sets of questions are more politically sensitive. One focuses on problems in Beijing in sixteen specific issue areas. This is an important and fairly time-consuming set of questions. Respondents are asked whether there is a problem in this issue area; if they respond "yes," they are asked whether the problem is serious. They are then asked to name the issue areas with the three most serious problems in Beijing. In 1999 and 2000, the BAS added open-ended questions that probed the exact nature of the problem for every issue area where respondents indicated a problem existed. This fourth set of questions sets up the most explicitly political set of core questions, which focuses on the Beijing Municipal Government. These questions ask about policy measures taken by the municipal government to address each of the three most serious problems noted by the respondent: whether the government took action, the effectiveness of the action (if taken), whether the government has sufficient power to address the problem, and whether the government has sufficient resources to address the problem.

These core questions, asked annually, allow analysts to gauge change and stability of views on basic issues of livelihood over time, something that is not possible with other sorts of Chinese data. For example, focusing simply on frequency distributions on a couple of policy-relevant and political items, we find that the evaluations of benefits to the household from "reform and opening" diverged greatly in the mid-1990s, with the preponderance of respondents reporting few benefits; by the end of the 1990s, however, roughly half of respondents reported few benefits and half reported many benefits. In another area, we find the "floating population" and social stability dominating the three most serious problems in Beijing for successive years; unemployment, health services, and housing are also among the most serious problems for high proportions of respondents. Finally, we find stability of responses on the effectiveness of the Beijing Municipal Government at solving the city's most serious problems: except in 1998, when the proportions are roughly equal, about 60 percent of respondents rate government response as effective. Obviously, with these and all core items, the BAS demographic data also allow us to analyze data (i.e., rather than simply report descriptive findings) and to examine change over time across different subsets (e.g., by age, income, education) of Beijing residents.

Core questions in a second category are now asked annually but were added to the BAS after its initial inception. A large battery of questions on views about foreign countries is an example of this. These questions were added to the BAS in 1998 and asked annually thereafter. They include use of a "feeling thermometer" to gauge feelings toward more than a dozen countries (some added after 1998); evaluations of Japan, China, and the United States as well as Japanese, Chinese, and Americans; and questions on the degree of

Measuring Change and Stability over a Decade 241

bellicosity of various powerful countries. Media consumption patterns are another issue area in which questions were added to the BAS after 1995 but then asked annually.

Core questions in a third category are asked regularly, but not annually. Items measuring a wide range of values are a good example of this category of questions. Values tend to be fairly stable, which suggests that they do not need to be measured annually. At the same time, with major socioeconomic change in China, it is important to investigate the degree of value change and stability as an empirical question. The BAS measures specific values every three years. These include equality of the sexes, income equality, equality of opportunity, post-materialism, moral conduct, competitive conduct, traditional Chinese values (e.g., collectivism), nationalism, and the relationship between the state and the individual. Each value is measured with several questions.

Questions Asked Infrequently

In addition to core questions, the BAS asks some questions infrequently, usually only once. For example, in 1998, to commemorate the twentieth anniversary of reform, the BAS asked three open-ended questions that called on respondents to reflect on the past two decades and report three important events since 1978, three people with significant influence since 1978, and three important changes in ways of thinking since 1978. Interestingly, the highest proportion of respondents (39 percent) recalled June 4, 1989, as one of three important events.

Most questions that appear in only one year have to do with current "hot issues," with several items used to measure orientations toward a single issue. These include corruption (1995), social stability (1995 and 1996), environmental protection (1997 and 2001), transfer of Hong Kong sovereignty (1997), worker furloughs and a guaranteed minimum income (1997), the Asian financial crisis (1998), China's application to host the 2008 Olympics (2000), Chinese entry into the World Trade Organization (2002), Severe Acute Respiratory Syndrome (2003), and the "Three Represents."[2] These issues are potentially politically sensitive. The BAS designers simply use their own judgment in deciding what sorts of questions are too sensitive to include, but this is always an imprecise art. For example, in 1995, when the first BAS was being designed, corruption was by far the "hottest" issue for ordinary Chinese in the capital. Beijing party secretary and Politburo member Chen Xitong was under investigation for corruption, his longtime associate and Beijing deputy mayor Wang Baosen had committed suicide in advance of questioning, and

---

[2] The "Three Represents," enshrined in the Chinese Communist Party constitution in 2002, are the doctrinal contribution of Jiang Zemin, party leader at the time. They assert that the party represents advanced social productive forces, advanced culture, and the interests of the majority. By this doctrine, the party shifted its identity from a Leninist revolutionary vanguard; the change also paved the way for admission of capitalists into the party.

the Central Discipline Inspection Commission had launched a nationwide anticorruption campaign. Not surprisingly in this context, BAS designers considered questions about corruption too politically sensitive to include in the questionnaire – only to have the Beijing Municipal Government suggest their addition.

SAMPLING

Sampling is perhaps the most challenging issue faced by BAS designers, eliciting regular minor adjustments and (in 2007) two major adjustments. The BAS uses cross-sectional sampling to select a probability sample: every year, a similar sample is newly drawn from the same population of Beijing residents. Up through 2007, sampling procedures ensured generalizability of the sample to the population of individuals aged 18 to 65 years, with a nonagricultural Beijing residence permit, living in a fixed domicile in one of Beijing's eight districts.[3] Based on previous experience with surveys, the RCCC expected a response rate of 80 percent to 85 percent. Taking this into account, to reach a 95 percent confidence level that the sample is generalizable to the population, BAS samplers drew a sample of 1,200 households (with a target of about 1,000 completed interviews) using probability proportionate to size (PPS) sampling, with two-stage sampling selection.

Within each of the eight districts of Beijing are multiple street offices (街道办事处), each of which manage dozens of neighborhood committees (居民委员会); under each neighborhood committee are residential small groups (居民小组) of varying numbers. After long consideration about appropriate primary sampling units (PSUs), the BAS chose neighborhood committees as PSUs and individual households registered with the neighborhood committees as secondary sampling units (SSUs). BAS samplers initially selected a PPS sample of 65 (from a total of 3,500–4,800) neighborhood committees. BAS field supervisors then confirmed that the committees had not disappeared in a major administrative reorganization within the city and that they did not include committees in which nongovernment surveys are prohibited (residences owned by the military, for example). From the neighborhood committees that survived these checks, PPS methods (with households as the scale measure) were used to select 50. From the 50 selected neighborhood committees, a probability sample of 1,200 households was selected, 24 in each neighborhood committee. BAS field supervisors recorded adult resident name-lists corresponding to the selected households, and then randomly selected respondents from the lists. The number of interviews completed and response rates are shown in Table 13.2. Actual response rates have varied from a high of 87 percent in 1995 to a low of 66 percent in 2003, with generally lower rates in recent years.

---

[3] In 1995 the age range was defined as 18 to 74 years; in 1996 and 1997 it was redefined as 18 to 70 years. Beginning in 1998, the BAS used 18 to 65 years as the age range for respondents.

Measuring Change and Stability over a Decade

TABLE 13.2. *Overview of sampling and survey implementation in BAS first decade*

Year	Sample size	Requirements unmet	Requirements met	Interview completed	Response rate
1995	1,189	134	1,055	916	87%
1996	1,074	132	942	811	86%
1997	1,048	108	940	791	84%
1998	1,075	104	971	756	78%
1999	1,010	69	941	712	76%
2000	1,101	96	1,005	757	75%
2001	1,072	218	854	615	72%
2002	1,055	181	874	662	76%
2003	1,019	185	834	551	66%
2004	1,099	213	886	617	70%

Note: Response rate refers to completed interviews as a proportion of sampled individuals who, at the time of the interview attempt, actually met survey requirements. Interviews with these individuals may not be completed if the respondent is not at home on several interview attempts, if the respondent's health does not permit an interview, or if the respondent refuses to be interviewed. See Table 13.3 on incomplete surveys due to unmet requirements.

Each year a proportion of selected respondents cannot be interviewed. Some incomplete interviews are due to respondents who are not found at home on several interview attempts; an increasing proportion is respondents who refuse to be interviewed. These problems are endemic to survey research. In 1995, BAS interviewers were instructed to make three attempts to interview respondents; in 1998 this was changed to five attempts. In addition, however, many incomplete interviews were due to reasons associated with reliance on outdated household registration lists, as shown in Table 13.3.

Minor sampling adjustments in the BAS have included changes to the neighborhood committee sampling frame on the basis of city administrative reorganization; also, in 1999 and 2004, the BAS directly obtained from the Beijing government the most up-to-date sampling frame. Neither of these adjustments addressed the source of the noninterview problem: reliance on household registration lists.

On the one hand, relaxation of the household registration system (户口) has produced greater population mobility in the past couple of decades. More than 100 million rural-to-urban migrants, the "floating population" (流动人口), are an important part of this, with the result that a large proportion of the Beijing population has official residence outside Beijing. Further, among those with official residence in Beijing, a large number do not live at their official household residence (人户分离). The traditional BAS sampling method did not pick up these migrants and movers. This is a significant population: about 45 percent (25 percent migrants and 20 percent movers) of a Beijing sample

TABLE 13.3. *Incomplete interviews due to unmet requirements in BAS first decade*

Year	Requirements unmet	Incorrect address	Mismatch of household and dwelling	Survey status unmet
1995	134	54%	43%	2%
1996	132	67%	29%	4%
1997	108	74%	19%	7%
1998	104	63%	24%	13%
1999	69	57%	43%	0
2000	96	57%	43%	0
2001	218	12%	82%	6%
2002	181	40%	55%	4%
2003	185	50%	42%	8%
2004	213	77%	15%	9%

Note: Incorrect address includes instances of relocation (搬迁); mismatch of household and dwelling means the selected respondent does not reside at the dwelling listed for official residency (i.e., 空挂户 or 人户分离). Survey status unmet refers to a situation where the selected respondent turns out to be older than 86 years old and there is no other individual in the household who meets survey status.

Percentages may not add up to 100 due to rounding.

selected by the global positioning system (GPS) in 2000 could not be reached using the traditional BAS sampling method (Landry and Shen, 2005).[4] Beginning in 2007, the BAS has used GPS sampling.

The increased pace of urbanization poses a second major sampling challenge. The original eight districts surveyed in 1995 no longer represent the core city districts of Beijing. Beginning in 2007 the BAS added six new city districts to the sample. The targeted sample size was increased to 1,500 to accommodate addition of the districts.

SURVEY IMPLEMENTATION

The BAS is assigned high priority as an RCCC special project each year, with a single project leader responsible for directing all its aspects. Survey implementation involves two teams: field supervisors and interviewers. BAS field supervisors are RCCC research assistants or Peking University graduate students; BAS interviewers are students recruited from six universities in Beijing. Interviewer training includes an initial day and a half of training, followed by a substantial survey pretest, followed by further training. The survey pretest serves two functions: to pretest the questionnaire (which changes annually) for readability and understandability, and to provide practical experience for

[4] On GPS sampling, see Chapter 12 of this volume and Landry and Shen (2005).

interviewers. After the pretest, the questionnaire is adjusted, based on the debriefing of interviewers and looking for signs of problems suggested by the response distributions across questions (e.g., no variation, high "no response" rates, etc.).

The actual survey is conducted in two stages. The first, intensive stage involves the 8–17 field supervisors leading their teams of interviewers (50–83 altogether) into the neighborhoods to conduct interviews all at the same time. The second stage focuses on recontacting households where identified respondents could not be interviewed in the first stage (e.g., because they were not at home); this stage is not intensive but takes cost into account and is often preceded by arranging appointments with respondents.

To ensure interview quality, interviewers are compensated by the hour, not by the interview. Also, completed questionnaires are checked in the field (by interviewers and field supervisors) and by the project manager at the RCCC – all of whom must "sign off" on the completed questionnaire itself. A further check is conducted during data input: logical inconsistencies in responses and suspicious questionnaires are tagged and checked again.

The BAS has faced challenges in survey implementation since 1995, some noted above. Other challenges include difficulty in access to sampled households due to the rise of gated communities and continually rising costs associated with survey work (e.g., printing of questionnaires, transportation of interviewers). Over the years, the BAS has been funded from various sources – including private foundations, the Beijing Municipal Government, and foreign scholars who add research modules of their own questionnaire items to the survey.

14

Quantitative Research and Issues of Political Sensitivity in Rural China

Lily L. Tsai

Political sensitivity is always a challenge for the scholar doing fieldwork in nondemocratic and transitional systems, especially when doing surveys and quantitative research. Not only are more research topics likely to be politically sensitive in these systems, but in trying to collect precise and unbiased data to give us a quantitative description of a population, we are sometimes doing exactly what the government – and sometimes certain members of that population – would like to prevent. In this chapter, I discuss some of the methodological and ethical issues that face researchers working in these contexts and describe strategies for dealing with these issues. I argue that in these contexts a "socially embedded" approach to survey research that carefully attends to the social relationships inherent in the survey research process can help alleviate problems of political sensitivity, protect participants and researchers in the survey research process, and maximize data quality.

For this chapter I draw on my experience conducting a village-level survey on village conditions of officials in 316 villages in rural China in 2001 as part of the twenty months of fieldwork I conducted for my doctoral dissertation and book, *Accountability without Democracy: Solidary Groups and Public Goods Provision in Rural China* (2007a). Unlike an individual-level opinion survey of the mass public, this survey focused on village-level institutions and outcomes and interviewed one or more village officials in each village as informants on their village's economy, politics, and society.

After an overview of the project's objectives and research design, I discuss the difficulties I encountered in trying to conduct quantitative research in rural China generally, and in studying politically sensitive questions more specifically. These difficulties will be familiar to anyone who tries to collect quantitative data, whether on individuals or communities, in rural China. I then describe the methods I used to try to overcome these difficulties and evaluate their strengths and shortcomings when used for a village-level informant survey. I conclude with a brief discussion of the appropriateness of these methods for individual-level attitudinal surveys and how the trade-offs between bias and variability, interviewer and respondent effects, validity and generalizability, and allocation of resources may differ.

OVERVIEW OF THE RESEARCH PROJECT

For this project, I was interested in accounting for variation in local governmental performance and public goods provision. More specifically, I was interested in evaluating the effects of formal bureaucratic and democratic institutions of accountability and informal institutions of accountability provided by community religious and lineage groups. After conducting preliminary fieldwork in seven provinces, I decided on a multistage, multimethod research strategy combining ethnographic study of a single set of villages in Fujian province over four months, a survey of 316 villages and 948 households in four provinces – Shanxi, Hebei, Jiangxi, and Fujian – and a structured comparison of in-depth village case studies selected from the same four provinces. The fieldwork took place over twenty months from 1999 and 2002.

In the first stage of my fieldwork, I focused on developing a detailed understanding of local governance and political processes. During this period, I was based in Xiamen and repeatedly visited four villages in the area almost every week (and villages in other parts of China less frequently). Sometimes I interviewed villagers and village officials. At other times, I simply observed everyday interactions between villagers and daily administrative work by village officials. I also periodically attended village meetings, participated in community festivals and social gatherings, and followed the informal politicking behind the scenes of the village elections in the year 2000. Through these visits, I discovered a variety of community groups and institutions that often dominate village life and village politics but are sometimes hidden. Officially, community groups were required to be registered with the state. Unofficially, township and county governments often looked the other way. In one village, for example, residents and village officials alternately referred to the unregistered community council of villagers associated with the village's temples as the village council, the temple council, the senior citizens' association (老年人协会), the village elders, or the state-approved wedding and funeral council (红白理事会).

My time in Xiamen gave me a basic understanding of political and social interactions at the village level, but it was based on only four villages. The next step was to collect data that would enable me to generalize about village governmental performance and public goods provision for a broad range of villages. The National Bureau of Statistics does not collect data on the provision of public services at a level as low as the village, and few studies of rural governance had systematically addressed this topic. I thus designed an original village survey to collect statistics on village-level provision of public services, village public finance, township-village relations, village democratic institutions, and community social institutions.

Since foreigners are not allowed to administer surveys in China, I needed to find Chinese researchers who would be willing to act as guarantors and help me administer my survey. I pursued discussions with three researchers who had contacts in four different provinces: one, a researcher in the Ministry of Agriculture, who had contacts in Shanxi and Hebei provinces; another, a professor in Jiangxi, who could arrange for a survey in that province; and a third, a professor in Fujian, who could potentially expand the sample for a survey he was already conducting in that province to accommodate my survey and sampling requirements.

These four provinces – Shanxi, Hebei, Jiangxi, and Fujian – varied along two important macro-level dimensions. Coastal and inland regions differ significantly from each other in terms of economic development, and north and south China vary greatly in their institutional history and social organization. To make my findings as generalizable as possible, I sought to conduct the survey in two provinces in north China and two provinces in south China. Within each pair, one province was coastal and one was inland. Pursuing leads for administering the survey in these four particular provinces also made sense in terms of backup plans because the survey design would still make sense if one or two of the leads were to fall through. Administering the survey in two northern provinces or two southern provinces, for example, would allow me to hold geographical factors constant while varying the level of development. (For more detailed information on the research design, see the first chapter of my book *Accountability without Democracy*, 2007a).

To my surprise, however, all three of these people eventually agreed to help me administer my survey. Within each of the four provinces – Shanxi, Hebei, Jiangxi, and Fujian – two counties were selected purposively according to a combination of theoretical and practical requirements. Although selecting counties within each province randomly would have increased the generalizability of my findings, my primary concern was maximizing the validity of the data. To control the quality of the data, I wanted to supervise the survey administration personally. The Chinese researchers who had agreed to assist me thus had to draw on local government contacts who would be willing to host a foreign graduate student, and the only contacts they had who were willing to do so were in county governments. I thus decided to select two neighboring counties in each province that were as similar as possible except that one would be a model county for village elections and the other would not (see book for details). With the help of these Chinese researchers, I was fortunate to have complete control over questionnaire design and survey sampling within each of the eight counties. Within each county, a random stratified sample of forty villages was selected.

For the Shanxi and Hebei portion of the survey, I selected and trained a team of eleven graduate and undergraduate students from Beijing. In Jiangxi, I trained a team of twenty graduate students from the provincial party school, and in Fujian, I trained a team of twelve or so undergraduate students from

Xiamen University. The survey took approximately eighteen days per province to administer in Shanxi, Hebei, and Fujian. In Jiangxi, we had twice as many survey interviewers so administration time was cut in half. In each province, I traveled with the interviewers to the countryside to supervise the administration of the survey directly. Every night or two, I met with the survey interviewers to discuss problems and issues arising in the field and to check through the questionnaire. When I found errors or skipped questions, survey interviewers called or revisited the respondents to make corrections and fill in the blanks. To correct problems in the field, an assistant and I used laptop computers to code and input the questionnaires each day.

In the final stage of my fieldwork, I wanted to evaluate whether community social institutions really affect village governmental performance in the ways that findings from the survey suggested. To check whether these findings really made sense in a variety of different cases, I put together a set of in-depth village case studies selected from the same four provinces in which the survey had been conducted. These case studies allowed me to explore the causal processes underlying the correlations identified by statistical analysis, make inferences about interaction effects between different explanatory variables, and gather more observations of the implications of the theories being tested. Gathering data through case studies also helped to trace the evolution of a village's political and social institutions and understand how local historical and cultural contexts shaped these institutions.

THE CHALLENGES OF QUANTITATIVE RESEARCH AND POLITICAL SENSITIVITY IN RURAL CHINA

First, the greatest challenge to doing quantitative research on nondemocratic and transitional systems like China is to obtain high-quality data. In the case of rural China, if we want village-level data, we have to collect them ourselves. Official statistical yearbooks published by the National Bureau of Statistics contain data aggregated at only the county level (with a little data aggregated at the township level). Another major problem is that nondemocratic and transitional systems rarely collect – or if they collect them, rarely publish – data on many of the political and social variables in which we are interested. In my case, official data on voluntary associations, for example, which are available for many Organisation for Economic Co-operation and Development (OECD) countries, are not available for rural China for two reasons. First, the government does not collect such data. Second, many groups that we might think of as voluntary associations are unregistered and often deliberately try to avoid notice by the official authorities.

These two reasons correspond to two different ways in which the collection of quantitative data is politically sensitive. First, as in other nondemocratic and transitional systems, survey research *itself* is politically sensitive in China. Quantitative descriptions of a population can often be used as a measure of the performance of particular officials or local governments. Not surprisingly, all levels of the state thus seek to control the collection and flow of statistical data (Cai, 2000; Huang, 1995). Local officials have strong incentives to manipulate the reporting of statistics – grain output during the Great Leap Forward, income per capita and industrial output during the reform period – so as to portray their performance in the best light possible. China's level-by-level reporting of official statistics facilitates this manipulation. Because government officials have so much at stake when it comes to statistical data, citizens also find survey research a politically sensitive matter. As Belousov et al. (2007: 163) note for Russia and other post-Soviet states, "there is still a general fear of answering questions per se." This political context makes survey research by both Chinese and foreign academics a politically sensitive matter.

Nevertheless, survey research and quantitative data collection by foreigners is a particularly sensitive issue. As Melanie Manion discusses in more detail in Chapter 10 of this volume, the Interim Measures for Administration of Foreign-Related Social Survey Activities issued by the National Bureau of Statistics in 1999 list numerous restrictions on survey research with foreign participation. Any foreigner contemplating survey research in China should look at the regulations in full.[1]

Second, the collection of quantitative data can also be politically sensitive when the *content* of our research topics is politically sensitive. To complicate matters, in an authoritarian or transitional system all sorts of topics may be considered politically sensitive, and a researcher does not always know which topics are politically sensitive. Topics that do not seem explicitly political may be politically sensitive. What is considered politically sensitive may also vary across regions and over time. Once, while chatting with a village official in Fujian, I offhandedly observed that ancestral graves were interspersed with the village fields, and the official suddenly fell silent and then changed the subject. I later found out that local officials in that area had been struggling to enforce a new regulation requiring cremation as well as trying to convince villagers to cremate the remains of already buried ancestors in order to increase arable land. The conflict had already led to more than one violent clash between villagers and officials. In another village, in Jiangsu province, I asked officials if I could use the village's public toilet. Again, the village officials fell silent. We had been talking about public projects in the village, and the officials had highlighted their investment in the large new public toilet – centrally located in the village, beautifully tiled, with a flushing system. They had, they emphasized, gone above and beyond the targets set by the county's recent sanitation campaign for village public toilets. Instead of showing me to the toilet, however, I was politely ushered out of the village. Confused, I asked the driver as we left the village why I hadn't been allowed to use the public toilet. The driver explained that, in clear contravention of the spirit (if not the letter) of the county's campaign, village officials kept the toilet locked up so that villagers

---

[1] These regulations are available online from the Supreme People's Court of the PRC, at http://en.chinacourt.org/public/detail.php?id=3897, accessed August 2009.

would not dirty it. The man with the key was away that day so they were unable to unlock it for me.

These examples highlight the distinction between topics that are politically sensitive to government officials and topics that are politically sensitive to villagers. Residents of the Jiangsu village were happy to point out that village officials had constructed the new public toilet only for show, whereas village officials were understandably reluctant to highlight this fact. In the case of the Fujian village, the new cremation and burial regulations were a sensitive topic for both villagers and officials. If I had been surveying on the topic, I would have had to frame my questions differently depending on whether my respondents were villagers or officials. On the one hand, villagers might not have responded well if I had asked them whether they were "complying" with the new regulations, whereas officials would have been less likely to object to this wording. Officials, on the other hand, might have responded poorly if I asked how well they were enforcing the new regulations.

These examples also illustrate how questions can sometimes be politically sensitive because disclosure of the truth can potentially harm the respondent and sometimes because people feel uncomfortable talking about certain topics. In the case of the public toilet, village officials did not want to admit to locking the toilet because their behavior was contrary to the policy objectives of higher levels. The issue of digging up ancestral graves was not only politically charged for policy-related reasons but for normative and historical ones as well. Digging up ancestral graves violates deeply held moral and spiritual convictions and also reminds villagers of the state's often violent efforts to stamp out what it considered "feudal superstitions" during the Maoist period.

There is one last point worth making about political sensitivity and one's research questions: it is critical to know where the line is between subjects that are politically sensitive and subjects that are taboo. *Asking questions about subjects that are taboo can destroy your ability to ask questions about subjects that are politically sensitive.* In his research on the guerrilla warfare of the Irish Republican Army (IRA), Sluka (1990) found that he could ask people questions about their support for and criticisms of the IRA but not questions about arms or explosives, or who might actively be a guerrilla (Sluka, 1990: 114–126). In the context of rural China, some questions related to the birth control policy, for example, are politically sensitive; others are taboo. In one Hebei village I visited, I talked with officials of the village's branch of the state-mandated women's association about their responsibilities and activities. As they became more comfortable with me, they described how one of the ways in which they encouraged villagers to follow the birth control policy was to perform comedy skits (小品) that mocked "out-of-quota birthing guerrillas" (超生游击队), villagers who go into hiding in order to give illegal out-of-quota births. They were comfortable gossiping about frequent cases like these in their locality. If, however, I had asked questions about illegally coerced abortions and sterilizations, they might very well have stopped telling colorful stories and reported me to the local authorities. Similarly, questions about underground Christian churches were politically sensitive but questions about the Falungong were taboo. In another area of Hebei, a township official felt comfortable telling me that the greatest fear of the county government was the proliferation of underground household churches in the area. Shortly after this discussion, however, he volunteered that of course there were no Falungong activities in the area. Since I had not asked about the subject, his comment gave me the impression that probing into Falungong activities would be taboo.

In short, issues of political sensitivity complicate the collection of quantitative data in rural China in various ways. First, arranging for the administration of a survey is a challenge. Foreign researchers have to find Chinese collaborators who are willing to take responsibility for conducting the survey, able to gain access to research sites and respondents in the sample, and willing to vouch for your trustworthiness. Second, researchers have to worry about getting respondents to give truthful and precise responses to politically sensitive questions. We have to know what the political incentives and sanctions are for giving certain answers. Sometimes there may be pressures on respondents to decline answering a question or to give only a vague answer. At other times, there may be pressure for respondents to avoid answering a question and yet appear as if they are answering the question to the best of their ability.

Third, researchers have to accommodate a suspicion of survey research in general. Both local officials and villagers can be uncomfortable and wary of being interviewed by people they do not know from outside their locality. For some people, the basic format of a survey interview may be unfamiliar or reminiscent of unpleasant interrogations by state agents. In these contexts, innovative question formats and questionnaire designs such as anchoring vignettes (King, 2004: 197–207) or list experiments (Streb, 2008) may actually raise suspicions and undermine data quality. When I tried a simplified version of the political efficacy vignette described by King et al. (2003), I not only had trouble securing the cooperation of respondents but also when they agreed to participate, they were extremely confused by the format. A few even reacted by walking away, leaving me alone in their house. List experiments raised suspicions among respondents that they were being tricked in some way because they found it hard to understand how the question worked. Finally, as with almost everything about doing research in China, there can be tremendous variation in political sensitivity issues across regions and individuals.

STRATEGIES FOR ACCOMMODATING POLITICAL SENSITIVITY ISSUES IN QUANTITATIVE RESEARCH

Before I go on to discuss some of the methods I used to accommodate the difficulties associated with the various issues of political sensitivity in collecting quantitative village-level data in rural China, I want to emphasize that *one should always be willing to change research topics due to issues of political sensitivity*. No academic project is more important than the safety and security of the people involved in the project.[2] We have an ethical imperative to "do no harm." As Elisabeth Wood notes, "there are some settings where research cannot be ethically conducted and should not be attempted or should be curtailed" (Wood, 2006: 373–386). Wood provides a valuable discussion of the research procedures that she followed in order to implement the "do no harm" ethic during her fieldwork in El Salvador.

An important strategy for learning how to "do no harm" and when to change research topics is to *do qualitative research before attempting the collection of quantitative data*. The initial stages of my fieldwork – a preliminary two-month trip, six months in Fujian, and several short trips to Shanxi and Hebei – were invaluable in helping me to design and pretest survey questions (Park, 2006:128). During these stages, I allocated much of my time simply to chatting conversationally with villagers and local officials in the different provinces about their lives and their communities in general. Like Wood, I found that rural residents I interviewed had far more political expertise than I did and a far better sense of what was politically risky. The more time and opportunity I gave them to teach me about the specifics of political sensitivity, the safer and more productive my subsequent research was (Wood, 2006: 380).

Although I always had my main research questions in the back of my mind, I also just wanted to get to know people as much as possible. When I knew I would have multiple chances to talk to someone, I often waited until later meetings to ask the person the questions on my structured interview schedule or on my draft surveys. The sociologist Ned Polsky's first rule of field research worked well: "Before you can ask questions, or even speak much at all other than when spoken to, you should get the 'feel' of their world by extensive and attentive listening – get some sense of what pleases them and what bugs them, some sense of their frame of reference, and some sense of *their* sense of language." At the same time, it was also important to answer their questions about my background. As Polsky also writes, "it is important that [the interviewee] will be studying you, and to let him study you.… He has got to define you satisfactorily to himself if you are to get anywhere" (Polsky, 2006: 128, 132).

This approach allowed me to find out which topics were easy to bring up and which topics were off limits, and how the line between sensitive and taboo varied from region to region. Often I would ask people to give me tours of their neighborhoods, which often gave me the occasion to ask about something that we saw – an abandoned road project, a Catholic church in the center of town, a twenty-foot gully full of garbage, or a burned-out storefront. This strategy resulted in interesting stories involving corruption, competition for congregants between local Catholic and Protestant churches, conflict between villagers and officials, and conflict among lineage groups. Chatting socially with people also allowed them to bring up local current events, which sometimes touched on my research interests – a scandal in a neighboring county where a local journalist reporting on local government investment in irrigation

---

[2] See Howell (1990), Sluka (1990), and Barrett and Cason (1997).

reached down to show TV cameras a new irrigation pipe and it came out of the ground, attached to nothing; or rumors about a contentious village election in the area that had resulted in one of the candidates being lured to a karaoke bar and stabbed. Although these kinds of rumors did not constitute reliable data, they gave me a valuable sense of the political climate and a context for gauging the topics people felt were politically sensitive and the ways in which they were willing to talk about these topics.

A period of qualitative research also taught me about regional variation in the political sensitivity of particular topics. The topic of underground Christian house churches was very sensitive in Hebei but openly discussed in Fujian. In some Fujian villages where conflict between lineages had erupted into physical fights among villagers, local officials explicitly warned me not to ask about it. By contrast, in Hebei, villagers freely recounted the long-standing feuds among a village's sublineages and found amusing the different ways in which the sublineages tried to sabotage each other. There was also variation within provinces. In eastern Fujian, I found that local officials felt they had to justify the existence of unregistered village temple councils by talking about how they contributed to village public goods provision and social stability. In western Fujian I talked to local officials who simply stated that villagers did not trust township and village cadres and informal villager councils were now running the villages.

After this first stage of fieldwork, it became clear to me that I would have to *attend to data quality before pursuing generalizability*. Getting survey respondents to give accurate and truthful answers to politically sensitive survey questions was going to be a primary concern. I therefore made a conscious decision to maximize the validity and reliability of the data rather than the generalizability of the findings. Drawing more valid conclusions about a smaller population seemed like a more sensible way to build knowledge than drawing less valid conclusions about a larger population. In theory I could have hired a market research firm to administer the survey nationally or piggybacked on an existing national survey by adding questions to an existing survey instrument. However, after witnessing firsthand how much responses to politically sensitive questions could vary depending on how comfortable respondents were and how they perceived the person doing the asking, I decided that I needed as much freedom, control, and participation in the actual administration of the survey as possible. This decision guided my sampling for the survey. Within each of the eight counties in the survey I used a multilevel stratified random sampling strategy to select villages, but I selected both the provinces and counties purposively based on where the Chinese researchers assisting me had personal contacts who would allow me to conduct a large-scale survey freely. Strictly speaking, this strategy limited the generalizability of the findings from the survey data analysis to these eight counties, but it was crucial to maintaining the quality of the data.

In the case of rural China, one is often forced to choose between obtaining a nationally representative sample and controlling the local conditions under which the survey is administered so that the accuracy of the data is maximized. Surveys based on nationally representative samples have become possible in China, but once the terms of survey administration have been negotiated, foreign researchers participating in these surveys often have limited control and leverage over the local conditions of the survey administration. The actual administration of the survey is outsourced and often takes place quickly.

The extent to which one has to choose between data quality and generalizability, or internal validity and external validity, depends in part on the kinds of questions one is trying to study. For research questions that are relatively uncontroversial, controlling the local conditions of survey administration may be less important. For these projects, the researcher may not have to choose between obtaining a nationally representative sample and obtaining accurate data. But for projects on potentially politically sensitive topics, researchers have to worry not only about securing access to sampled research sites and respondents but about creating an interview environment in which respondents feel comfortable giving truthful responses to survey questions. In these cases, obtaining a probability sample of a more limited population may be a reasonable choice.

Conducting "Socially Embedded" Survey Research

To create this kind of environment and maximize the quality of quantitative data collected on politically sensitive topics, I argue that *researchers need to recognize that survey research is embedded in social relationships among researchers, official authorities, interviewers, and respondents. Moreover, researchers need to invest in building and shaping these social relationships so that they generate trust and mutual obligations.*[3] While this approach may sound obvious, many survey research projects in fact try to render the survey research process as impersonal as possible. Researchers often pay firms or domestic research institutions to conduct their surveys, treat official approvals as purely bureaucratic hurdles, and seek to "standardize" interviewers and depersonalize interviewer-respondent interactions to minimize interviewer error. Rather than thinking about how to foster social relationships based on trust and reciprocal obligations with domestic collaborators and official authorities, survey researchers often think in terms of principal-agent problems, incentives, and monitoring (Fowler, 1993).

In the following sections, I discuss four types of social relationships that influence the process of survey research and quantitative data collection, and consider the ways in which these social relationships can generate trust and

---

[3] The concept of social embeddedness I use here comes from Granovetter's (1985) article on economic exchange. Granovetter's emphasis on the "role of concrete personal relations and structures (or 'networks') of such relations in generating trust and discouraging malfeasance" is the point I highlight here.

obligation to influence the quality of data on politically sensitive research topics (Granovetter, 1985: 482, 490).

1. Relationships between Foreign and Chinese Researchers

To collect quantitative data in China, foreign researchers must work with Chinese researchers who are willing to take official responsibility for conducting the survey. In the case of surveys on potentially politically sensitive topics, this responsibility is an especially serious one. It is not to be taken lightly by the Chinese researcher or by the foreign researcher asking for the assistance of the Chinese researcher. The fact that the Chinese researcher bears official responsibility does not let foreign researchers off the hook. In asking for the help of a Chinese researcher to collect data on potentially politically sensitive issues, the foreign researcher is obligated to take responsibility for the security and well-being of the Chinese researcher. Not only should we always listen to and defer to our collaborators' judgment on what is too politically sensitive, but if our collaborators seem more daring than seems sensible, then it is also our responsibility to rein them in. Although these collaborators may be right in judging something to be perfectly safe, our responsibility for them requires us to listen to our own judgment as well. It goes without saying that one should never do something without the full knowledge and consent of one's collaborator.

It is impossible to collect high-quality data without a skilled and reliable collaborator. As Albert Park, an economist working on China, notes: "Nearly all successful surveys in developing countries depend on the support of energetic, capable research collaborators from the host country who know how to get things done within the country's institutional, political, and social environment; are skilled at interacting with government officials and community leaders; have developed reputations within the country that build trust, and have valuable substantive insights into the research question. On the flip side, collaborators pursuing agendas at cross-purposes with those of the researcher can easily frustrate research plans" (Park, 2006: 122–123).

The more potentially politically sensitive one's research topics are, the more important it is to work with a collaborator whom one trusts. I grew to know my collaborators and their families. We moved in the same professional circles within China, we had mutual friends and acquaintances, which reinforced the mutual trust and confidence necessary to collaborate on politically sensitive survey research, and we continue to keep in touch.

Research collaborations always carry an ethical obligation to reciprocate the other party's time and efforts. As Park discusses, one can reciprocate by providing intellectual benefits (providing them with useful ideas and tools for their own research, acting as a guest lecturer, coauthoring papers, or facilitating a visit to one's own research institution), material benefits (adequate compensation for services), or personal benefits (developing personal relationships and being friendly) (Park, 2006: 123). When, however, the research project involves politically sensitive topics and political risk, relying solely on material compensation is unlikely to work – and if it seems to work, one should be extremely cautious about proceeding.

One's collaborator also has to have a finely honed sense of what political concerns different types and levels of officials may have about the research project. I usually found that researchers working for state ministries and government organs were better informed about the political sensitivity of particular issues and more experienced at negotiating people's concerns. As a result, they were generally more confident about tackling politically sensitive questions than researchers in universities or academic research institutes.

2. Relationships between Researchers and Official Authorities

After forging a research collaboration based on mutual trust and obligation, the next step is to build relationships with government officials whose approval and support are needed. In many cases, the informal support is far more important than the official approval. As Belousov et al. comment, "fieldwork in difficult to access places often needs to be facilitated by key 'gatekeepers.'" Belousov et al. note that after their gatekeeper was murdered, his "personal patronage" and "this informal status disappeared, even though the formal agreements remained intact. While no-one now attempted to prevent our research activity, in contrast with the earlier stage, nobody went out of their way to help us either" (Belousov et al., 2007: 166).

Collecting valid and reliable data on potentially politically sensitive subjects requires extremely careful attention to how the survey is administered and how relationships between interviewers and respondents are structured. Control over these aspects of survey administration in turn required a very high degree of trust and confidence from local officials in the counties where I conducted the survey. To achieve this level of comfort from local officials so that they would not intervene in our survey of village officials, I had to work in places where my Chinese collaborators had relationships with provincial, municipal, and county officials. My collaborators generally went through contacts they had made in their previous field research. When my sampling strategy required us to work in a county where they did not have a contact, they would go through a contact at the municipal or provincial level instead. Because my collaborators had already established relationships with local authorities that they had worked at maintaining over time, local officials were willing to trust me and to take more time to get to know us and our project, which also increased their level of comfort with the survey administration.

As a result, we were given relatively free rein within each county, and county and township officials did not attempt to intervene in the administration of the survey. We were allowed to administer the survey in a village immediately after it was sampled so that higher level officials had little opportunity to call up sampled villages and debrief them on how they should respond to our questions. In most cases, I or one of my assistants accompanied the higher level officials making arrangements for us and witnessed most of their telephone interactions with lower levels. We were allowed to spend as much time as we wanted in whatever area we wanted, which enabled us to probe the responses of village officials to make sure they were giving us the most accurate answers possible. We were allowed to talk with multiple village officials and, in some cases, former village officials to corroborate information about village-level conditions. Without this degree of freedom and the flexibility to adjust the administration of the survey to local conditions, it would have been much more difficult to ensure the accuracy of data on sensitive subjects such as the existence of village religious activity or the collection of illegal local levies.

3. Relationships between Researchers and Interviewers

While forging relationships based on trust and reciprocity among researchers and official authorities is essential for setting up the survey and setting up the conditions for collecting high-quality quantitative data on politically sensitive subjects, *the people who are most important for ensuring the quality of the data are the interviewers.* They are the ones who are doing the actual collection of the data. In the field, I realized that the efforts of the interviewers depended heavily on my relationship with them. Even if my funds had not been limited, it would have been hard to compensate them enough for undergoing the hardship of administering a rural survey. Personally supervising administration of the survey and traveling to research sites along with the interviewers allowed me to build stronger relationships with them and to strengthen bonds of mutual obligation and reciprocity. The more I was able to convince them of the intellectual and social value of the project, the more effort they invested in trying to obtain accurate data *and the more they felt that they had a responsibility to invest in this effort.*

Leading by example and doing things to express my gratitude for their work helped immeasurably to improve the quality of survey administration. These things ranged from advising them on their theses to staying in the same accommodations to hand-washing their laundry when they were busy with survey administration. I traveled with them to each locality and took all of the same long-distance bus and train trips. When I spot-checked enumerators by dropping in on them, I picked villages that were difficult to access as often as ones that were easy to access. The more effort I showed, the more they realized how important data quality was to me, and the more they realized how important and valuable they were to the process, which in turn motivated them to put in more effort.

4. Relationships between Interviewers and Respondents

The relationship between interviewer and respondent is the most immediate and critical context for the generation of valid and accurate data. While in the village, interviewers maximized the quality of the data from village officials by spending a large amount of time visiting the village. Even though the survey focused on interviewing village officials as informants on village conditions, interviewers also talked with villagers as well as current and former village officials. Interviewers typically spent half a day to a day in each village. Depending on the time it took to travel to the village, interviewers sometimes stayed in a village overnight.

We administered the survey as a genuine two-way conversation between interviewers and village officials. When village officials gave responses that seemed to conflict with their previous responses or with the personal impressions enumerators had gained from walking around the village and talking with villagers, interviewers would ask follow-up questions to probe their responses more deeply and to reconcile contradictions. To corroborate the responses of village officials, interviewers also asked for and were typically able to look at supplementary village documents, including village account books, village receipts, minutes from village government meetings, village election ballots, and election records.

Conducting the survey as a conversation and spending a significant amount of time visiting each village also helped interviewers and village officials get to know each other as people. Not only did this process make village officials more comfortable talking to the survey enumerators, but it also enabled us to repay the village officials a little by providing them with information and answering their questions about us, our research, and our backgrounds. The more we were able to create a relationship based on reciprocity and trust, the higher was the quality of the data we collected.

Several other factors also helped to build a relationship between interviewers and respondents and maximize the comfort of village officials with our research on potentially politically sensitive topics. We were able to stress the purely academic nature of the survey to village officials credibly. The survey was in fact purely academic, and the data were not collected for policy-making purposes. All of the interviewers and I looked like, and in fact were university students. In the vast majority of cases, interviewers were not accompanied by higher level officials when interviewing village officials. We also administered the survey at the convenience of the village officials. We scheduled the survey so that it did not coincide with peak times for agricultural work such as harvesting or administrative work such as tax collection or village elections. When interviewers arrived in a village and village officials were busy, they waited around until the village officials had sufficient time to sit down with them for a lengthy conversation.

Perhaps most important, the high quality of the data was due in large part to the skilled and diligent administration of the survey by the student interviewers. All of the interviewers underwent two to five days of training in the classroom and in practice administrations of the survey in the field. Most of the students had grown up in villages themselves. A number of them had worked as enumerators on previous rural surveys. Because of their personal backgrounds, they were particularly adept at putting the village officials at ease by talking about their own experiences growing up in a village and drawing on their personal knowledge of rural life. Many of them applied to work on the survey because they were writing theses on rural issues and could take advantage of the time in the field to collect information for their own research projects.

Choosing a Mode of Interviewing: Conversational or Flexible Interviewing versus Standardized Interviewing

One of the most important factors for data quality in this survey was the choice to use conversational or flexible interviewing rather than standardized interviewing. In standardized interviewing the ideal interviewer is a simple reader of the questions as they are written in the survey instrument. Lavrakas (1993:132) describes the standardized interviewer as an "intelligent automaton," and as Weisberg (2005:47) comments, "the emphasis often is more on the interviewer as automaton than as intelligent." The standardized approach to interviewing characterizes the relationship between interviewer and respondent as a professional relationship in which the interviewer seeks to obtain high-quality data from the respondent by providing incentives, appealing to the respondent's own values, and teaching respondents how to play their expected role in the survey interview and what good answers should be like (Weisberg, 2005:48).

The standardized mode of interviewing has a number of advantages. If conducted properly, it minimizes interviewer variance (Groves, 1987:164). Having interviewers adhere strictly to a script reduces the demands on interviewer skills and comprehension of the research project and the costs of training interviewers (Weisberg, 2005:48). Standardized interviewing is also much faster than conversational interviewing and decreases administration time (Biemer and Lyberg, 2003:154).

There are few systematic studies providing data on the circumstances under which standardized or conversational interviewing produces higher quality data, and more such studies are sorely needed (Weisberg, 2005:62). Based on my experience with my 2001 village survey, standardized interviewing presented a number of problems when conducting research in rural China on potentially politically sensitive topics.

Some of these problems existed irrespective of the research topics and arose because interviews and surveys were completely unfamiliar to most rural residents. Many villagers in China lack experience with multiple-choice questions, standardized tests, interviews, or even informal conversations with strangers from outside their locality. Even when dialect was not a problem, simple misunderstandings were particularly common. Village officials would, for example, confuse "preliminary" or "primary" village election candidates and "final" or "formal" village election candidates, regardless of how clearly and thoroughly we defined the concepts for them. During a question about preliminary candidates, for example, it might become clear that the respondent was thinking about final candidates because the number of candidates he had in mind matched the final slate rather than the primary slate. In a standardized interview the interviewer should simply record the respondent's answer exactly as given, even if he knows it does not represent the facts accurately (Groves,

2004: 289). In conversational interviewing the interviewer can ask the respondent whether he is definitely thinking about preliminary candidates or actually thinking about final candidates and can clarify that the current question concerns preliminary candidates.

One of the main arguments for using conversational interviewing rather than standardized interviewing parallels the issue of translating cross-national surveys into different languages: using the same words does not guarantee the same meanings to different respondents (Iarossi, 2006: 85–86; Suchman and Jordan, 1990: 233). Schober and Conrad (1997) demonstrate in a laboratory experiment that while both standardized and conversational interviewing produce high levels of accuracy when respondents are certain about how concepts in a question map onto their own circumstances, conversational interviewing produces higher response accuracy when respondents are unsure about these mappings and interviewers can provide additional assistance and explanation. Unclear mappings are a particularly salient problem for China. Because of the immense amount of regional variation, it is particularly difficult to anticipate all the possible questions and definitional issues that might arise, regardless of how thoroughly one pretests the survey instrument. In this context, conversational interviewing may offer significant advantages over standardized interviewing. As Groves (1987) notes, "many of the normal mechanisms of assuring clear communication, of correcting misimpressions, of addressing the questions of the listener have been stripped away from the 'standardized' interview." Moreover, standardized interviewing may reduce interviewer-related error at the expense of increasing respondent-related bias: "The effects of [standardized interviewing] may have been to minimize interviewer variance but to increase bias, due to poor comprehension or minimal memory search for relevant information" (Groves, 1987: S164).

Standardized interviewing in contexts where respondents lack experience with surveys and strangers can also have a dramatic effect on response rates and data accuracy. A stranger who appears on a villager's doorstep and wants him to provide answers to questions read mechanically from a prepared script may elicit a number of reactions that are not conducive to the collection of high-quality data. One reaction, as Suchman and Jordan observe, is simple disinterest: "As respondents realize that their expectations for ordinary conversation are violated (and violated without recourse), they may react with boredom (with consequent intellectual if not physical withdrawal) and impatience (with answers designed to 'get it over with')" (Suchman and Jordan, 1990: 233). As a result, response rates go down, and missing data and "don't know" responses go up.

Another reaction that I experienced when I tried to conduct standardized interviews in rural China was related to the political sensitivity of survey research itself. Villagers and village officials often did a suspicious "double take" if I refused to deviate from the prepared script. Even if the respondent's initial reaction to my request for an interview and explanation of the process was good-natured willingness, as soon as I explained that I had to follow the script in order to make sure that I had collected information in the same way as all the other interviewers, the respondent would often ask, "Who did you say you were again? What did you say this was for again?" or "Is this for a government office (政府部门)?" Even if I attempted at that point to reiterate reassurances that this research was purely academic and this practice was simply to ensure that all the interviewers collected the same information, respondents usually remained visibly disturbed or disengaged for the rest of the interview, especially if I continued to refuse to deviate from the script.

Trying to get me to deviate from a standardized script was in fact a way of equalizing the power dynamics in the interviewer-respondent relationship. Deviating from the script was like agreeing to drink 白酒 (strong liquor) at lunch – a concession that both symbolically and practically allowed the other person to exercise power over my behavior, which in turn made him more inclined to agree to my requests. Moreover, because formal interviews and the collection of quantitative data themselves are politically sensitive matters in China, the more formal and professional the process is, the more the experience smacks of political and governmental authority. Respondents assume that the authority that the script has over the interviewer is because the study is actually being commissioned by government authorities.

Conversational interviewing also had a number of other advantages over standardized interviewing when it came to asking questions about politically sensitive topics.[4] Giving respondents the opportunity and conversational space to explain and justify their behavior often made them feel better about giving truthful answers about politically incorrect behavior. In one Hebei village, for example, village officials were willing to admit to using floating ballot boxes instead of the officially mandated fixed polling stations. However, they wanted to spend some time explaining to us that floating ballot boxes worked much better in their village because many villagers worked on fishing boats that went out to sea at different times of the day. Conversational interviewing also allowed interviewers to cross-check responses and allowed respondents to relate anecdotes that provided interviewers with information about the validity of the data. More than once, respondents changed their minds later on in the interview when they felt more comfortable and then indicated that an earlier answer they had provided was false. In a standardized interview, this kind of later admission of the truthful answer would be ignored.

Finally, the conversational mode of interviewing permits interviewers to ask questions using terms that are not politically sensitive to respondents but may be politically sensitive to the official authorities. Some Chinese researchers, for example, are wary about putting questions on government corruption on the written questionnaire. Their solution is to write a question about something like "problems of public administration," which will not raise the eyebrows of

---

[4] Kish (1962) finds that interviewer effects are not necessarily greater for politically sensitive questions.

official authorities, and then have interviewers explicitly explain to the respondents that the question actually asks about problems of corruption. Paluck (2007) used a similar technique in Rwanda to collect survey data on opinions about ethnicity. Since the Rwandan constitution bans speech about ethnicity, Paluck had to replace the word "ethnicity" with "types of people" in her survey. She notes: "Researchers followed up these questions with an explanation that implied the significance of this term. I am confident that these questions were understood to implicate ethnicity, because Rwandans are accustomed to using such 'coded' language to refer to ethnicity on a daily basis, and because it was clear from our participants' responses that they understood the question, as many dismissed the coded language altogether and referred directly to Hutus, Tutsis, and Twa" (Paluck, 2007: 54).

REFLECTIONS ON CONDUCTING INDIVIDUAL-LEVEL ATTITUDINAL SURVEYS

Although these observations are drawn from my administration of a politically sensitive village-level informant survey, they may also be applicable to the administration of public opinion surveys on politically sensitive topics. As with village-level surveys, we need to attend to the problem of data quality before pursuing generalizability.

Since individual-level public opinion surveys can be even more politically sensitive to official authorities than village-level surveys, using a socially embedded approach to survey administration is perhaps even more critical. Creating relationships with Chinese researchers, official authorities, interviewers, and respondents that are based on mutual trust and obligation is doubly important for creating an environment in which respondents feel less pressure to give politically desirable responses.

In sum, the conclusion that I drew from my survey experience was that a conversational mode of interviewing, which preserved the neutrality guidelines associated with but not inherently exclusive to standardized interviewing (Dijkstra and van der Zouwen, 1987), created a mutually trusting relationship between interviewer and respondent that maximized the quality of the quantitative data collected. It is not surprising that studies find that experienced interviewers instructed to use standardized interviewing often use elements of conversational interviewing anyway. Viterna and Maynard's (2002) study of twelve university survey centers that purported to use the standardized approach found that only one consistently followed standardized interviewing procedures. Houtkoop-Steenstra observes (2000: ch. 7) that interviewers have a strong tendency to try to maintain rapport with respondents by breaking the rules of standardized interviewing. In a survey on illiteracy, interviewers tried to make respondents more comfortable by rephrasing questions frequently, praising their achievements, and indicating that they sometimes shared some of the respondents' problems with reading.

Interviewers should be nonjudgmental of respondents, and probing should be neutral. Depending on the circumstances, interviewers might act "bland and naïve," or matter-of-fact and knowledgeable about corruption and other characteristic qualities of rural politics (Wood, 2006: 382). Conversational interviewing enabled respondents to ask interviewers questions about what survey questions meant and why we were interested in asking them. It enabled respondents to obtain often-detailed information about us and our research that helped to alleviate their concerns and suspicions and helped to build a relationship governed by reciprocity of frankness. Dijkstra (1987: 312) also finds that conversational interviewing in which the interviewer shows interest and empathy helps to motivate the respondent to try harder to understand the question, retrieve the information needed to answer the question, and to repeat this process until an adequate response is provided.

Conversational interviewing gave respondents power and control not only over the decision to participate in the survey but also during the survey interview process itself. This sense of equality in the survey interviewing relationship was critical to the willingness of the respondents to volunteer truthful information on politically sensitive subjects.

Using conversational interviewing for attitudinal surveys may require even more intensive training of interviewers, but I argue that this investment will help us advance the study of public opinion in China more systematically. Interviewers can be trained to answer factual questions about the survey and definitional questions about terms and concepts in survey questions without giving their opinions. They can be trained to answer, "I don't know," or "I'm not sure" if respondents ask for their own opinions. Like standardized surveys that include questions with statements like, "Some people do this, while others do that," interviewers can be trained to make conversation that refers matter-of-factly to the existence of both politically desirable and undesirable behaviors and attitudes. It is true that conversational interviewing may sometimes be less likely to introduce additional bias or variance when we are collecting factual information than when we are collecting attitudinal data since there is a definite "right" or "wrong" answer to factual questions. However, if the danger of political desirability bias is high, the decrease in political desirability bias may be worth the risk of increased interviewer variance. Training interviewers to use conversational interviewing for attitudinal surveys may also be more costly than using standardized interviewing, but again, it may be important to spend resources on improving data quality before we spend resources on maximizing sample size.

Finally, starting with smaller scale attitudinal surveys can free up resources for collecting systematic data on interviewers and interviewer-respondent interactions. Instead of using standardized interviewing to allow us to ignore or assume away interviewer variance, a better strategy is to collect data on the interviews and interviewers and *to study these effects explicitly*.

ADDITIONAL NOTES ON STRATEGIES FOR DEALING WITH POLITICALLY SENSITIVE ISSUES

Several other nuts-and-bolts strategies were also very helpful when conducting survey research in rural China on potentially politically sensitive subjects. One important strategy was to send teams of two interviewers to conduct survey interviews. One interviewer could try to draw away any higher level authorities monitoring the interview by asking them for a tour of the environs, leaving the other interviewer free to conduct the survey without interference. Another strategy was to try to corroborate responses by collecting supplementary data on things that could be seen. For example, in addition to asking about lineage activities, I also asked about the existence of lineage hall buildings and, if they existed, whether we could go and visit them. Similarly, survey interviewers also collected various documents from the villages they surveyed, such as election ballots and reports, villager tax receipts, and cadre responsibility contracts.

CONCLUSION

In the end, surveys are inherently compromises (Groves, 1987: S167). In making decisions about survey design and administration, researchers make endless trade-offs — between data quality and generalizability, time and money, interviewer effects and respondent effects, bias and variance, conducting pretests and the main survey, and more. This chapter offers some thoughts on how to make these trade-offs in nondemocratic and authoritarian contexts where political sensitivity is a central issue. I argue that data quality is of both paramount importance and concern in these contexts and that central to maximizing data quality is conducting survey research that is "socially embedded." Survey researchers in any context take on multiple roles and invest in different interpersonal relationships: "The decision to conduct a survey is a decision to become not just a scholar but also a project manager, a fundraiser, a survey methodologist, and a motivator and supervisor of others" (Park, 2006: 128). Prioritizing the investment of time, resources, and attention into constructing these social relationships so that they are based on mutual obligation and trust can be invaluable for overcoming the methodological and ethical challenges associated with politically sensitive quantitative research.

Reflections on the Evolution of the China Field in Political Science

Kenneth Lieberthal

The current volume highlights the range and vibrancy of current studies of China by political scientists in the United States. This is a field that has become relatively mature in terms of the number and types of institutions that produce good China-related research, the array of generations of scholars engaged in that research, the variety of sources available to understand developments in China, and the methodological richness of the field overall. All of this represents a situation very different from and much better than that in the 1960s. But the changes over the past four decades have also introduced problems that require the ongoing attention of the field.

THE EVOLUTION OF THE FIELD

The world of the 1960s differed fundamentally from that of 2010 in terms of how China is studied. China studies in the earlier period were just reviving in the wake of the devastation wrought by the anti-Communist efforts most memorably associated with Senator Joseph McCarthy, who, in February 1950, asserted that he had a list of 205 Communists being protected in the State Department. The senator – along with others asking "Who lost China?" – decimated the ranks of China specialists in the State Department and questioned the loyalty of scholars such as John K. Fairbank and Owen Lattimore, arguing that they were at least Communist dupes and in some cases active secret members of the Communist Party (Fairbank, 1982). The results were such that Fairbank, generally regarded as the dean of the China field, addressed a conference of China scholars in the early 1970s and advised the younger participants to be sure to always keep a daily diary. He explained that this would prove important when they are investigated by a congressional committee and must explain what they were doing and thinking at any particular point in their past.[1]

---

[1] Author's personal recollection from that meeting.

The senior faculty in the 1960s generally had lived in China before 1949. Some were offspring of YMCA officials[2] or missionaries,[3] whereas others became engaged in China via their service in World War II.[4] Columbia University's A. Doak Barnett was not atypical. He had been raised in China (his father directed the YMCA in Shanghai), attended Yale University in the United States for a B.A. and later for an M.A. in International Relations, then returned to Asia in basically reportorial positions in China in the late 1940s, and in Hong Kong in the early 1950s. He then moved to the United States, where by the 1960s he had become a key member of the Columbia University faculty. This background gave him an intimate knowledge and "feel" for China, but relatively modest formal training in political science.

Those who began their studies of China in the 1960s had better formal training, virtually all studying for Ph.D.s in political science at major American universities.[5] Many came to the China field from having studied the Soviet Union and were driven by abiding interests in communism, Marxism-Leninism, and the dynamics of revolution. But the world of the China scholar at that time in many ways differed vastly from that of today.

For these young scholars, China was an abstraction – Americans were not permitted to travel to the PRC (then universally called "Communist China"). Scholars learned about China completely via sources, not from firsthand experience. Those sources were quite limited.[6]

China research initially relied primarily on U.S. government translations, along with analytical work, publications, and documents from Hong Kong and Taiwan. The U.S. government provided voluminous translation series of media broadcasts and articles in publications.[7] But these were not indexed well. For example, the most widely used source, the Foreign Broadcast Information Service *Daily Report*, provided only single entries at the beginning of each

[2] For example, A. Doak Barnett of Columbia University.
[3] For example, Lucian Pye of MIT.
[4] For example, Robert Scalapino of UC-Berkeley and Benjamin Schwartz of Harvard. John Stewart Service was both a YMCA child and a U.S. government employee in China during World War II. Harvard's John K. Fairbank also served in the State Department in China during World War II.
[5] Steven Andors, Phyllis Andors, Richard Baum, Gordon Bennett, Thomas Bernstein, Parris Chang, Edward Friedman, Steven Goldstein, Harry Harding, Ying-mao Kau, Steven Levine, Andrew Nathan, Michel Oksenberg, Susan Shirk, Richard Solomon, Frederick Teiwes, James Townsend, Lynn White, and the author, among others.
[6] Oksenberg (1970) provides an excellent overview and analysis of the English-language sources available to study China during this period.
[7] Foreign Broadcast Information Service's *China Daily Report* translated radio broadcasts and newspaper articles, producing a daily "book" five times a week that often contained over eighty single-spaced pages. Longer articles tended to be captured in the *Survey of China Mainland Press* and *Selections from China Mainland Magazines*, also U.S. government translation series. Items were selected for translation based on their potential value to U.S. government analyses. Three other series also provided translations that many scholars used: the Joint Publications Research Service (which included a far wider array of types of materials), the U.S. (Hong Kong) Consulate General's *Current Background*, and the BBC's *Summary of World Broadcasts*.

daily "book" and quarterly single-entry compendia. Researchers often allocated months in their research schedules to identifying articles that now can be located literally in seconds via readily available search engines. These early studies tended to focus on the analysis of documents, ideological framings, and newspapers/media broadcasts.

China itself published some periodicals, such as *China Pictorial*, *China Reconstructs*, *Peking Review*, and *Hong Qi*, but many of these stopped publication during the Cultural Revolution. The Cultural Revolution produced a tide of Red Guard publications, which began (albeit in extremely polemical ways) to reveal the policy debates and elite conflicts that had taken place in earlier years.[8] The U.S. government acquired many of these publications by purchase and, not surprisingly, Hong Kong-based counterfeiters quickly sensed a gold mine and began to churn out fakes.

With the Cultural Revolution, as more refugees began to appear in Hong Kong, refugee interviews became increasingly important as a source of information. Refugees, by definition, are an unrepresentative lot, though. Out of concerns about assuring personal safety, most scholars did not identify the refugees they interviewed. This could present its own set of problems. Three scholars who did important interviewing in Hong Kong one after the other, and who developed relatively compatible views of how the Chinese system was operating, only years later learned that they had been relying on the same key refugee as a source.[9]

Communications were very poor and physical materials hard to obtain. Copying technology other than microfilm and microfiche basically did not yet exist, and electronic communications beyond telephone and telegraph were still unavailable. Most young entrants to the China field went to Taiwan to study language (and perhaps do some research in the few carefully guarded rooms permitted to hold mainland "Communist bandit" materials), and then on to Hong Kong, in many cases to the Universities Service Centre (USC) in Kowloon, for their dissertation research. USC provided office space, a sense of community, a network for finding refugees to interview about conditions across the border, and good clippings files of mainland newspapers compiled by the nearby Union Research Institute.[10] Given the absence of copying facilities, protecting the physical safety of one's research notes from loss or inadvertent damage was a matter of serious concern.

---

[8] Many universities now have microfilm and microfiche collections of Red Guard papers and other materials. These materials provided a major basis for such studies as Chang (1978). The present author (1971) sought to evaluate the accuracy of some of these materials as they pertained to past elite debates.

[9] A. Doak Barnett (1967), not one of the three scholars mentioned in this paragraph, wrote the most detailed volume on the government system. Virtually the entire volume was based on interviews with refugees who were ex-cadres. The interviews were conducted among refugees who had left China before the Cultural Revolution.

[10] The Union Research Institute also held extensive files of notes compiled from interviews of refugees from the mainland.

The Evolution of the China Field in Political Science 269

Ideology and politics intruded deeply into scholarship. The Cultural Revolution in China coincided with America's escalation of the Vietnam War and the extremely bitter, in 1968 bordering on revolutionary, politics that ensued in the United States. These disputes deeply affected the China field. A number of scholars in the Asia field formed their own progressive association, called the Committee of Concerned Asian Scholars, which held its own annual meeting and published a journal, the *CCAS Bulletin*, and some books. Profound political and resulting personal disagreements divided the scholarly community, with a great deal of pressure exerted by some to take a stand against "American imperialism." These political fissures ran deep, and ideological differences ripped the field apart well into the late 1970s.

Students almost without exception entered graduate school with no previous background in Chinese-language study. Acquiring the language, therefore, occupied a significant part of the graduate training program.

The study of China was concentrated at a few leading centers because of a dearth of both scholars and materials. Harvard, Columbia, University of California-Berkeley, and Stanford (especially because of the Hoover Institution collection) played especially large roles in developing the field.

Each major university took a quintessentially area studies approach to understanding China. Ph.D. students in political science who focused on China often obtained an M.A. or certificate in China area studies along the way. Their programs included courses in the history, sociology, and language of modern China, in addition to dedicated courses on Chinese politics.[11]

Despite these limitations, a great deal of very careful work produced serious analyses of developments in the PRC. These tended to be richly contextual studies of individual cases, locations, or policy developments,[12] with insights generated by careful consideration of the potential implications of the studies' empirical findings.[13] That reflected in part the way political science was taught in the 1960s and in part the almost total lack of reliable statistical information from China at the time.[14] During the Cultural Revolution, of course, even Chinese officials no longer had access to remotely reliable data.[15] Earlier

---

[11] Courses in economics became more important only after China moved well along its path of reform.
[12] For example, Barnett (1969), Baum and Teiwes (1968), Shirk (1982), and Vogel (1969).
[13] The brief comments in this chapter do not seek to match the depth and richness of Oksenberg's (1970) essay.
[14] The excellent series edited by Robert F. Dernberger for the Joint Economic Committee of the U.S. Congress provided inadvertent testimony to how limited the concrete data were. Most Chinese statistics consisted of statements concerning percentage increases over the previous year in broad aggregates, where the base numbers for the series and concrete definitions of the categories were never revealed.
[15] At the height of the Cultural Revolution, the State Statistical Bureau had only fourteen people left in its central office. On the rehabilitated statistical system, see the series of articles in FBIS *Daily Report: People's Republic of China*, February 17, 1984, pp. K17–K21.

periods, such as the Great Leap Forward, produced statistical black holes of almost equally enormous scope.[16]

The field has subsequently evolved as a result of changes in virtually every parameter noted here. First, access to China has been transformed. Very limited visits by scholars began to take place as early as 1971, and these increased gradually during the 1970s. These afforded opportunities to meet with various Chinese officials from local to central levels, but those officials generally provided only carefully vetted information. Travel opportunities were so limited that in many cases pictures taken by recent visitors were of not only the same cities but also of the same rooms in the same buildings as those taken by visitors in earlier years. Visas were scarce, and the Chinese often paid all land expenses and provided the guides and entertainment. The purpose was hardly unfettered inquiry. But even these choreographed experiences began to lift the veil on the realities behind the propaganda in China.

A personal anecdote illustrates this. I was in Shanghai in 1977 at the time of the conclusion of the Eleventh Party Congress. Our minders had gathered all foreigners into a large room at the Peace Hotel to watch on TV the coverage of Hua Guofeng's Political Work Report to the congress.[17] Many Chinese hotel staffers were also with us. When Hua announced the formal conclusion of the Great Proletarian Cultural Revolution, a spontaneous cheer went up from the Chinese present. Hua then went on to say that there would be another such movement every seven or eight years – which was met by dead silence in the room.

Deng Xiaoping's reemergence in a commanding position by the end of 1978 and normalization of diplomatic relations with the United States at the beginning of 1979 opened up new vistas. Chinese, many of whom had spent roughly twenty years in prison camps as Rightists, were now released and found themselves attending conferences at plush sites such as Airlie House in Virginia.[18]

By the early 1980s China had begun to admit American scholars to do limited research and spend real time at Chinese institutions, and Chinese scholars began to visit and study at American universities. These opportunities made scholars aware of the enormously difficult lives that their Chinese counterparts led and the extent to which bureaucracy and political oppression weighed on virtually everything they did. One often heard Chinese colleagues explain patiently that "In China, little things are difficult and difficult things are impossible," as personal dependence on bureaucrats to accomplish even the simplest things characterized every dimension of the system. In addition, during the 1980s, China began to open up to foreign businesses, and an increasing range of people grappled with trying to get things done in the

---

[16] See Becker (1998), which details how absurd the reported statistics became during the Great Leap Forward.
[17] Text carried by New China News Agency, August 22, 1977.
[18] Many of these were people who had learned English before 1949 and were the most "presentable" people China could produce for international conferences at the time.

Chinese context. Harry Harding captured the resulting change in perspectives in an essay of that period (Harding, 1982).

The 1980s proved to be an extremely exciting period of reforms, and various American scholars were sought out by reformers to provide advice and insights. In political science, Americans advised on the development of the field in China (political science had been disestablished as a discipline in the 1950s, and in the 1980s individuals such as Yan Jiaqi, who had no previous training in the discipline, were assigned to be political scientists and to develop the field). Organizations such as the Committee on Scholarly Communications with the PRC (of the National Academy of Sciences) and the Social Science Research Council played significant roles in these efforts. America was then held in very high repute in China, in part because it was seen as the quintessentially modern country and in part because it was viewed as an ally against the Soviet Union. Reformers of all stripes often visited American scholars in search of good counsel. American knowledge of Chinese politics and policy process began to grow. In addition, the World Bank and other international organizations began to establish ties with China, and the World Bank especially began to publish figures on the economy that previously were unavailable even to most Chinese economists. At the same time, the World Bank and others worked with China to improve the quality of economic reporting there.[19]

With some disruptions, most notably in the wake of June 4, 1989, access to China has continued to grow. By 2010, many students entering Ph.D. programs in political science with a focus on China have already lived in the PRC for a year or more and have developed a good personal feel for the country, along with significant language skills. Most academics studying the country have spent extensive time there in both academic institutions and various other units. Chinese, both in China and in the United States, talk relatively freely about their views and concerns and provide a wide variety of perspectives.

Second, changes in China and in sources have produced related changes in the topics that are studied. The 1960s and 1970s saw many volumes devoted primarily to analysis of elite politics and ideological battles.[20] The 1980s brought studies of the reforms and of bureaucratic organization,[21] in addition to ongoing analyses of personal politics at the top of the Communist Party. Toward the end of that decade, interviewing began to produce enough of a basis to permit concrete explication of policy process.[22] As access further increased and the reforms produced major changes in the way the economy functioned, attention increasingly focused on analysis of the country's evolving political economy, along with a vast array of local studies based on interviews and participant observation.[23] Most of these developments have been

---

[19] Oksenberg and Jacobson (1990) provide an overview of this.
[20] Two of many examples are MacFarquhar (1974, 1983, 1997) and Teiwes (1979).
[21] See, for example, Harding (1981).
[22] See, for example, Lieberthal and Oksenberg (1988) and Lieberthal and Lampton (1992).
[23] See, for example, Blecher and Shue (1996), Oi (1998a), and Gallagher (2005).

additive, with perhaps only ideological studies largely disappearing from the literature in the past decade. By 2010, moreover, studies of Chinese politics, as illustrated by the contributions to this volume, have increasingly joined the mainstream of political science literature in terms of methods and topics.

Third, sources of data have multiplied in every way. In the 1980s, former top officials began to write memoirs that were sometimes very revealing. Over the years, the volume and scope of memoir literature, both autobiographical and through various types of party publications and reportage, have continued to mushroom.[24] The Chinese media have diversified and multiplied, and they have become enormously more informative. The statistical agencies have become far more adept at collecting data (despite ongoing serious problems), and far less of what they collect is considered secret. Publications abound for all types of state units, including ministries, local governments, the Central Party School, the Central Committee Party History Office, and others. Trade associations and other groups publish specialized journals, as do foreign NGOs, businesses, and news sources. And the various research units and academic centers produce a veritable avalanche of published analytical work, especially now that publications are considered a key metric of productivity.

As Allen Carlson and Hong Duan's chapter in this volume explains in the foreign policy realm, the Internet has introduced a phenomenal additional array of sources, from personal blogs to Web sites for all types of publications and bodies. A large percentage of government units, for example, now have Web sites, from which it is possible to obtain data that in the early years of study would have been difficult, if not impossible, to access.[25]

Search engines are making information in publications available in a way that could not have been imagined in earlier years. The CNKI databases hosted by EastView (中国知识资源总库 – – CNKI 系列数据库), for example, contain full-text digital access to Chinese publications, including 7,200 journals starting from 1915 (containing over 23 million articles), nearly 4,000 academic journals dating back to 1887, and about 1,000 newspapers published since 2000. Other datasets focus on specialized areas such as laws and regulations. The Internet has also enabled regular exchanges of information among large groups of scholars of China organized through listservs.

Surveys are now feasible, and many are conducted. The authorities still impose limits on what they deem to be sensitive inquiries, but these limits are fundamentally looser than in earlier years.[26]

In-depth interviews provide far wider and deeper access to information than in earlier times. Many more officials and knowledgeable outsiders are

---

[24] See, for example, Jin (1989) and Zong (2008).
[25] The Congressional-Executive Commission on China provides a useful list of links to government Web sites in its PRC E-Government Directory, at http://www.cecc.gov/pages/prcEgovDir/dirEgovPRC.php.
[26] For details, see the contribution to this volume by Mingming Shen and Ming Yang, with Melanie Manion.

prepared to talk with scholars, and in this author's experience many are willing to meet informally. Access is now available to leaders and staff in vastly more units than previously, most are far more open in their discussions as rules governing secrecy have narrowed in scope enormously, and social science scholarship is now regarded with less a priori suspicion than was the case in the early days of the reforms.

In short, China has gone from being a basically inaccessible, very low-information society to being a relatively accessible, high-information society since the 1960s. The major problems now are to gain control over the primary and secondary sources. In the 1960s, a scholar could reasonably aspire to read everything published in English on China – or at a minimum all serious scholarly work – in addition to keeping up with the major Chinese-language sources. Now it is no longer feasible to do either.

Fourth, technology has transformed the study of China. Scholars communicate with each other globally and instantaneously, and that includes many scholars in China itself. Materials are now available, in many cases electronically, to far more institutions and scholars than was previously feasible. The Web, scanning technologies, and other developments have changed the situation fundamentally. And computer programs now permit automated content analysis and sophisticated data analysis that in earlier years were extremely labor-intensive exercises.[27]

Even travel has changed dramatically, becoming far less expensive and more rapid. That is true both between the United States and China and within China itself. When this author first flew to Taiwan in 1969 from New York, for example, it required two stops in the continental United States, a third in Hawaii, and a fourth in Japan before landing in Taipei. When China began to open up in the 1970s, internal flights were infrequent and equipment was primitive (typically, old Aeroflot planes). Because there were no major highways, most travel necessarily was by train. Transportation generally had to be booked via the China Travel Service, which conducted operations only in person and could take weeks to make even simple arrangements. Airplane tickets had to be reconfirmed in person or they were canceled, and this often required waiting in line for hours at the appropriate office. Getting into a city from an airport could take hours if ground transportation had not been arranged ahead of time. And major areas of every province were off limits to foreigners.

Fifth, changes in the discipline of political science have changed the scholarship on China. To put it in somewhat oversimplified terms, in the 1960s "political science" was primarily an analysis of politics in order to generate inductively insights of more general applicability – that is, it was basically the

---

[27] For example, Yoshikoder, which can be downloaded for free from http://www.yoshikoder.org/, can do frequency counts of terms, provide the context in which keywords appear, and do simple evaluations of content (for example, ratio of positive-to-negative references to particular terms), among other functions. See also Daniela Stockmann's contribution in the present volume.

study of politics without science. By 2010, that situation has largely reversed itself. Now the discipline privileges survey research, large-N studies, statistical analyses, game theory, and formal modeling. Highly contextualized, granular case studies do not easily lead to favorable tenure decisions in many of the most highly ranked political science departments. And issues that inherently are difficult to put into quantitative frameworks – such as cultural dimensions of issue framing, policy making, and elite politics – receive less attention.

Finally, the content of graduate education for political scientists who want to study China has changed significantly. The discipline now privileges methodology, and courses in that subfield consume substantial graduate program time. Combined with increasing pressure in many Ph.D. programs to shorten the time from matriculation to degree, the opportunity costs of taking courses in the history, sociology, economics, culture, and language of modern China have risen to the point that relatively few students put these together as part of their political science Ph.D. programs. Indeed, many graduate programs have abolished foreign language requirements in favor of requirements on methodology. As a result, one or two courses on Chinese politics/foreign policy typically suffice, with much of the rest of the learning about China relegated to dissertation proposal preparation and in-country dissertation research. Many Ph.D. programs discourage students from pursuing an area-studies M.A. on their way to obtaining a Ph.D.

CURRENT ISSUES

Overall, the above-noted changes have moved forward the America-based China field in political science enormously. Scholars generally have taken effective advantage of the facts that China itself is more open and accessible, the available data are of higher quality and greater variety, methods of analysis have become more rigorous and sophisticated, and the field itself has become more "democratic" in that serious studies are no longer confined primarily to a few leading universities and centers. Another change, that scholars who grew up in China are now important members of the American political science community studying China, has deepened the insights and broadened the perspectives available in the U.S. academy. The chapters in the present volume testify to the serious progress and types of results that have been achieved.

But all is not well. Some of the trends over the years have diminished approaches that can provide rich insights and in the process threaten to reduce the fruitful synergy between the study of China in particular and of politics more generally. Four issues warrant particular attention.

First, the data standards demanded by the discipline often still cannot be met in China. In some instances this reflects the unavailability of data series of sufficient length or the simple lack of systematic data on various issues. Scholars of the Americas or Europe who want to benefit from survey research, for example, can often count on access to existing datasets, fully documented, with which they can do their work. As Melanie Manion explains in her contribution to this volume, the same is not true for such work on China. This reflects in part the inherent difficulties of doing research in this type of authoritarian system, where many types of data are considered sensitive, the datasets produced cannot be accessed by others, and key information is often missing concerning the sample and the Chinese partners involved in the research effort. In part, this also reflects the rapid changes in China and the lack of reliable time-series data. In addition, data quality frequently suffers from many of the problems inherent in dealing with a country that is still in transition from third world to first world institutions and capabilities.

Consequently, many graduate students who have completed courses in methodology despair when they try to develop sufficiently "rigorous" research projects on China. The overlap between available high-quality statistical data and important, interesting questions to ask is still uncomfortably small in developing countries. Where students of China must develop their data from scratch, as is most frequently the case, they must spend enormous amounts of time in questionnaire construction and pretests, gaining access to the relevant populations, developing their sample frames, implementing their surveys, and then analyzing and writing up the results. The same applies to many other types of research that require in-country data collection. In this context, there can be a lot of pressure to ask questions that are driven by data availability, rather than asking different, challenging questions that can yield significant results.

There is now tremendous focus on framing questions that can be pursued in a methodologically rigorous fashion. But framing good questions is a necessary first step in producing worthwhile outcomes. Thus, there needs to be serious focus, too, on first understanding politics and deriving from that understanding the key questions that need to be raised; then, within that universe, trying to structure the questions so as to be most amenable to formal analytical enhancements of the analysis. Otherwise, the rigor with which one can pursue an issue tends to drive what issues are pursued. Since rigor itself is not directly proportional to importance, its pursuit can weaken the field as a whole. As a colleague of the author memorably commented during a heated discussion of a tenure review case, "the most common form of 'rigor' is 'mortis.'"

Second, ideas, culture, history, and social constructs can shape outcomes in China profoundly. The ways issues are structured cognitively and how they relate to other factors in the environment are influenced significantly by culture and history. Even terminology affects intellectual constructs differently in different languages. As Lily Tsai's chapter in this volume explains, for example, there are advantages to conversational interviewing over standardized interviewing, as the former assures that survey questions are understood correctly by respondents. But these dimensions in general are not readily applicable to the types of rigorous inquiry and analysis increasingly demanded by American political science departments. And graduate programs, as noted above, train students less well to understand and analyze these types of factors than was the case for their predecessors.

Third, students of Chinese politics who still utilize more traditional approaches to understanding their topic often gravitate to think-tanks and schools of public policy instead of leading political science departments.[28] This is potentially a major loss to both the study of Chinese politics and to the development of political science as a discipline. A more hospitable posture by the discipline toward more traditional approaches to the study of China would potentially make young scholars feel more comfortable in gradually adopting more formal methods of analysis as the data from China warrant doing so.

In addition, the development of China studies in political science holds out serious opportunities for the overall development of political science. Political science developed from the study of Western historical experience, and many of its most fundamental assumptions deeply reflect that background. But things in China (and many non-Western areas) often do not fit into the conceptual categories typically employed in the West. For example, Bruce Dickson's work in this volume and elsewhere (Dickson, 2003)[29] has shown that entrepreneurs in China do not, as was the case in modern Western history, seek to challenge the regime. Rather, they tend to try to draw close to the state, viewing their capacity to deal with the state as a competitive advantage in the Chinese economy. Others have found through surveys that political trust in the authoritarian Chinese system is actually higher than that in democratic Taiwan (Shi, 2001). Thus, one of the major potential scholarly values of a more open and accessible China is that it provides opportunities to test fundamental conclusions that have grown out of years of social science work based primarily on Western developmental experience. Therefore, good studies of China may contribute real insight into areas in which the conventional wisdom in political science unknowingly reflects a more uniquely Western developmental experience than universal laws concerning political systems.

In sum, as the China field matures, it has an enormous amount to offer to the rest of the political science – and to broader social science – disciplines. But those disciplines must be able to value the reality that different parts of the world yield different types of data and pull things together in ways that may differ substantially from those in the Western experience. Therefore, the value of a maturing China field is in part that it can engage the broader discipline in a serious analysis of fundamentals. This requires that the broader discipline not impose too tight a boundary on defining the kinds of work that are valued. Only in this context can the training programs and career incentives nurture the full value of a mature scholarly community that is able to bring China's experience into the mainstream of political science.

Fourth, although things have changed enormously since John King Fairbank issued the warning to younger China scholars in the early 1970s noted earlier, there arguably is still an important need to have some students of Chinese

---

[28] To name but a few: Erica Downs, Elizabeth Economy, David M. Lampton, James Mulvenon, Jonathan Pollack, Anthony Saich, Michael Swaine, Murray Scot Tanner.
[29] See also Kellee Tsai (2007).

politics who have a good grasp of overall developments in China and who are able to articulate this to a broad public. Ironically, this is in part because the American public is now deluged by presentations on China in the media and by businesspeople, travelers, language teachers, and others. Too much of this coverage of China succumbs to caricature and a focus on the colorful and dramatic versus what is systematic. With the flood of coverage of things Chinese, there is an acute need for informed judgments to create context and perspective; these must be proffered in ways that reach and engage general audiences.

The pressures, both from better accessibility and data and from the demands of the discipline, however, move in the opposite direction – toward developing a particular specialty that permits increasingly sophisticated analysis over time. This is valuable and certainly should be nurtured. However, failure to develop some public intellectuals among each generation of students of Chinese politics can diminish the quality of public discourse on China; this, in turn, can reduce the resources available for ongoing development of the field. This is also a problem for policy-making purposes. The more formal the research methods used by political scientists are, the less likely it is that the results of that work will inform in any serious way the deliberations of policy makers. Public intellectuals who are able to translate such work into terms readily accessible to the policy community, and to place their presentations in outlets that command community attention, can play a vital role in making academic work on China inform better public policy.

In sum, despite the reality that a volume of this scope and substance could not possibly have been put together two decades ago, there are still troubling questions that scholars of Chinese politics and those in other areas of political science can and should address. These issues are, of course, not completely unique to China, and in many ways they reflect the tremendous advances in both the China field and the discipline of political science in the United States. The maturity of the China field, and the enormous importance and visibility of the country itself, now make the study of China a good vehicle for addressing issues that should engage the entire discipline.

Glossary

爱国主义 *aiguo zhuyi* patriotism
白酒 *bui jiu* strong liquor
搬迁 *banqian* relocation
北京社会经济发展年度调查 *Beijing shehui jingji fazhan niandu diaocha* Beijing Annual Survey of Social and Economic Development
本地人 *bendi ren* locals
表现 *biaoxian* political behavior
比武 *biwu* "match of skill," contest
布什 *Bushi* Bush
长假 *changjia* long vacation
超生游击队 *chaosheng youjidui* out-of-quota birthing guerrilla
朝鲜 *Chaoxian* North Korea
处 *chu* bureau
打工妹 *dagongmei* factory girl
党员 *dangyuan* party member
但是 *danshi* however
单位 *danwei* work unit
地 *di* below the departmental/prefecture level
调查 *diaocha* survey
地方志 *difangzhi* gazetteer
动态 *dongtai* trend
锻炼 *duanlian* training
妇联 *Fulian* Women's Federation
复员军人 *fuyuan junren* veteran
改善政治体制 *gaishan zhengzhi tizhi* improve the political structure

改革开放 *gaige kaifang* reform and opening
个体户 *geti hu* individually owned enterprise
关系 *guanxi* connections
国际问题研究 *Guoji wenti yanjiu* Journal of International Studies
国际资料信息 *Guoji ziliao xinxi* International Data Information
国情 *guoqing* national condition
和平崛起 *heping jueqi* peaceful rise
和平论坛 *Heping luntan* Peace Forum
红白理事会 *hongbai lishihui* state-approved wedding and funeral council
户口 *hukou* household registration system
检查 *jiancha* inspection
街道 *jiedao* neighborhood
街道办事处 *jiedao banshichu* street office
解放军报 *Jiefangjun bao* PLA Daily
精神 *jingshen* spirit
局 *ju* below the departmental/prefecture level
居民委员会 *jumin weiyuanhui* neighborhood committee
居民小组 *jumin xiaozu* residential small group
军属 *junshu* military dependent
开放档案 *kaifang dang'an* open archives
科 *ke* section
空挂户 *konggua hu* does not live at official household residence
空话 *konghua* empty verbiage
块/政府 *kuai/zhengfu* horizontal coordinating governing bodies at various levels
老户 *laohu* long-term petitioner
老年人协会 *laonianren xiehui* senior citizens association
邻长 *linzhang* block captain (Taiwan)
流动人口 *liudong renkou* floating population
利用处 *liyong chu* user services
里长 *lizhang* neighborhood head (Taiwan)
民族主义 *minzu zhuyi* nationalism
内部 *neibu* internal
片儿警 *piarjing* "beat cop"
强国 *qiangguo* strong nation
强国论坛 *Qiangguo luntan* Strong Country Forum

Glossary

企业 *qiye* enterprise
区 *qu* district
群众 *qunzhong* masses
群体访 *quntifang* group petition
人户分离 *renhu fenli* does not live at official household residence
人民日报 *Renmin ribao* People's Daily
人民网 *Renmin wang* People's Net
认同 *rentong* identity
三乱 *san luan* "three disorders" (illegitimate fees)
社会调查 *shehui diaocha* social survey
社区居民委员会 *shequ jumin weiyuanhui* residents' committee or community residents' committee (PRC)
涉外调查 *she wai diaocha* foreign-affiliated survey
涉外调查许可证 *she wai diaocha xuke zheng* permit for survey research involving foreign affiliates
市场调查 *shichang diaocha* business survey
世界经济与政治 *Shijie jingji yu zhengzhi* World Economics and Politics
事业 *shiye* institute
事业单位 *shiye danwei* service unit
司 *si* departmental position
特护期 *tehuqi* specially protected period
天津信访 *Tianjin xinfang* Tianjin Petitioning
天益学术网 *Tianyi xueshuwang* TECN Academic Net
条/部门 *tiao /bumen* vertical bureaucracies of governance
厅 *ting* office
统计公报 *tongji gongbao* statistical report
突发性群体事件 *tufaxing qunti shijian* explosive mass incident
网民 *wangmin* netizen
委托 *weituo* jointly
维稳办 *weiwenban* Social Stability Maintenance Office
我感到担心 *wo gandao danxin* I feel worried
我感到害怕 *wo gandao haipa* I feel afraid
我感到骄傲 *wo gandao jiao'ao* I feel proud
毋忘国耻 *wuwang guochi* "Never Forget the National Humiliation"
下海 *xiahai* going "into the sea" of the private sector
现代国际关系 *Xiandai guoji guanxi* Contemporary International Relations

小品 *xiaopin* comedy skit

信访 *xinfang* petitioning

信访信息 *Xinfang xinxi* Petitioning Information

新华网 *Xinhua wang* Xinhua Net

学科建设 *xueke jianshe* constructing the discipline

以前什么都靠司长，后来谁都要看市场 *yiqian shenmme doukao sizhang, houlai shei douyao kan shichang* "before, everything depended on the bureau chief, afterward, everyone had to look to the market"

政法委 *zhengfawei* Politics and Law Committee

政府部门 *zhengfu bumen* government office

正式体制改善 *zhengshi tizhi gaishan* improve the political structure

政治改革 *zhengzhi gaige* political reform

指南 *zhinan* guidebook

中国国关在线 *Zhongguo guoguan zaixian* IR China

中国国际关系研究网 *Zhongguo guoji guanxi yanjiu wang* Chinese IR Study Network

中国军网 *Zhongguo jun wang* China Military Online

中国外交论坛 *Zhongguo waijiao luntan* Forum on China's Foreign Relations

中国网 *Zhongguo wang* China Net

中国知识资源总库系列数据库 *Zhongguo zhizhi ziyuan zongku xilie shujuku* CNKI databases hosted by EastView

中国重要报纸全文数据库 *Zhongguo zhongyao baozhi quanwen shujuku* China Core Newspapers Full-Text Database

中华人民共和国外交部 *Zhonghua renmin gongheguo waijiao bu* Ministry of Foreign Affairs

资助 *zizhu* funded

总结报告 *zongjie baogao* work summary

座谈会 *zuotanhui* group discussion

References

Aberbach, Joel D., Robert D. Putnam, and Bert A. Rockman. 1981. *Bureaucrats and Politicians in Western Democracies*. Cambridge, MA: Harvard University Press.

Adams, Laura. 2003. "Cultural Elites in Uzbekistan: Ideology Production and the State," in Pauline Jones Luong (ed.), *The Transformation of Central Asia: States and Societies from Soviet Rule to Independence*. Ithaca, NY: Cornell University Press: 93–119.

Adolph, Christopher. 2003. *Paper Autonomy, Private Ambition: Theory and Evidence Linking Central Bankers' Careers and Economic Performance*. Paper presented at the annual APSA Conference, Philadelphia, PA.

Allina-Pisano, Jessica. 2004. "Sub Rosa Resistance and the Politics of Economic Reform: Land Redistribution in Post-Soviet Ukraine." *World Politics*, vol. 56, no. 4: 554–581.

Almond, Gabriel A. and Sidney Verba. 1963. *The Civic Culture*. Princeton, NJ: Princeton University Press.

Alonso, William and Paul Starr. 1983. *The Politics of Numbers*. New York: Russell Sage Foundation.

Anderson, Elijah. 1990. *Streetwise: Race, Class, and Change in an Urban Community*. Chicago: University of Chicago Press.

Anderson, Jeffrey J. 1992. *The Territorial Imperative: Pluralism, Corporatism, and Economic Crisis*. Cambridge: Cambridge University Press.

Ash, Robert, David Shambaugh, and Seiichiro Takagi (eds.) 2007. *China Watching: Perspectives from Europe, Japan, and the United States*. New York: Routledge.

Bachman, David M. 1991. *Bureaucracy, Economy, and Leadership in China: The Institutional Origins of the Great Leap Forward*. Cambridge: Cambridge University Press.

Banfield, Edward C. 1958. *The Moral Basis of a Backward Society*. Glencoe, IL: Free Press.

Bar-Tal, Daniel. 1998. "The Rocky Road toward Peace: Beliefs on Conflict in Israeli Textbooks." *Journal of Peace Research*, vol. 35, no. 6: 723–742.

Barnard, Chester. 1968. *The Functions of the Executive*. 30th anniv. ed. Cambridge, MA: Harvard University Press.

Barnett, A. Doak. 1985. *The Making of Foreign Policy in China*. Boulder, CO: Westview.

(ed.). 1969. *Chinese Communist Politics in Action*. Seattle: University of Washington Press.

Barnett, A. Doak, with a contribution by Ezra Vogel. 1967. *Cadres, Bureaucracy and Political Power in Communist China*. New York: Columbia University Press.

Barrett, Christopher B. and Jeffrey W. Cason. 1997. *Overseas Research: A Practical Guide*. Baltimore, MD: Johns Hopkins University Press.

Barron, Erma W. and Robert H. Finch, Jr. 1978. "Design Effects in a Complex Multistage Sample: The Survey of Low Income Aged and Disabled (SLIAD)." *Proceedings of the Survey Research Methods Section, American Statistical Association*: 400–405.

Bartke, Wolfgang. 1997. *Who Was Who in the People's Republic of China: With More than 3100 Portraits*. 2 vols. München: K.G. Saur.

Bartke, Wolfgang and Institut für Asienkunde (Hamburg, Germany). 1991. *Who's Who in the People's Republic of China*. 3rd ed. New York: K.G. Saur.

Bates, Robert, Avner Greif, Margaret Levi, Jean-Laurent Rosenthal, and Barry Weingast. 1998. *Analytic Narratives*. Princeton, NJ: Princeton University Press.

Baum, Richard. 2007. "Studies of Chinese Politics in the United States," in Robert Ash, David Shambaugh, and Seiichiro Takagi, (eds.) 2007. *China Watching: Perspectives from Europe, Japan and the United States*. New York: Routledge: 147–168.

1998. "The Fifteenth National Party Congress: Jiang Takes Command?" *China Quarterly*, no. 153:141–156.

1994. *Burying Mao: Chinese Politics in the Age of Deng Xiaoping*. Princeton, NJ: Princeton University Press.

Baum, Richard and Alexei Shevchenko. 1999. "The 'State of the State,'" in Merle Goldman and Roderick MacFarquhar (eds.), *The Paradox of China's Post-Mao Reforms*. Cambridge, MA: Harvard University Press: 333–362.

Baum, Richard and Frederick Teiwes. 1968. *Ssu-Ch'ing: The Socialist Education Movement of 1962–1966*. Berkeley: Center for Chinese Studies, University of California.

Bayard de Volo, Lorraine. 2001. *Mothers of Heroes and Martyrs: Gender Identity Politics in Nicaragua, 1979–1999*. Baltimore, MD: Johns Hopkins University Press.

Bayard de Volo, Lorraine and Edward Schatz. 2004. "From the Inside Out: Ethnographic Methods in Political Research." *PS: Political Science and Politics*, vol. 37, no. 2: 417–422.

Becker, Jasper. 1998. *Hungry Ghosts*. New York: Macmillan.

Bellin, Eva. 2000. "Contingent Democrats: Industrialists, Labor, and Democratization in Late-Developing Countries." *World Politics*, vol. 52, no. 2: 175–205.

Belousov, Konstantin, et al. 2007. "Any Port in a Storm: Fieldwork Difficulties in Dangerous and Crisis-Ridden Settings." *Qualitative Research*, vol. 7, no. 2: 155–175.

Ben-Eliezer, Uri. 1995. "A Nation-in-Arms: State, Nation, and Militarism in Israel's First Years." *Comparative Studies in Society and History*, vol. 37, no. 2: 264–285.

Bensel, Richard F. 2000. *The Political Economy of American Industrialization, 1877–1900*. Cambridge: Cambridge University Press.

1984. *Sectionalism and American Political Development*. Madison: University of Wisconsin Press.

Benton, Gregor. 1992. *Mountain Fires: The Red Army's Three-Year War in South China, 1934–1938*. Berkeley: University of California Press.

Berns, Walter. 2001. *Making Patriots*. Chicago: University of Chicago Press.
Bernstein, Thomas P. and Xiaobo Lü. 2003. *Taxation without Representation in Contemporary Rural China*. Cambridge: Cambridge University Press.
Bestor, Theodore C. 1989. *Neighborhood Tokyo*. Stanford, CA: Stanford University Press.
Bewley, Truman F. 2004. "The Limits of Rationality," in Ian Shapiro, Rogers Smith, and Tarek Masoud (eds.), *Problems and Methods in the Study of Politics*. Cambridge: Cambridge University Press: 381–5.
Bian, Yanjie. 1999. "Getting a Job through a Web of *Guanxi* in China," in Barry Wellman (ed.), *Networks in the Global Village: Life in Contemporary Communities*. Boulder, CO: Westview: 255–278.
Biemer, Paul P. and Lars E. Lyberg. 2003. *Introduction to Survey Quality*. Malden, MA: Wiley-Interscience.
Blecher, Marc and Vivienne Shue. 1996. *The Tethered Deer: Government and Economy in a Chinese County*. Stanford, CA: Stanford University Press.
Bo, Zhiyue. 2004a. "The 16th Central Committee of the Chinese Communist Party: Formal Institutions and Factional Groups." *Journal of Contemporary China*, vol. 39, no. 13: 223–256.
  2004b. "The Institutionalization of Elite Management in China," in Barry Naughton and Dali L. Yang (eds.), *Holding China Together: Diversity and National Integration in the Post-Deng Era*. Cambridge: Cambridge University Press: 70–100.
  2002. *Chinese Provincial Leaders: Economic Performance and Political Mobility, 1949–1998*. Armonk, NY: M. E. Sharpe.
Bobrow, Davis B. 2001. "Visions of (In)Security and American Strategic Style." *International Studies Perspectives*, vol. 2, no. 1: 1–12.
Bodnar, John (ed.). 1996. *Bonds of Affection: Americans Define Their Patriotism*. Princeton, NJ: Princeton University Press.
Boylan, Delia M. 2001. *Defusing Democracy: Central Bank Autonomy and the Transition from Authoritarian Rule*. Ann Arbor: University of Michigan Press.
Brace, Paul. 1993. *State Government and Economic Performance*. Baltimore, MD: Johns Hopkins University Press.
Brady, Henry E. 2004. "Doing Good and Doing Better: How Far Does the Quantitative Template Get Us?" in Henry E. Brady and David Collier (eds.), *Rethinking Social Inquiry: Diverse Tools, Shared Standards*. Lanham, MD: Rowman and Littlefield: 53–68.
Bruun, Ole. 1993. *Business and Bureaucracy in a Chinese City: An Ethnography of Private Business Households in Contemporary China*. Berkeley: Institute of East Asian Studies, University of California.
Bueno de Mesquita, Bruce, Alastair Smith, Randolph M. Silverson, and James D. Morrow. 2003. *The Logic of Political Survival*. Cambridge, MA: MIT Press.
Burawoy, Michael. 2000. *Global Ethnography: Forces, Connections, and Imaginations in a Postmodern World*. Berkeley: University of California Press.
  1998. "The Extended Case Method." *Sociological Theory*, vol. 16, no. 1: 4–33.
  1985. *The Politics of Production: Factory Regimes under Capitalism and Socialism*. London: Verso.
Burden, Barry C. and Joseph Neal Rice Sanberg. 2003. "Budget Rhetoric in Presidential Campaigns from 1952–2000." *Political Behavior*, vol. 25, no. 2: 97–118.
Cai Wenzhong. 1995. "Dubi jiangjun Cai Shufan" [One-Armed General: Cai Shufan]. *Dangshi tiandi* [Party History World], no. 3: 28–31.

Cai, Yongshun. 2000. "Between State and Peasant," *China Quarterly*, no. 163: 783–805.
Calhoun, Craig. 1994. *Neither Gods nor Emperors: Students and the Struggle for Democracy in China*. Berkeley: University of California Press.
Cambridge History of China, vols. 14, 15. 1987. 1991. Ed. John King Fairbank and Roderick MacFarquhar. Cambridge: Cambridge University Press.
Cammett, Melani. 2007. *Globalization and Business Politics in Arab North Africa*. Cambridge: Cambridge University Press.
 2005. "Fat Cats and Self-made Men: Globalization and the Paradoxes of Collective Action." *Comparative Politics*, vol. 37, no. 4: 379–400.
Carlson, Allen. 2009. "A Flawed Perspective: The Limitations Inherent within the Study of Chinese Nationalism." *Nations and Nationalism*, vol. 15, no. 1: 20–35.
CASS. 2009. "Chinese Academy of Social Sciences," at http://bic.cass.cn/English/InfoShow/Arcitle_Show_Cass.asp?, accessed June 2009.
 2007. "Surveying Internet Usage and Its Impact in Seven Chinese Cities." Research Center of Social Development, at http://www.wipchina.org/?p1=content&p2=07122508155, accessed June 2009.
Central Organization Department and Party History Research Center of the CCP CC. 2004. *Zhongguo gongchandang lijie zhongyang weiyuan da cidian, 1921–2003* [The Dictionary of Past and Present CCP Central Committee Members]. Beijing: Dangshi chubanshe.
Chan, Alfred L. and Paul Nesbitt-Larking. 1995. "Critical Citizenship and Civil Society in Contemporary China." *Canadian Journal of Political Science*, vol. 28, no. 2: 293–309.
Chan, Anita, Richard Madsen, and Jonathan Unger. 2009. *Chen Village: Revolution to Globalization*. 3rd ed. Berkeley: University of California Press.
 1992. *Chen Village under Mao and Deng*. Berkeley: University of California Press.
Chang, Parris S. 1978. *Power and Policy in China*. 2nd enlg. ed. University Park: Pennsylvania State University Press.
Chang, Yu-Tzung, Yun-han Chu, and Frank Tsai. 2005. "Confucianism and Democratic Values in Three Chinese Societies." *Issues and Studies*, vol. 41, no. 4: 1–33.
Charmaz, Kathy. 2006. *Constructing Grounded Theory: A Practical Guide through Qualitative Analysis*. London: Sage.
Chase, Michael and James Mulvenon. 2002. "You've Got Dissent." Rand, at http://www.rand.org/pubs/monograph_reports/MR1543/index.html, accessed June 2008.
Chen, An. 2002. "Capitalist Development, Entrepreneurial Class, and Democratization in China." *Political Science Quarterly*, vol. 117, no. 3: 401–422.
Chen, Calvin. 2008. *Some Assembly Required: Work, Community, and Politics in China's Rural Enterprises*. Cambridge, MA: Asia Center, Harvard University.
 2006. "Work, Conformity, and Defiance: Strategies of Resistance and Control in China's Township and Village Enterprises," in Jacob Eyferth (ed.), *How China Works: Perspectives on the Twentieth Century Workplace*. New York: Routledge: 124–139.
Chen, Jie. 2005a. "Popular Support for Village Self-government in China." *Asian Survey*, vol. 45, no. 6: 865–885.
 2005b. "Sociopolitical Attitudes of the Masses and Leaders in the Chinese Village: Attitude Congruence and Constraint." *Journal of Contemporary China*, vol. 14, no. 4: 445–464.

2004. *Popular Political Support in Urban China*. Washington, DC and Stanford, CA: Woodrow Wilson Center Press and Stanford University Press.

2001. "Urban Chinese Perceptions of Threats from the United States and Japan." *Public Opinion Quarterly*, vol. 65, no. 2: 254–266.

2000. "Subjective Motivations for Mass Political Participation in Urban China." *Social Science Quarterly*, vol. 81, no. 2: 645–662.

1999. "Comparing Mass and Elite Subjective Orientations in Urban China." *Public Opinion Quarterly*, vol. 63, no. 2: 193–219.

Chen, Jie and Bruce J. Dickson. 2010. *Allies of the State: Democratic Support and Regime Support among China's Capitalists*. Cambridge, MA: Harvard University Press.

Chen, Jie, Chunlong Lu, and Yiyin Yang. 2007. "Popular Support for Grassroots Self-Government in Urban China." *Modern China*, vol. 33, no. 4: 505–528.

Chen, Jie and Yang Zhong. 2002. "Why Do People Vote in Semicompetitive Elections in China?" *Journal of Politics*, vol. 64, no. 1: 178–197.

2000. "Research Note. Valuation of Individual Liberty vs. Social Order among Democratic Supporters: A Cross-validation." *Political Research Quarterly*, vol. 53, no. 2: 427–439.

1999. "Mass Political Interest (or Apathy) in Urban China." *Communist and Post-Communist Studies*, vol. 32, no. 3: 281–303.

Chen, Jie, Yang Zhong, and Jan William Hillard. 1997. "The Level and Sources of Political Support for China's Current Regime." *Communist and Post-Communist Studies*, vol. 30, no. 1: 45–64.

Chen, Jie, Yang Zhong, Jan Hillard, and John Scheb. 1997. "Assessing Political Support in China: Citizens' Evaluations of Governmental Effectiveness and Legitimacy." *Journal of Contemporary China*, vol. 6, no. 16: 551–566.

Chen, Nancy N. 2003. *Breathing Spaces: Qigong, Psychiatry, and Healing in China*. New York: Columbia University Press.

Chen, Shenghuo. 2004. *The Events of September 11 and Chinese College Students' Images of the United States*. Paper presented at the Center for Strategic and International Studies Conference on "Chinese Images of the United States."

Chen, Xi. 2009. "The Power of 'Troublemaking': Chinese Petitioners' Tactics and Their Efficacy." *Comparative Politics*, vol. 41, no. 4: 451–71.

2008. "Collective Petitioning and Institutional Conversion," in Kevin O'Brien (ed.), *Popular Protest in China*. Cambridge, MA: Harvard University Press: 54–70.

Chen, Xueyi and Tianjian Shi. 2001. "Media Effects on Political Confidence and Trust in the People's Republic of China in the Post-Tiananmen Period." *East Asia: An International Quarterly*, vol. 19, no. 3: 84–118.

Cheng, Peter T.Y., Jae Ho Chung, and Zhimin Lin (eds.). 1998. *Provincial Strategies of Economic Reform in Post-Mao China*. Armonk, NY: M. E. Sharpe.

Christensen, Thomas J., Alastair Iain Johnston, and Robert S. Ross. 2006. "Conclusions and Future Directions," in Alastair Iain Johnston and Robert S. Ross (eds.), *New Directions in the Study of China's Foreign Policy*. Stanford, CA: Stanford University Press: 379–420.

Chu, Yun-han and Yu-tzung Chang. 2001. "Culture Shift and Regime Legitimacy: Comparing Mainland China, Taiwan, and Hong Kong," in Shiping Hua (ed.), *Chinese Political Culture, 1989–2000*. Armonk, NY: M. E. Sharpe: 320–347.

CNNIC. 2008. "The 21st Statistical Survey Report on the Internet Development in China," at http://www.cnnic.net.cn/index/oE/oo/11/index.htm, accessed July 2008.

CNNIC. 2007. "Surveying China's Blogging Market in 2007," at http://www.cnnic.net.cn/uploadfiles/pdf/2007/12/26/113902.pdf, accessed August 2008.
Congressional-Executive Commission on China. 2006. *China's Household Registration System: Sustained Reform Needed to Protect China's Rural Migrants*. Washington, DC.
Cornelius, Wayne A., Todd A. Eisenstadt, and Jane Hinley (eds.). 1999. *Subnational Politics and Democratization in Mexico*. La Jolla: Center for U.S.-Mexican Studies, University of California.
CPCR. 2005. *Zhongguo shichanghua baokan quanguo toufang cankao 2005 (I)* [Market Intelligence Report on China's Print Media Retail Distribution 2005 (I)]. Beijing: CPCR Kaiyuan Celue [Opening Strategy Consultation].
Cyert, Richard and James March. 1992. *A Behavioral Theory of the Firm*. 2nd ed. Cambridge: Blackwell.
Damm, Jen and Simona Thomas. 2006. *Chinese Cyberspaces: Technological and Political Effects*. New York: Routledge.
Davis, Deborah S. (ed.). 2000. *The Consumer Revolution in Urban China*. Berkeley: University of California Press.
Davis, Deborah, Pierre Landry, Yusheng Peng, and Jin Xiao. 2007. "Gendered Pathways to Rural Schooling: The Interplay of Wealth and Local Institutions." *China Quarterly*, no. 189: 60–82.
Dever, Jill A., Jun Liu, Vincent G. Iannacchione, and Douglas E. Kendrick. 2001. "An Optimal Allocation Method for Two-Stage Sampling Designs with Stratification at the Second Stage." *Proceedings of the Annual Meeting of the American Statistical Association*, August 5–9.
Diamant, Neil J. 2009. *Embattled Glory: Veterans, Military Families, and the Politics of Patriotism in China, 1949–2007*. Lanham, MD: Rowman and Littlefield.
  2000. *Revolutionizing the Family: Politics, Love, and Divorce in Urban and Rural China, 1949–1968*. Berkeley: University of California Press.
Diao Jiecheng. 1996. *Renmin xinfang shilue* [A Brief History of People's Letters and Visits]. Beijing: Xueyuan chubanshe.
Dickson, Bruce J. 2008. *Wealth into Power: The Communist Party's Embrace of China's Private Sector*. Cambridge: Cambridge University Press.
  2007. "Integrating Wealth and Power in China: The Communist Party's Embrace of the Private Sector." *China Quarterly*, no. 192: 827–854.
  2003. *Red Capitalists in China: The Party, Private Entrepreneurs, and Prospects for Political Change*. Cambridge: Cambridge University Press.
  2002. "Do Good Businessmen Make Good Citizens? An Emerging Collective Identity among China's Private Entrepreneurs," in Merle Goldman and Elizabeth J. Perry (eds.), *Changing Meanings of Citizenship in Modern China*. Cambridge, MA: Harvard University Press: 255–287.
Dijkstra, Wil. 1987. "Interviewing Style and Respondent Behavior: An Experimental Study of the Survey-Interview." *Sociological Methods and Research*, vol. 16, no. 2: 309–334.
Dijkstra, Wil and Johanese van der Zouwen. 1987. "Styles of Interviewing and the Social Context of the Survey Interview," in Hans-J. Hippler, Norbert Schwartz, and Seymour Sudman (eds.), *Social Information Processing and Survey Methodology*. New York: Springer.
DiMaggio, Paul, (Eszter Hargittai, W. Russell Neuman, and John P. Robinson. 2001. "Social Implications of the Internet." *Annual Review of Sociology*, vol. 27: 307–336.

Dittmer, Lowell. 2001. "The Changing Nature of Elite Power Politics." *China Journal*, no. 45: 53–68.
  1983. "The 12th Congress of the Communist Party of China." *China Quarterly*, no. 93: 108–214.
Dittmer, Lowell and William Hurst. 2002/2003. "Analysis in Limbo: Contemporary Chinese Politics amid the Maturation of Reform." *Issues and Studies*, vol. 38, no. 4/vol. 39, no. 1: 11–48.
Dowd, Daniel V., Allen Carlson, and Mingming Shen. 1999. "The Prospects for Democratization: Evidence from the 1995 Beijing Area Study." *Journal of Contemporary China*, vol. 8, no. 22: 365–380.
DRC [Guowuyuan fazhan yanjiu zhongxin]. 2001. "'Dongbei xianxiang' de xin chulu" [A New Way Out of the "Northeast Phenomenon"]. *Guowuyuan fazhan yanjiu zhongxin diaocha yanjiu baogao*, no. 60.
  1999a. "Shenyang shuibengchang qiye gaige yu xiagang zhigong wenti diaocha" [Investigation into the Shenyang Water Pump Factory's Problems with Reform and *Xiagang* Workers]. *Guowuyuan fazhan yanjiu zhongxin diaocha yanjiu baogao*, no. 84.
  1999b. "Shanghai dianhua shebei zhizaochang qiye gaige yu xiagang zhigong wenti diaocha" [Investigation into the Shanghai Telephone Equipment Production Plant's Problems of Enterprise Reform and *Xiagang* Workers]. *Guowuyuan fazhan yanjiu zhongxin diaocha yanjiu baogao*, no. 86.
  1999c. "Baoshan gangtie (jituan) gongsi de qiye fazhan yu renyuan zhuangkuang diaocha" [Investigation into the Enterprise Development and Employee Situation of Baoshan Steel]. *Guowuyuan fazhan yanjiu zhongxin diaocha yanjiu baogao*, no. 87.
Druckman, Daniel. 1995. "Social-Psychological Aspects of Nationalism," in John Comeroff and Paul Stern (eds.), *Perspectives on Nationalism and War*. Amsterdam: Gordon and Breach: 47–98.
Druckman, James N., Donald P. Green, James H. Kuklinski, and Arthur Lupia. 2006. "The Growth and Development of Experimental Research in Political Science." *American Political Science Review*, vol. 100, no. 4: 627–635.
Duriau, Vincent J., Rhonda K. Reger, and Michael D. Pfarrer. 2007. "A Content Analysis of the Content Analysis Literature in Organization Studies: Research Themes, Data Sources, and Methodological Refinements." *Organizational Research Methods*, vol. 10, no. 1: 5–34.
Earl, Jennifer, Andrew Martin, John D. McCarthy, and Sarah Soule. 2004. "The Use of Newspaper Data in the Study of Collective Action." *Annual Review of Sociology*, vol. 30: 65–80.
Eaton, Kent. 2004. *Politics beyond the Capital: The Design of Subnational Institutions in Latin America*. Stanford, CA: Stanford University Press.
Eckstein, Harry. 1975. "Case Study and Theory in Political Science," in Fred Greenstein and Nelson Polsby (eds.), *Handbook of Political Science, Vol. 7: Strategies of Inquiry*. Reading, MA: Addison-Wesley: 79–138.
Edwards, Richard. 1977. *Contested Terrain: The Transformation of the Workplace in the Twentieth Century*. New York: Basic Books.
Eldersveld, Samuel J. and Mingming Shen. 2001. *Support for Political and Economic Change in the Chinese Countryside: An Empirical Study of Cadres and Villagers in Four Counties, 1990 and 1996*. Lanham, MD: Lexington Books.

Emerson, Robert, Rachel Fretz, and Linda Shaw. 1995. *Writing Ethnographic Fieldnotes*. Chicago: University of Chicago Press.
Esarey, A. 2009. *Who Controls the Message? Propaganda, Pluralism, and Press Freedom in China*. Paper presented at the Media in Contemporary Chinese Politics workshop, Harvard University, April.
Fairbank, John King. 1982. *China Bound: A Fifty-Year Memoir*. New York: Harper and Row.
Farrer, James. 2002. *Opening Up: Youth Sex Culture and Market Reform in Shanghai*. Chicago: University of Chicago Press.
Fenno, Richard F., Jr. 1990. *Watching Politicians: Essays on Participant Observation*. Berkeley: Institute of Governmental Studies, University of California.
  1978. *Home Style: House Members in their Districts*. Boston and Toronto: Little, Brown.
Fewsmith, Joseph. 1994. *Dilemmas of Reform in China: Political Conflict and Economic Debate*. Armonk, NY: M. E. Sharpe.
Fitzgerald, John. 1996. *Awakening China: Politics, Culture, and Class in the Nationalist Revolution*. Stanford, CA: Stanford University Press.
  (ed.). 2002. *Rethinking China's Provinces*. New York: Routledge.
Fletcher, George. 1993. *Loyalty: An Essay on the Morality of Relationships*. New York: Oxford University Press.
Fong, Vanessa. 2004. *Only Hope: Coming of Age under China's One Child Policy*. Stanford, CA: Stanford University Press.
Forster, Keith. 1990. *Rebellion and Factionalism in a Chinese Province*. Armonk, NY: M. E. Sharpe.
Foster, Kenneth C. 2002. "Embedded within State Agencies: Business Associations in Yantai." *China Journal*, no. 47: 41–65.
Fowler, Floyd. 1993. *Survey Research Methods*. Thousand Oaks, CA: Sage.
Fravel, M. Taylor. 2007. "Securing Borders: China's Doctrine and Force Structure for Frontier Defense." *Journal of Strategic Studies*, vol. 30, no. 4/5: 705–737.
  2000. "Online and On China: Research Sources in an Information Age." *China Quarterly*, no. 163: 821–842.
Frazier, Mark. 2003. *The Making of the Chinese Industrial Workplace: State, Revolution, and Labor Management*. Cambridge: Cambridge University Press.
Friedman, Edward. 1975. "Some Political Constraints on a Political Science: Quantitative Content Analysis and the Indo-Chinese Border Crisis of 1962." *China Quarterly*, no. 63: 528–538.
Friedman, Edward, Paul G. Pickowicz, and Mark Selden. 2005. *Revolution, Resistance, and Reform in Village China*. New Haven, CT: Yale University Press.
Friedman, Sara. 2006. *Intimate Politics: Marriage, the Market, and State Power in Southeastern China*. Cambridge, MA: Asia Center, Harvard University.
Gallagher, Mary. 2005. "'Use the Law as Your Weapon!' Institutional Change and Legal Mobilization in China," in Neil Diamant, Stanley Lubman, and Kevin O'Brien (eds.), *Engaging the Law in China*. Stanford, CA: Stanford University Press: 54–83.
Galvan, Dennis. 2004. *The State Must Be Our Master of Fire: How Peasants Craft Culturally Sustainable Development in Senegal*. Berkeley: University of California Press.
Geertz, Clifford. 1983. *Local Knowledge: Further Essays in Interpretative Anthropology*. New York: Basic Books.

1973. *The Interpretation of Cultures: Selected Essays*. New York: Basic Books.
George, Alexander L. 1979. "Case Studies and Theory Development: The Method of Structured, Focused Comparison," in Paul Gorden Lauren (ed.), *Diplomacy: New Approaches in History, Theory, and Policy*. New York: Free Press: 43–68.
George, Alexander L. and Andrew Bennett. 2004. *Case Studies and Theory Development in the Social Sciences*. Cambridge, MA: MIT Press.
Gerring, John. 2004. "What Is a Case Study and What Is it Good For?" *American Political Science Review*, vol. 98, no. 2: 341–354.
  2001. *Social Science Methodology: A Critical Framework*. Cambridge: Cambridge University Press.
Gladney, Dru C. 1996. *Muslim Chinese: Ethnic Nationalism in the People's Republic*. Cambridge, MA: Council on East Asian Studies, Harvard University.
Goffman, Erving. 1959. *The Presentation of Self in Everyday Life*. Garden City, NY: Doubleday.
Gold, Thomas. 1998. "Bases for Civil Society in Reform China," in Kjeld Erik Brødsgaard and David Strand (eds.), *Reconstructing Twentieth-Century China: State Control, Civil Society, and National Identity*. Oxford: Oxford University Press: 163–188.
  1989. "Guerrilla Interviewing among the *Getihu*," in Perry Link, Richard Madsen, Paul Pickowicz (eds.), *Unofficial China: Popular Culture and Thought in the People's Republic*. Boulder, CO: Westview: 175–192.
Gold, Thomas, Doug Guthrie, and David L. Wank. 2002. *Social Connections in China: Institutions, Culture, and the Changing Nature of Guanxi*. Cambridge: Cambridge University Press.
Goldstein, Alice, Sidney Goldstein, and Shenyang Guo. 1991. "Temporary Migrants in Shanghai Households, 1984." *Demography*, vol. 28, no. 2: 275–291.
Goldstein, Sidney. 1987. "Forms of Mobility and Their Policy Implications: Thailand and China Compared." *Social Forces*, vol. 65, no. 4: 915–942.
Goodkind, Daniel and Loraine A. West. 2002. "China's Floating Population: Definitions, Data and Recent Findings." *Urban Studies*, vol. 39, no. 12: 2237–2251.
Goodman, Byrna. 2004. "Networks of News: Power, Language and the Transnational Dimensions of the Chinese Press, 1850–1949." *China Review*, vol. 4, no. 1: 1–10.
Granovetter, Mark. 1985. "Economic Action and Social Structure: The Problem of Embeddedness." *American Journal of Sociology*, vol. 91, no. 3: 481–510.
  1973. "The Strength of Weak Ties." *American Journal of Sociology*, vol. 78, no. 6: 1360–1380.
Gray, Clive. 1994. *Government beyond the Centre: Subnational Politics in Britain*. London: MacMillan.
Gries, Peter Hays. 2005a. "Chinese Nationalism: Challenging the State." *Current History*, vol. 104, no. 683: 251–256.
  2005b. "Nationalism, Indignation and China's Japan Policy." *SAIS Review*, vol. 25, no. 2: 105–114.
  2004. *China's New Nationalism: Pride, Politics, and Diplomacy*. Berkeley: University of California Press
Gries, Peter Hays, Kaiping Peng, and H. Michael Crowson. Under review. "Determinants of Security and Insecurity in International Relations: Symbolic and Material Gains and Losses: A Cross-national Experimental Analysis," in Vaughn Shannon (ed.), *Ideational Allies: Constructivism, Political Psychology, and IR Theory*. Ann Arbor: University of Michigan Press.

Gries, Peter Hays, Quigmin Zhang, H. M. Michael Cronson, and Huajian Cai. Under review. "Patriotism, Nationalism, and Perceptions of U.S. Threat: Structures and Consequences of Chinese National Identity."

Grodzins, Morton. 1956. *The Loyal and the Disloyal: Social Boundaries of Patriotism and Treason*. Chicago: University of Chicago Press.

Groves, Robert M. 2004. *Survey Errors and Survey Costs*. Malden, MA: Wiley-Interscience.

  1987. "Research on Survey Data Quality." *Public Opinion Quarterly*, vol. 51, part 2 (Supplement): S156-S172.

Gu, Edward X. 1996. "The *Economics Weekly*, the Public Space and the Voices of Chinese Independent Intellectuals." *China Quarterly*, no. 147: 860–888.

Guo, Gang. 2007. "Organizational Involvement and Political Participation in China." *Comparative Political Studies*, vol. 40, no. 4: 457–482.

Guo Liang. 2002. "'Qiangguo luntan': 9.11 kongbu xiji hou de 24 xiaoshi" ["Strong Country Talk": The First Twenty-four Hours after the Terrorist Attacks]. *Xinwen yu chuanbo yanjiu* [Research in Journalism and Communications], no. 4: 2–13.

Guthrie, Douglas. 1999. *Dragon in a Three-piece Suit: The Emergence of Capitalism in China*. Princeton, NJ: Princeton University Press.

Harding, Harry. 1994. "The Contemporary Study of Chinese Politics: An Introduction." *China Quarterly*, no. 139: 699–703.

  1982. "From China, with Disdain: New Trends in the Study of China." *Asian Survey*, vol. 22, no. 10: 934–958.

  1981. *Organizing China: The Problem of Bureaucracy, 1949–1976*. Stanford, CA: Stanford University Press.

Hartford, Kathleen. 2000. "Cyberspace with Chinese Characteristics." *Current History*, vol. 99, no. 638: 255–262.

Hassid, Jonathan. 2007. *Poor and Content Is Rich: A Computer-Assisted Content Analysis of Twenty-Six Chinese Newspapers, 2004–2006*, presented at the 9th annual conference of the Hong Kong Sociological Association, Hong Kong.

He, Baogang. 1997. *The Democratic Implications of Civil Society in China*. New York: St. Martin's Press.

He, Zhou and Jian-hua Zhu. 2002. "The Ecology of Online Newspapers: The Case of China." *Media, Culture and Society*, vol. 24, no. 1: 121–137.

Heckman, James J., Hidehiko Ichimura, Jeffrey Smith, and Petra Todd. 1998. "Characterizing Selection Bias Using Experimental Data." *Econometrica*, vol. 66, no. 5: 1017–1098.

Heimer, Maria. 2006. "Field Sites, Research Design and Type of Findings," in Maria Heimer and Stig Thøgersen (eds.), *Doing Fieldwork in China*. Honolulu: University of Hawaii Press: 58–77.

Heimer, Maria and Stig Thøgersen (eds.). 2006. *Doing Fieldwork in China*. Honolulu: University of Hawaii Press.

Heller, Patrick. 1999. *The Labor of Development: Workers and the Transformation of Capitalism in Kerala, India*. Ithaca, NY: Cornell University Press.

Hendrischke, Hans and Chongyi Feng (eds.). 1999. *The Political Economy of China's Provinces: Comparative and Competitive Advantage*. London: Routledge.

Herrigal, Gary. 1996. *Industrial Constructions: The Sources of German Industrial Power*. Cambridge: Cambridge University Press.

Hertz, Ellen. 1998. *The Trading Crowd: An Ethnography of the Shanghai Stock Market*. Cambridge: Cambridge University Press.

Hetherington, Marc J. 1998. "The Political Relevance of Political Trust." *American Political Science Review*, vol. 92, no. 4: 791–808.

Hjellum, Torstein. 1998. "Is a Participant Culture Emerging in China?" in Kjeld Erik Brødsgaard and David Strand (eds.), *Reconstructing Twentieth-Century China: State Control, Civil Society, and National Identity*. Oxford: Clarendon Press: 216–250.

Ho, David Yau-fai. 1976. "On the Concept of Face." *American Journal of Sociology*, vol. 81, no. 4: 867–884.

Hoddie, Matthew. 2008. "Ethnic Difference and Survey Cooperation in the People's Republic of China." *Asian Survey*, vol. 48, no. 2: 303–322.

Hong, Zhaohui. 2004. "Mapping the Evolution and Transformation of the New Private Entrepreneurs in China." *Journal of Chinese Political Science*, vol. 9, no. 1: 23–42.

Honig, Emily. 2003. "Socialist Sex: The Cultural Revolution Revisited." *Modern China*, vol. 29, no. 2: 143–175.

Houtkoop-Steenstra, Hanneke. 2000. *Interaction and the Standardized Survey Interview: The Living Questionnaire*. Cambridge: Cambridge University Press.

Howell, Nancy. 1990. *Surviving Fieldwork: A Report of the Advisory Panel on Health and Safety in Fieldwork*. Arlington, VA: American Anthropological Association.

Hu, Hsien-chin. 1944. "The Chinese Concepts of 'Face.'" *American Anthropologist*, vol. 46, no. 1, pt. 1: 45–64.

Huang, Yasheng. 2008. *Capitalism with Chinese Characteristics: Entrepreneurship and the State*. Cambridge: Cambridge University Press.

  1996. *Inflation and Investment Controls in China: The Political Economy of Central-Local Relations during the Reform Era*. Cambridge: Cambridge University Press.

  1995. "Administrative Monitoring in China." *China Quarterly*, no. 143: 828–843.

  1994. "Information, Bureaucracy, and Economic Reforms in China and the Soviet Union." *World Politics*, vol. 47, no. 1: 102–134.

Huntington, Samuel P. 1987. "The Goals of Development," in Myron Weiner and Samuel P. Huntington (eds.), *Understanding Political Development: An Analytic Study*. Boston: Little, Brown: 3–32.

Hurst, William. 2009. *The Chinese Worker after Socialism*. Cambridge: Cambridge University Press.

Iarossi, Giuseppe. 2006. *The Power of Survey Design: A User's Guide for Managing Surveys, Interpreting Results, and Influencing Respondents*. Washington, DC: World Bank.

Inglehart, Ronald. 1997. *Modernization and Postmodernization: Cultural, Economic, and Political Change in 43 Societies*. Princeton, NJ: Princeton University Press.

Jacka, Tamara. 2004. *On the Move: Women and Rural-to-Urban Migration in Contemporary China*. New York: Columbia University Press.

Jankowiak, William R. 1993. *Sex, Death and Hierarchy in a Chinese City: An Anthropological Account*. New York: Columbia University Press.

Jennings, M. Kent. 2003. "Local Problem Agendas in the Chinese Countryside as Viewed by Cadres and Villagers." *Acta Politica*, vol. 38, no. 4: 313–332.

  1998a. "Gender and Political Participation in the Chinese Countryside." *Journal of Politics*, vol. 60, no. 4: 954–973.

1998b. "Political Trust and the Roots of Devolution," in V. A. Braithwaite and M. Levi (eds.), *Trust and Governance*. New York: Russell Sage Foundation: 218–244.

1997. "Political Participation in the Chinese Countryside." *American Political Science Review*, vol. 91, no. 2: 351–372.

Jennings, M. Kent and Kuang-Hui Chen. 2008. "Perceptions of Injustice in the Chinese Countryside." *Journal of Contemporary China*, vol. 17, no. 55: 319–337.

Jennings, M. Kent and Ning Zhang. 2005. "Generations, Political Status, and Collective Memories in the Chinese Countryside." *Journal of Politics*, vol. 67, no. 4: 1164–1189.

Jervis, Robert. 1976. *Perception and Misperception in International Politics*. Princeton, NJ: Princeton University Press.

Jiang Zemin. 1999. *Jianding jinxin shenhua gaige, kaichuang guoyou qiye fazhan de xin jumian: Zai dongbei he huabei diqu guoyou qiye gaige he fazhan zuotan huishang de jianghua, 1999 nian 8 yue 12 ri* [Keep the Faith, Deepen Reform, Initiate a New Phase of SOE Development: Speech at the Conference on Reform and Development of SOEs in the Northeast and North China Regions, August 12, 1999]. Beijing: Renmin chubanshe.

Jin Chongji (ed.). 1989. *Zhou Enlai zhuan, 1898–1949* [A Biography of Zhou Enlai]. Beijing: Zhongyang wenxian chubanshe.

Jing, Jun. 1996. *The Temple of Memories: History, Power, and Morality in a Chinese Village*. Stanford, CA: Stanford University Press.

Johnston, Alastair Iain. 2006. "The Correlates of Beijing Public Opinion toward the United States, 1998–2004," in Alastair Iain Johnston and Robert S. Ross (eds.), *New Directions in the Study of China's Foreign Policy*. Stanford, CA: Stanford University Press: 340–377.

2004. "Chinese Middle Class Attitudes towards International Affairs: Nascent Liberalization?" *China Quarterly*, no. 179: 603–628.

1996. "Cultural Realism and Strategy in Maoist China," in Peter J. Katzenstein (ed.), *The Culture of National Security*. New York: Columbia University Press: 216–256.

Johnston, Alastair Iain and Daniela Stockmann. 2007. "Chinese Attitudes toward the United States and Americans," in Peter J. Katzenstein and Robert O. Keohane (eds.), *Anti-Americanism in World Politics*. Ithaca, NY: Cornell University Press: 157–195.

Jones, Benjamin and Benjamin Olken. 2005. "Do Leaders Matter? National Leadership and Growth since World War II." *Quarterly Journal of Economics*, vol. 120, no. 3: 835–864.

Judd, Ellen R. 1994. *Gender and Power in Rural North China*. Stanford, CA: Stanford University Press.

Kang, David C. 2002. *Crony Capitalism: Corruption and Development in South Korea and the Philippines*. Cambridge: Cambridge University Press.

Kateb, George. 2000. "Is Patriotism a Mistake?" *Social Research*, vol. 67, no. 4: 901–924.

Kennedy, John James. 2002. "The Face of 'Grassroots Democracy' in Rural China: Real Versus Cosmetic Elections." *Asian Survey*, vol. 42, no. 3: 456–482.

Kennedy, John James, Scott Rozelle, and Shi Yaojiang. 2004. "Elected Leaders and Collective Land: Farmers' Evaluation of Village Leaders' Performance in Rural China." *Journal of Chinese Political Science*, vol. 9, no. 1: 1–22.

Kennedy, Scott. 2005. *The Business of Lobbying in China*. Cambridge, MA: Harvard University Press.

Kertzer, David and Dominique Arel. 2006. "Population Composition as an Object of Political Struggle," in Robert E. Goodin and Charles Tilly (eds.), *The Oxford Handbook of Contextual Political Analysis*. Oxford: Oxford University Press: 664–680.

Kidder, Tracy. 2003. *Mountains beyond Mountains: The Quest of Dr. Paul Farmer, a Man Who Would Cure the World*. New York: Random House.

Kilwein, John C. and Richard A. Brisbin, Jr. 1997. "Policy Convergence in a Federal Judicial System: The Application of Intensified Scrutiny Doctrines by State Supreme Courts." *American Journal of Political Science*, vol. 41, no. 1: 122–148.

Kim, Samuel. 1979. *China, the United Nations and World Order*. Princeton, NJ: Princeton University Press.

King, Gary. 2004. "Enhancing the Validity and Cross-Cultural Comparability of Measurement in Survey Research." *American Political Science Review*, vol. 98, no. 1: 191–207.

King, Gary, Robert Keohane, and Sidney Verba. 1994. *Designing Social Inquiry: Scientific Inference in Qualitative Research*. Princeton, NJ: Princeton University Press.

King, Gary, Christopher J. L. Murray, Joshua A. Salomon, and Ajay Tandon. 2003. "Enhancing the Validity and Cross-cultural Comparability of Measurement in Survey Research." *American Political Science Review*, vol. 97, no. 4: 567–583.

King, Neil Jr. 2005. "A Scholar Shapes Views of China." *Wall Street Journal*, September 8: 1.

Kipnis, Andrew B. 1997. *Producing Guanxi: Sentiment, Self, and Subculture in a North China Village*. Durham, NC: Duke University Press.

Kish, Leslie. 1962. "Studies of Interviewer Variance for Attitudinal Variables." *Journal of the American Statistical Association*, vol. 57, no. 297: 92–115.

Kissinger Transcripts: The Top Secret Talks with Beijing and Moscow. 1998. Ed. William Burr. New York: New Press.

Kline, Rex B. 2005. *Principles and Practice of Structural Equation Modeling*. 2nd ed. New York: Guilford Press.

Kluver, Randy and Chen Yang. 2005. "The Internet in China: A Meta-review of Research." *Information Society*, vol. 21, no. 4: 301–308.

Kohli, Atul. 1987. *The State and Poverty in India: The Politics of Reform*. Cambridge: Cambridge University Press.

Kooghe, Liesbet. 1996. *Subnational Mobilization in the European Union*. Florence: European University Institute Working Paper RSC 95/6.

Kosterman, Rick and Seymour Feshbach. 1989. "Toward a Measure of Patriotic and Nationalistic Attitudes." *Political Psychology*, vol. 10, no. 2: 257–274.

Kou, Chien-wen. 2008. *Chinese Political Elites Database*. Taipei: National Chengchi University.

Krebs, Ronald. 2006. *Fighting for Rights: Military Service and the Politics of Citizenship*. Ithaca, NY: Cornell University Press.

Krug, Barbara. 2004. *China's Rational Entrepreneurs: The Development of the New Private Business Sector*. New York: RoutledgeCurzon.

Ku, Hok Bun. 2003. *Moral Politics in a South Chinese Village: Responsibility, Reciprocity, and Resistance*. Lanham, MD: Rowman and Littlefield.

Ku, Lun-Wei, Tung-Ho Wu, Li-Ying Lee, and Hsin-Hsi Chen. 2005. *Construction of an Evaluation Corpus for Opinion Extraction*. Paper presented at the NTCIR-5 workshop, December, Tokyo.

Kuan, Hsin-chi and Lau Siu-kai. 2002. "Traditional Orientations and Political Participation in Three Chinese Societies." *Journal of Contemporary China*, vol. 11, no. 31: 297–318.

Kuran, Timur. 1995. *Private Truths, Public Lies: The Social Consequences of Preference Falsification*. Cambridge, MA: Harvard University Press.

Lacy, Stephen, Daniel Riffe, Staci Stoddard, Hugh Martin, and Kuang-Kuo Chang. 2001. "Sample Size for Newspaper Content Analysis in Multi-Year Studies." *Journalism and Mass Communication Quarterly*, vol. 78, no. 4: 836–845.

Lamb, Malcolm. 2003. *Directory of Officials and Organizations in China*. Armonk, NY: M. E. Sharpe.

Landry, Pierre F. 2008a. *Decentralized Authoritarianism in China: The Communist Party's Control of Local Elites in the Post-Mao Era*. Cambridge: Cambridge University Press.

2008b. "The Institutional Diffusion of Courts in China: Evidence from Survey Data," in Tom Ginsburg and Tamir Moustafa (eds.), *Rule by Law: The Politics of Courts in Authoritarian Regimes*. Cambridge: Cambridge University Press: 207–234.

Landry, Pierre F. and Mingming Shen. 2005. "Reaching Migrants in Survey Research: The Use of the Global Positioning System to Reduce Coverage Bias in China." *Political Analysis*, vol. 13, no. 1: 1–22.

Langman, Lauren. 2005. "From Virtual Public Spheres to Global Justice: A Critical Theory of Internetworked Social Movements." *Sociological Theory*, vol. 23, no. 1: 42–74.

Laver, Michael and John Garry. 2000. "Estimating Policy Positions from Political Texts." *American Journal of Political Science*, vol. 44, no. 3: 619–634.

Lavrakas, Paul J. 1993. *Telephone Survey Methods: Sampling, Selection, and Supervision*. Thousand Oaks, CA: Sage.

Lee, Ching Kwan. 1998. *Gender and the South China Miracle: Two Worlds of Factory Women*. Berkeley: University of California Press.

Lee, Hong Yung. 1991. *From Revolutionary Cadres to Party Technocrats in Socialist China*. Berkeley: University of California Press.

Lee, Taeku. 2002. *Mobilizing Public Opinion: Black Insurgency and Racial Attitudes in the Civil Rights Era*. Chicago: University of Chicago Press.

Lee, Tahirih V. (ed.) 1997. *Contract, Guanxi, and Dispute Resolution in China*. New York: Garland.

Levi, Margaret. 2004. "An Analytic Narrative Approach to Puzzles and Problems," in Ian Shapiro, Rogers Smith, and Tarek Masoud (eds.), *Problems and Methods in the Study of Politics*. Cambridge: Cambridge University Press: 201–226.

1999. "The Problem of Trust." *American Journal of Sociology*, vol. 104, no. 4: 1245–1246.

Levi, Margaret and Laura Stoker. 2000. "Political Trust and Trustworthiness." *Annual Review of Political Science*, vol. 3: 475–507.

Li, Cheng. 2004. "Political Localism versus Institutional Restraints: Elite Recruitment in the Jiang Era," in Barry Naughton and Dali L. Yang (eds.), *Holding China Together: Diversity and National Integration in the Post-Deng Era*. Cambridge: Cambridge University Press: 29–69.

2001. *China's Leaders: The New Generation.* Lanham, MD: Rowman and Littlefield.

2000. "Jiang Zemin's Successors: The Rise of the Fourth Generation of Leaders in the PRC." *China Quarterly*, no. 161: 1–40.

1994. "University Networks and the Rise of Qinghua Graduates in China's Leadership." *Australian Journal of Chinese Affairs*, no. 32: 1–30.

Li, Cheng and Lynn White, III. 1991. "China's Technocratic Movement and the *World Economic Herald*." *Modern China*, vol. 17, no. 3: 342–388.

Li, Hongbin, Lingsheng Meng, and Junsen Zhang. 2006. "Why Do Entrepreneurs Enter Politics? Evidence from China." *Economic Inquiry*, vol. 44, no. 3: 559–578.

Li, Hongbin and Li-An Zhou. 2005. "Political Turnover and Economic Performance: The Incentive Role of Personnel Control in China." *Journal of Public Economics*, vol. 89, no. 9–10: 1743–1762.

Li, Lianjiang. 2008. "Political Trust and Petitioning in the Chinese Countryside." *Comparative Politics*, vol. 39, no. 4: 209–226.

2004. "Political Trust in Rural China." *Modern China*, vol. 30, no. 2: 228–258.

2003. "The Empowering Effect of Village Elections in China." *Asian Survey*, vol. 43, no. 4: 648–662.

2002. "Elections and Popular Resistance in Rural China." *China Information*, vol. 16, no. 1: 89–107.

2001. "Support for Anti-Corruption Campaigns in Rural China." *Journal of Contemporary China*, vol. 10, no. 29: 573–586.

Liang, Zai and Zhongdong Ma. 2004. "China's Floating Population: New Evidence from the 2000 Census." *Population and Development Review*, vol. 30, no. 3: 467–490.

Liao, Kuang-sheng and Allen S. Whiting. 1973. "Chinese Press Perceptions of Threat: The U.S. and India, 1962." *China Quarterly*, no. 53: 80–97.

Lieberthal, Kenneth. 1995. *Governing China*. New York: W.W. Norton.

1971. "Mao Versus Liu? Policy Towards Industry and Commerce, 1946–1949." *China Quarterly*, no. 47: 494–520.

Lieberthal, Kenneth and David M. Lampton (eds.). 1992. *Bureaucracy, Politics, and Decision Making in Post-Mao China*. Berkeley: University of California Press.

Lieberthal, Kenneth and Michel Oksenberg. 1988. *Policy Making in China: Leaders, Structures, and Processes*. Princeton, NJ: Princeton University Press.

Linz, Juan J. and Armando de Miguel. 1966. "Within-Nation Differences and Comparisons: The Eight Spains," in Richard L. Merritt and Stein Rokkan (eds.), *Comparing Nations: The Use of Quantitative Data in Cross-National Research*. New Haven, CT: Yale University Press: 267–320.

Litzinger, Ralph. 2000. *Other Chinas: The Yao and the Politics of National Belonging*. Durham, NC: Duke University Press.

Liu, Xin. 2000. *In One's Own Shadow: An Ethnographic Account of the Condition of Post-Reform Rural China*. Berkeley: University of California Press.

Luhtanen, Riia and Jennifer Crocker. 1992. "A Collective Self-Esteem Scale: Self-Evaluation of One's Social Identity." *Personality and Social Psychology Bulletin*, vol. 18, no. 3: 302–318.

Luo, Xiaopeng. 1994. "Rural Reform and the Rise of Localism," in Jia Hao and Lin Zhimin (eds.), *Changing Central-Local Relations in China: Reform and State Capacity*. Boulder, CO: Westview: 115–134.

MacFarquhar, Roderick. 1997. *The Origins of the Cultural Revolution: 3. The Coming of the Cataclysm, 1961–1966*. New York: Columbia University Press.
  1983. *The Origins of the Cultural Revolution: 2. The Great Leap Forward 1958–60*. New York: Columbia University Press.
  1974. *The Origins of the Cultural Revolution: 1. Contradictions among the People 1956–7*. New York: Columbia University Press.
MacFarquhar, Roderick and Michael Schoenhals. 2006. *Mao's Last Revolution*. Cambridge, MA: Belknap Press of Harvard University Press.
MacLean, Lauren Morris. 2004. "Empire of the Young: The Legacies of State Agricultural Policy on Local Capitalism and Social Support Networks in Ghana and Cote d'Ivoire." *Comparative Studies in Society and History*, vol. 46, no. 3: 469–496.
Mahoney, James and Dietrich Rueschmeyer (eds.). 2003. *Comparative Historical Analysis in the Social Sciences*. Cambridge: Cambridge University Press.
Mainland China Research Center. 2006. *Zhongguo jingying ziliao ku* [Database on Chinese Elites]. Taipei: National Chengchi University.
Malinowski, Bronislaw. 1922. *Argonauts of the Western Pacific: An Account of Native Enterprise and Adventure in the Archipelagoes of Melanesian New Guinea*. New York: E. P. Dutton.
Manion, Melanie. 2006. "Democracy, Community, Trust: The Impact of Chinese Village Elections in Context." *Comparative Political Studies*, vol. 39, no. 3: 301–324.
  1996. "The Electoral Connection in the Chinese Countryside." *American Political Science Review*, vol. 90, no. 4: 736–748.
  1994. "Survey Research in the Study of Contemporary China: Learning from Local Samples." *China Quarterly*, no. 139: 741–765.
  1993. *Retirement of Revolutionaries in China: Public Policies, Social Norms, Private Interests*. Princeton, NJ: Princeton University Press.
  1991. "Policy Implementation in the People's Republic of China: Authoritative Decisions versus Individual Interests." *Journal of Asian Studies*, vol. 50, no. 2: 253–279.
Marcus, George E. 1998. *Ethnography through Thick and Thin*. Princeton, NJ: Princeton University Press.
Marshall, Eliot. 1993. "U.S. May Renew Collaboration after China Relents on Data." *Science* (August 6): 677.
Martin, Lanny W. 2004. "The Government Agenda in Parliamentary Democracies." *American Journal of Political Science*, vol. 48, no. 3: 445–461.
Maryland Study. 2002. "Perspectives Towards the United States in Selected Newspapers of the People's Republic of China." *Report for the U.S. China Security Report Commission*.
McDermott, Rose. 2006. "Editor's Introduction." *Political Psychology*, vol. 27, no. 3: 347–358.
McGregor, Richard. 2006. "Data Show Social Unrest on the Rise in China." *Financial Times*, at http://www.ft.com/cms/s/0/171fb682-88d6-11da-94a6-0000779e2340.html, accessed January 2010.
McKinnon, Rebecca. 2008. "Flatter World and Thicker Walls: Blogs, Censorship and Civic Discourse in China." *Public Choice*, vol. 134, no. 1/2: 31–46.
Medeiros, Evan and M. Taylor Fravel. 2003. "China's New Diplomacy." *Foreign Affairs*, vol. 82, no. 6: 22–35.
Mengin, Françoise. 2004. *Cyber China: Reshaping National Identities in the Age of Information*. New York: Palgrave.

Michelmann, Hans J. and Pnayotis Soldatos (eds.). 1990. *Federalism and International Relations: The Role of Subnational Units*. Oxford: Clarendon Press.

Mooney, Paul. 2005. "Internet Fans Flames of Chinese Nationalism." *Yale Global*, at http://yaleglobal.yale.edu/display.article?id=5516, accessed February 2009.

Murphy, Rachel. 2002. *How Migrant Labor Is Changing Rural China*. Cambridge: Cambridge University Press.

Nathan, Andrew and Bruce Gilley. 2002. *China's New Rulers: The Secret Files*. New York: New York Review of Books.

Nathan, Andrew and Tianjian Shi. 1996. "Left and Right with Chinese Characteristics: Issues and Alignments in Deng Xiaoping's China." *World Politics*, vol. 48, no. 4: 522–550.

  1993. "Cultural Requisites for Democracy in China: Some Findings from a Nationwide Survey." *Daedalus*, vol. 122, no. 2: 95–123.

National Bureau of Statistics of the PRC. 2009. "2008 nianmo quanguo nongmingong zongliang wei 22542 wan ren," at http://www.stats.gov.cn/tjfx/fxbg/t20090325_402547406.htm, accessed August 2009. See a translation and discussion of this document in Boxun News, "Chinese Migrant Workers Totaled 225.42 Million at the End of 2008," at http://www.boxun.us/news/publish/chinanews/Chinese_Peasant_Workers_Totaled_225_42_Million_at_the_End_of_2008.shtml, accessed August 2009.

  2004a. "She wai diaocha guanli banfa" [Measures for the Administration of Foreign-Affiliated Surveys]. October 13, 2004, at http://www.stats.gov.cn/tjgl/swdcglgg/xgfg/t20041118_402209105.htm, accessed June 2008.

  2004b. "Tongjiju jiu gongbu 'she wai diaocha guanli banfa' dajizhe wen" [National Bureau of Statistics Official Responds to Journalists' Questions about Measures for the Administration of Foreign-Affiliated Surveys]. October 19, at http://www.chinacourt.org/public/detail.php?id=135541, accessed August 2009.

  2004c. "Guanyu 'she wai diaocha guanli banfa' de ershiliu tiao" [On Article 26 of the Measures for the Administration of Foreign-Affiliated Surveys]. November 18, 2004, at http://www.stats.gov.cn/tjgl/swdcglgg/spwb/t20041118_402209303.htm, accessed June 2008.

Naughton, Barry. 1996. *Growing Out of the Plan: Chinese Economic Reform 1978–1993*. Cambridge: Cambridge University Press.

Neuendorf, Kimberly A. 2002. *The Content Analysis Guidebook*. Thousand Oaks, CA: Sage.

"Never Forget the National Humiliation" [*Wuwang guochi*]. 1992. *History Book Series*. Beijing: Zhongguo huaqiao chubanshe.

Nevitt, Christopher. 1996. "Private Business Associations in China: Evidence of Civil Society or Local State Power?" *China Journal*, no. 36: 25–45.

Nicholson-Crotty, Sean and Kenneth J. Meier. 2002. "Size Doesn't Matter: In Defense of Single-State Studies." *State Politics & Policy Quarterly*, vol. 2, no. 4: 411–422.

Nisbett, Richard. 2003. *The Geography of Thought: How Asians and Westerners Think Differently, and Why*. New York: Free Press.

Nohria, Nitin and Ranjay Gulati. 1994. "Firms and their Environments," in Neil Smelser and Richard Swedberg (eds.), *The Handbook of Economic Sociology*. Princeton, NJ: Princeton University Press: 529–555.

Nolan, Peter. 2001. *China and the Global Economy: National Champions, Industrial Policy, and the Big Business Revolution*. New York: Palgrave.

Notar, Beth E. 2006. *Displacing Desire: Travel and Popular Culture in China.* Honolulu: University of Hawaii Press.

Nyiri, Pal and Joanna Briedenbach. 2005. *China Inside Out: Contemporary Chinese Nationalism and Transnationalism.* New York: Central European University Press.

O'Brien, Kevin. 2006. "Discovery, Research (Re)design and Theory-Building," in Maria Heimer and Stig Thøgersen (eds.), *Doing Fieldwork in China.* Honolulu: University of Hawaii Press: 27–41.

2003. "Neither Transgressive nor Contained: Boundary-Spanning Contention in China." *Mobilization,* vol. 8, no. 1: 51–64.

1996. "Rightful Resistance." *World Politics,* vol. 49, no. 1: 31–55.

O'Brien, Kevin J. and Lianjiang Li. 2006. *Rightful Resistance in Rural China.* Cambridge: Cambridge University Press.

Oi, Jean C. 1998a. "The Evolution of Local State Corporatism," in Andrew Walder (ed.), *Zouping in Transition The Process of Reform in Rural North China.* Cambridge, MA: Harvard University Press: 35–61.

1998b. *Rural China Takes Off: Institutional Foundations of Economic Reform.* Berkeley: University of California Press.

1986. "Commercializing China's Rural Cadres." *Problems of Communism,* vol. 35, no. 5: 1–15.

Oi, Jean C. and Scott Rozelle. 2000. "Elections and Power: The Locus of Decision-Making in Chinese Villages." *China Quarterly,* no. 162: 513–539.

Oksenberg, Michel. 1970. *A Bibliography of Secondary English Language Literature on Contemporary Chinese Politics.* New York: East Asian Institute, Columbia University.

1964. "Sources and Methodological Problems in the Study of Contemporary China," in A. Doak Barnett (ed.), *Chinese Communist Politics in Action.* Seattle: University of Washington Press: 577–606.

Oksenberg, Michel and Harold Jacobson. 1990. *China's Participation in the IMF, the World Bank, and the GATT: Toward a Global Economic Order.* Ann Arbor: University of Michigan Press.

O'Leary, Cecilia. 1999. *To Die For: The Paradox of American Patriotism.* Princeton, NJ: Princeton University Press.

Olzak, Susan. 1989. "Analysis of Events in the Study of Collective Action." *Annual Review of Sociology,* vol. 15: 119–141.

Orleans, Leo A. 1974. "Chinese Statistics: The Impossible Dream." *The American Statistician,* vol. 128, no. 2: 47–52.

Paluck, Elizabeth Levy. 2007. *Reducing Intergroup Prejudice and Conflict with the Mass Media: A Field Experiment in Rwanda.* Ph.D. dissertation, Yale University.

Park, Albert. 2006. "Using Survey Data in Social Science Research in Developing Countries," in Ellen Perecman and Sara R. Curran (eds.), *A Handbook for Social Science Field Research: Essays and Bibliographic Sources on Research Design and Methods.* Thousand Oaks, CA: Sage: 117–134.

Parris, Kristin. 1993. "Local Initiative and National Reform: The Wenzhou Model of Development." *China Quarterly,* no. 134: 242–263.

Pearson, Margaret. 1994. "The Janus Face of Business Associations in China: Socialist Corporatism in Foreign Enterprises." *Australian Journal of Chinese Affairs,* no. 31: 25–46.

Pei, Minxin. 2006. *China's Trapped Transition: The Limits of Developmental Autocracy*. Cambridge, MA: Harvard University Press.
    1998. "Is China Democratizing?" *Foreign Affairs*, vol. 77, no. 1: 68–82.
People's Daily. 2006. "Private Business People Gain More Influence in China." October 30, at http://english.peopledaily.com.cn/200610/30/eng20061030_316473.html, accessed August 2009.
Perecman, Ellen and Sara R. Curran (eds.). 2006. *A Handbook for Social Science Research: Essays and Bibliographic Sources on Research Design and Methods*. Thousand Oaks, CA: Sage.
Perkins, Tamara. 2002. *Village, Market and Well-Being in a Rural Chinese Township*. New York: Routledge.
Perreault, William D., Jr. and Laurence E. Leigh. 1989. "Reliability of Nominal Data Based on Qualitative Judgments." *Journal of Marketing Research*, vol. 26, no. 2: 135–148.
Perry, Elizabeth J. 2007. "Studying Chinese Politics: Farewell to Revolution?" *China Journal*, no. 57: 1–22.
    2006. *Patrolling the Revolution: Worker Militias, Citizenship and the Modern Chinese State*. Lanham, MD: Rowman and Littlefield.
    1994a. "Shanghai's Strike Wave of 1957." *China Quarterly*, no. 137: 1–27.
    1994b. "Trends in the Study of Chinese Politics: State-Society Relations." *China Quarterly*, no. 139: 704–713.
Perry, Elizabeth and Xun Li. 1997. *Proletarian Power: Shanghai in the Cultural Revolution*. Boulder, CO: Westview.
    1993. "Revolutionary Rudeness: The Language of Red Guards and Rebel Workers in China's Cultural Revolution." *Indiana East Asian Working Paper Series on Language and Politics in Modern China*, no. 2.
Pierson, Paul. 2004. *Politics in Time: History, Institutions, and Social Analysis*. Princeton, NJ: Princeton University Press.
Polsky, Ned. 2006. *Hustlers, Beats, and Others*. Piscataway, NJ: Transaction.
Popper, Karl R. 2001. *All Life Is Problem Solving*. New York: Routledge.
Porter, Bruce. 1994. *War and the Rise of the State: The Military Foundations of Modern Politics*. New York: Free Press.
Posner, Daniel N. 2004. "The Political Salience of Cultural Difference: Why Chewas and Tumbukas Are Allies in Zambia and Adversaries in Malawi." *American Political Science Review*, vol. 98, no. 4: 529–545.
Przeworski, Adam and Henry Teune. 1970. *The Logic of Comparative Social Inquiry*. New York: Wiley-Interscience,
Pun, Ngai. 2005. *Made in China: Women Factory Workers in a Global Marketplace*. Durham, NC: Duke University Press.
Putnam, Robert D. 1993. *Making Democracy Work: Civic Traditions in Modern Italy*. Princeton, NJ: Princeton University Press.
Pye, Lucian W. 1968. *The Spirit of Chinese Politics: A Psychocultural Study of the Authority Crisis in Political Development*. Cambridge, MA: M.I.T. Press.
Ragin, Charles. 1987. *The Comparative Method: Moving beyond Qualitative and Quantitative Strategies*. Berkeley: University of California Press.
Ramseyer, J. Mark and Frances McCall Rosenbluth. 1998. *The Politics of Oligarchy: Institutional Choice in Imperial Japan*. Cambridge: Cambridge University Press.

Remick, Elizabeth. 2004. *Building Local States: China during the Republican and Post-Mao Eras*. Cambridge, MA: Asia Center, Harvard University.

Renmin chubanshe. 1997. *Zhongguo gongchandang dishiwuci quanguo daibiao dahui wenjian huibian* [Collection of Documents from the Fifteenth Party Congress of the CCP]. Beijing.

Riffe, Daniel, Stephen Lacy, and Michael W. Drager. 1996. "Sample Size in Content Analysis of Weekly News Magazines." *Journalism and Mass Communication Quarterly*, vol. 73, no. 3: 635–644.

Riffe, Daniel, Stephen Lacy, and Frederick G. Fico. 1998. *Analyzing Media Messages: Using Quantitative Content Analysis in Research*. Mahwah, NJ: Lawrence Erlbaum.

Roberts, Carl W. 2000. "A Conceptual Framework for Quantitative Text Analysis." *Quality & Quantity*, vol. 34, no. 3: 259–274.

  1989. "Other than Counting Words: A Linguistic Approach to Content Analysis." *Social Forces*, vol. 68, no. 1: 147–177.

Robertson, Graeme B. 2007. "Strikes and Labor Organization in Hybrid Regimes." *American Political Science Review*, vol. 101, no. 4: 799–809.

Rofel, Lisa. 1999. *Other Modernities: Gendered Yearnings in China after Socialism*. Berkeley: University of California Press.

Roitman, Janet. 2004. *Fiscal Disobedience: An Anthropology of Economic Regulation in Central Africa*. Princeton, NJ: Princeton University Press.

Rong, Hu. 2005. "Economic Development and the Implementation of Village Elections in Rural China." *Journal of Contemporary China*, vol. 14, no. 44: 427–444.

Rosenau, Pauline. 1992. *Post-modernism and the Social Sciences: Insights, Inroads and Intrusions*. Princeton, NJ: Princeton University Press.

Ross, Robert S. 2001. "Introduction," in Robert S. Ross and Jiang Changbin (eds.), *Re-Examining the Cold War: U.S.-China Diplomacy, 1954–1973*. Cambridge, MA: Asia Center, Harvard University.

Rueschemeyer, Dietrich, Evelyne Huber Stephens, and John D. Stephens. 1992. *Capitalist Development and Democracy*. Chicago: University of Chicago Press.

Saich, Tony. 1992. "The Fourteenth Party Congress: A Programme for Authoritarian Rule." *China Quarterly*, no. 132: 1136–1160.

Saunders, Robert A. and Sheng Ding. 2006. "Digital Dragons and Cybernetic Bears." *Nationalism and Ethnic Politics*, vol. 12, no. 2: 255–290.

Schatz, Edward. 2006. *The Problem with the Toolbox Metaphor: Ethnography and the Limits to Multiple-Methods Research*. Paper prepared for the 2006 annual meeting of the American Political Science Association, Philadelphia, PA.

  2004. *Modern Clan Politics: The Power of "Blood" in Kazakhstan and Beyond*. Seattle: University of Washington Press.

Schein, Louisa. 2000. *Minority Rules: The Miao and the Feminine in China's Cultural Politics*. Durham, NC: Duke University Press.

Schober, Michael F. and Frederick G. Conrad. 1997. "Does Conversational Interviewing Reduce Survey Measurement Error?" *Public Opinion Quarterly*, vol. 61, no. 4: 576–602.

Schram, Stuart R. 1989. *The Thought of Mao Tse-Tung*. Cambridge: Cambridge University Press.

Schrank, Andrew. 2006. "Case-Based Research," in Ellen Perecman and Sara R. Curran (eds.), *A Handbook for Social Science Research: Essays and Bibliographic Sources on Research Design and Methods*. Thousand Oaks, CA: Sage: 21–45.

References

Schumacker, Randall E. and Richard G. Lomax. 2004. *A Beginner's Guide to Structural Equation Modeling.* 2nd ed. Mahwah, NJ: Lawrence Erlbaum.
Schwartz, Benjamin. 1966. *Chinese Communism and the Rise of Mao.* Cambridge, MA: Harvard University Press.
Scott, James C. 1998. *Seeing like a State: How Certain Schemes to Improve the Human Condition Have Failed.* New Haven, CT: Yale University Press.
  1990. *Domination and the Arts of Resistance: Hidden Transcripts.* New Haven, CT: Yale University Press.
  1985. *Weapons of the Weak: Everyday Forms of Peasant Resistance.* New Haven, CT: Yale University Press.
Shambaugh, David (ed.). 1993. *American Studies of Contemporary China.* Armonk, NY: M. E. Sharpe.
Shapiro, Gilbert and John Markoff. 1998. *Revolutionary Demands: A Content Analysis of the Cashier de doléances of 1789.* Stanford, CA: Stanford University Press.
Shatz, Robert T., Ervin Staub, and Howard Levine. 1999. "On the Varieties of National Attachment: Blind Versus Constructive Patriotism." *Political Psychology*, vol. 20, no. 1: 151–174.
Shi, Tianjian. 2001. "Cultural Values and Political Trust: A Comparison of the People's Republic of China and Taiwan." *Comparative Politics*, vol. 33, no. 4: 401–419.
  2000. "Cultural Values and Democracy in the People's Republic of China." *China Quarterly*, no. 162 (June): 540–559.
  1999a. "Economic Development and Village Elections in Rural China." *Journal of Contemporary China*, vol. 8, no. 22: 425–442.
  1999b. "Mass Political Behavior in Beijing," in Merle Goldman and Roderick MacFarquhar (eds.), *The Paradox of China's Post-Mao Reforms.* Cambridge, MA: Harvard University Press: 145–169.
  1999c. "Voting and Nonvoting in China: Voting Behavior in Plebiscitary and Limited-Choice Elections." *Journal of Politics*, vol. 61, no. 4: 1115–1139.
  1997. *Political Participation in Beijing.* Cambridge, MA: Harvard University Press.
  1996. "Survey Research in China," in Michael X. Delli Carpini, Leonie Huddy, and Robert Y. Shapiro (eds.), *Research in Micropolitics: Rethinking Rationality.* vol. 5. Greenwich, CT: JAI Press: 216–220.
Shie, Tamara Renee. 2004. "The Tangled Web." *Journal of Contemporary China*, vol. 13, no. 40: 523–540.
Shih, Victor. 2004. "Factions Matter: Personal Networks and the Distribution of Bank Loans in China." *Journal of Contemporary China*, vol. 13, no. 38: 3–19.
Shirk, Susan. 1993. *The Political Logic of Economic Reform in China.* Berkeley: University of California Press.
  1982. *Competitive Comrades: Career Incentives and Student Strategies in China.* Berkeley: University of California Press.
Shue, Vivienne. 1988. *The Reach of the State: Sketches of the Chinese Body Politic.* Stanford, CA: Stanford University Press.
Sil, Rudra. 2004. "Problems Chasing Methods or Methods Chasing Problems? Research Communities, Constrained Pluralism, and the Role of Eclecticism," in Ian Shapiro, Rogers Smith, and Tarek Masoud (eds.), *Problems and Methods in the Study of Politics.* Cambridge: Cambridge University Press: 307–331.

2000a. "Against Epistemological Absolutism: Toward a 'Pragmatic' Center?" in Rudra Sil and Eileen M. Doherty (eds.), *Beyond Boundaries? Disciplines, Paradigms, and Theoretical Integration in International Studies*. Albany: SUNY Press: 145–175.

2000b. "The Foundations of Eclecticism: The Epistemological Status of Agency, Culture, and Structure in Social Theory." *Journal of Theoretical Politics*, vol. 12, no. 3: 353–387.

Sinha, Aseema. 2003. "Rethinking the Developmental State Model: Divided Leviathan and Subnational Comparisons in India." *Comparative Politics*, vol. 35, no. 4: 459–476.

Sluka, Jeffrey. 1990. "Participant Observation in Violent Social Contexts." *Human Organization*, vol. 49, no. 2: 114–126.

SMA1. 1964. (Shanghai Civil Affairs Party Organization to Shanghai CCP) "Guanyu baohu junren hunyin qingkuang de jiancha" [An Investigation Concerning the Protection of Soldiers' Marriages]. 1964. Shanghai Municipal Archives B168–1–223.

SMA2. 1966. (Shanghai Civil Affairs Party Organization to Shanghai CCP) "Guanyu junren hunyin caoshou pohuai qingkuang baogao" [An Investigation Report Concerning the Situation of Soldiers' Marriages that Have Been Violated]. Shanghai Municipal Archives B168–1–132.

SMA3. 1966. (Shanghai Civil Affairs Party Organization to Shanghai CCP) "Guanyu guanche shixing zuigao fayuan guanyu junren hunyin caoshou pohuai qingkuang baogao zuotanhui jiyao" [Notes on a Meeting Regarding the Implementation of the Supreme People's Court's Investigation Concerning the Situation of Soldiers' Marriages that Have Been Violated]. Shanghai Municipal Archives B168–2–132.

Smith, Arthur H. 1890. *Chinese Characteristics*. Shanghai: North China Herald.

Snyder, Richard. 2001a. *Politics after Neoliberalism: Reregulation in Mexico*. Cambridge: Cambridge University Press.

2001b. "Scaling Down: The Subnational Comparative Method." *Studies in Comparative International Development*, vol. 36, no. 1: 93–110.

So, Ying Lun and Anthony Walker. 2006. *Explaining Guanxi: The Chinese Business Network*. New York: Routledge.

Solinger, Dorothy J. 1999. *Contesting Citizenship in Urban China: Peasant Migrants, the State and the Logic of the Market*. Berkeley: University of California Press.

1995. "China's Urban Transients in the Transition from Socialism and the Collapse of the Communist 'Urban Public Goods Regime.'" *Comparative Politics*, vol. 27, no. 2: 127–146.

1977. *Regional Government and Political Integration in Southwest China, 1949–1954*. Berkeley: University of California Press.

Spencer-Rodgers, Julie, Kaiping Peng, and Lei Wang. 2004. "Dialectical Self-Esteem and East-West Differences in Psychological Well-being." *Personality and Social Psychology Bulletin*, vol. 30, no. 11: 29–44.

Starr, John Bryan. 1976. "From the 10th Party Congress to the Premiership of Hua Kuo-feng: The Significance of the Colour of the Cat." *China Quarterly*, no. 67: 457–488.

Starr, Paul. 1992. "Social Categories and Claims in the Liberal State." *Social Research*, vol. 59, no. 2: 263–296.

1983. "The Sociology of Official Statistics," in William Alonso and Paul Starr (eds.), *The Politics of Numbers*. New York: Russell Sage Foundation: 7–58.

State Council. 2005. "Guanyu xiugai 'Zhonghua renmin gongheguo tongji fa' shishi xize" [Revised Detailed Regulations on Implementation of the Statistics Law of the People's Republic of China]. December 16, at http://china.findlaw.cn/fagui/jj/25/101390.html, accessed August 2009.

Steinfeld, Edward S. 1998. *Forging Reform in China: The Fate of State-owned Industry*. Cambridge: Cambridge University Press.

Stempel, Guido H. 1952. "Sample Size for Classifying Subject Matter in Dailies." *Journalism Quarterly*, vol. 29, no. 3: 333–334.

Stockmann, Daniela. Forthcoming-a. "Who Believes Propaganda? Media Effects during the Anti-Japanese Protests in Beijing." *China Quarterly*.

Forthcoming-b. "What Kind of Information Does the Public Demand? Getting the News during the 2005 Anti-Japanese Protests," in Susan Shirk (ed.), *Changing Media, Changing China*. Under Review. Oxford University Press.

2009. Political Voices in the Chinese Press: Does Media Commercialization Change the Position of the Authoritarian State? Paper presented at the Media in Contemporary Chinese Politics workshop, Harvard University, April.

2007. *Propaganda for Sale: The Impact of Newspaper Commercialization on News Content and Public Opinion in China*. Ph.D. Dissertation, University of Michigan.

Stockmann, Daniela and Mary E. Gallagher. 2007. *Mass Media Mobilization as a Means of Legal Reform in China*. Paper presented at the annual meeting of the American Political Science Association, Chicago.

Stone, Philip James. 1997. "Thematic Text Analysis: New Agendas for Analyzing Text Content," in Carl W. Roberts (ed.), *Text Analysis for the Social Sciences: Methods for Drawing Statistical Inferences from Texts and Transcripts*. Mahwah. NJ: Lawrence Erlbaum: 35–54.

Stone, Philip James, Dexter C. Dunphy, Marshall S. Smith, and Daniel M. Ogilvie. 1966. *The General Inquirer: A Computer Approach to Content Analysis*. Cambridge, MA: MIT Press.

Stoner-Weis, Kathryn. 1997. *Local Heroes: The Political Economy of Russian Regional Governance*. Princeton, NJ: Princeton University Press.

Strand, David. 1990. "Protest in Beijing: Civil Society and the Public Sphere in China." *Problems of Communism*, vol. 39, no. 3: 1–19.

Straus, Scott. 2006. *The Order of Genocide: Race, Power, and War in Rwanda*. Ithaca, NY: Cornell University Press.

Strauss, Julia. 2002. "Paternalist Terror: The Campaign to Suppress Counterrevolutionaries and Regime Consolidation in the People's Republic of China, 1950–1953." *Comparative Studies in Society and History*, vol. 44, no. 1: 80–105.

Streb, Matthew. 2008. "Social Desirability Effects and Support for a Female American President." *Public Opinion Quarterly*, vol. 72, no. 1: 76–89.

Su, Fubing and Dali L. Yang. 2000. "Political Institutions, Provincial Interests, and Resource Allocation in Reformist China." *Journal of Contemporary China*, vol. 9, no. 24: 215–230.

Suchman, Lucy and Brigitte Jordan. 1990. "Interactional Troubles in Face-to-Face Survey Interviews." *Journal of the American Statistical Association*, vol. 85, no. 409: 232–241.

Svolik, Milan. 2006. *A Theory of Leadership Dynamics in Authoritarian Regimes*. Paper presented at the Annual Midwest Political Science Association, Chicago, Il.

Swaine, Michael D. 1992. *The Military and Political Succession in China: Leadership, Institutions, Beliefs*. Santa Monica, CA: Rand.
Tai, Zixue. 2006. *The Internet in China: Cyberspace and Civil Society*. New York: Routledge.
Tamir, Yael. 1997. "Reflections on Patriotism," in Daniel Bar-tal and Ervin Staub (eds.), *Patriotism in the Lives of Individuals and Nations*. Chicago: Nelson Hall: 23–41.
Tan, Qingshan and Xin Qiushui. 2007. "Village Elections and Governance: Do Villagers Care?" *Journal of Contemporary China*, vol. 16, no. 53: 581–599.
Tang Diaodeng. 2003. *Zhongguo chengshi pinkun yu fanpinkun baogao* [Report on Poverty and Anti-Poverty in Urban China]. Beijing: Huaxia chubanshe.
Tang, Wenfang. 2005. *Public Opinion and Political Change in China*. Stanford, CA: Stanford University Press.
  2003. "Research Guide: An Introduction to Survey Research in China." *Issues and Studies*, vol. 39, no. 1: 269–288.
  2001a. "Political and Social Trends in the Post-Deng Urban China: Crisis or Stability?" *China Quarterly*, no. 168: 890–909.
  2001b. "Religion and Society in Taiwan and China: Evidence from Survey Data," in Shiping Hua (ed.), *Politics and Political Culture in Contemporary China*. Armonk, NY: M. E. Sharpe: 298–319.
  1993. "Workplace Participation in Chinese Local Industrial Enterprises." *American Journal of Political Science*, vol. 37, no. 3: 920–940.
Tang, Wenfang and William L. Parish. 2000. *Chinese Urban Life under Market Reform: The Changing Social Contract*. Cambridge: Cambridge University Press.
  1996. "Social Reaction to Urban Reform in China." *Problems of Post-Communism*, vol. 43, no. 6: 35–47.
Tang, Wenfang, William L. Parish, and Tongqing Feng. 1996. "Chinese Labor Relations in a Changing Work Environment." *Journal of Contemporary China*, vol. 5, no. 13: 367–389.
Tang, Wenfang and Qing Yang. 2008. "The Chinese Urban Caste System in Transition." *China Quarterly*, no. 196: 759–777.
Taubman, Geoffry. 1998. "A Not-So World Wide Web: The Internet, China, and the Challenges to Non-Democratic Rule." *Political Communication*, vol. 15, no. 2: 255–272.
Taylor, Charles. 1989. "Cross-Purposes: The Liberal Communitarian Debate," in Nancy L. Rosenblum (ed.), *Liberalism and the Moral Life*. Cambridge, MA: Harvard University Press: 159–182.
Teiwes, Frederick. 1993. *Politics and Purges in China: Rectification and the Decline of Party Norms, 1950–1965*. Armonk, NY: M. E. Sharpe.
  1979. *Politics and Purges in China*. White Plains, NY: M. E. Sharpe.
Tendler, Judith. 1997. *Good Governance in the Tropics*. Baltimore, MD: Johns Hopkins University Press.
Thelen, Kathleen. 2004. *How Institutions Evolve: The Political Economy of Skills in Germany, Britain, the United States, and Japan*. Cambridge: Cambridge University Press.
Thelwall, Mike and Alastair Smith. 2002. "Interlinking between Asia-Pacific Web Sites." *Scientometrics*, vol. 55, no. 3: 363–376.

Thøgersen, Stig and Soren Clausen. 1992. "New Reflections in the Mirror: Local Chinese Gazetteers (*difangzhi*) in the 1980s." *Australian Journal of Chinese Affairs*, no. 27 (January): 161–184.
Thomas, William I. and Florian Znaniecki. 1918–1920. *The Polish Peasant in Europe and America*. 2 vols. Chicago: University of Chicago Press.
Thornton, Patricia. 2007. *Disciplining the State: Virtue, Violence and State-making in Modern China*. Cambridge, MA: Asia Center, Harvard University.
Thurston, Anne F. 1983. "The Social Sciences and Fieldwork in China: An Overview," in Anne F. Thurston and Burton Pasternak (eds.), *The Social Sciences and Fieldwork in China: Views from the Field*. Boulder, CO: Westview: 3–36.
Tikhonov, Vladimir. 2007. "Masculinizing the Nation: Gender Ideologies in Traditional Korea and in the 1890s-1900s Korean Enlightenment Discourse." *Journal of Asian Studies*, vol. 66, no. 4: 1029–1065.
Tilly, Charles. 2002. "Event Catalogs as Theories." *Sociological Theory*, vol. 20, no. 2: 248–254.
　1978. *From Mobilization to Revolution*. Reading, MA: Addison-Wesley.
Tilly, Charles, Louise Tilly, and Richard Tilly. 1975. *The Rebellious Century, 1830–1930*. Cambridge, MA: Harvard University Press.
Tong, Yanqi. 2007. "Bureaucracy Meets the Environment: Elite Perceptions in Six Chinese Cities." *China Quarterly*, no. 189: 100–121.
Tsai, Kellee S. 2007. *Capitalism without Democracy: The Private Sector in Contemporary China*. Ithaca, NY: Cornell University Press.
　2005. "Capitalists without a Class: Political Diversity among Private Entrepreneurs in China." *Comparative Political Studies*, vol. 38, no. 9: 1130–1158.
　2002. *Back-Alley Banking: Private Entrepreneurs in China*. Ithaca, NY: Cornell University Press.
Tsai, Lily L. 2007a. *Accountability without Democracy: How Solidary Groups Provide Public Goods in Rural China*. Cambridge: Cambridge University Press.
　2007b. "Solidary Groups, Informal Accountability, and Local Public Goods Provision in Rural China." *American Political Science Review*, vol. 101, no. 2: 355–372.
　2002. "Cadres, Temple and Lineage Institutions, and Governance in Rural China." *China Journal*, no. 48: 1–28.
Tsui, Lokman. 2005. "Introduction: The Sociopolitical Internet." *China Information*, vol. 19, no. 2: 181–188.
Tullock, Gordon. 1987. *Autocracy*. Boston: Kluwer Academic.
U, Eddy. 2003. "The Making of *Zhishifenzi*: The Critical Impact of the Registration of Unemployed Intellectuals in the Early PRC." *China Quarterly*, no. 173: 100–121.
Ulbig, Stacey G. 2002. "Policies, Procedures, and People: Sources of Support for Government?" *Social Science Quarterly*, vol. 83, no. 3: 789–809.
Unger, Jonathan. 1996a. "'Bridges': Private Business, the Chinese Government and the Rise of New Associations." *China Quarterly*, no. 147: 795–819.
　(ed.). 1996b. *Chinese Nationalism*. Armonk, NY: M. E. Sharpe.
　1987. "The Struggle to Dictate China's Administration: The Conflict of Branches vs. Areas vs. Reform." *Australian Journal of Chinese Affairs*, no. 18: 15–45.
Uslaner, Eric. 2002. *The Moral Foundations of Trust*. Cambridge: Cambridge University Press.
van Evera, Stephen. 1997. *Guide to Methods for Students of Political Science*. Ithaca, NY: Cornell University Press.

Varshney, Ashutosh. 2002. *Ethnic Conflict and Civic Life: Hindus and Muslims in India*. New Haven, CT: Yale University Press.
Verba, Sidney, Norman H. Nie, and Jae-on Kim. 1971. *The Modes of Democratic Participation: A Cross-National Comparison*. Beverly Hills, CA: Sage.
Vermeer, Edward. 1992. "New County Histories: A Research Note on Their Compilation and Value." *Modern China*, vol. 18, no. 4: 438–467.
Viroli, Maurizio. 1995. *For Love of Country: An Essay on Patriotism and Nationalism*. Oxford: Clarendon.
Viterna, Jocelyn and D. W. Maynard. 2002. "How Uniform Is Standardization? Variation Within and Across Survey Research Centers Regarding Protocols for Interviewing," in Douglas W. Maynard, et al. (eds.), *Standardization and Tacit Knowledge: Interaction and Practice in the Survey Interview*. Malden, MA: Wiley-Interscience: 365–397.
Vogel, Ezra. 1969. *Canton under Communism*. Cambridge, MA: Harvard University Press.
Walder, Andrew, G. 1986. *Communist Neo-traditionalism: Work and Authority in Chinese Industry*. Berkeley: University of California Press.
  1979. "Press Accounts and the Study of Chinese Society." *China Quarterly*, no. 79: 568–592.
Walder, Andrew and Yang Su. 2003. "The Cultural Revolution in the Countryside: Scope, Timing and Human Impact." *China Quarterly*, no. 173: 74–99.
Walzer, Michael. 1970. *Obligations: Essays on Disobedience, War and Citizenship*. Cambridge, MA: Harvard University Press.
Wang, Hongying and Honggang Tan. 2008. *Chinese Media and the Judicial System under Soft Authoritarianism*. Paper presented at the annual meeting of the Association for Asian Studies, Atlanta.
Wang Jianying. 1995. *Zhongguo gongchandang zuzhishi ziliao huibian* [A Collection of Material Related to CCP Organizational History]. Beijing: Zhongyang dangxiao chubanshe.
Wang, Shaoguang. 1995. "The Rise of the Regions: Fiscal Reform and the Decline of State Capacity," in Andrew Walder (ed.), *The Waning of the Communist State: Economic Origins of Political Decline in China and Hungary*. Berkeley: University of California Press: 87–114.
Wang, Xiaopeng. 2006. *Exploring Sample Sizes for Content Analysis of Online News Sites*. Paper presented at the annual meeting of the Association for Education in Journalism and Mass Communication.
Wang, Yanlai, Nicholas Rees, and Bernadette Andreosso-O'Callaghan. 2004. "Economic Change and Political Development in China: Findings from a Public Opinion Survey." *Journal of Contemporary China*, vol. 13, no. 39: 203–222.
Wang, Zhengxu. 2007. "Public Support for Democracy in China." *Journal of Contemporary China*, vol. 16, no. 53: 561–579.
  2006. "Explaining Regime Strength in China." *China: An International Journal*, vol. 4, no. 2: 217–237.
Wank, David L. 1999. *Commodifying Communism: Business, Trust, and Politics in a Chinese City*. Cambridge: Cambridge University Press.
  1998. "Political Sociology and Contemporary China: State-Society Images in American China Studies." *Journal of Contemporary China*, vol. 7, no. 18: 205–228.

1995. "Private Business, Bureaucracy, and Political Alliance in a Chinese City." *Australian Journal of Chinese Affairs*, no. 33: 55–71.
Watson, James L. and Rubie S. Watson. 2004. *Village Life in Hong Kong: Politics, Gender, and Ritual in the New Territories*. Hong Kong: Chinese University Press.
Wedeen, Lisa. 2004. "Concepts and Commitments in the Study of Democracy," in Ian Shapiro, Rogers Smith, and Tarek Masoud (eds.), *Problems and Methods in the Study of Politics*. Cambridge: Cambridge University Press: 274–306.
  2002. "Conceptualizing Culture: Possibilities for Political Science." *American Political Science Review*, vol. 94, no. 4: 713–728.
Weisberg, Herbert F. 2005. *The Total Survey Error Approach: A Guide to the New Science of Survey Research*. Chicago: University of Chicago Press.
White, Gordon, Jude Howell, and Shang Xiaoyuan. 1996. *In Search of Civil Society: Market Reform and Social Change in Contemporary China*. Oxford: Oxford University Press.
Whiting, Susan H. 2001. *Power and Wealth in Rural China: The Political Economy of Institutional Change*. Cambridge: Cambridge University Press.
Wich, Richard. 1974. "The Tenth Party Congress: The Power Structure and the Succession Question." *China Quarterly*, no. 58: 231–248.
Wood, Elisabeth Jean. 2006. "The Ethical Challenges of Field Research in Conflict Zones." *Qualitative Sociology*, vol. 29, no. 3: 373–386.
Wood, Linda A. and Rolf O. Kroger. 2000. *Doing Discourse Analysis: Methods for Studying Action in Talk and Text*. Thousand Oaks, CA: Sage.
Wu, Xu. 2007. *Chinese Cyber Nationalism: Evolution, Characteristics and Implications*. Lanham, MD: Lexington Books.
Xu Xiqiang. 2005. "'Zuolian' 'wulieshi' anqing xintan" [New Exploration of the Situation Surrounding the "Five Martyrs" of the "Left Association"]. *Nanjing shifan daxue wenxueyuan xuebao* [Journal of the School of Humanities at Nanjing University], no. 12: 61–68.
Yan, Yunxiang. 2003. *Private Life under Socialism: Love, Intimacy, and Family Change in a Chinese Village, 1949–1999*. Stanford, CA: Stanford University Press.
  1996. *The Flow of Gifts: Reciprocity and Social Networks in a Chinese Village*. Stanford, CA: Stanford University Press.
Yang, Guobin. 2003. "The Co-Evolution of the Internet and Civil Society in China." *Asian Survey*, vol. 43, no. 3: 405–422.
Yang, Mayfair Mei-hui. 1994. *Gifts, Favors, and Banquets: The Art of Social Relationships in China*. Ithaca, NY: Cornell University Press.
Yang, Ming, et al. 2007. *1995–2004 Beijing shehui jingji fazhan niandu diaocha shuju baogao* [Report on Annual Statistical Survey of the Social and Economic Development of Beijing, 1995–2004]. Beijing: Beijing chubanshe.
Yang, Xiushi. 1993. "Household Registration, Economic Reform and Migration." *International Migration Review*, vol. 27, no. 4: 796–818.
Yanow, Dvora. 2003. "Interpretive Political Science: What Makes This Not a Subfield of Qualitative Methods." *Qualitative Methods* (Newsletter of the American Political Science Association Organized Section on Qualitative Methods), vol. 1, no. 2: 9–13.
Ye, Wa and Joseph W. Esherick. 1996. *Chinese Archives: An Introductory Guide*. Berkeley: Institute of East Asian Studies, University of California.

Yin Jizuo. 2001. *Tizhi gaige shehui zhuanxing: 2001 nian Shanghai shehui fazhan lanpi shu* [System Reform, Social Transition: 2001 Blue Book of Shanghai's Social Development]. Shanghai: Shanghai shehui kexueyuan chubanshe.

Zhang Houyi. 2004. "Jinru xin shiqi de Zhongguo siying qiyezhu jiceng" [Chinese Private Entrepreneurs Enter a New Era], in Ru Xin, et al. (eds.), *2004 nian: Zhongguo shehui xingshi fenxi yu yuce* [Blue Book of China's Society 2004: Analysis and Forecast of China's Social Development]. Beijing: Shehui kexue wenxian chubanshe.

Zhang, Li. 2001. *Strangers in the City: Reconfigurations of Space, Power and Social Networks within China's Floating Population*. Stanford, CA: Stanford University Press.

Zhang, Weimin, Li Xiru, and Cui Hongyan. "China's Inter-census Survey in 2005," at http://www.ancsdaap.org/cencon2005/Papers/China/China.Zhang.Weimin.etal.pdf., accessed August 2009.

Zhejiang nianjian. 2002 [Zhejiang Yearbook 2002]. Hangzhou: Zhejiang nianjian bianweihui, 2002.

Zheng, Yongnian. 2008. *Technological Empowerment: The Internet, State, and Society in China*. Stanford, CA: Stanford University Press.

2004. *Will China Become Democratic? Elite, Class, and Regime Transition*. Singapore: Eastern Universities Press.

Zhong, Yang and Jie Chen. 2002. "To Vote or Not to Vote: An Analysis of Peasants' Participation in Chinese Village Elections." *Comparative Political Studies*, vol. 35, no. 6: 686–712.

Zhong, Yang, Jie Chen, and John M. Scheb. 1998. "Mass Political Culture in Beijing: Findings from Two Public Opinion Surveys." *Asian Survey*, vol. 38, no. 8: 763–783.

Zhongguo laodong tongji nianjian [China Labor Statistical Yearbook]. *Various Years*. Beijing: Zhongguo tongji chubanshe.

Zhou, Yongming. 2005a. "Living on the Cyber Border." *Current Anthropology*, vol. 46, no. 5: 779–803.

2005b. "Informed Nationalism: Military Websites in Chinese Cyberspace." *Journal of Contemporary China*, vol. 14, no. 44: 543–562.

Zhu, Jian-Hua. 1996. "'I Don't Know' in Public Opinion Surveys in China: Individual and Contextual Causes of Item Non-Response." *Journal of Contemporary China*, vol. 5, no. 12: 223–244.

Zong Fengming. 2008. *Zhao Ziyang: Ruanjin zhong de tanhua* [Zhao Ziyang: Captive Conversations]. Hong Kong: Kaifang chubanshe.

Zweig, David. 1999. "Undemocratic Capitalism: China and the Limits of Economism." *National Interest*, no. 56: 63–72.

Zweig, David and Siu Fung Chung. 2007. "Elections, Democratic Values, and Economic Development in Rural China." *Journal of Contemporary China*, vol. 16, no. 50: 25–45.

Index

archival research, 18, 33–6
  gaining access, 15, 20–21, 30, 36–7, 38
  intra-disciplinary debates, 37
  study of military dependents, 45–49
  study of patriotism and nationalism, 41–5, 49–50
  types, 38–41
Archives Law, 20–1
area studies, 4, 269, 274
  and survey research, 198
authoritarian regimes
  data quality, 15, 30, 249
  elite studies, 51–3
  information collection by government, 23–4
  necessity of approval from Chinese authorities, 130
  necessity of collaboration with Chinese partners, 30, 87, 152, 207, 248, 252, 255–7
  research in, 7–8, 152, 161, 250

Barnett, A. Doak, 88, 267
Beijing Area Study (BAS), 52, 71–3, 83, 135–8, 181, 190, 219–35, 236–45
Belousov, Konstantin, 250, 257
Bernstein, Thomas, 165
blogs, 100, 104–05
bulletin boards (BBs), 98–9
bureaucratic politics, 17, 24–6, 205, 210–12

capitalists. *See also* private entrepreneurs
Carlson, Allen, 83
case selection, 168, 169, 202–3
case-study research, 162–77, 249
  single case studies, 173
causal mechanisms, 76, 86, 143, 173–4, 249
causal process observations, 155.
  See also causal mechanisms
causality, 69, 76, 85, 130, 132, 151
Central Committee
  Central Committee Database, 53–57
  changes in characteristics over time, 60–65
  factional influence, 65–7
Chen, Calvin, 154
Chen, Jie, 194–6
Chen, Yun, 53–4, 62, 65, 67
China Institute of Contemporary International Relations, 94
China Institute of International Studies, 94
China Military Online, 92
China National Knowledge Infrastructure (CNKI) database, 103, 112, 272
China Net, 91, 99
China studies and the political science discipline, 273–7
"China threat", 83–4
Chinese Academy of Social Sciences (CASS), 93, 152, 183
  researchers in Wenzhou, 135–8

Chinese Communist Party (CCP), 201–2, 204–7, 209–10, 214–15, *See also* Central Committee
Chinese politics
  and history as a discipline, 33–5
  and the comparative politics subfield, 4–7
Chinese university Web sites, 95
coding, 51, 54–60, 67, 86, 116, 121, 125
collective self-esteem (CSE) scale, 70, 77
Computer aided text analysis (CATA), 122, 125. *See also* Yoshikoder
concepts, 49, 153, 156, 174, 218, 261
content analysis, 18, 102–3, 107–10, 116–17, 122–5
  drawing samples, 113–16
  electronic sources, 110–13
  examples, 117–22
  source biases, 124
contentious politics, 15–18, 20, 27, 30
conversational interviewing, 16, 260–3
county gazetteers, 20, 31, 36
Cultural Revolution, 34, 48, 52, 270
  effects on research, 107, 268–9
  leadership changes, 53, 61, 64
cybermedia, 90–92

data
  accessibility, 15, 151
  limitations, 274–5
  multiple types, 17, 209
  quality, 6, 31, 151, 210, 248, 254–5
democratization, 193, 200, 201, 203, 214, 217
Deng, Xiaoping, 61–2, 65, 67, 236, 270

EastView. *See* China National Knowledge Infrastructure (CNKI) database
electronic aids. *See* Computer aided text analysis (CATA)
elites, focus on, 41, 43–4, 50, 132, 203
epistemology, 129, 130, 148
ethnography, 18, 129–34, 143–4, 247, *See also* site-intensive methods
  contrasted with more deductive approaches, 136–8, 143
  contrasted with site-intensive methods, 148
  and institution-building, 138–43
  and labor politics, 134–8
  and multiple methods research, 131
event analysis, 16, 18, 22
event catalogs, 18–19
everyday interactions, 41, 45, 132, 237, 247
experimental methods, 69–70, 83–7
  Chinese national identity, 76–83
  "face" and foreign policy, 69–70
  exploratory factor analysis, 78, 85
external validity. *See* generalizability

"face", 86
  Chinese foreign policy, 70–6
Fairbank, John K., 266
Fenno, Richard F., Jr., 147, 149–50, 153–4, 156, 157, 159
flexible interviewing.
  See conversational interviewing
Foreign Broadcast Information Service (FBIS), 107, 267
foreign policy, 84
Friedman, Edward, 123–4

Geertz, Clifford, 41, 129, 133
generalizability, 87, 174, 176, 177, 217, 218, 242
  as a goal, 37, 109, 125, 130, 146, 173–4, 217, 248
  vs. data quality, 87, 248, 254–5, 263–4
Global Positioning System (GPS), 190, 223, 244
governmental materials. *See also* state-generated data
Great Leap Forward, 22, 52, 270
guanxi. *See* personal connections

Heimer, Maria, 162
Home Style, 147, 157
Hu, Yaobang, 51, 65–7
Hua, Guofeng, 51, 66–7, 270
hukou, inaccuracy due to migration, 219, 220–22, 235, 243
human subjects 73, 209.
  See also respondents

Index

hypotheses
  generation, 153, 174
  testing, 130–1, 137, 154, 174

information
  increasing availability, 2, 88, 107–10, 123, 272–3
  information dependence, 24–5
  information distortion, 23, 24–6, 30
  lack of, 2, 88, 107
  usefulness of newly available materials, 89
informed consent, 184
institutional diffusion, 227–35
Institutionalization of Legal Reforms in China (ILRC), 227–32
Interim Measures for Administration of Foreign-Related Social Survey Activities, 184, 250
Internal Review Board (IRB), 87, 209
internal validity, 87, 254–5
internationalism, 77, 80–1
Internet, 88–9, 105–6, 272
  foreign policy materials, 89–100
  uses of Internet data, 100–5
interviews, 16, 268, *See also* standardized interviewing, *See also* conversational interviewing
  elite interviews, 102, 159, 271–2
  and ethnography, 135, 158
  and multiple methods, 147, 155
  political sensitivity, 261–2
  response rate, 243
  suggestions, 239, 265
  and survey research, 223, 245
invalid part-to-whole mappings, 164–5, 174, 176
IR China Web site, 96–7

Jiang, Zemin, 171–2
Johnston, Alastair Iain, 85, 102, 190, 238

labor politics, 134–43
laid-off workers, 167–73
Lattimore, Owen, 266
Likert scale, 72, 77, 83

local people's congresses, 214–15, 217
  elections, 194–6
Long March, 56, 60, 62–4
Lü, Xiaobo, 165

MacFarquhar, Roderick, 34
Mao's Last Revolution, 34
Maryland Study, 110, 113–15
May Fourth generation, 61–2
McCarthy, Joseph, 266
measurement, 83, 85
Measures for the Administration of Foreign-Affiliated Surveys, 183
mechanism of causation. *See* causal mechanisms
military dependents, 35, 46–49
Ministry of Foreign Affairs (MFA), 90, 92–4, 99, 101, 104
  Web site, 93
mixed methods. *See* multiple methods
modernization theory, 69, 200
multiple methods, 18, 147, 155, 217, 253–4

National Bureau of Statistics (NBS), 183, 184, 220, 250
national identity, 69, 76–7, 78–80, 83
nationalism, 41, 43–4, 49, 69, 76–84
  "threshold problem", 83–4
neighborhood organizations, 152–3, 159
newspaper databases, 112–13

O'Brien, Kevin J., 133, 156
observable implications, 154, 249
observations, 68, 130, 182
Oksenberg, Michel, 123–4
organizational change, 138–43
outliers, 131, 162, 165, 169, 176

Park, Albert, 256
parsimony, 38, 130, 132, 137
participant observation, 138–9, 271. *See also* site-intensive methods
  contrasted with site-intensive methods, 149
party-affiliated mass organizations, 138–43
path analysis, 81–3

patriotism, 41–6, 49, 69, 70, 76–84
  blind patriotism, 76, 77, 80–1
Peking University, 76, 183, 190, 207, 236, 238
People's Daily, 90–1, 112, 114
People's Liberation Army (PLA), 35, 45, 49, 92. See also military dependents
People's Net, 90–1
People's University, 191
personal connections, 30, 36, 166, 228
petitioning system, 16–17, 25–6, 27–32
political culture, 69, 189
political participation, 189, 194
private entrepreneurs, 200–01, 210–18
  data collection, 207–10
  survey design, 201–6
process tracing, 130, 155
provincial yearbooks, 20
psychological measures.
    See experimental methods
Pye, Lucian, 70

qualitative methods, 18, 116, 124–5, 147–8, 154. *See also* content analysis. *See also* case study research. *See also* interviews. *See also* archival research. *See also* site-intensive methods. *See also* participant observation. *See also* ethnography
quantitative methods, 117, 273,
    See also content analysis.
    See also survey research.
    See also statistical methods.
questionnaires, 87, 207–9, 237–42
  Chinese regulations, 184–5

red capitalists, 194, 205, 210, 215, 217
reform era, 62, 65, 270–1
replicability, 87, 125, 130
Research Center for Contemporary China (RCCC), 190, 207, 236, 238, 244
research design, relation to research goals, 87
respondents, 73
  building trust, 150–3, 158–61, 255, 258–63
  eliciting responses, 18

  protecting safety of, 134, 252–3
Ross, Robert S., 85
"ruining a solider marriage", 46–9

sample size, 114–16, 217
sampling, 132, 157, 203–6
  biased samples, 221
  constructed-week sampling, 113–16, 123
  efficient samples, 123
  final (spatial) sampling units (FSUs), 223, 229
  multistage stratified samples, 222, 231
  nonrandom samples, 87, 113
  primary sampling units (PSUs), 242
  probability proportionate to size (PPS), 222–3, 242
  probability samples, 181–3, 188–9, 242–4, 255
  purposive selection, 203–4, 217, 248, 254
  random samples, 87, 109, 203–6, 248, 254
  representative samples, 112, 190, 236
  secondary sampling units (SSUs), 242
  spatial probability samples, 219–35
  systematic random sampling, 113, 115
satellite imagery, 225–7
Scott, James, 23, 131, 146–7, 149–50, 154, 157
security studies, materialist vs. symbolic, 71–2, 74
selection bias, 111–12, 132
sensitive research topics, 7–8, 15, 207, 208, 218, 240, 241, 250–1
  framing, 36
  information accessibility, 16, 20, 30, 36–7
  protecting Chinese collaborators, 256
  regional variation, 253–4
  socially embedded survey research, 255–63
  vs. taboo research topics, 251
Shanghai Institutes of International Studies, 94
Shi, Tianjian, 188–9, 194–6
site-intensive methods, 129–34, 138–9, 143–4. *See also* participant observation, See also ethnography

Index

contrasted with interviews, 159
contributions to theory, 153
definition of term, 148
optimizing validity, 158–60
trade-offs between breadth and
    depth, 146, 156–7
when to use, 150–3
Snyder, Richard, 164
"soaking and poking", 149, 153
social networks, 142–3, 228–31, 232
standardized interviewing, 260–3
state-generated data. See also archival
    research
  accessibility, 15, 20
  availability, 30
  contrasted with newspaper data, 18,
    19, 22
  information collection and
    processing, 28–30
  published materials, 19–20
  quality of statistical information,
    29, 31
  reliability, 15, 22–7, 30–1
  upstream sources, 31–2
state-owned enterprises (SOEs), 167–9,
  170–3
statistical methods
  challenges, 86
  overemphasis on statistical
    significance, 86
subnational comparative analysis.
    See also case-study research
  application of, 163, 176–7
  contrasted with large-N quantitative
    analysis, 174–5
  contrasted with single-city case
    studies, 173–4
  identifying antecedent conditions,
    163, 166, 174, 176
survey research. See also Beijing Area
    Study (BAS)
  access to gated communities, 235,
    245
  advantages and limitations, 192, 218
  contrasted with interviews and
    archival research, 218
  contrasted with qualitative research,
    196–8
  conversational interviewing, 263–4

face-to-face interviewing, 185, 237,
    244–5
  individual-level attitudinal surveys,
    263–4
  longitudinal, 236
  political sensitivity of surveys
    in non-democratic regimes,
    246–65
  regulatory regime, 183–5
  socially embedded survey research,
    255–63
  village-level, 247

Technorati, 104–5
TECN Academic Net, 97
thick description, 10, 129, 131
Tilly, Charles, 16, 18
time-series analysis, 67, 112, 206
Touch Graph, 104
trust, 276. See also respondents,
    building trust
  collaborators, 255–8
  inter-personal and system-based,
    227–29
Tsai, Kellee, 165, 194, 198, 201, 204,
    215
Tsai, Lily L., 155, 198

University of Michigan, 191, 237

variation, 146
  individual variation, 203–6
  regional variation, 6, 68, 202–3,
    261
  temporal variation, 206

Walder, Andrew, 123–4
Weapons of the Weak, 147, 154, 156
Whiting, Allen, 88, 123
Wood, Elisabeth, 253

xiahai red capitalists, 205, 214, 217
xinfang. See petitioning system
Xinhua Net, 91
Xinhua News Agency, 91, 117–20

Yoshikoder, 4, 103, 116, 119–22, 125

Zhong, Yang, 194–96